D0712421

EVANGELICALS
INCORPORATED

EVANGELICALS INCORPORATED

BOOKS and the BUSINESS of RELIGION in AMERICA

Daniel Vaca

Harvard University Press

Cambridge, Massachusetts | London, England | 2019

For Julia

Publication of this book has been supported through the generous provisions of
the Maurice and Lula Bradley Smith Memorial Fund

First printing

Library of Congress Cataloging-in-Publication Data

Names: Vaca, Daniel, 1980– author.
Title: Evangelicals incorporated : books and the business of religion in
America / Daniel Vaca.
Description: Cambridge, Massachusetts : Harvard University Press, 2019. |
Includes bibliographical references and index.
Identifiers: LCCN 2019032163 | ISBN 9780674980112 (cloth)
Subjects: LCSH: Christian-owned business enterprises—United States. |
Evangelicalism—Economic aspects—United States. |
Christianity—Economic aspects—United States. | Christian
literature—Publishing—United States. | Church and mass media—United States.
Classification: LCC BR115.E3 V33 2019 | DDC 277.3/082—dc23
LC record available at https://lccn.loc.gov/2019032163

Contents

Introduction

WITHIN A FEW YEARS of its release in 2002, a book entitled *The Purpose Driven Life: What on Earth Am I Here For?* became known as the best-selling hardcover of all time.[1] An inspirational self-help manual written in the style of a guide for daily devotional reflection, the book sold almost thirty million copies in the United States during the three years following its initial publication. This outsized success inevitably raises a question: why did so many people buy it?

You could answer this question in at least two ways. First, you could examine the book itself, chronicling its most appealing or distinctive features. Written in a direct and earnest tone, each of the book's forty chapters is only a handful of pages long, which makes its chapter-a-day regimen easy to undertake. The chapters end with study questions that facilitate group discussion or individual introspection. The book underlines its transformative potential in its first few pages, inviting readers to pledge themselves to forty days of reading by physically signing their own signatures alongside a reproduction of the signature of the book's author, the Southern Californian megachurch pastor Rick Warren. Figuring as a sort of life coach and prophet, Warren presents his book as a singular solution to an age-old problem: "The search for the purpose of life," he explains, "has puzzled people for thousands of years." Buying the book affords you the opportunity to determine whether it solves this perennial puzzle in your own life.[2]

A second method of explaining the book's success focuses less on the peculiar appeal of its content than on the scope of the book's market. How did its tens of millions of consumers become receptive to this product? The easiest answer is to acknowledge that the book sold especially well among consumers who participate in a mode of Protestant Christianity known as evangelicalism, which surveys since the 1970s have estimated to account for anywhere from a quarter to almost half of the adult population of the United States.[3] Despite the almost laughable imprecision of those figures, they complement a survey's finding in 2005 that a quarter of American adults reported having read *The Purpose Driven Life*.[4] That seemingly settles it: evangelicals are abundant, and most of them bought Warren's book. This explanation seems so obvious because it hews to typical understandings of the relationship between religious life and consumer practice. That model generally treats consumer behavior as an expression of a dominant religious identity, which compels people to consume things that fulfill their needs.[5] If best sellers were so easy to create, however, many more books would sell tens of millions of copies. But neither the market for religious books nor the evangelical population is a stable social body, and the two do not operate in lockstep.

Both the evangelical market and the evangelical population have taken shape continually, through commercial and cultural effort. And if evangelicalism's growth has fueled industries that have supplied the demand of evangelical consumers, the inverse also has occurred: industries have helped generate evangelical demand, evangelical identities, and the very idea of a coherent evangelical population. Without a doubt, part of the appeal of Warren's book lay in its ability to engage and exemplify evangelical devotional cultures. But those cultural ideas and practices saturated American society through commercial media, which publishers, salespeople, editors, and other agents of industry persistently have labored to make and sell.

This book is about the making of markets and the forms of social life that markets make. As one popular economics textbook relates, mainstream economic theory typically defines a market not just as a group of buyers and sellers for a particular set of commodities but also as a group that takes shape primarily on the basis of price and the rational self-interest of its participants.[6] In such formulations, terms like "self-interest" tend to portray markets as features of contemporary society that we participate in by choice. Yet in a consumer society, where virtually all aspects of social life involve commodification and consumption, we invariably make our consumer choices in response to sets of social obligations, which we perceive alongside social identities that take shape within and through the marketplace itself.[7] By exploring the history of a media industry dedicated to creating and selling religious books and bibles, I illustrate how commercial attempts to create and expand the market for particular kinds of consumer products have depended upon parallel efforts to cultivate complementary networks, identities, and obligations.

The evangelical book industry's commercial success did not merely follow the growth of evangelical Christianity during the postwar decades of the twentieth century. To the contrary, contemporary evangelicalism took shape and steadily expanded through commercial efforts to generate new media markets and build successful media corporations.[8] Recently, several histories of evangelicalism have chronicled close relationships between evangelicalism and business. These studies have detailed how business practices have served as instruments of evangelical endeavor, and how evangelical ideas and initiatives meanwhile have sanctified business interests.[9] Building upon that scholarship in this book, I resist the tendency to treat evangelicalism as a static form of "conservative" Protestantism that operates in an independent yet dialogic partnership with other ideologies and interests. Instead, I emphasize the continual reproduction of evangelical religiosity and treat commercial activity as an engine of that process.

COMMERCIAL RELIGION

Evangelicalism exemplifies what I describe as "commercial religion," by which I refer primarily to forms of social organization commonly recognized as religion that take shape through the ideas, activities, and strategies that typify commercial capitalism.[10] Commercial religion involves more than "the commodification of religion," a phrase that both scholars and pundits have used to describe what they have seen as the modern transformation of religions into commodities, which people literally and metaphorically buy and sell.[11] Typically portraying religions as traditions that adapt or succumb to market forces, narratives of commodification often imply that religions can or should transcend the social contexts in which they are practiced. By contrast, I understand religions as forms of social organization and authority that continually take shape through realms of social life that include commodities and their circulation. Terms like "evangelicalism" are abstractions that we use to refer to these forms.[12]

Recognizing the rich theological and devotional traditions that historians and theologians long have associated with the idea of evangelicalism, I argue that those traditions and associations continually have been drawn together through commercial technologies and initiatives, which have enabled consumers to cultivate shared ideas, practices, and sensibilities across denominational, ecclesiastical, and geographic contexts. Through bookstores, supermarket checkout aisles, television talk shows, and more, a diverse spectrum of spiritual seekers have participated in evangelical markets. Although some critics argue that such expansive commercial activity has diluted, "juvenilized," or otherwise corrupted what they understand as an evangelical tradition, this activity is what allowed evangelicalism to loom so large in American religious history and culture during the twentieth century.[13] While commercial activity has served as the spirit that has animated the incorporation of evangelicalism's social body, practices of profit-making, branding, selling, financing, and marketing have served as fields of religious faith.[14]

At the heart of "commercial" activity is the pursuit of financial profit through devotion to the act of selling.[15] Although humans perennially have sold goods of all kinds, Christians also have expressed persistent anxiety about the money and wealth that sales can generate. Many of the teachings attributed to Jesus in the New Testament have proven difficult for Christians to interpret and apply to their own contexts, and few imperatives have proven more vexing than the injunction against serving both God and "mammon," a term typically understood as money or material wealth (see Matthew 6:24). Although this teaching seems to explicitly condemn the parallel pursuit of God and money, Christians have spent 2,000 years asking and answering countless clarifying questions. What exactly does service to God or mammon entail? Is wealth truly antithetical to service to God, or can one sphere of service remain subservient to the other? Can money actually serve God?[16] Answers to such questions have varied due to more than hermeneutical creativity or individual disingenuousness. Above all, answers have depended upon shifting conceptions of what constitutes service to God and service to mammon.[17] Throughout the history of the evangelical book industry, its participants have sought to interpret and portray their commercial objectives and activities as forms of divine service.[18] But those participants have not always agreed about how to understand and describe their effort.

Consider a conflict that took shape in 2005, pitting Rick Warren against the marketing professional Greg Stielstra. Before their disagreement took shape, Stielstra had served as a senior marketing director at Zondervan, one of the world's preeminent publishers of evangelical books, bibles, and other media. Founded in 1931 in Grand Rapids, Michigan, Zondervan was purchased in 1988 by the media conglomerate News Corporation, which went on to own such media properties as Fox Broadcasting Company, Fox News Channel, and the *Wall Street Journal*.[19] Both before and after that acquisition, Zondervan published some of the best-selling titles of the twentieth and twenty-first centuries. In the 1970s, for instance, Zondervan's *The Late Great Planet Earth* (1970) became that decade's best-selling book, outselling religious and nonreligious books alike. In the late 1970s, Zondervan released the New International Version (NIV) of the Bible, which became the best-selling English-language translation.[20] And in 2002 Zondervan published *The Purpose Driven Life*. During his tenure at Zondervan, Stielstra had helped market books by such well-known evangelical authors as Philip Yancey, Lee Strobel, Joni Eareckson Tada, Billy Graham, Dan Quayle, Oliver North, and C. Everett Koop. But *The Purpose Driven Life* became his crowning achievement. Its success convinced him to write a marketing textbook based largely on his experience marketing Warren's book. Published in 2005, *PyroMarketing: The Four-Step Strategy to Ignite Consumer Evangelists and Keep Them for Life* refers to *The Purpose Driven Life* every few pages. Before Stielstra's book came out, however, Rick Warren had demanded that Stielstra strip all references to him and his book.

In principle, Warren had no quarrel with Stielstra's marketing strategies. As the book's pyrotechnic title suggests, *PyroMarketing* argued that "the best way to understand marketing . . . is to think of it as fire." This meant that marketing professionals should seek to "gather the driest tinder" (identify the people most likely to purchase), for example, and "fan the flames" (help consumers tell others about the product).[21] Although reviews of Stielstra's book praised the clarity of his metaphors, they generally recognized his strategy as a synopsis of common market segmentation strategies. "The idea of equating marketing to fire," one marketing professional remarked, "isn't new."[22]

Instead of objecting to Stielstra's marketing practices, Warren opposed Stielstra's basic claim that marketing contributed to the success of *The Purpose Driven Life*. As one of Warren's representatives explained, the author did not want his book "associated with the word 'marketing' in any way, shape or form." Speaking for himself in a public statement released to the industry magazines *Christian Retailing* and *Publishers Weekly,* Warren argued that Stielstra should "not use *The Purpose Driven Life* as [an] example of 'pyromarketing,' since that would be inaccurate." Warren added that his "only concern was that no one, neither Zondervan nor myself, claim credit for the astounding success of *The Purpose Driven Life* book. The worldwide spread of the purpose-driven message had nothing to do with marketing or merchandizing." Instead of conferring credit upon marketing efforts, Warren argued that his book's success "was the result of God's supernatural and sovereign plan, which no one anticipated."[23]

Although I testify throughout this book to the social power of marketing and merchandizing by exploring a century of commercial enterprise, I do not seek to prove Warren wrong. Taking for granted that marketing and merchandizing had something to do with his book's best-seller status, I not only consider how commercial initiatives have circulated evangelical ideas and cultivated evangelical identities but also explain how such a strong disavowal of commercial influence became possible. For as long as evangelical publishers, editors, investors, wholesalers, authors, and book clerks have pursued profit, responded to consumer demand, built bookstores in shopping malls, sold their corporate stock to the public, and segmented their consumer markets, they meanwhile have sought to interpret their commercial effort as nothing less than manifestations of "God's supernatural and sovereign plan." By animating their religious endeavor with commercial logic, their religion and their commerce became indistinguishable from each other.[24]

Any assessment of marketing's contribution to Warren's success ultimately depends upon what you recognize as marketing. Both Warren and Greg Stielstra would agree that his book benefited tremendously from the extensive network of churches he had developed following the release of his previous book, *The Purpose Driven Church* (Zondervan, 1995), which taught pastors to secure their church's growth by nurturing the spiritual purpose and health of their congregation. After that book far exceeded sales expectations, Warren set out to cement a connection to his consumers by launching the website pastors.com in 2001. Boasting as many as 200,000 members by the following year and knitting together what it describes today as "global coalition of congregations," the website allowed Warren to invite churches and their respective "small groups" or study groups to adopt *The Purpose Driven Life* and its forty-day regimen upon its release in September 2002.[25] This arrangement helped sell out the book's first print run of 500,000 before it even reached stores, which drew additional attention to the book and its author.[26] Did pastors.com and Warren's network of churches constitute a marketing campaign? According to Greg Stielstra and the marketing professionals who assessed his book, Warren's strategy typified key marketing imperatives, such as engaging likely consumers and retaining a connection to them. According to Warren, however, his success testified exclusively to the power of a God who endorsed the purpose-driven program and inspired the faithful to adopt it.

By examining business activity as well as understandings of it, this book documents how evangelicals successively have had their God effect his will through commercial ideas and practices. I focus above all on participants in the evangelical book industry, within which the executives and editors of publishing companies have possessed outsized influence. Although I analyze the content of many evangelical books, I focus far less on particular books and readers than on the ideas, infrastructures, and innovations that have oriented book production, circulation, and reception. Complementing studies of evangelical print culture that have focused particularly on readers' experience, I explore the lived religious experiences and endeavors of salespeople, ministers, investors, institutional leaders, authors, and others who have worked within or alongside the industry.[27] The author Rick Warren could disavow any reliance on marketing and merchandizing not because he condemned fields of commercial activity, but instead because evangelical thought and practice had subsumed the ideas and strategies that the terms "marketing" and "merchandizing" identify. And his consumers in turn became part of his expansive audience through the pathways that marketing, merchandizing, finance, and other commercial activities generated. Their evangelicalism was a paragon of commercial religion, and this book examines some of the ways in which it took shape.

EVANGELICAL MARKETS AND PUBLICS

Who are evangelicals? For perspective on that question, consider the following story:

> The morning of March 11, 2005, Brian Nichols was beginning the final day of a trial on rape charges. While changing from prison clothes to attire appropriate for court, he managed to overpower his deputy, take her gun, and kill two people. After escaping Atlanta's Fulton County Courthouse, he shot and killed two more.
>
> Nichols spent the day on the run from authorities. Late that night, at a suburban apartment complex, Nichols ran into Ashley Smith. At gunpoint, Nichols forced his way into Smith's apartment and bound her with tape. Then they began talking.
>
> They talked for about seven hours. For much of the time, they talked about Smith's five-year-old daughter, and about how her husband had been stabbed to death four years earlier. But then they talked about *The Purpose Driven Life*. Smith had been working her way through the book, and she decided to read Chapter Thirty-three aloud to Nichols. "We serve God by serving others," Warren's chapter begins.
>
> Smith read all eight pages. After she finished, Nichols asked her to read it again. Before long, he let her go free, and he surrendered to the police.[28]

Based on what this story has told you about Ashley Smith or Brian Nichols, do you consider them evangelical? For the purposes of this book, I do. But that answer depends upon how I approach "evangelicalism," a term that has remained relentlessly subject to scholarly definition and redefinition.

For decades, scholars often have portrayed evangelicalism as a diverse but discrete religious tradition that has cohered across space and time despite the diversity of denominations, doctrines, and devotional sensibilities within its expanse.[29] To describe and identify examples of that coherence, many scholars have invoked versions of a definition with four main criteria: conversion, activism, biblicism, and crucicentrism.[30] By regularly applying these theological criteria to people in times and places where the term "evangelical" rarely was used, historians have been able to identify and trace an evangelical tradition across centuries of European and American history. Yet as scholars like the historian Douglas Winiarski have pointed out, the definition often "masks far more than it illuminates" about the lived religious lives of the people it seeks to describe.[31] Often premised upon the notion that religious groups take shape and persist primarily due to their participants' explicit or implied ability to endorse particular doctrinal principles, the definition minimizes histories and peoples that manifest its criteria uneasily.

If trying to apply the fourfold definition to Smith and Nichols, we would need more information. We might ask: did they seem invested in the definition's commitments? Did Smith's recitation of Warren's book count as an attempt to convert Nichols? Had Smith already converted? Although they read or listened to a book that quoted the Bible, did they revere the Bible's authority? While answers to these questions might help us determine whether Smith and her captor fit within the evangelical tradition that scholars have posited, other questions would do more to help us understand the religious identities and attachments that Smith and Nichols experienced, or the significance of their encounter with *The Purpose Driven Life*.[32]

At least one fact is clear: both Smith and Nichols participated in the amorphous audience that Rick Warren, his book, and his publisher generated. By participating in that audience, Smith and Nichols participated in evangelicalism. We can even say that they were evangelicals. If it sounds absurd to apply that label so easily, remember that in many surveys a primary criterion for evangelical identity is just one question: "Would you describe yourself as a 'born-again' or evangelical Christian, or not?" Since this question first appeared during the 1970s, it never has measured evangelical identity with any theological precision.[33] What it has measured above all is survey respondents' willingness to describe themselves as "born-again" or "evangelical," however they understand the meaning of those terms and the social constituency that they think the terms denote. Taken together, the people who answer affirmatively make up an amorphous social body. But their answers nevertheless gesture toward a form of common consciousness, shared self-awareness, or ecumenism, all of which the idea of evangelicalism helps denote.

Just as surveys ask us to associate ourselves with categories and constituencies that exist principally in our imaginations, media objects perpetually invite us to affiliate ourselves with people whom we imagine as the ideal audience for that media. To be sure, we often serve as the audience for media that carry content we do not endorse. When we pay attention to media and imagine ourselves as the people they address, however, we become more than members of an audience; we become members of a social phenomenon sometimes described as a "public." As the literary theorist Michael Warner explains to his readers, and as any author might explain to their own: "If you are reading this, or hearing it or seeing it or present for it, you are part of this public." Publics do not take shape through central institutions or subscription to any particular criteria. They are the product of active participation, attention, and imagination. At any time, people might imagine themselves as members of multiple publics.[34]

Instead of understanding religions primarily as bounded groups that possess four-part definitions or firm membership criteria, we can see religions as publics. Of course, religions also take shape within institutions, such as temples, churches, monastic orders, and denominations. Their sociality involves more than mere attention. But religions also exceed any particular institutions or set of institutions. Although the terms "Christianity," "Judaism," "Islam," "Buddhism," and "Hinduism" are widely recognized as denoting paradigmatic religions, those terms do not necessarily describe any fixed set of people. Nor are they defined by any particular institutions, or by firm sets of doctrines and practices. They are imagined groupings, which take shape above all through the willingness of people to recognize themselves and their religious cultures as part of social groups to which other ostensible Christians, Jews, Muslims, Buddhists, or Hindus also belong.[35]

Today, no less than in centuries past, evangelicalism can be understood as an expansive social public, which participants conceive of alongside any number of other religious and cultural attachments, including narrower evangelical publics. Etymologically, "evangelical" Protestantism names a mode of Christianity that reflects the message of the *evangelion*—the Greek word for the "good news" or "gospel" of Jesus Christ. But virtually any Christian fits that description. In practice, Christians since the sixteenth century have used the word "evangelical" and its variants as an adjective that describes people and activities that they have seen as true to their own understandings of the gospel message and the biblical texts within which they find that message.[36] For centuries, then, the heart of evangelical imagination has lain not in any stable set of doctrines or practices but rather in an effort to associate authentic Christian faith and authority within an individual's own experience, judgment, and personal relationship with God.

Although evangelicals typically have received instruction from such ecclesial bodies as denominations, churches, and congregations, they consistently have prioritized individual choice and conviction.[37] This is why the historian Timothy Gloege uses the term "evangelical" to denote a cultural orientation that has ebbed and flowed over time in contradistinction with a "churchly" orientation. While churchly Protestants have insisted that "an authentic faith required sincere and active membership in a particular church and that religious authority," evangelicals have insisted that "it was the act of choosing specifically that made one's faith authentic."[38] This emphasis on individual authority has tended to find fullest expression through some of the ideas and cultural practices for which evangelicalisms have been known, which also have preoccupied religious historians. Those ideas and practices include the conversionist notion that individuals should bring others into the faith and the biblicist emphasis on having individuals engage the Bible for themselves. The priority of individual authority also is why evangelicalisms always have seemed to take shape through markets, which perennially have nurtured the ideal of individual choice.[39]

As constituencies in the past and present, evangelical publics have developed primarily through the willingness of their participants to identify the religious practices and social concerns of other ostensible evangelicals as their own.[40] In different times and places, those social concerns have included such diverse issues as the defense of slavery, patriarchal gender ideals, fear of immigrants, and the power of the state.[41] Although pundits typically portray evangelicals as social and theological conservatives, the wide array of people commonly understood as evangelicals never have conserved any particular ideologies or imperatives systematically. Today some prominent evangelical organizations admit this fact, even though they tend to make that admission with the hope that evangelicals might close what the executive director of one evangelical research organization described in 2017 as the "gap between who evangelicals say they are and what they believe."[42] But if propositional beliefs define evangelical publics, why have so many African American and Latino Protestants often seemed united with white evangelicals theologically but not sociologically?[43] Which doctrines theologically united the 80 percent of avowed evangelicals who voted for Donald Trump in 2016? Rather than theological ideas alone, evangelicalisms have comprised identities shaped through politics of race, gender, and class, all of which have developed in dialogue with consumer behavior and patterns of media consumption.

Whatever Ashley Smith and Brian Nichols thought about the doctrine of the substitutionary atonement or the inerrancy of the Bible in its original autographs, they came to recognize themselves as part of a broad evangelical public, and Rick Warren affirmed their senses of self. After Nichols released her, Smith reported that Nichols had admitted that "I was his sister and he was my brother in Christ. And that he was lost and God led him right to me to tell him that he had hurt a lot of people." Smith also reported that she had told Nichols, "I was a child of God and that I wanted to do God's will."[44] Acknowledging familiarity with the style of these stories, Rick Warren reached out to Smith and her captor. Warren pledged to visit Nichols in prison to "see where he is spiritually," and Warren reportedly began talking and praying with Smith every day. He remarked that "Ashley is very aware of the fact that God chose her to be used in this particular situation."[45]

Yet even as Warren recognized both Nichols and Smith as fellow evangelicals, he seemed to find Smith most recognizable. Highlighting his comfort with Smith's mode of evangelical self-presentation, Warren claimed that he had heard stories like hers "over and over." Perceptions of race and gender undoubtedly enhanced Warren's recognition. In the mid-2000s, just 6 percent of self-identified evangelicals identified as black, while 81 percent of self-identified evangelicals described themselves as white, and 53 percent of those evangelicals identified as women.[46] As a black man, Nichols did not fit an evangelical mold as effortlessly as did Smith, a white woman. Although any number of logistical reasons might explain why Nichols received a smaller share of Warren's attention than Smith, Warren clearly situated her closer to the center of an evangelical public.

But Warren also helped Smith and her story reach consumers beyond the ranks of evangelical pastors and their core evangelical constituencies. Following her ordeal, Smith told her story to a variety of news organizations, and their reports inspired so many consumers to purchase Warren's book that it jumped to second place on sales charts for both Barnes & Noble and Amazon, where the book had fallen since 2002 to a rank in the 50s and 60s.[47] Her story's salience inspired a competition among publishers for the rights to a book about her experience.[48] Zondervan eventually secured the contract, and the company published her *Unlikely Angel: The Untold Story of the Atlanta Hostage Hero* in 2005. The press tour for the book included appearances not just on explicitly evangelical networks but also on such mainstream outlets as *Good Morning America*, *Today*, and the shows hosted by Larry King, Paula Zahn, and Oprah. During most appearances, Ashley Smith appeared alongside Warren, who took the opportunity to amplify his own book's message of individual purpose.

Through these commercial broadcasts, figures like King and Oprah also conjured evangelical publics. True, many avowed "conservative" evangelicals might have distanced themselves theologically or culturally from both Larry King and Oprah. Offering an average daily audience of nine million viewers what she described as "illumination," Oprah especially had drawn a reputation for preaching a "liberal" mode of spiritual seeking and ecumenism.[49] And yet as Oprah, Warren, and Smith collaboratively encouraged the viewers in Oprah's media market to pursue individual transformation, they simultaneously called those viewers to embrace shared priorities and self-understandings. On the day when Oprah hosted Smith and Warren, no less than on countless other days, Oprah's commercial religion became difficult to distinguish from that of her guests. A decade later, transformative principles would animate the feature film *Captive* (2015), starring the actors Kate Mara and David Oyelowo. "The greatest tragedy is not death," Mara's explains to Oyelowo in the movie's trailer, "but life without purpose." With these words, Mara could have been quoting Oprah. But she was playing the character of Ashley Smith, offering advice to Oyelowo's Brian Nichols. The message that Mara voiced, via Smith and Warren, does not fit neatly within the definitional criteria that scholars of evangelicalism regularly have recited. But anyone who had proverbial ears to hear or eyes to see the film might be understood as participants in evangelicalism.

"Is your company 'evangelical'?" I once asked an experienced evangelical executive and editor this question, and he responded by dismissing any illusion of descriptive precision. "Don't you know?" he jokingly asked me. "'Evangelicalism' is just a marketing slogan." To be clear, the point of his quip was not to claim that evangelicals exist only in marketing executives' imaginations. Instead, the editor explained that his own understanding of the evangelical public both included and exceeded the consumer markets that actually applied the term to themselves. In this book I not only explore how commercial media companies have engaged those markets but also chronicle how companies have sought to knit them together by cultivating common consciousness through commercial endeavor. By cultivating evangelical markets, they have generated evangelical publics.[50]

BOOK PEOPLE

For centuries, books have served as engines of transdenominational evangelical consciousness. Rick Warren and Ashley Smith provide just two instances of that textual tradition. Looking back as far as evangelicalism's etymological origins, the books and tracts produced by early European printing presses helped generate Protestant publics that transcended local attachments.[51] In the nineteenth-century United States, the historian Candy Brown argues, circulations of print "mediated and structured seemingly private experiences," generating an "evangelical textual community."[52] Conceptualizing evangelicalism as a larger social phenomenon than the notion of "community" colloquially conjures, the historian John Modern explains that "evangelical media practices . . . made possible particular conceptions of the self, the social, and the means to understand them both." Media had this effect, in part, by generating "sensual criteria for evaluating the true, the good, and the beautiful—for others, to be sure, but, more importantly, for themselves."[53] Large and ambitious publishing enterprises like the American Bible Society (founded in 1816) and the American Tract Society (1825) produced much of the media that Brown and Modern have in mind.

As a variety of scholars have documented, evangelicals in the twentieth and twenty-first centuries have continued to understand and approach the reading of books and bibles as a primary practice of cultivating personal faith and individual intimacy with God.[54] Through a study of evangelical romance fiction, for example, Lynn Neal illustrates how Protestant women who affiliate with a variety of denominations "read (and write) evangelical romance novels as a way to demonstrate and maintain their religious identities."[55] Criticizing the tradition of portraying evangelicalism as a tightly bounded "subculture," Amy Johnson Frykholm presents the best-selling apocalyptic fiction series *Left Behind* as a form of popular culture, through which readers become part of interpretive communities that render particular understandings of self and salvation "plausible and even urgent."[56] Other scholars have examined how popular books by evangelical authors like Max Lucado have cultivated a shared emphasis on feeling and sentimentality.[57] The anthropologist Tanya Luhrmann credits books such as *The Purpose Driven Life* with helping to teach religious seekers to assert an intimate, individual relationship with God, which Luhrmann presents as a primary evangelical sensibility.[58] Conceiving of "conversion" as the process through which individuals adopt new modes of thinking and being, several anthropologists have presented such discursive practices as group bible and book studies as a primary means of conversion.[59]

Building upon these and other studies of evangelical print cultures and reading practices in this book, I help explain why books became key objects of evangelical initiative and attention. One reason is that the form and concept of the book complement evangelical emphasis on individual authority and introspection. Although countless historians of the book have detailed how reading and interpretation occur within webs of social inter-action, the idea of reading perennially privileges readers' individual effort and interpretive judgment, and their ultimate ability to put the ideas they read about into personal practice.[60] During the modern period, this indi-vidual ideal became ascendant especially after the invention of the printing press made reading materials more widely available, which not only fueled a rise in rates of literacy but also presented solitary reading as the path toward both intellectual and spiritual salvation. While Martin Luther is known for urging members of his "evangelical" church to practice lay priest-hood by reading the Bible for themselves, other heralds of the modern era affirmed Luther's claim that authentic religion emerged out of the free in-quiry that reading afforded. Even as newer and cheaper printing technolo-gies made reading material more abundant throughout the nineteenth century, many American Protestants continued to view reading as a sort of sacred activity.[61]

A second reason that books have preoccupied evangelicals involves the status of books as commodities, or articles of purchase. Although they come into being through complex networks of individuals and ideas, books do not especially invite reflection about what causes people to create or con-sume them.[62] Even more than other commodities, books appeal to the ideal that consumption derives not from corporate manipulation of consumers and markets but instead from the object's quality and its alignment with consumers' authentic interests, convictions, or needs. Of course, publishers, booksellers, and even readers recognize that consumers do not always read the books that they purchase, appreciate, or display. But the notion of reading idealizes both the merit of a book's content and the virtue of a book's reader.[63] For this reason, marketing materials for evangelical books often have presented reading as a matter of personal piety, spiritual duty, or divine intervention in readers' lives. During the late 1970s, for instance, one of the Zondervan Corporation's slogans offered consumers the omi-nous warning: "Read for Your Life."[64]

Yet for at least as long as printing presses have made possible the mass production of books, publishers have labored to persuade consumers to purchase their products. This persuasion often has cultivated and capital-ized upon religious and cultural concerns, which have circulated through commercial strategies and infrastructures no less than through the content of books themselves. In examining the book business in eighteenth-century France, for instance, the historian Robert Darnton argues that the publishers and promoters of the multivolume *Encyclopédie* initially presented their product as a challenge to traditional forms of knowledge and intellectual authority. But Darnton also notes that the *Encyclopédie*'s publishers were entrepreneurs who participated in a "brutal business," and that they accordingly sought to maximize their profits with "almost mathematical rationality." Publishers "knew they were agents of Enlightenment," Darnton explains, "not because they felt committed" necessarily to the ideas in particular books but instead "because they made a business of it."[65] While this claim might sound like an indictment of cynical cupidity, Darnton's point is that businesses consistently have recognized that particular ideas, discourses, and publics complement their commercial objectives and imperatives.

Applying Darnton's phrasing to the nineteenth-century United States, many American publishers became advocates of evangelicalism because they made a business of it. During the early nineteenth century, several practical developments had primed the publishing business for what would become exponential growth, with the number of titles in circulation multiplying from approximately 1,300 in 1804 to at least 25,000 between 1820 and 1850.[66] Practical developments included new steam-power and papermaking technologies, which made printing presses and printing processes less expensive and more productive. Meanwhile, canals, railways, and a more reliable postal system made the transportation of raw printing materials and final printed products cheaper and easier than ever. As these changes reduced the unit cost of books and periodicals, books no longer seemed like luxuries that only the wealthiest consumers could afford.[67] Despite all of these practical improvements, however, book production and distribution continued to require significant capital investment and steady revenue. Not until the recent rise of digital design and distribution technologies have books become dramatically less expensive to make and sell.

To address these business imperatives, nineteenth-century associations and entrepreneurs took advantage of legal and cultural developments. In addition to disestablishing their official churches, many states had set about devising statutes that allowed voluntary associations and entrepreneurs to incorporate more easily. This enabled new corporations to receive donations, amass wealth, and own valuable property, such as printing presses.[68] With those resources, corporations competed to conjure publics among whom they could claim religious and moral authority. That authority allowed corporations to encourage purchases that helped generate required revenue.

In order to persuade consumers, publishers and booksellers presented book buying and reading as primary disciplines of authentic Christian faith. Lamenting that the book market's expansion had created what the historian David Nord describes as "the literature of wickedness, sensation, dissipation, and error," publishers of religious literature portrayed their products as sources of ideas, teachings, and stories that true Christians should choose for themselves.[69] Hoping to maximize their market reach, publishers and sales agents encouraged consumers to make their selections without regard to denominational or ecclesiastical distinctions. Both a religious and a commercial strategy, this ecumenical imperative depended upon and amplified the idea of an evangelical public. Evangelicalism served, in short, as a marketing slogan and strategy.

Because the commercial scale of the book industry and the social scale of evangelicalism both seemed to boom during the nineteenth century, historians of evangelicalism often depict that era as the heyday of both evangelicalism and its print culture.[70] The prevailing story has held that evangelicalism contracted during the first decades of the twentieth century as fundamentalist evangelicals lost theological and cultural credibility during the 1920s, while more liberal "modernist" Protestants increased their social standing and entrenched their cultural power.[71] All along, however, book businesses continued to cultivate broad consumer markets and corresponding publics, and the idea of evangelicalism continued to serve as a means of conjuring common consumer consciousness. Beginning especially in the 1940s, as new techniques of production, distribution, and retail multiplied the number of people and places that publishers and booksellers could reach, both the evangelical book industry and the evangelical public blossomed. By the 1970s, when mainstream news media began reporting that nearly a third of all American adults could be considered evangelical, the commercial clout of the evangelical book industry evidenced those claims. Standout best sellers included Kenneth Taylor's *The Living Bible* (1971), which ranked as the best-selling book nationwide in 1972 and 1973, Hal Lindsay's *The Late Great Planet Earth* (1970), and Marabel Morgan's *The Total Woman,* the best-selling nonfiction book of 1974.[72]

Although relatively few scholars of American religion have devoted attention to the relationship between evangelicalism's social profile and its market reach, media corporations have recognized this dialogue for decades.[73] Between the 1980s and today, many of the world's largest media conglomerates—such as Bertelsmann, Lagardère, and Amazon—have acquired or created their own religion divisions or imprints. For these corporations, "religion" typically has meant "evangelicalism." This trend became pronounced beginning in 1988, when Rupert Murdoch's News Corporation acquired the Zondervan Corporation, making it subsidiary of the publishing firm Harper & Row (renamed HarperCollins in 1990).[74] Founded in western Michigan almost sixty years earlier, Zondervan initially had catered to that region's Dutch Reformed immigrant community, before going on to establish itself as a preeminent publisher of evangelical media. In

2012, News Corporation acknowledged the persistent profitability of the evangelical market and the cross-promotional possibilities of subsidiaries like the cable news network Fox News Channel by having HarperCollins acquire one of Zondervan's principal competitors, the evangelical publisher Thomas Nelson. Zondervan and Thomas Nelson continued to function independently as brands, but they both became imprints of a new company, HarperCollins Christian.

Conglomerates have found the expansive evangelical market attractive due largely to its amorphousness. Before HarperCollins finalized its acquisition of Thomas Nelson, the U.S. Department of Justice launched an investigation to determine whether the acquisition would give HarperCollins such outsized influence over the evangelical market that it might violate antitrust law. One experienced evangelical editor and executive estimated that the merger provided HarperCollins with control over as much as half of the evangelical market and 75 percent of the bible market. Due to the ambiguity of terms like "religious," "Christian," and "evangelical," however, HarperCollins was able to insist that the companies possessed "different, though complementary, missions" and published across a wide range of genres. Because antitrust policy is based on market concentration, these nebulous categories made anticompetitive behavior difficult to prove.[75]

As large publishing subsidiaries like Penguin Random House, Hachette, and Simon & Schuster all have developed their own evangelical divisions, Zondervan has exemplified and even pioneered the symbiosis of religion and business that they have put into practice. For this reason, I focus in this book especially on Zondervan and the constellation of companies that have cooperated, competed, and merged with it. Those other companies include Fleming H. Revell Company, Moody Publishers, Thomas Nelson, Tyndale House, and InterVarsity Press. Especially prominent within this constellation are the other Michigan-based publishers with Dutch Reformed roots, such as Baker Publishing Group and the William B. Eerdmans Company. Together these companies have generated evangelical publics not only though books but also through the commercial infrastructure they created over the course of the twentieth century. Far more than any particular author, book, or parachurch institution, this infrastructure became the bedrock of evangelical cultures. Biblical texts, interpretive methods, worship songs, Christian music, doctrinal debate, celebrity status: the evangelical book industry has provided all of this and more for the fundamentalist evangelicals sometimes seen as evangelicalism's center no less than for the liberal evangelicals who champion social justice on biblicist grounds.

Drawing upon editorial correspondence, sales records, marketing plans, personal archives, and private interviews collected everywhere from university archives to corporate headquarters, the following chapters illustrate how business strategies continually have guided evangelical book production, distribution, and culture. The chapters begin in the nineteenth century, when evangelical publishers embraced for-profit commercialism and began approaching their potential evangelical markets as their evangelical publics (Chapter 1). As those for-profit publishers sought to reach beyond their local markets in the 1930s, they cultivated new brand identities that prioritized theological and cultural "distinctiveness," which not only served as a euphemism for white Christian identity but also helped lay the foundation for the "new evangelicalism" of the 1940s (Chapter 2). To account for distribution constraints and to generate an audience that could recognize their products, the evangelical book industry collaborated with evangelical leaders during the 1940s and 1950s to create new trade associations devoted to cultivating shared "evangelical" identity and common commercial purpose (Chapter 3). These efforts allowed supermarket-style evangelical bookstores to proliferate throughout the suburban United States, which allowed retail infrastructures and practices to circulate evangelical understandings of gender, family, and individual choice (Chapter 4). In order to enable growth in the 1970s and 1980s, evangelical publishers cultivated a sacred tradition that put faith in corporate finance, dramatically reshaping their corporate obligations and priorities (Chapter 5). And during the century's final decades, evangelical companies capitalized upon their new financial capacities by pursuing growth through new market segments or "niches," which multiplied the variety of constituencies that could serve as evangelical publics (Chapter 6). By segmenting the general evangelical market, evangelical companies not only found commercial cause to cultivate African American and Latino consumer segments but also began focusing especially on consumers who endorsed a strident mode of social and political conservatism.[76]

Recently some scholars have censured historians and histories of evangelicalism for often treating evangelicalism as "ecclesiastically, theologically, or racially homogeneous."[77] As I illustrate, however, evangelicalism's apparent homogeneity has taken shape not just through historiography but also through evangelical businesses, which have focused primarily on engaging and incorporating white authors and consumers. Seeking to account for evangelicalism's homogeneous constituencies and categories without accepting those categories as analytically or historically definitive, I continually ask how business imperatives have nurtured evangelicalism's whiteness through "distinctive" branding strategies, suburban retail settings, editorial practices, and more.

According to some scholars, evangelicalism's social prominence has seemed to decline during these first decades of the twenty-first century. Detailing this decline, the historian Steven Miller argues that the "age of evangelicalism" began to "wind down" around 2012, after decades during which "born-again Christianity provided alternately a language, a medium, and a foil by which millions of Americans came to terms with political and cultural changes."[78] Narrating decline more statistically, one study found in 2017 that white evangelical Protestants composed 23 percent of the adult population in 2006, yet only 17 percent a decade later.[79] These studies attribute their diagnosed decline to a variety of demographic and cultural changes, including generational transition, immigration, increased religious pluralism, and growing proportions of the population who claim no religious affiliation.

Because evangelicalism recurrently has taken shape through media and the markets within which media circulate, its apparent decline has stemmed in part from the rise of new modes of media and market circulation, including such phenomena as social media, ebooks, and online shopping. After all, online bookstores like Amazon do not nurture subcultural identity with the same curatorial intensity as evangelical bookstores in suburban shopping malls once did. And younger generations do not have the same relationship with books that their parents and grandparents possessed.

Yet evangelicalism continues to comprise more than the seemingly shrinking demographic and cultural constituencies that have helped constitute it. Even as online bookstores and advertisements have undermined commercial pathways through which particular evangelical publics once took shape, they have made it easier in the twenty-first century for mainline Christians and religious seekers of all kinds to take part in new media publics. Today the realm of commercial religious media both within and beyond the United States remains preoccupied with evangelical authors, ideas, and idioms.[80] With that fact in mind, how should we distinguish between the evangelical market, the mainline Protestant market, the broad market of spiritual seekers, and the common consciousness that each of those markets help conjure?[81] As this story shows, the business of religion undermines such distinctions.

1

Finding Profit

THE ASCENDANCE OF COMMERCIALISM

"THERE IS BIG MONEY to be made in the book business in this country," Arthur Fitt explained to his board of directors in 1909. Yet rather than highlighting potential riches with the hope of acquiring them, Fitt disavowed monetary motive. Founded in 1894 as an agency of what became Chicago's Moody Bible Institute and incorporated independently in 1899, Fitt's Bible Institute Colportage Association (BICA) had pledged in its charter to "circulate, distribute, make public, buy, sell and give away books, pamphlets, tracts, singing books, bibles, testaments and evangelical religious publications, and to use any surplus funds of the Association in and about bible and evangelical work."[1] Testifying to his belief in that mission, Fitt insisted that "the object of the Association is not, as I understand it, to make money."[2] While he acknowledged that any corporation must generate enough money to support its activities, he insisted, "We are a religious corporation, evangelical and evangelistic in character, not aiming for financial profit, but only for the widest sale and distribution of Gospel literature on a self-supporting margin of profit."[3]

Fitt disavowed big money because his corporation's financial struggles recently had made significant profit especially alluring. Throughout most of the nineteenth century, however, most book publishers had struggled to make a profit, and many avoided profit without intending to. Although the firm Harper & Brothers became the most successful commercial trade publisher of the nineteenth century, for example, it also amassed so much debt that it fell into receivership in 1899.[4] Yet even more than general trade publishers, companies that specialized in religious literature perennially struggled to raise enough money to realize their ambitions. BICA exemplified this fact.

Publishers found profit illusory largely because books were expensive to produce and distribute. To defray those expenses, publishers had limited options, each of which required interlocking compromises. They could charge high prices, but then only the wealthy could afford their books. Publishers could solicit donations, but donors always faced competing charitable obligations. Although economies of scale could lower costs, that required large groups of consumers. And publishers could secure more consumers by selling books that a wider range of consumers might find more appealing. But that strategy required a company to reconsider its mission and identity.

Rather than prioritize products designed primarily to align with potential consumer desire, religious publishers tended to locate their "religious" mission in the project of cultivating what they understood as the right kind of desire.[5] As the historian Candy Gunther Brown explains, Protestant publishers perennially sought to achieve greater "presence" in the market, but they did so while also attempting to cultivate moral and spiritual "purity."[6] To maintain purity and ensure that evangelical publishers helped oppose "ungodliness, immorality and crime," Arthur Fitt called upon the Colportage to avoid "commercialism," which he defined as the impulse to "to do business because there is money in it."[7] To be sure, Christian ministers and their publishing allies long had used commercial methods to circulate religious literature and cultivate religious authority.[8] But Fitt did not disclaim the mere practice of selling. At the heart of the commercialism that he decried lay the impulse to prioritize profit, especially by emphasizing products that were the most likely to sell. Fitt condemned that kind of commercialism because he suspected that it would undermine the purity of his firm's publications and abandon the imperative to provide his audience with the doctrinal and moral orientations he believed they needed. And he was not alone. Toward the end of the nineteenth century, many commercial publishers lamented that "commercialism" led companies to cater to the whims of a mass market, at the expense of qualities like literary merit.[9]

Yet the ascendance of commercialism enabled the rise of the twentieth century's for-profit evangelical book industry. Even as Fitt called upon evangelical publishers to avoid a commercialism that sought financial solvency by creating products designed to appeal to the mass market, other evangelical publishers sought to maximize profit by engineering new consumer constituencies for their products. Whereas Fitt worried that commercialism would promote "ungodliness," other evangelical publishers treated the task of locating and engaging profitable consumer constituencies as the heart of a commercial strategy that promised to help true Christians identify the needs and preferences that united them.

Today evangelical publishers often treat this kind of commercialism as a sort of common sense. When I spoke with the CEO of a leading evangelical publishing firm in 2016, for example, I invited him to respond to the common claim that avowedly Christian companies ideally should operate without commercial motive. Unequivocally dismissing that idea, the CEO claimed that commercialism enhances rather than undermines an evangelical company's religious mission. Insofar as nonprofit companies possess the legal and financial luxury of soliciting charitable donations to help cover financial shortfalls, he explained, that model leads a company to "lose its connection to the Church, because you're not responsive to it." He criticized companies that focused on giving people "what you think they should read," which he described as the strategy that most denominational publishers pursued.[10]

According to this logic, consumer engagement and corresponding profits not only serve as the measure of a company's service to "the Church" but also determine who belongs to that imagined group. Since no company possibly can reach everyone, commercial evangelical corporations devote their attention to those consumers who seem most receptive to their products. Rather than simply commodifying religion in service of the Church, commercial publishers define their consumer constituency as the Church. Their evangelical market serves as their evangelical public.[11]

To chronicle the ascendance of evangelical commercialism, this chapter contrasts Arthur Fitt's Colportage with another evangelical publisher: the Fleming H. Revell Company, described in 1904 as "one of the largest publishers of evangelical literature in the world, if not the largest."[12] The companies' differences took shape alongside all they held in common. The Revell Company's eponymous founder, Fleming H. Revell, served with Fitt as a trustee of Moody Bible Institute, and Revell's company printed many of the Colportage's books for them. Both institutions also attributed their existence and their success to the best-known evangelist of his era, Dwight Lyman Moody, who was Fitt's father-in-law and Revell's brother-in-law. Moody had helped create both publishing institutions, and he involved himself intimately in their affairs.

But it was Revell's company that most fully transformed Moody's mode of evangelical ecumenism into a kind of commercialism. With Moody advocating a Protestant posture that deemphasized sectarianism and called upon laypeople to unite around a common commitment to the "Christian work" of sharing the gospel, the Revell Company presented itself as a platform through which individuals and institutions endorsing varied Protestant perspectives could address ecumenical audiences by publishing and distributing "evangelical literature." After Moody's death in 1899, the Revell Company increasingly cultivated markets that embraced "liberal" evangelicals more generously than many of Moody's "fundamentalist" heirs. But their contrasting strategies would only testify to the power of commercial markets to conjure new religious publics, and the arc of Revell's commercialism exemplifies this fact of religion in modernity.

BENEVOLENCE, BOOKS, AND PRECARIOUS PROFIT

During the first few decades of the nineteenth century, a wide range of institutions claimed "beneficent" or "benevolent" intention as the animating ideal behind initiatives that included missionary work, the promotion of temperance, the "suppression of vice," and more. Reflecting in 1855 on his experience living in the United States for the previous decade, the Swiss historian and theologian Philip Schaff explained that Americans seemed to display a "noble liberality toward all sorts of benevolent objects." Even "the business man," Schaff observed, "considers his pecuniary gain only a means 'to do good.'"[13] As Schaff's exaggerated observation implies, benevolent institutions regularly called upon people with pecuniary wealth to fund "good" activities that did not generate sufficient revenue to cover their own costs. Valued as engines of both individual and social transformation, book publishing and print distribution ranked high among expensive benevolent activities, and antebellum evangelicalism took shape as the ecumenical premise for financial and industrial cooperation. By the second half of the nineteenth century, however, technological, economic, and cultural changes undermined evangelical ecumenism, which reorganized the market for evangelical books.

Although American book publishers and booksellers have always pursued profit, commercial success generally proved difficult to achieve before the middle of the nineteenth century. Until the early 1800s, American manufacturers struggled to produce or distribute most consumer goods at a lower cost than British manufacturers, who benefited from greater capital investment and more established transatlantic trade routes. Without comparably robust routes moving domestic goods from north to south between towns along the Eastern Seaboard, American manufacturers sold domestically produced goods to local and regional consumers. Even seemingly successful attempts to pursue greater commercial ambitions did not necessarily generate greater revenue. In 1796, for example, the Philadelphia publisher Matthew Carey found that he had printed too many copies of large and expensive books on geography and nature, each comprising multiple illustrated volumes. After failing to sell his surplus books to booksellers in Philadelphia and its environs or to generate interest through regional newspaper advertisements, he commissioned a traveling bookseller to find new consumers constituencies. That bookseller, the famed Anglican minister Mason Locke Weems, traveled south and canvassed the Chesapeake for three months, during which time he secured 1,000 subscription orders and placed books on consignment with storekeepers throughout the region. Altogether, Weems generated almost $20,000 of sales. And yet neither Weems nor Matthew Carey profited from those sales. The problem was that sales revenue had to cover Carey's initial investment, the cost of shipping stock from Philadelphia to sales sites, Weems's personal expenses, and sales commissions for all of the diffuse shopkeepers and individuals whom Weems enlisted to manage subscriptions and sales after he left the towns he visited. As this example illustrates, the practical and financial challenges of distribution persistently limited the domestic book industry's potential profitability, which in turn undermined any commercial incentive to address those challenges.[14] As the book historian Ronald Zboray notes, the publishing and bookselling businesses proved so difficult that they drove away even such famously speculative entrepreneurs as the showman P. T. Barnum.[15]

Despite these financial and logistical constraints, antebellum benevolent institutions treated publishing and bookselling as means by which they might effect their social and soteriological objectives. As religious disestablishment and new legal statutes made it easier for the voluntary associations of the early Republic to incorporate, own property, and amass wealth, benevolent institutions had set out to confront what they recognized as the opportunity and obligation to establish the kingdom of God on earth.[16] Viewing both common faith and cultural consensus as a precondition for that kingdom's realization, advocates of benevolence treated print and its distribution as a method of achieving those goals. "No man can love God any farther than he know what God is," a Baptist minister explained to a gathering of the American Bible Society in 1820. For that reason, he insisted, "true religion can prevail in this world to an extent no wider than the actual circulation of the Holy Scriptures give it a vehicle for its prevalence." Without such initiative, and without the "vast co-operation of benevolent individuals," true religion could "wind its way into no more of the recesses of that territory which it nominally occupies."[17]

Although every benevolent institution pursued distinct priorities, virtually every institution responded in varied ways to forms of real and perceived social instability. In such cities as Philadelphia, New York, Boston, Newport, Charleston, and Baltimore, for example, African Americans created benevolent societies that provided forms of social and economic assistance that white Americans and institutions withheld from them.[18] Meanwhile, as European and American migrants colonized the western frontier, displacing and decimating Native American civilizations, religious itinerants and institutions competed to establish themselves as agents of social order in new settlements. In urban centers, white Protestants became increasingly preoccupied by rising rates of Roman Catholic immigration, which they addressed through domestic missionary work and campaigns of moral reform.[19] Although historians sometimes have debated whether or not these efforts to cultivate social consensus merit condemnation as strategies of "social control," proponents of consensus understood their own social control as a form of freedom. As the historian Finbarr Curtis explains, the revivalist Charles Finney and other antebellum evangelicals acted upon the conviction that "people were most free when they made the same choices as their Christian neighbors."[20]

To pursue their dreams of conformity most effectively, benevolent institutions encouraged collaboration across the regional and ecclesiastical attachments that might otherwise undermine common concern. Reflecting in 1843 on the previous twenty years of benevolent effort, for example, an advocate of the American Sunday School Union praised Episcopalians, Methodists, Baptists, Presbyterians, and Congregationalists for proving that they could "all come together on the elevated ground of their common faith, leaving behind them their peculiarities, . . . and present an united front to the armies of the aliens."[21] Testifying to the need for ecumenical "evangelical" effort, an advocate of the American Tract Society (ATS) proclaimed in 1838 that "this enterprise for the supply of an American evangelical literature, to the whole population, should be prosecuted till not a family in all our borders shall be unsupplied."[22] Inviting Protestants from any denominational background to support their efforts, organizations like the ATS cultivated support for their cause by often avoiding what their leaders perceived as controversial or sectarian issues, including and especially debates over the abolition of slavery.[23]

Like other publishers and booksellers, benevolent institutions persistently struggled with the logistical and financial challenges of printing and distribution. Their struggle became especially steep because they sought to distribute their printed work as widely as possible, at low or even no cost to potential readers. As the first bible and tract societies took shape during the first decades of the nineteenth century, it was taken for granted that they would give their bibles and pamphlets away freely, just as other charitable associations donated alms to those in need. Bible and tract societies accordingly raised funds through membership dues, bought bibles and pamphlets from local printers and importers, and distributed those products to the poor. In its ninth annual report, for example, the American Tract Society underlined its need for more membership revenue. Insisting that "the Society *must* have GREATER FUNDS," the report detailed the value of every contribution. If 2,000 ministers across the United States would organize an auxiliary tract society of eighty "benevolent individuals" who contributed 25 cents each, one example suggested, they could produce as many as 3,999,000 tracts. And yet even this would not "supply the world," the report admitted.[24] The ATS's need for greater funds became more acute after 1827, when it began publishing full-length books in addition to their simple and short pamphlets.[25]

For both bible and tract societies, the limits of a strictly charitable model quickly became clear. Virtually every strategy designed to do more with limited financial resources ultimately called for additional money. Seeking not only to solicit as much membership revenue as possible but also to multiply the ranks of people willing to distribute their texts, bible and tract societies allied with and established smaller auxiliary societies. But in order to take fullest advantage of those auxiliaries' resources, publishers needed to print and distribute their products at lower cost per unit. To do so, they required capital to build regional distribution depots and to purchase new printing technologies, such as stereotype printing plates and steam-powered presses. And as they achieved what looked like success, they steadily elevated their ambitions. In 1829, for instance, the American Bible Society announced its "general supply" campaign, which set out to distribute a bible to every family in the United States, even as it steadily expanded to the west.[26]

All of this led both bible and tract societies to seek more revenue by selling literature to readers who seemed capable of paying. Those payments subsidized free literature for readers less able to pay.[27] This system allowed paying customers to subsidize free books and bibles, and it encouraged people who received free works to pay for them in the future. "When we find a family that has no book," one ATS agent explained in 1852, "we generally have to grant one: at the next visit they will usually buy one; and at the next a number, and so on, increasing their purchases as a thirst for knowledge and habits of reading increase."[28] In this way, selling became an effective method of allowing individuals to choose their way into conformity.

To be sure, not everyone endorsed the logic behind a shift toward selling. Writing in 1836, for example, one critic complained that "methods of business-doing" had cultivated a "bias of the heart toward money-making," which often generated "too much *trust* in money." Although he acceded that the "treasures [*sic*] of all the benevolent societies are full," the critic cautioned readers to pay attention to the moral compromises so often made under the guise of the excuse that financial "necessity compels us."[29] Indicting the American Tract Society's use of traveling, salaried agents known as colporteurs, another critic lamented in 1859 that "the *main* business of the colporteurs is book-*selling*," while "their religious influence is incidental and secondary." Detailing some of the corruptions that an emphasis on sales revenue engendered, the critic accused the ATS of avoiding the subject of slavery due to fear of alienating customers and supporters who endorsed slavery. "Every bookseller knows," he explained, "that if the colporteurs were not book *peddlers,* but only tract visitors carrying the Gospel, there would be no such timidity at the bare mention of slavery."[30]

Yet if evangelical anxieties about balancing charitable and commercial concerns had developed in response to the financial and logistical challenges of book publishing and distribution, the need for that balance became far less pronounced during the second half of the nineteenth century. During the 1820s and 1830s, evangelical publishers had pioneered advances in papermaking, power printing, mass production, and corporate communication. By 1855 they collectively produced 16 percent of all books published in the United States.[31] Over the same period, however, commercial publishers increasingly embraced the same advances, while also heralding their own innovations.[32] Taking advantage of regional railroad networks created in the 1850s, for example, commercial publishers established more constant communication between central printing plants and local booksellers, which facilitated commission-based sales arrangements and nurtured marketing strategies tailored to regional consumer preferences. As commercial publishers grew, they co-opted evangelical institutions' prior posture as engines of American consensus and community.[33] Testifying in 1861 to the general book trade's growing influence on evangelical publishers, one editorialist praised the American Tract Society not only for "circulating a fresh and vigorous evangelical literature throughout the land" but also for taking advantage of "the regular channels of trade both in the manufacture and in the distribution of its books." By using those channels, the ATS had established a model to which others should aspire. Any institutions that ignored that model, the writer concluded, should hear a censorious message from their benefactors: "Dismiss your costly agencies; reduce your expenses; and conduct your business *as a business,* and according to the times."[34]

In addition to enhanced business efficiency, shifting understandings of evangelical ecumenism also undermined the power of antebellum evangelical publishers. Beginning around 1840, an array of issues inspired what the historian James Bratt describes as a "new birth" of denominational consciousness. In 1837, for example, the United States experienced a significant financial collapse, which precipitated one of the most severe economic depressions prior to the Great Depression of the 1930s.[35] The panic limited the financial resources that wealthy donors could give to benevolent causes. Meanwhile, divergent understandings of slavery and society not only undermined cooperation within and across denominational divisions but also led both denominations and evangelical associations to divide. In 1857 the American Tract Society of Boston seceded from the national American Tract Society due to its reluctance to condemn slavery. In lieu of supporting ecumenical evangelical publishing enterprises, denominations increasingly created or enhanced their own initiatives. By 1863 the Methodist Book Concern described itself as the largest publishing house in the world, even though Southern Methodists had seceded and established their own book concern in 1854. Recalling an earlier era of evangelical ecumenism, an advocate of the Book Concern complained in 1889 that institutions like the ATS and American Sunday School Union had been "exclusively Calvinistic."[36]

During the second half of the nineteenth century, denominational publishers and commercial publishers essentially divided the market that benevolent evangelical publishers had pioneered. Denominational publishers continued to distribute literature to more rural regions of the expanding United States, funding that expensive undertaking by drawing on their denominations' financial and administrative resources. The Methodist Book Concern continued to grow, for example, by using traveling Methodist ministers as distribution agents. But denominational publishers lamented that denominational identity constrained their market. The Methodist leader James M. Buckley complained in 1889, "The limitations of a denominational literature are that the general public will invariably consider the institution a part of Methodist machinery, . . . and its imprint will constantly confirm that impression." From "a commercial point of view," Buckley noted, denominational identity functioned as "an element of restriction."[37] Meanwhile, commercial trade publishers like Harper & Brothers focused their attention on markets more likely to generate profit—primarily middle-class urban consumers—and supplemented their revenue from religious books by selling a wide range of other genres.[38] Many commercial trade publishers' emphasis on variety reflected their origins as booksellers. The publishing firm D. Appleton & Company, for example, began as a chain of dry goods shops, and Daniel Appleton's sense of sales potential allowed his firm to become a leading seller of devotional and theological books before his death in 1849.[39]

Whatever they sold and however they sold it, both denominational and commercial publishers asked the same question: How can we sell more books to more people? During the final decades of the nineteenth century, new fields of advertising and marketing devised answers to that question, designing strategies that sought to convince potential consumers to view particular goods as items that "most people" seemed to desire and that they too should acquire.[40] But other fields of activity generated parallel answers. Capitalizing upon the emergence of a middle-class consumer culture, Dwight L. Moody would champion a form of evangelical ecumenism that encouraged American Protestants to view themselves as the kind of people who could and should desire particular cultural products.[41] Moody's ecumenism would serve as the heart of a commercialism that became the operating logic for a new evangelical book industry.

THE MOODY MARKET

Early on the morning of August 14, 1875, a small barge approached the steamship *Spain*, off the shore of Manhattan. The barge carried a welcoming party of reporters, evangelical leaders, and prominent businessmen, all of whom had come to greet Dwight L. Moody and his song-leader partner Ira Sankey. The revivalists had been in Great Britain two years, during which time they had led hundreds of revival meetings and reportedly addressed millions of Britons. Over the course of four months in London alone, Moody held as many as 285 meetings and spoke to more than two million attendees.[42] With both surprise and fascination, American newspapers reported almost daily on Moody's activities. "We believe we may fairly say that the extraordinary successes of Messrs. Moody and Sankey in England have been a source of great astonishment over here," the *New York Times* reported shortly before their return. Moody's astonishing appeal not only made him a celebrity but also generated a market for goods by and about him.

Part of Moody's appeal lay in his deliberate inoffensiveness. As the historian Timothy Gloege explains, "Moody was happy to cooperate with whomever embraced a personal relationship to God, some sort of plain interpretation of the Bible, and a desire to have a practical impact, especially through evangelism." Moody actively avoided any teachings that might draw "sectarian" disagreement, focusing instead on issues that united

Protestants.[43] One contemporaneous observer noted that Moody avoided "the characteristic delusion of the average revival preacher, whose stock in trade consists of threats and denunciations, . . . whose favorite inducements are fire and brimstone."[44] Instead of focusing on any issues that might shock or censure, Moody especially addressed ideas of forgiveness and reconciliation with God and fellow man. Often relating stories about the Civil War, the historian Edward Blum explains, Moody presented a "depoliticized, sentimentalized, and distanced version of the struggle that diminished differences between the warring sections."[45] Moody's contemporaries sometimes interpreted this avoidance of political issues as a form of humility, in that he put matters of faith before personal opinion. In addition to avoiding politics, Moody avoided potential criticisms of his new "old fashioned Gospel"; as one colleague explained, Moody preached his sermons "with most impressive directness, not as by a man half convinced and who seems always to feel that a sceptic is looking over his shoulder."[46]

Moody's inoffensive posture and ecumenical palatability enhanced the circulation of stories, books, and consumer goods related to him. During the final decades of the nineteenth century, as news increasingly functioned as a commodity, newspapers had become preoccupied with the task of raising enough revenue to meet their escalating capital costs. To secure consistent revenue streams, newspapers cultivated reliable consumer constituencies by prioritizing predictable and palatable stories. The historian of journalism Gerald Baldasty describes this strategy as an emphasis on "least-offensive programming." And stories about Moody fit this description.[47] "Mr. Moody is evidently in earnest," a reporter for the *New York Times* explained in 1875, "and he endeavors to make the great truths of religion clear to the comprehension of the most illiterate of his audience. He encourages everybody to believe that the instant conversion and security of eternal peace are within their reach. No time need be lost. No doubts need be entrenched." The reporter insisted that Moody's message deserved "the respect and encouragement of all denominations of Christians."[48]

While Moody's nonsectarian posture encouraged stories about his exploits, his style of preaching helped make his teachings easy to consume in person and in print. Beginning in 1872, Moody had adopted a style of preaching pioneered especially by the Brethren evangelist Henry Moorehouse. Whereas Protestant preachers traditionally had put the ideal of *sola scriptura* into practice by crafting sermons that took individual bible passages as their primary object of analysis, Moorehouse crafted sermons that focused on single topics. Speaking on a topic like God's love, Moorehouse knit together passages that seemed to speak to that idea, without much regard for those passages' textual context. Moody had become familiar with

Moorehouse's method when Moorehouse preached at Moody's Illinois Street Church. Leading up to his trip to Britain, Moody had practiced using this technique by speaking at YMCAs in the United States.[49] This topical approach allowed Moody not only to dwell on his preferred themes and to cite disparate bible passages that supported his views but also to conform his teachings to what he perceived as his audience's preferences, anxieties, or interests.

In response, many of Moody's listeners came to see his sermons as incomparably engaging. "One of the most common experiences, perhaps, of those who have had the privilege of listening to Mr. Moody," the editor of an unauthorized 1875 sermon collection explained, "is that his words carry with them a recurrent power, continually cropping up afterwards with somewhat of their original force; a sure token of vigorous and effective speech, albeit, occasionally it may be, crude and homely in form." Offering this principle as the idea behind the sermon collection, the editor speculated that "the compilation in a book form of some of the more striking passages of his discourses would be gladly welcomed by many"[50] Due to their topical focus, Moody's sermons made excellent book chapters, and editors easily packaged several thematic sermons together around broader themes. One 1877 collection contained only Moody's anecdotes about children.[51]

As these collections illustrate, Moody regularly appealed to evangelical ideals of motherhood and womanhood. "More than any other preacher of our time," the introduction to *D. L. Moody's Child Stories* testified, "Mr. Moody possesses the power of appealing to the domestic affections, and using them for the purposes of religious persuasion."[52] Often teaching that women should prioritize their work in the domestic realm, Moody meanwhile used his ministerial stature and previous business experience to present himself an exemplar of masculine authority outside the home.[53] Although these gender ideals theoretically restricted women to the "woman's sphere" of the home, women negotiated such restrictions throughout the nineteenth century not only by participating in varied religious and benevolent associations and activities but also by developing new methods of living out the spirit of domesticity itself.[54]

Women took advantage of Moody's appeal to "domestic affections" in a variety of ways. At his revival meetings, for example, women staffed "inquiry rooms" in which they convicted other women of their sin and taught them how a relationship with Jesus could transform their lives and families.[55] At Moody's church in Chicago, Emma Dryer elaborated upon this model by creating the "Chicago Bible Work" initiative, which trained women to teach the city's working-class families about the Bible and to offer

D. L. MOODY'S

CHILD STORIES

RELATED BY HIM IN HIS

REVIVAL WORK

IN

EUROPE AND AMERICA,

WITH

PICTORIAL ILLUSTRATIONS.

———

EDITED BY

Rev. J. B. McCLURE,

Compiler of "MOODY'S ANECDOTES."

CHICAGO:
RHODES & McCLURE,
94 Washington St.
1877.

Love of Children. [Modern.]

Dwight Moody's sermons and anecdotes regularly addressed themes of evangelical motherhood and womanhood.

From Dwight L. Moody, *D. L. Moody's Child Stories*, 1877. Reproduced from a copy in Google Books.

charitable assistance. It heralded the creation of what became Moody Bible Institute, where women would receive training in missions, pastoral care, preaching, education, and more.[56] The notion of pious domesticity also justified religious consumerism in the age of consumer capitalism's emergence. By buying books, bibles, magazines, and other consumer goods, women cultivated ideas and resources that could nourish their families. This belief in the alignment of consumerism and domesticity generated new forms of social authority for women. That authority animated what became known as the science of home economics, the dominance of women in retail and sales, and the proliferation of consumer goods designed to serve women's own understandings of domestic duty.[57] Those consumer goods included Dwight Moody's books.

Recognizing Moody's potential appeal to both women and men, a wide array of merchants and publishers joined newspapers in cultivating and capitalizing upon the Moody market. In Great Britain, some shops even sold trinkets such as rings that displayed the names Moody and Sankey.[58] Following the evangelists' return to the United States, publishers and printers raced to produce books by and about Moody. As early as the middle of 1874, biographies of Moody, collections of his sermons, and accounts of his campaigns appeared regularly in newspapers and books. By the year's end, a collection of "Moody and Sankey hymns" had become well known in the United States.[59] As Moody traveled from Brooklyn to Philadelphia to New York to Chicago during his subsequent two-year-long revival tour, additional collections of his sermons, often culled from shorthand notes written by revival attendees, appeared throughout both the United States and Britain. According to some reports, opportunists even used unauthorized texts to imitate Moody's performances. One Methodist minister in New York reported in 1876 that he had discovered a meeting where "Moody and Sankey . . . are advertised, at which Moody's sermons will be read, Moody and Sankey hymnbook used, etc., then someone dashes out like Bro. Moody, or tries to sing a solo like Bro. Sankey—perfect copyist, and always more or less a failure."[60]

As the Moody market grew, Moody initially objected to the flood of merchandise associated with him. But his objection did not reflect disapproval of merchandising itself. Among his worries were potential accusations that his ministry served as a moneymaking scheme. This fear had become reality in 1873, when he and Sankey published a hymnbook that compiled songs used at their meetings. Because Sankey wrote many of his hymns himself, standard hymnals had not included them. But with the popularity of Moody's meetings generating demand for their book, its sales inspired successive editions and generated approximately $35,000 in revenue—which is equivalent to more than $750,000 in contemporary terms, according to one estimate.[61] This scale of success inspired accusations that Moody and Sankey had undertaken their revivals for the purpose of making money. Noting that Moody's revivals had "proved to be an astonishing success pecuniarily," some critics even circulated satirical stories—which some newspapers reprinted as news—that the showman and P. T. Barnum had "resolved to found a new religion, and he has introduced the work through Moody and Sankey."[62] To respond to suspicions of commercial intent, Moody entrusted the hymnal's subsequent revenue and charitable disbursements to businessmen. After returning to the United States, Moody made a similar arrangement with a committee of businessmen that included Cyrus McCormick and John Farwell—who long had underwritten Moody's activities.[63] They vouched for Moody's true intentions, just as he vouched for theirs. "We do not want your money," Moody explained in 1875. "Our one object in coming here is to preach

Christ," he insisted, "and that with God's blessing we shall see many brought into His fold."[64]

It may seem odd for Moody to turn to businessmen in order to allay suspicions of commercialism. But businessmen evidenced good intention, in part, because Moody saw the business principles of individual choice and responsibility as sanctified solutions to both individual and social suffering. Following the end of the Civil War, rapid industrialization not only propelled urbanization but also fueled racial, ethnic, and class conflict, as cities experienced unprecedented immigration, inequality, and injustice.[65] Whereas liberal Protestants increasingly attributed growing urban unrest to economic and political problems, which they attempted to address through hermeneutical techniques such as higher criticism and theological notions such as a "social gospel," Moody and his allies presented individuals as the source of social ill and the primary means of potential change.[66] This idea had become manifest especially during the 1850s, when downtown prayer meetings—subsequently known collectively as the "Businessmen's Revival"—cultivated the idea that a business sensibility could strengthen both individual piety and Christian society by wedding robust emotions to strict self-control, in the name of an optimized relationship with God. As the historian John Corrigan explains, revival participants came to see "an emotional relationship with God as a contractual, transactional matter."[67] Although Moody admitted that particular businesses and businessmen might sometimes deserve criticism, he insisted that such criticisms did not extend to any systemic qualities of capitalism.[68] Both the problem and the solution, Moody argued, lay within individuals. In one sermon, Moody compared an individual's spiritual journey to a ride in a hot-air balloon, with money functioning as the ballast that weighs a balloon down. "There are some Christians who, before they rise higher," Moody explained, "will have to throw out some ballast. It may be money, or any worldly consideration."[69] Free of burdensome moral or spiritual weight, individuals were able to take full advantage of what the historian Brendan Pietsch describes as "the salvific power of technology." As a mode of quantification, measurement, and application, business seemed to possess that power.[70]

Moody presented the businessmen who served as his as trustees and helped organize his revivals as exemplars of individual behavior and masculine authority. For two decades Moody had taught that every individual had the same opportunity and obligation to control society by controlling themselves. First in Boston and then in Chicago, Moody had been involved in the local YMCA. Founded in London in 1844, with outposts subsequently established in major American cities, the YMCA had emerged out of the "deep concern and anxiety" its founders reported feeling in response to "the almost totally neglected spiritual condition of the mass of young men engaged in the pursuits of business." In order to "discountenance immorality and vice" among the working classes, YMCAs in both Britain and the United States offered lectures, classes, reading rooms, and activities designed to cultivate "humble and unpretending Christian men" who would "work in harmony on the broad basis of our common Christianity" without "distinction of creed."[71] Acknowledging his working-class background and his experience nurturing individual and social reform among the working classes, wealthy business elites supported Moody in the hope that his message of individual discipline might help solve "the problem of the masses."[72]

Yet even if the premise of Moody's message seemed especially suited to working-class audiences, it ultimately made the most sense to middle-class laypeople. Moody nurtured that audience. Whereas "churchly" Protestants often sought to effect social reform through churches in working-class neighborhoods, the heart of Moody's method of reform lay in evangelism. He accordingly urged followers from any denominational background to undertake the "Christian work" of evangelism and to equip themselves for evangelism by developing a deeper understanding of the Bible's plain meaning. Just as a business might train its employees to enhance their productivity, Moody presented training as means by which Christian workers could achieve better results. Laypeople could train themselves, for example, through "Bible institute" courses that Moody began offering in Chicago in the 1880s. But they also could train themselves through books.[73] As reliable, mass-produced articles that women and men could chose to purchase and read for themselves, books enabled evangelistic and educational efficiency by allowing disparate readers to engage the same authorized information and by attuning readers to the processes of their own knowing. A related emphasis on efficiency and standardization had fueled demand during the 1870s for standardized ecumenical Sunday-school literature.[74]

This emphasis on reliability provides another reason Moody initially opposed books associated with him that lacked his endorsement.[75] Although in both Chicago and Britain he had taken extensive advantage of print to publicize events and raise awareness about his teachings, earlier print publicity had consisted primarily of announcements and articles that contained brief quotations or descriptions of his approach.[76] As collections of his sermons and stories appeared in the 1870s, Moody worried that those more comprehensive books might contain inaccuracies or might otherwise fail to accurately represent his message. Admitting that his speaking schedule limited his opportunities to produce new sermon content, Moody also speculated that readers might come to prefer other preachers after growing weary of seeing and hearing the same sermons.[77]

AUTHORIZING BUSINESS

Around 1875 Moody decided to exert control over the supply that fed the consumer demand for his teachings and celebrity. Moody provided his brother-in-law, Fleming Hewitt Revell, with the exclusive opportunity to produce his "authorized publications." Treating Moody's strain of middle-class ecumenism as an operating logic, Revell would capitalize on the Moody market as well as reach beyond it, cultivating a broader readership and engaging a more expansive evangelical public.

Revell received his opportunity after evidencing sound evangelical intentions and sharp commercial instincts. Born in Chicago in 1849, Revell first met Moody in 1860, when the revivalist came to speak at his school. And they grew closer in 1862, when Moody married Emma Revell, Fleming's older sister. Revell's father, a ship builder from England, had died just a couple years earlier, and Fleming reportedly lived with the newly wed Moodys for several years. Ten years older than Revell, Moody mentored him throughout his adolescence.[78] In 1869 Moody invited Revell to serve the Chicago YMCA by editing and publishing the periodical *Everybody's Paper*.[79] Moody had founded the paper in his capacity as vice president of the YMCA, on behalf of which he had raised money both for periodicals and for the construction of a new library for the public.[80] To achieve greater circulation, Revell cut the price by 25 percent in January 1871, which led sales to grow from 40,000 copies in December 1870 to 100,000 by March. Selling subscriptions by paying personal visits to Sunday schools and YMCA centers across the Midwest and Northeast, Revell reported in April 1871 that his magazine had sold 647,600 copies during the previous year. But lowering the price also reduced the paper's revenue, which led Revell to consider new ways of achieving a larger circulation.[81] One solution involved the creation of new periodicals, including *Words of Life* and *Temperance Tales,* which reprinted content between themselves in addition to circulating stories from other sources.[82] To secure images for *Everybody's Paper,* Revell reportedly traveled to England and asked the publisher of *The Christian Plowman* to sell him some woodcuts; as the story goes, the editor initially refused but eventually sold Revell several boxes of woodcuts after learning that Revell's Chicago office had been destroyed by the fire of 1871.[83]

After turning to book publishing, Revell strategically cultivated and capitalized on the company's access to Moody. In an 1877 issue of the *Chicago Daily Tribune,* for example, Revell placed an ad for three books. At the top of list was *Gospel Hymns No. 2*. The ad touted "the gems of the old book, together with a large amount of new material," promising that this particular volume "will hereafter be used by Moody and Sankey."[84] Immediately below this promise, another ad announced, in large letters, the "Last week of MOODY AND SANKEY at the Tabernacle." The ad explained that "Mr. Moody will Preach and Mr. Sankey will Sing every night this week, at 8 o'clock (except Saturday)," and it provided a detailed schedule of additional meeting times during the day, including the subjects that Moody would discuss. A few days after these advertisements and these meetings, an ad in another periodical touted the book of hymns and a collection of addresses delivered in Chicago, drawn from stenographic reports. "In justice to the public," the ad explained with a kind of compassionate commercialism, "we beg to announce that the only complete and authorized sermons . . . are in the above-named book."[85] Cementing the evangelical public's awareness of his company's rank in Moody's eyes, Revell distributed tickets for Moody's lectures through his company's bookstore, occasionally led noon prayer meetings in Chicago, and regularly served as a sort of public spokesperson for Moody himself.[86] As late as 1892, when Moody made plans to hold large revival meetings alongside the following year's World's Fair, the press identified Revell as one of two people closest to Moody, and Revell spoke on Moody's behalf.[87] Occasionally, as in Biloxi, Mississippi, in 1897, Revell delivered lectures as an authority on "Mr. Moody and his Evangelistic Work."[88]

For his company's first book-length publication, Revell chose a title that had proven its sales potential during Moody's revivals in Great Britain. A Scottish pastor and hymn writer who served at a church in Hull, England, and had participated in and supported Moody's revivals, William P. Mackay originally published his *Grace and Truth under Twelve Different Aspects* in Edinburgh. But when the Brethren firm of Pickering & Inglis released a new edition in 1872, Revell asked to reprint it through stereotype reproduction. In the preface to the 1874 "American edition," Mackay thanked "my beloved brother, Mr. Moody of Chicago," for enabling its publication.[89] Sympathetic to Mackay's emphasis on the notion that the hubristic "grace of man" too often keeps humans from recognizing God's true grace, Moody encouraged his revival volunteers to use *Grace and Truth* as a resource for anyone who sought to preach the gospel but possessed little doctrinal training or knowledge.[90] He often instructed his workers to give a book to meeting attendees who had spent time hearing "the truth as God gives it" in his revival's inquiry rooms.[91] Recounting her work as a volunteer during an 1874 meeting, for example, Jane MacKinnon recalled giving the book to a woman who had seemed "full of trouble." Admitting that she always had "fancied the 'lapsed mass' meant the poor," MacKinnon was surprised to encounter a woman like herself seeking assistance. After the woman admitted to having last attended church eight years prior,

MacKinnon read to her from Matthew 21:28 ("Come unto Me, and I will give you rest") and then handed her a copy of *Grace and Truth*.

In addition to publishing books used in Moody's meetings, Revell published collections of sermons delivered at those meetings. Moody explained that he published his sermons "in compliance with the wishes of many friends" and shared a self-deprecating assessment of his writing. "I deeply feel how partially and insufficiently the Glorious Gospel of the blessed God is represented in them," Moody remarked. To be sure, sermon collections were no innovation. Sermon collections had circulated since the first centuries of Christianity.[92] For Revell, however, sermon collections held commercial promise due especially to their potential to capitalize upon Moody's celebrity. At the heart of celebrity status lies the attention of a mass public, and Moody not only possessed such attention but also nurtured it.[93] Although he initially expressed anxiety that sermon collections could undermine his appeal, Moody had become comfortable presenting written sermons as part of an experience that he might amplify in person. Supporters eventually agreed that his sermons rewarded repeated reflection, commenting that the message "always came quite fresh and home to the heart and conscience, with power."[94] Moody also explained in the preface to *Addresses of D. L. Moody* (1875) that he hoped that his sermons "may be the means in their printed form of winning more souls to Christ than they have been when spoken." His focus on multimediation found a parallel in contemporaries like Henry Ward Beecher, who cultivated his own national public by speaking on lecture circuits and publishing collections of his own sermons, in which he offered "living truth aimed at living men."[95] Recognizing the commercial potential behind this model, commercial trade publishers like Harper, Macmillan, and Scribner's came to dominate the market for sermon collections by the early twentieth century.[96]

The Revell Company touted Moody's celebrity as well as his exclusive endorsement of the firm. In books by Moody, Revell always followed Moody's introductory remarks with a copy of his signature. And in advertisements for Moody's books, Revell pointed out that "all former books issued in Mr. Moody's name have been mere compilations, issued without his consent and notwithstanding his protest." For this reason, advertisements explained, only Revell's books should "be widely circulated."[97] Using demand for Moody's words as evidence of merit and utility, Revell's advertisements emphasized its high sales figures no less than the authorized status of its books. In 1884, for example, an ad in *The Ladies' Home Journal and Practical Housekeeper* boasted that the book *The Way to God and How to Find It* had sold "nearly two thousand copies per week for six weeks since issued. We publish only authorized books by Mr. Moody."[98]

PREFACE.

In compliance with the wish of many friends I have consented to the publication of the following Addresses.

I deeply feel how partially and insufficiently the Glorious Gospel of the blessed God is represented in them, but I lay them at the Master's feet, praying, and asking all my Christian friends to pray, that they may be the means in their printed form of winning more souls to Christ than they have been when spoken.

D L Moody

—All former books issued in Mr. Moody's name have been mere compilations, issued without his consent and notwithstanding his protest. The following are the only

AUTHORIZED PUBLICATIONS BY

D. L. MOODY.

SECRET POWER or the Secret of Success in Christian life and Christian work. "A book of intense interest and practical suggestion." Cloth, 60 cents; paper, 30 cents.

TWELVE SELECT SERMONS, by D. L. MOODY. Carefully revised, and containing those gospel addresses most blessed in Evangelistic work. 128 pp., cloth, rich gilt stamp, 60 cents; paper edition, 30 cents. *Ready May 1st.*

HEAVEN—*Where it is; Its Inhabitants and how to Get There,* by D. L. MOODY. Cloth, rich gold stamp, 112 pp., 60 cents; paper covers, 30 cents. *25th thousand.*

The clear, scriptural, common-sense treatment of this subject by Mr. Moody has been commended in the highest terms by leading theologians in Europe and America, while the common people have heard them everywhere with gladness.

How to Study the Bible. By D. L. MOODY. Revised. A valuable little work, which should be carefully read and studied by all who desire to enjoy the study of the Word. Paper cover, 10 cents; per doz., $1.00. Cloth, flexible, 15 cts.

The Way and the Word. By D. L. MOODY. Paper cover, 15 cents; cloth, 25 cents.

This is a neat little volume, containing a treatise on Mr. Moody's favorite topic, Regeneration; together with his thoughts on Bible study; the whole prefaced with a personal introduction by Mr. Moody.

The Second Coming of Christ. By D. L. MOODY. Revised from original notes. 32 pages and cover. Price, 10 cents. Per dozen, $1.00.

Should be widely circulated, calling attention to this important subject and most precious truth.

For sale by all Booksellers, or will be sent post free by return Mail on receipt of price by the publisher.

F. H. REVELL, 148 and 150 Madison St., Chicago.

Revell cultivated a reader's connection with Moody through its "authorized" branding and by including signed messages from Moody himself.

From Dwight L. Moody, *Twelve Select Sermons*, 1881. Reproduced from a copy in Google Books.

By 1890 the Revell Company published a wide range of other books that aided Moody's ministry and circulated within his orbit. These books included hymnbooks devoted to "every phrase of Christian experience and work," how-to books for holding events like prayer meetings and revivals, collections of poetry by authors like the English writer Frances Ridley Havergal, and an assortment of aids for studying the Bible.[99] Bible study aids included *Studies in the Book,* by Revere F. Weidner, who based his book on lectures delivered to students at Moody's school in Chicago.[100] In addition to study aids, Revell published bibles. During the 1890s, for example, Revell published a popular version of the Bible known as the "Bagster Bible" for distribution through the YMCA. Named after the English publisher who designed it, the Bagster Bible featured large type, wide margins for notes, tables with which to convert Jewish measurements and money, and thousands of marginal cross-references. It was the bible that most commonly drew the endorsement of Moody and his associates before their own Cyrus Scofield published his reference bible in 1909.[101] But some of Revell's most popular books were biographies of preachers and missionaries. Often prioritizing the virtues of simple living, pious masculinity, and the importance of devotion over doctrine, these biographies presented consumers with a template for Christian life in a changing world.[102] Short books containing "sweet stories" for children sought similar effect among young readers. And Revell advertised all of these books in the periodical *Record of Christian Work,* which the company published in partnership with Dwight Moody beginning in 1881.[103]

THE BUSINESS OF ECUMENISM

By the end of the 1880s, many observers had come to see Fleming Revell's company as the unofficial publication division of Moody's expansive empire. Commenting on this close partnership in 1888, the Baptist minister J. H. Gilmore gently chided Moody, his fellow pastors, and the Revell Company, joking that "many a book which does not bear the imprint of our good brother Revell, and which Mr. Moody would utterly condemn, may, to a man of greater mental breadth and more generous culture, be eminently helpful and suggestive in fathoming the meaning of the Book of Books."[104]

But the bedrock of Revell's partnership with Moody always had lain not just in Revell's allegiance to his brother-in-law and his teachings but also in the profitability of Moody's market and its attendant public. An 1891 profile of notable "books and bookmakers" in *The American Bookseller* testified that "the works of Mr. D. L. Moody have attained a sale of over six hundred thousand copies." That figure more than doubled the number of copies of the best-selling novel *Ben-Hur: A Tale of the Christ* that sold between 1880 and 1887.[105] And as the report noted, those figures included "only the volumes prepared by Mr. Moody and issued by his only authorized publisher, Fleming H. Revell, New York and Chicago, and does not include the large numbers of unauthorized and garbled reports of sermons, sketches, etc., that have been issued by irresponsible publishers."[106] In 1898 an article about Moody's achievement as a producer of books described Moody's *Gospel Hymns* in particular as "perhaps exceeding in money value any other individual literary property in the world."[107]

Even at the apex of his company's connection to the Moody market, however, Fleming Revell shifted from primarily publishing books by Moody and his immediate associates to pursuing business opportunities that elaborated upon Moody's mode of ecumenism. To convey its identity as a firm concerned above all with that ecumenical objective, Revell described itself on title pages and in advertisements as a "Publisher of Evangelical Literature." The slogan began appearing around 1880.[108] These new "evangelical" markets brought Revell new sources of revenue and enhanced its commercial reputation and reach.

Capitalizing upon an evangelical ideal, the Revell Company offered its services to diverse denominations, associations, churches, and ministers. Later reflecting on his earlier role as an executive at the Revell Company, the publisher George Doran recounted, "There were at least thirty other and minor denominations and sects, and as most of these had their beginnings in evangelical zeal and were relatively small and struggling, they could not produce their own literature. Here was a fertile and fruitful field for the independent evangelical publisher." Doran recalled that he accordingly began his career as an "ambassador from the house of Revell to all of these denominational houses west of the Alleghenies." For many individual ministers, Revell served as a sort of Protestant vanity press, often requiring ministers to finance substantial portions of their books' printing costs. Doran would explain that preachers often had approached him and boasted that their congregations had "begged of him to give to the wider world the blessing of his exhortations." By publishing their books, Revell simultaneously supplied the potential demand behind such boasts and transformed ministers' pride into profit.[109]

Yet not all individuals sought to publish for vanity alone. Some had more practical reasons. Itinerant evangelists, for example, often sought to publish books as a way of legitimizing themselves or supplementing their incomes. In Doran's view, some of these authors seemed "genuinely interested in the spiritual welfare of their fellows and thought not at all of financial results." The majority, however, "were shrewd and bargaining, more especially the traveling evangelist who took copies of his books with him for sale on his journeys to the members of his audiences—the profits to swell the income from collections and all to go to the purse of the evangelist, now a regular recognized and established merchant, or shall I say peddler."[110]

Both settled and itinerant ministers sought Revell's services, not simply because Revell offered more robust book production and distribution infrastructure but also because they hoped to associate themselves with the same respectability and legitimacy that Moody cultivated among his public. In return for extending that association, Revell was able to fold new churches, ministerial associations, and tract societies into its distribution network. Describing an agreement with the Seventh-Day Adventists, for example, Doran noted that the denomination already possessed a "thorough-going printing and publishing plant for the publication of their denominational papers and supplies, and for the selling of books by subscription." Doran even recalled that they had established "a branch in the capital city of each state," with each branch serving as "headquarters for proselyting and sales" that employed "a small army of men and women book-agents." By establishing a relationship with Revell, the Seventh-Day Adventists sought greater respect at a time when they were dismissed as "ascetic zealots." Meanwhile, Revell gained access to what Doran described as the denomination's "golden field for operation."[111]

This commercial strategy reflected Moody's own approach to denominational division. Although denominational loyalty often reflected ethnic or national identities no less than theological convictions, doctrinal distinctions often proved central to how Protestant groups articulated their social identities. An emphasis on doctrine led even small denominations to create periodicals that manifested their ideal perspective. With "a magazine or church paper with its editor for every shade of belief," Doran explained, "they fought their battles and washed their dirty linen in full view of a public which loved a religious fight."[112] Moody's avoidance of doctrinal issues reflected his recognition that doctrinal distinctions were socially divisive, and he called for evangelical alliance across those divisions. Manifesting that evangelical logic, Revell simultaneously catered to denominations' desire for particularity while also allowing them to participate in an ecumenical evangelical network.

To be sure, other new institutions joined the Revell Company in cultivating interdenominational ecumenism. Chief among those institutions were varied conferences on prophecy and the Bible. These events proliferated in the United States and Britain during the second half of the nineteenth century. Examples included the Interdenominational Bible Conferences and the International Seaside Bible Conferences, both held in New Jersey, as well as the Niagara Bible Conferences, held in Niagara-on-the-Lake in Ontario, Canada.[113] The Revell Company sought to capitalize upon these conferences for at least two reasons. First, they provided lucrative opportunities for bookselling.[114] As late as 1906 Fleming Revell remarked that he sold ten times more books at revival meetings and conferences than he sold at bookstores.[115] But second, these events provided opportunities to recruit new authors. Wealthy laypeople sometimes attended Bible conferences, and many conferences eventually invited families to treat summer meetings as inexpensive family vacation destinations. Yet early Bible conferences primarily drew ministers and professional Christian workers, who used conferences as opportunities not only to learn, worship, and relax but also to associate with people who might be able to offer opportunities for speaking, guest preaching, administration, or publishing. Reuben A. Torrey, for instance, became the first superintendent of the Bible Institute of Chicago and a Revell author after Revell met him at a convention.[116] Still today, conferences are engines of evangelical ecumenism and authorship.

By cultivating close relationships with conferences and their participants, the Revell Company extended legitimacy to the concerns that preoccupied those events, thereby allowing the company to build a market around those preoccupations. Beginning in the late 1870s, premillennial teachings ranked high among the articles of interdenominational faith that Bible conferences examined, and Revell circulated and elevated premillennial ideas more than any other company. In 1878, for example, a group of prominent premillennialists from the Northeast held a conference in New York to share what the conference's organizers described as "mutual encouragement in the maintenance of what they believe to be a most vital truth for the present times." After the New York *Tribune Extra* sold as many as 50,000 copies of the conference's proceedings, Fleming Revell published some of the event's addresses in a collection of "premillennial essays."[117] Following the book's publication, some reviews disparaged the book's "biblical criticisms and exegetical reasoning," insisting that "the essays are of small worth" and disparaging "the endeavor to literalize" key passages of the Bible as "absurd and self-contradictory." But the same reviewer also insisted that "one must be glad that they have been published," so that the ideas themselves might be understood and interrogated. In that spirit of ecumenical debate, the reviewer praised "the enterprising publisher and bookseller, F. H. Revell."[118]

As premillennial theories took shape in the decade following the end of the Civil War, they varied substantially. But they all emerged from the apocalyptic notion that Jesus Christ would return imminently and begin a millennial reign. Or, as the premillennialist William Blackstone explained in the title and content of a pamphlet that Revell published in 1878: "Jesus Is Coming." Whereas Dwight Moody avoided addressing the divisive idea publicly before 1877, Revell had begun publishing premillennial books and supporting premillennial networks as early as 1873, when the company reprinted *Notes on the Book of Exodus*, by the British scholar Charles Henry Mackintosh. In that book, Mackintosh encouraged readers to prepare for the "glorious advent" of Jesus in the same way that the Israelites prepared for the imminent death of firstborn children in Egypt.[119] Revell published Mackintosh's book not only because it drew interest from people in Moody's network but also because Revell could reprint the book without paying royalties to the original English publisher.[120]

Revell would achieve far greater success with William Blackstone's book. Described in an 1879 advertisement as a collection of "seven arguments in favor of the pre-millennial coming," Blackstone's ninety-six-page booklet sought "to furnish in an abbreviated form, a handbook that might serve as a convenient reference volume in the study of this truth." Priced aggressively at 25 cents for a cloth cover and 10 cents for paper, the booklet became one of Revell's early best sellers. A year after its publication, it had sold 10,000 copies.[121] In 1898 the company re-released Blackstone's book as a revised and significantly expanded book. In those later editions, leading evangelicals would recall the influence that the booklet initially had on them. Reuben A. Torrey described it as "the first book that made the coming of Jesus Christ a living reality to me. . . . It was this that first brought me to definite convictions and made the doctrine not only clear, but very precious." Claiming that the book "revolutionized my thinking, the evangelist J. Wilbur Chapman explained that he "had no defined method of Bible study" before reading Blackstone's book. And Robert E. Speer, the secretary of the Presbyterian Church's board of foreign missions, recounted reading the booklet twenty years earlier at a summer conference at Dwight Moody's Northfield retreat. "That summer was the first time," Speer admitted, "the truth of our Lord's return came to me."[122]

In assessing the popularity of premillennialism, historians have noted that the number of denominations endorsing premillennial principles proliferated at the turn of the century. They include the Christian and Missionary Alliance and the Church of God in Christ. But an emphasis on denominations should not shift attention away from the interdenominational constituency that those ideas inspired. This constituency became manifest not only at the New York conference and subsequent Niagara Bible Conferences but also as a market. Matthew Sutton notes that premillennialism was "not a church or a denomination"; it was, Sutton argues, "a conviction and an ideology."[123] But convictions and ideologies achieve social significance only to the extent that publics take them up. By identifying and nurturing a market for premillennial convictions and ideologies, Revell gave premillennialism social stature.

For Dwight Moody no less than for Revell's consumers, part of the appeal of premillennial ideas involved their therapeutic effect. Centered on the notion that people can enhance and improve themselves beyond predetermined social or cultural limitations, therapeutic culture blossomed toward the end of the nineteenth century. With industrial capitalism continually reorganizing relationships and obligations within communities, households, and other social networks, therapeutic ideas and practices allowed Americans to seek a sense of relief, stability, and certainty by focusing on the self rather than society.[124] For Americans at the end of the nineteenth century, premillennialism offered relief in a variety of ways. Premillennialists taught, for example, that the Bible contained a seamless message that suited a "plain" interpretation of the text, which allowed the

Bible to serve as a sort of guidebook for Christian living.[125] This method of reading the Bible led premillennialists to expect Jesus's literal and imminent second coming, which offered some certainty in the face of dramatic social changes. Those changes included attempts to integrate former slaves into an interracial political order during Reconstruction; conflict over racist efforts to enforce segregation; new waves of immigration from southern and eastern Europe; the perceived decline of white Protestant dominance; and such revolutionary technologies as electric lighting, telegraphy, and train travel.[126]

During the 1890s a version of premillennial thought known as dispensationalism amplified premillennialism's therapeutic power. Presenting their approach to the Bible as nothing less than a "science" of biblical interpretation, dispensationalists claimed that their interpretive principles allowed humans to understand the arc of human history and the specific conditions of Jesus's impending return. But many premillennialists initially proved reluctant to champion dispensationalism, and Moody himself waited until 1897 to do so. Long before that, however, the Revell Company began selling related literature.[127] In 1886, for example, Revell published Arthur T. Pierson's *Many Infallible Proofs,* in which Pierson adopted what he described as "a truly impartial and scientific spirit" to detail his "evidences of Christianity." Insisting that his argument qualified as science insofar as science "compels a clear comprehension of truth or facts," Pierson devoted special attention to the biblical prophecies from which he and others would develop robust dispensational schema in the next decade.[128] In addition to Pierson, Revell authors like Robert Cameron and the Southern Baptist preacher Len Broughton would help codify dispensational teachings during the 1890s and early 1900s.[129] These and other books allowed dispensational ideas to circulate far beyond the bible and prophecy conferences where they initially flourished.

By investing early in both premillennialism and dispensationalism, the Revell Company not only presented its books as means by which Christians could acquire the certainty they sought but also championed the therapeutic orientation of consumer capitalism. Having developed through a longer history of religious introspection, therapeutic culture complemented consumer capitalism's emphasis on identifying and satisfying individual desires and needs through the purchase of commodities. Like other commercial publishers, Revell and its authors argued that their books offered the assistance that consumers needed. "The only motive inspiring this small volume," Moody explained in the preface to his book *Heaven: Where It Is, Its Inhabitants, and How to Get There* (1880), "is that souls may be helped." This sales pitch helped Revell sell nearly 90,000 copies of the book within four years.[130] Although dispensationalist literature might seem less straight-forwardly therapeutic than books about heaven and "how to get there," both genres of books invited consumers from across the spectrum of de-nominational attachments to treat their consumption as a means of achieving relief from uncertainty. The historian David Watt describes the evangelicalism of the 1960s and 1970s as "a variant of the therapeutic cul-ture" rather than a bulwark against it, but commercialism conjured thera-peutic evangelicalism long before the rise of modern psychology.[131]

THE VIRTUES OF COMMERCIALISM

"Look how our great book houses have captured this proud and haughty avenue (Fifth) to Twenty-third street," a report in the *New York Evangelist* boasted in 1898. The writer, Henry Robinson, took pride in seeing evan-gelical publishers located alongside leading commercial publishers. Heaping special praise upon the Fleming H. Revell Company, Robinson noted that the company's books always proved "specially tasteful to the eye." Because the "eye is such a critic," he mused, "a book had better always please it."[132] Both the company and its books reflected what Robinson described as a "certain spic and spanness." As this assessment suggests, Revell became re-nowned by the standards of Fifth Avenue by establishing itself as a pur-veyor of books that appealed to middle-class, urban Protestants. Although that public included the Moody market and other "evangelical" constitu-encies, Revell's commercialism eventually would lead the company to re-cast those attachments.

Among Fifth Avenue's commercial publishing companies, a focus on the middle-class market did not seem peculiar. High distribution costs continued to make urban bookstores primary distribution outlets, and those book-stores secured their cultural significance by presenting themselves as cita-dels of commercial and civic citizenship.[133] Revell's middle-class emphasis drew support from Dwight Moody, who addressed the same demographic. During the second half of the 1890s, however, Moody and his closest sup-porters implemented a new social strategy that conflicted with the princi-ples of commercialism that Revell practiced.

For most of his career, Dwight Moody, along with his immediate allies, primarily addressed a public comprised of people who worried more about their spiritual welfare than their material welfare. Moody virtually never spoke or wrote about addressing social suffering through material means.[134] In 1893, when responding to a question about whether there was "much actual suffering among the poor of Chicago," Moody insisted that "by far

1. E. P. Dutton & Co.
2. G. P. Putnam's Sons.
   Frederick A. Stokes & Co.
   Henry Holt & Co.
3. A. D. F. Randolph & Co.
4. American Tract Society.
5. Charles Scribner's Sons.
6. Dodd, Mead & Co.
   American Baptist Publication Society.
7. Methodist Book Concern.
8. Houghton, Mifflin & Co. (New York Agency.)
9. The Forum.
   Cassell Publishing Company.
10. The Century Company.
    Thomas Nelson & Son.
11. James Pott & Co.
12. Fleming H. Revell Company.
13. Baker and Taylor Company.
14. The Illustrated American.
15. The John Church Company.
16. Longmans, Green & Co.
17. The Evangelist.
18. William Evarts Benjamin.
    George H. Richmond & Co.
19. The Aldine Club.
20. North American Review.
21. The Merriam Company.
    Leach, Shewell & Sanborn. (N. Y. Agency.)
    Charles L. Webster & Co.
22. J. Selwyn Tait & Son.
23. Merrill and Baker.
24. D. Appleton & Co.
25. Ginn & Co. (N. Y. Agency.)
26. Macmillan & Co.
27. T. Y. Crowell & Co. (N. Y. Agency.)

In close proximity to the above are:

Harper and Brother's uptown agency, at 766 Broadway, near the corner of Ninth street.
Rand, McNally & Co., 61 East Ninth street.
A. C. Armstrong & Son, 51 East Tenth street.
Maynard, Merrill & Co., 43 East Tenth street.
A. S. Barnes & Co., 56 East Tenth street.
Fords, Howard & Hulbert, 47 East Tenth street.

By 1894 the Fleming H. Revell Company had achieved both metaphorical and physical standing alongside some of New York's most prominent publishing companies. Located west of Union Square, Revell is indicated with an arrow.

"The New Publishing District," *New York Evangelist*, November 29, 1894, 48. This reprint is from an image that originally appeared as part of ProQuest® American Periodicals product. Reprinted with permission from digital images produced by ProQuest LLC. www.proquest.com

the greater part of it comes from intemperance, improvidence and laziness." Arguing that the city's regular worker demonstrations had threatened to "injure trade" and "cause money to be hoarded up" at the expense of the working class itself, Moody offered unemployed workers advice by paraphrasing Matthew 6:33. "Seek the kingdom of God and His righteousness," Moody recommended, "believing His promise . . . that all things will be added unto them."[135] Even Moody's patrons came to acknowledge that "the problem of the masses" was something Moody seemed uninterested in or unable to solve.[136]

Virtually from the start, Revell's best sellers accordingly focused on addressing middle-class concerns. Originally published in 1875, for example, Hannah Whitall Smith's *The Christian's Secret of a Happy Life* became one of Revell's best-selling titles by providing consumers with accessible and therapeutic methods of seeking certainty in their own lives. To be sure, Smith approached her book from a distinct devotional perspective.[137] Born a Quaker but converted to an evangelical orientation during revivals in 1857, Smith and her husband Robert initially achieved prominence in 1874 after traveling to England and serving as evangelists for the Keswick or "Higher Life" movement. A strain of the Holiness tradition, the Keswick movement emphasized the need for individuals to commit their lives to God and invite sanctification before God would give them what Smith describes as lives "of abiding rest and of continual victory."[138] But Smith ultimately insisted that she had "not tried . . . to make my book theological." Instead, she explained in the preface to an 1888 edition, "the truths I have to tell are not theological, but practical." Presenting her ideas about God as reliable "facts," Smith offered readers "fundamental truths of life and experience." But the majority of her examples took for granted that her readers "have plenty" and require spiritual rather than material certainty.[139]

Addressing female readers in particular, Smith regularly used illustrative anecdotes from her own life and the lives of other real or imagined women to explain how Christians could seek and find transformative closeness to God through all aspects of their mundane lives. She praised one woman for yielding "herself up as heartily to sweep, and dust, and bake, and sew, as she would have done to preach, or pray, or write for the Lord."[140] Having initially drafted the book in the early 1870s while pregnant and nursing her husband back to health after a nervous breakdown, Smith recurrently reflected upon the struggles of motherhood and marriage.[141] Consistently, she argued that the way to achieve "happy and effectual service" is to put trust in God. "Trust and worry cannot go together," she explained.[142] Relatable and encouraging, Smith's book sold over 175,000 copies by 1889 and more than 500,000 copies by 1944. During the twentieth century, such prominent evangelical authors as Catherine Marshall and Marabel Morgan cited Smith as inspiration.[143]

Revell's singular focus on middle-class consumers inspired the creation of the Bible Institute Colportage Association. According to the origins story often recounted in BICA's promotional literature, the Association took shape following a series of revival meetings that Dwight Moody held in Wisconsin during the fall of 1894. Toward the end of that meeting, some of the men and women who had been "making decisions to live for Christ" asked for additional guidance that they could use after the revival's conclusion. While considering how to provide those young converts with "help for the future," Moody received a message from an old friend. "I'm desperate," the friend reportedly wrote, asking Moody for "spiritual help" from afar. As a promotional flyer from the 1940s later narrated, Moody concluded that these two problems had a common solution: "Books! That was it. Christians needed definite, helpful books of guidance for their spiritual life." And yet Moody reportedly had trouble locating the books he desired. At local bookstores in Wisconsin, for example, he found that "the shelves were loaded with fiction of all kinds," but "he could not procure a single religious book." Moody dismayingly discovered that only one bookstore in all of Wisconsin even "pretended to carry even a limited assortment of religious books." Only after returning to Chicago and rushing "from bookstore to bookstore" did Moody locate appropriate products. And he found those books at the Revell Company store in Chicago, where Moody purchased "a bundle of Christian books for three dollars and one for five." Moody subsequently established the Association so that others would not have such difficulty supplying their own demand for Christian literature.[144]

The Colportage set out to supply rural regions and their residents with literature that Revell chose to sell primarily in cities. To that end, BICA published and distributed inexpensive and free versions of books by Moody and his associates. The Association's superintendent, Arthur Fitt, presented its books not only as articles that could supply unmet demand but also as opportunities for "the masses" to choose the right kind of religion. Among the masses Fitt counted "prisoners, lumbermen, seamen, railroad men and miners." Arguing in 1903 that "the need is as great as it ever was for the distribution of evangelical literature in this and other lands," Fitt boasted that "no society has better books than ours for reaching the masses."[145] Focusing especially on prisoners, the Colportage's administrators tried in 1898 to identify every prison in the country and to determine whether it possessed a library. Using this information, the Colportage offered sets of books to prisons that requested them and encouraged subscriptions to its periodical *Record of Christian Work* by offering three months free.[146] A journal devoted to prisoner welfare reported that a prisoner in New York's Sing Sing Prison said that he "had no thought of the necessity of a change of heart when committed, but . . . was attracted to reading Moody's book, *The Way to God* (copies of which have been furnished each prisoner). From this he got to reading the Bible, and feeling that he had no friends led him to seek the friendship of Christ, and on being put into a cell with a new convert he feels that he is now a child of God."[147]

Although Fitt portrayed the Colportage's understanding of evangelical print culture as an objective with a long precedent, its emphasis on rural consumers stemmed largely from new theological concerns within the Moody network. Especially after the financial crisis of 1893, new Populist movements called more pressingly for radical economic changes and justified their appeal with radical evangelical ideas and rhetoric. Populist constituencies spanned the working and middle classes, including economically aggrieved industrial workers, farmers, and the owners of various small businesses. Many from these constituencies blamed the professional classes for low wages, falling commodity prices, and rising debt—which farmers and proprietors often found more necessary for financial survival, and yet more difficult to repay. Radical evangelicals borrowed Populist principles from many of the notions that Moody had encouraged them to embrace—including notions of individual sanctification, a personal relationship with God, and a plain interpretation of the Bible. These ideas encouraged radicals to emphasize the spiritual authority and worth of every individual, while also training them to read such scriptural passages as Jesus's criticisms of wealth in their plainest, condemnatory sense.[148] The Colportage thus served as a means of engaging more actively with rural working classes.

But the problem with selling books in rural settings and targeting consumers who had little means to pay is that sales revenue struggled to cover the cost of production and distribution. That is precisely why the Revell Company and other commercial publishers avoided that model. The Colportage accordingly relied on charitable donations to cover its operating costs. Requesting money in periodicals and through correspondence with potential donors, the Colportage established charity funds dedicated to the distribution of books not just in prisons but also in lumber camps, fire stations, Alaska, China, India, and among "mountain whites."[149] During the 1930s, BICA would focus its efforts especially on rural public schools, establishing initiatives to distribute Christian literature to "many thousands of isolated homes in the mountain areas, on the vast plains, in the bayou and swamp regions, where children have never heard of Jesus Christ."[150] Its consistent emphasis on rural distribution ultimately earned the Colportage a prominent place in the homes of rural white evangelicals. "When I was a boy on a Missouri farm," Dale Carnegie, the author of the popular self-help book *How to Win Friends and Influence People* (1936), testified in 1943, "most of the books in the house were of the Moody Colportage Library books."[151]

Beginning with the aid that it offered after Moody's experience in Wisconsin, the Revell Company provided BICA with substantial support. Because Revell owned both the copyright and the printing plates to most of the books that the Colportage sought to circulate, BICA required Revell's cooperation. But that support also came at a cost. After all, with BICA specializing in distributing cheap, paperback versions of Revell's books, the Colportage undermined sales of Revell's more expensive editions of the same titles. Revell accordingly charged BICA at least 30 percent more than the market rate for printing.[152] Throughout the Colportage's first decade, payments to "F.H. Revell Co." were regularly one of the largest expenses in its annual reports.

To be sure, Revell benefited from their arrangement with the Colportage. But even if Revell profited by supplying the Colportage's demand, Revell did not share BICA's business strategy. Throughout the 1890s Revell steadily had intensified its emphasis on letting consumer demand serve as the index of what its ecumenical audience needed. "The demand . . . is not as large, relatively, for the distinctly devotional type of literature as it has been at other times," Fleming Revell remarked to an interviewer in 1904. Revell attributed this relative disinterest in devotional literature to what he saw at the time as "the great financial prosperity of the country." Noting that he had been in business during three financial panics, he explained that "the invariable rule has been that at the beginning of a panic there is at first a marked depression in all lines of the publishing business, and then a sudden increase in the demand for devotional literature until it has become enormous." Revell concluded by noting that "the total amount of religious literature sold does not decrease, . . . but the emphasis changes. Just now we are in a didactic and practical mood. The pendulum will doubtless swing back again."[153] Disavowing an obligation to shape consumer mood, Revell emphasized the need to help consumers perform their desire through acts of purchase. Reflecting on Revell's unwavering dedication to this profit principle and his defense of business agreements premised upon that principle, Fitt would lament in 1900 that "Mr. Revell has a reputation—or, rather, the *firm*—of being rather hard in business."[154]

Revell's pursuit of profit put an unbearable strain on the Colportage in 1903, when the postal service revised the policies it had used to classify mail and determine postage. For years the Colportage and many other low-cost publishers had bound their books in paper covers, which they designed to make the books look like periodicals. This allowed the books to qualify for the lower, second-class periodical postage rate. Convinced that these paperbacks undercut their sales, retail merchants and store owners complained about this practice. And after the department store magnate (and Moody supporter) John Wanamaker became postmaster general in 1889 and changed the policy to one that incidentally benefited department stores, only "legitimate periodicals" received second-class status after 1901.[155]

Writing to his board that November, A. P. Fitt noted that third-class status would require three cents per book, as opposed to the previous one-cent postage cost. "The loss of these privileges has consequently cut the ground from under our feet," Fitt lamented, "and has hurt our operations very seriously." Fitt reported that this financial problem would impair BICA's ability to reach regions "where the books were most helpful, namely: in frontier sections and neglected or sparsely settled districts, to which points express charges mean much extra expense to colporteurs." Even though it stopped publishing new monthly books in October 1901, the Association still generated a net loss of $1,448.10 that year—a substantial amount for a corporation whose net assets and credits totaled $26,637.75.[156]

Although initially unwilling to revise its licensing fees and printing charges, the Revell Company eventually helped BICA out of its financial crisis by offering better terms. At first Revell merely offered to sell BICA duplicates of its printing plates, at prices that Fitt considered "harsh and unjustifiable." Blaming the company's crisis and low stock of popular books on "the attitude of Fleming H. Revell Co.," Fitt asked Fleming Revell to discuss the matter in person in December 1903; Revell agreed, but Fitt reported that Revell insisted on meeting "in the presence of a third party (a business man)." Henry Parsons Crowell—the president of the Quaker Oats Company and soon-to-be president of Moody Bible Institute—agreed to serve. To Fitt's surprise, however, Revell welcomed Crowell merely as a "mutual friend whose advice might or might not be taken." As a result, "nothing practical came of the interview."[157] When Revell ultimately agreed to an arbitration a few months later, Fitt described the arbitrator's conclusions as a triumph for Revell. Revell held firm on printing prices, but it granted BICA discounts on subsequent editions and large orders of particular books, so long as BICA published at least one a month and ordered no fewer than 100,000 books per year. Revell retained the copyright to the most popular titles, and it insisted that BICA could only use its plates for paperback books. Revell alone possessed the right to publish comparably lucrative hardcover books.

When challenged to defend this policy, Revell insisted that Moody himself had sanctified his company's business tactics and its negotiating position. "Mr. Revell claimed," Fitt explained, "to have made certain agreements with Mr. D. L. Moody personally." Due to "Mr. Revell's intimate family and other relations" with Moody and BICA, many of those agreements had occurred "without being preserved in writing." Using what Fitt interpreted as a dismissive tone, Revell had insisted that Fitt lacked "documentary evidence to refute those claims." More than merely claiming that Moody had blessed its business, Revell argued that BICA could not expect

Revell to accept anything less than the full value of its property. "Much that we supposed was freely done for our Association by Mr. Revell as a friend and supporter," Fitt lamented, "he now claims had a commercial lien and value which he asserted to our loss before the arbitrator." Adding insult to injury, Revell had revealed its plans to begin publishing cheaper paperback editions of its books. The arbitrator had upheld its right to do so, despite Fitt's complaint that such an act would cut "into the market created by us with books which in many cases owe their existence to us."[158] True as this might have been, Revell possessed the legal right to cut into BICA's market, and two decades of activity had endorsed its unabashed pursuit of commercial profit.

By the end of the 1890s the Revell Company had concluded that its identity as a "publisher of evangelical literature" restricted its ability to cultivate lucrative consumer markets. One of the first Revell books to appear without the "evangelical" designation was a book that George Doran acquired—Roswell Field's novel *The Bondage of Bollinger* (1903), which the Revell Company advertised as the story of "a dear old New Englander whose passion for books leads him into many a trouble." According to Doran, the shift reflected the company's sense that the "evangelical" label limited its commercial potential.[159] During the 1890s, Revell's desire to remain in the good graces of the Moody market had obligated it to turn down a number of manuscripts because they endorsed the kinds of social critiques that Populists had affirmed. Those books reportedly included Charles Sheldon's *In His Steps* (1897), which Doran described as "too revolutionary, too intensely practical" for Moody and his allies. According to Doran, the Revell Company rejected it three times. "Evangelical as was our effort," Doran explained, "this did not extend to the point where we would present Jesus as Sheldon did, as the intimate and concerned personal friend of mankind." Yet because it engaged the popular evangelical idiom of personal encounter with God, Sheldon's book went on to become one of the best-selling books of its day.[160]

As Revell abandoned the label "evangelical," the company increasingly published books that manifested middle-class evangelical morality without explicit reference to Christian teachings or categories. The company created a line of popular fiction, for example, which offered what *Publishers Weekly* would describe as "clean, healthy stories." The novelist Ralph Connor proved especially popular. In a 1901 publishing roundup in the periodical *Zion's Herald*, Revell bragged about having sold 60,000 copies of Connor's *The Man from Glengarry* before publication day. A 1906 *Washington Post* advertisement claimed that the first edition of Connor's *The Doctor* had sold 100,000 copies. Reviews of Revell's books sometimes acknowledged the company's more implicit evangelical posture. One review noted that the company often published "didactic fiction with a pretty heavy touch of the obviously moral, not to say religious purpose in it." The review added that Revell's novels valorized "the merit of earnestness and simplicity."[161]

A similar approach oriented Revell's list of nonfiction titles. In 1903, for example, Revell published an American edition of a book by John Kelman originally published in London as *The Religious Message of Robert Louis Stevenson*. A Scottish writer and literary celebrity known above all for the novels *Treasure Island* and *The Strange Case of Dr. Jekyll and Mr. Hyde*, Stevenson did not have a religious reputation. Raised by a Presbyterian minister in a doctrinaire Calvinist household, Stevenson famously had disappointed his father by affirming an interest in atheism. Yet Kelman portrayed Stevenson as a paragon of "unconscious Christianity" and an exemplar of the true spirit of "modern Christianity." Insisting that "there are strong men whom God has girded though they have not known Him," Kelman argued that advocates of conventional "religion" often drew that concept's boundaries too narrowly. Calling for a broader appreciation of Stevenson's "faith," Kelman praised that faith for "its unconventionality, its freedom from dogmatic expression, and the inseparable weaving of it into the warp and woof of his life's various activities." Affirming this more capacious understanding of faith, Revell retitled Kelman's book *The Faith of Robert Louis Stevenson*, which better captured aspects of religious life "generally reckoned among things secular."[162] The *New York Times*, at least, found Kelman's book compelling enough to publish two reviews of it in the space of a few months. One review explained that "the 'faith' of which Mr. Kelman writes is to be taken in the largest sense. It is something more than religious, though the religious is also included in it."[163]

As the Revell Company's commercialism increasingly fixed its attention on the "more than religious," that shift required greater investment. "As evangelical publishers," George Doran later boasted, "we were specialists." Because the company had developed such elaborate networks for engaging authors and audiences, the company had been able to address its "comparatively compact public . . . at relatively low cost." To engage markets beyond its evangelical address, the company set out to conjure "a broad national public" by purchasing more advertising in more prominent periodicals.[164] That investment in a broader audience had begun much earlier. During the 1880s the company had acquired smaller publishing firms and established outposts in cities like Edinburgh and London.[165] New York appeared on the colophon of its books beginning in 1884, and Toronto appeared around 1888. By 1891 Revell had consolidated its administrative operations in New York, which had emerged as North America's publishing center. Chicago and Toronto served largely as hubs for more efficient retail and mail-order distribution.

Yet even as Revell pursued broader markets beyond "religion," it did not abandon the evangelical public. Just as the label "evangelical" had allowed the company to address an ecumenical constituency of evangelical consumers, the Revell Company applied the same style of commercial ecumenism to both adjacent and new markets. Adjacent markets took shape around authors like Newell Dwight Hillis and Harry Emerson Fosdick, who sometimes described themselves as "liberal evangelicals." The minister of Brooklyn's Plymouth Church, Hillis emphasized the importance of biblical morality but expressed little concern about doctrinaire issues like biblical inspiration.[166] Meanwhile, Fosdick became known above all as a paradigmatic "modernist."[167]

By the 1920s, Revell's devotion to these markets situated the company as an ally of publishing firms and religious leaders that collaboratively sought to claim social influence on behalf of a broader understanding of religion.[168] Aggressively marketing what the historian Matthew Hedstrom describes as "more expansive religious books," this collaboration helped revolutionize "the way religious books were marketed and sold in the United States." What the Fleming H. Revell Company's story illustrates, however, is that this revolution had been decades in the making. Long before its executives helped organize the first Religious Book Week, in 1921, the company's "commercialism served sacred ends."[169]

CONCLUSION

By the middle of the twentieth century, Revell's commercialism ultimately invited competition that the company could not overcome. Neither a general trade publisher nor a fundamentalist publisher, the Revell Company ultimately surrendered much of the liberal evangelical market to publishers like Harper & Brothers, which produced cheaper books and distributed them more broadly. Granted, Revell would experience a conservative renaissance around 1970, under the leadership of a new president. During the 1970s the company published books by such prominent evangelical conservatives as Anita Bryant, Marabel Morgan, Richard DeVos, and Francis Schaeffer. Yet as Revell wrung renewed evangelical value from its residual value, a series of evangelical firms acquired and resold the company in the 1980s. Zondervan bought it in 1983, then sold it to Guideposts in 1986. Baker Publishing Group bought Revell in 1992. Baker uses it to publish "practical books that would help bring the Christian faith to everyday life."[170]

But even if Revell struggled commercially, its commercialism ultimately reigned triumphant. Meeting in 1939, the Colportage's executive committee identified the meeting's central purpose clearly: "How to Increase the Income of the B.I.C.A." The Association recently had become unable to meet its financial obligations, with neither sales revenue nor donations compensating entirely for the shortfall. Much of the committee's conversation revolved around their most obvious option: to sell more books for profit, by developing more sophisticated sales strategies and by reducing the volume of books given away for free. But several committee members dismissed the idea. "I feel there is a danger of losing the vision," one committee member explained, "of selling books for profit. It is true we sell books, we have expenses and all that, but our vision should be continually a missionary one and our work should be run on faith principles."[171] Another committee member added: "I don't have any interest in selling somebody a book. . . . I can cannot warm up to the idea of inducing children, young people, and others to sell our books in order to get some trinket."[172]

Simultaneously affirming this unease while offering sobering truths, E. A. Thompson—one of two women on the nine-person committee—offered a perspective born of her experience as the person responsible for wholesale sales. "I feel, from the review of last year's figures," Thompson explained, "there must be something wrong with the material we offer . . . Therefore I believe there is some truth in the fact we ought to go after material these people want."[173] To secure more sales, Thompson suggested finding new material and new markets to whom the Colportage might sell its products. To that end she suggested, "We should work a little closer with Zondervan and Eerdman [sic]." Founded in 1931 and 1911, respectively, those companies had become adept at identifying and embracing potential consumer constituencies, which they addressed as avowedly "evangelical" publishers. As the Colportage debated whether to revise its approach to publishing and sales, Zondervan and Eerdmans became the primary inheritors of the commercialism that the Fleming H. Revell Company had heralded.

2

Brands of Distinction

CREATING VALUE THROUGH THE
FUNDAMENTALIST NETWORK

SOMETIME AROUND 1934, probably in Chicago, the evangelist Billy Sunday met with two businessmen after one of his revival meetings. For the three previous decades, Sunday had been a preeminent champion of a fundamentalist piety premised upon strident biblicism, strict personal morality, and fierce condemnation of what he portrayed as the corrosive effects of modern society.[1] Having achieved celebrity especially through his reputation for boisterous and convicting sermons, the aging evangelist's peak years of popularity had long passed. But the two businessmen hoped to capitalize on Sunday's residual fame by persuading him to publish a book with the publishing companies that they each led. Neither publisher had known beforehand, however, that the other would be attending; Sunday had kept details about the meeting and its agenda to himself.[2]

Once gathered with his guests, Sunday came right to the point. "I'm going to give the book to one of you two," Sunday revealed, "and we are going to decide today." Before either publisher could respond, Sunday added: "Let's pray about it." Looking up at the older, more refined man, Sunday pressed his finger to the publisher's chest and insisted: "You first." Smiling nervously, the first candidate bowed his head, collected his thoughts, and, in Dutch-accented English, offered a relatively formulaic prayer of thanksgiving and praise. Once he finished, the younger, more jocular, and accentless publisher dramatically removed his hat, bowed his head, and launched into an energetic extemporaneous prayer that blew away the first. It impressed Billy Sunday so much that when the second prayer ended, Sunday looked squarely at the younger man and announced: "You got the book."

The second publisher's triumph notwithstanding, he is not the hero of this story. Instead, the story venerates its loser, William B. Eerdmans Sr., the founder of the William B. Eerdmans Company. Eerdmans had founded his publishing firm in 1911, less than a decade after emigrating from the Netherlands. Initially focusing on Dutch-language and Reformed Protestant literature, Eerdmans's firm became one of the leading evangelical publishing companies in the United States. It remains in operation today. Despite that evangelical heritage, however, Eerdmans employees occasionally have told this story to me as a way of describing the company's ambivalent relationship with contemporary evangelicalism and the current landscape of evangelical publishing. Channeling their collective dissatisfaction with the popular devotionalism and social conservatism that evangelical firms regularly endorse today, the story of their founder's failure tells the listener that the Eerdmans Company never possessed an easy evangelical bearing. Today the company focuses primarily on more academic approaches to biblical, theological, and historical studies. By narrating distance between Billy Sunday and William Eerdmans, the tale of a failed authorial acquisition expresses the company's current brand.

Derived from the notion of burning or otherwise imprinting a distinguishing mark on livestock or other property, a brand not only involves the identity that a product or institution presents to its publics but also encompasses the identity that its publics perceive. As the marketing scholar Mara Einstein explains, "branding is about making meaning."[3] Although brands have existed for centuries, some scholars argue that brands became especially powerful during the second half of the twentieth century, when increased cultural freedom, rising disposable income, and greater exposure to mass media trained individuals to view their lives as a relentless series of opportunities to choose and consume objects, ideas, and attachments.[4] Especially in that context, brands have served as vessels of social authority, relying upon and requesting the assent of those who encounter them.

For centuries, however, evangelicals have taught to the world how to make and value brands. Since the Reformation era, branding strategies perennially have cultivated authority on behalf of the products and people around whom evangelical publics have taken shape. According to the historian Andrew Pettegree, Martin Luther was able to "capture the public imagination" of German Catholics not simply through the persuasiveness of his theological principles but especially through his use of print, which included innovative use of illustrations and graphic designs that taught consumers to associate themselves with his likeness and his name.[5] In the eighteenth century, the outdoor revivalist George Whitefield used emotive preaching, theater techniques, and self-promotion through news media to help audiences invest themselves in his persona and the religious experience he offered. Whitefield's brand splintered New England's churches and towns, leading to the creation of new evangelical denominations and sects.[6] Throughout the nineteenth and twentieth centuries, individual evangelical preachers and teachers continued to solicit attention and authority as brands. But as the histories of companies such as Revell and Eerdmans illustrate, those individuals' brands increasingly drew their power from corporate brands, which simultaneously capitalized upon and cultivated their authors' celebrity.

Although contemporary retellings of the Billy Sunday story gesture toward the Eerdmans Company's current distance from contemporary evangelicalism, it also depicts an earlier era, when the company found itself far closer to leading evangelical figures and faced tight competition from newer firms. So it was that William Eerdmans impressed Billy Sunday far less than his younger counterpart in the story, Peter "Pat" Zondervan. Not older than twenty-five in 1934, Zondervan was Eerdmans's nephew. Pat and his brother Bernard had worked for their uncle for several years before leaving in 1931 to found Zondervan Publishing House. Throughout the 1930s and 1940s, both companies shared a desire to secure wider consumer markets by reaching beyond their Dutch Reformed community, and they each pursued this ambition as brands that championed "distinctiveness."

The notion of distinctiveness served not just as a bridge between Dutch Reformed and fundamentalist cultures but also as a euphemism for middle-class whiteness. With that profile, the firms helped draw the Dutch Reformed into the fundamentalist network and heralded that network's transformation into the "neo-evangelical" movement of the 1940s. Cutting across and against denominational boundaries, that movement's commercial religion drew its intellectual and devotional logic from the economy of ideas, identity, and authority that Eerdmans and his entrepreneurial nephews created through their contrasting and collaborative brands.

CLAIMING PURPOSE

Countless publishing companies trace their origins not to publishing but instead to such merchant activity as importing, retailing, printing, or peddling. Founded in 1817 as a printer, for example, the firm Harper & Brothers spent its first decade mostly reprinting or rebinding British and European books. D. Appleton and Company began not as a printer but as a chain of dry goods shops. And Charles Scribner began his career as a general importer before focusing on books.[7] As these examples suggest, many merchants have shifted to publishing after their experience importing or selling has attuned them to consumer demand and convinced them to supply that demand with their own products, rather than reselling products created by others, at smaller margins of profit.

Yet publishers do not always tout these merchant origins and the commercial impulses behind them; more commonly, publishing companies emphasize the higher purposes that book publishing calls to mind.[8] Harper & Brothers described its books as "interesting, instructive, and moral," for example, and Henry Hoyt claimed that his company's books sought to "do good."[9] The sociologist Laura J. Miller argues that "publishers and book-sellers typically seek to operate as though "there is more than just economics at stake" because people generally see books as "carriers of ideas and embodiments of culture."[10] Although companies as varied as computer manufacturers, soap makers, and fast-food restaurants try to create the impression that their products serve consumers' authentic interests and needs, book industries trade in a commodity that encourages participants to obscure or mythologize the commercial calculations that orient their origins and ongoing activities. Publishers accordingly build brands devoted to moral, intellectual, or religious ideals.

The William B. Eerdmans Company built its brand on such higher purposes. The company often traces its history back to Benjamin Breckinridge "B. B." Warfield, a professor of theology at Princeton Theological Seminary at the time of Eerdmans's founding. Warfield ranked high in the pantheon of scholars whom conservative Reformed Protestants revered for strong piety, staunch orthodoxy, and intellectual scrupulousness. He had become known above all for his defense of the Westminster Confession and the inerrancy of the Bible in its original autographs.[11] As the story goes, William Eerdmans recently had dropped out of Calvin Theological Seminary, and he undertook a pilgrimage from Grand Rapids to visit Warfield. Eerdmans hoped that Warfield might offer advice and guidance for his next steps. After telling Eerdmans to lighten up and assuring him that he would find a worthy career, Warfield suggested that Eerdmans consider publishing serious philosophical and theological books as a service to fellow Christians. Warfield offered Kok Publishers in the Netherlands as a publishing model.[12] When told today, this story often begins with an admission that the meeting may not have happened. But it testifies to a desire to lend intellectual and spiritual justification to Eerdmans's entrepreneurial enterprise. Although a member of his family later would attribute Eerdmans's interest in religious publishing purely to its profit potential, Eerdmans himself came to describe his activities in less monetary terms; his company was, above all, a "book ministry."[13]

To be sure, not all of Eerdmans's origin stories claim a spiritual purpose so explicitly. Recalling an early memory of his father, William Eerdmans Jr. remembers visiting the Marshall Field's department store in Chicago when he was five years old. In the early years of the twentieth century, before the chain's national expansion, the original Marshall Field's in Chicago possessed a national reputation as a premier shopping destination. So it was with particular pride that William B. Eerdmans Sr. ventured to the store with his son sometime in the 1920s. Having developed a successful business importing and reselling a variety of consumer goods, Eerdmans stood with his son in front of one of the store's spectacular display windows and gestured proudly toward the domestic scene behind the glass. "Those are our blankets, son," Eerdmans Sr. boasted. As this story indicates, Eerdmans had continued working as a general importer even after shifting toward books. He traded in goods as diverse as vases, scissors, and knives.[14] But Eerdmans wrapped even this general merchant activity in religious ideals, presenting it as a form of service to his community.

Eerdmans belonged to the Dutch community in western Michigan, and his importing business helped provide immigrants with familiar goods from far away. During the second half of the nineteenth century, that region had become what Dutch-American writer David De Jong once described as a "new Jerusalem" for the Dutch.[15] Although Dutch immigrants had come to North America since the seventeenth century, they first arrived in western Michigan in 1847. The majority of them were farmers and laborers who had experienced hardship at home due to an economic downturn and an agricultural slump caused by the potato blight that also plagued other parts of Europe.[16] Far more Dutch immigrants arrived in the decades after the Civil War, and by the end of the nineteenth century they had achieved rising prosperity and purchasing power. Nevertheless, Dutch goods and Dutch-language literature remained relatively scarce. Because few Dutch books were printed in the United States, robust demand from the first generation and subsequent Dutch arrivals inspired local importers to specialize in Dutch-language books. Low tariffs on books offered merchants an additional incentive.

Some importers resold their books to peddlers and retailers, but others sold their books directly to consumers.[17] As the legend goes, William Eerdmans began his business as a student, selling imported books from the back of his bike. In 1911 he began a retail bookstore in partnership with Brant Sevensma, a local Dutch-American bookseller and publisher. Looking back in 1923 on his company's early trade, Eerdmans would estimate that his "business was 80 per cent Dutch and 20 per cent English."[18] Eerdmans even wrote and published one of those Dutch books—a 1912 book about the Titanic tragedy, an event that tugged at the proverbial heartstrings of a community whose families regularly traversed the Atlantic by ship. Eerdmans himself had arrived just eight years earlier, in 1904; "[I] came to America . . . with the purpose of visiting relatives," Eerdmans later explained, "and then stayed here."[19]

Eerdmans focused especially on supplying the Dutch demand for religious literature. As *Publishers Weekly* explained in 1920, the Dutch were "large consumers of books, especially in the field of religion and biblical study." Eerdmans recognized and nurtured this fact.[20] This appetite for religious literature reflected the particular mode of Protestantism that many of western Michigan's Dutch immigrants practiced. Although the first wave of immigration had reflected economic motivations above all, at least 35 percent of that initial population also identified themselves with the seceders who had left the Dutch Reformed Church, the national church of the Netherlands, in 1834. In addition to becoming convinced that a drift toward theological liberalism and rationalism had led the state church to abandon the Calvinistic or "Reformed" teachings "of our fathers, based on God's Word," seceders also opposed liturgical innovations and chafed under the hierarchical church authority that King William I had instituted in 1816.[21] Initially these newly arrived Dutch had found an ecclesial home within the denominational descendant of New Amsterdam's original Dutch Reformed Church—the Reformed Protestant Dutch Church (known after 1867 as the Reformed Church in America). Yet as their cultural and linguistic distinctiveness enhanced their secessionist spirit, many decided in 1857 to leave what they saw as a theologically compromised denomination. They created the Christian Reformed Church (CRC), headquartered in Grand Rapids, where in 1876 the CRC would found what became known as Calvin College and Theological Seminary to train its ministers. In addition to prioritizing an educated ministry, the Christian Reformed insisted that laypeople also should be theologically literate and thoroughly catechized in Reformed theology and challenges to it.

The Christian Reformed emphasis on doctrinal scrupulousness and devotional seriousness received renewed support during the 1880s, as the century's largest wave of Dutch immigrants brought with them the theological teachings and cultural priorities of the Dutch minister, journalist, and politician Abraham Kuyper. Beginning in the 1860s, Kuyper had championed a renewal of Calvinist theology in Dutch society. At the heart of Kuyper's "Neo-Calvinism" was the notion that Calvinism offered a total system of living that provided a comprehensive alternative to the forces of individualization and privatization that increasingly splintered modern society. Kuyper insisted that people who had received salvation through the "particular grace" of God were also called to witness for righteousness "in every domain of life" under the power of God's "common grace." He therefore emphasized the need for Christians not only to nurture their interior spiritual lives but also to expand Reformed theology into a "life-and-world view" that shaped their work in society. Insisting that Christians should not compartmentalize their lives into the dualistic categories of "religious" and "everyday" life, Kuyper argued that Christians should live according to the Calvinist doctrine that Jesus reigns over the whole world. Convinced that Christians should participate actively in public life, he became prime minister of the Netherlands in 1901. Yet Kuyper also argued that the fact of pluralism required Christian communities to guard their distinctiveness carefully and consistently. His commitment to this principle inspired him to split with the Dutch Reformed Church in 1886.[22]

Kuyper's emphasis on guarding distinctiveness echoed and affirmed the policies and practices that more traditional leaders in the CRC had designed for their members. Treating the social cohesion of their community as a soteriological priority, Christian Reformed leaders spoke out against changes that they saw as a threat to that cohesion. Until the 1910s, for example, many Christian Reformed churches continued holding services in Dutch; and as late as the 1950s, Christian Reformed leaders discouraged racial integration of their churches and supported the creation of separate African American congregations, on the logic that social differences between black and white Christians would loosen bonds within congregations and, ultimately, within the community more broadly. A more extreme interpretation of Kuyperian thought fed the Afrikaner religio-nationalism that animated apartheid in South Africa.[23] In the United States, an emphasis on distinctiveness inspired the creation of a variety of institutions, including publishing companies and schools.

Around Grand Rapids, Kuyperian Calvinism invigorated a growing market for religious literature. Ministers, laypeople, and students in parochial schools all required religious literature, and local publishers met that demand. Before 1910 those publishers included John B. Hulst, a Grand Rapids bookseller and publisher whose book stock Eerdmans and Brant Sevensma bought out when they began their firm. During the 1890s Hulst had become the official publisher of the Christian Reformed Church, and Eerdmans-Sevensma inherited that market. Hulst had become a successful publisher through his relationship with the CRC as well as by sending agents out to Dutch settlements, where they sold bibles, pamphlets, and religious books door-to-door.[24] To sell books to laypeople, publishers like Hulst and

Eerdmans capitalized upon the notion that children and adults alike regularly needed to reflect on and seek deeper understanding of Calvinism's principles and priorities. Although successive generations of immigrant families increasingly spoke English, the prevalence of Dutch-language theological literature ensured that many second-generation Dutch American readers retained greatest fluency in Dutch on matters of faith. This held especially true for women, who read most avidly.[25]

The Eerdmans brand embraced these principles, and the company became recognized as a champion of Dutch and Calvinist literature. Writing in 1931 as editor of the *Banner*—the official Christian Reformed magazine, often described in jest as the "paper pope"—Henry J. "H. J." Kuiper would lament that "many large publishers of religious literature accept books of the 'liberal' type" and "seem to be going out of the orthodox field." Recognizing this trend, Kuiper heaped praise upon the Eerdmans Company for publishing "a considerable number of worthwhile works during the past ten or fifteen years," cautioning that "our Christian Reformed Church will not survive as a Church of Reformed persuasion unless our distinctive principles are diligently propagated not only from our pulpits and in our classrooms, but also by means of the press." By providing "good literature of the orthodox, more specifically of the Reformed type," he explained, "is to make a real contribution to the preservation of the distinctiveness of our Church." Eerdmans affirmed this praise. "We Hollanders," Eerdmans later explained to an interviewer, "we are educators and I think that is the gift the Lord has given us."[26] Eerdmans made this comment not just with his own business in mind but also with a Kuyperian understanding of the task that God assigned to the righteous: to witness to the world for righteousness. The gift of that task required Christians to educate themselves. To cultivate an education that reached beyond theology and doctrine, Eerdmans also published works of fiction, which offered an education in Christian virtue through what he described as "good, wholesome, character-building, christian books."[27]

During the 1920s, however, Eerdmans shifted away from Dutch-language literature. Although the Christian Reformed Church would continue to use Dutch in synodical minutes as late as 1932, Eerdmans's embrace of English reflected a broader trend.[28] As the book trade periodical *Publishers Weekly* explained in a 1920 profile of Eerdmans, shifting immigration patterns and generational change attenuated the dominance of the Dutch language. "The flow of immigration to this country from Holland has largely ceased," the magazine explained, "and as the new generation grows up the demand for books in the Holland language has, to a large extent, changed to a demand for similar books in English." As a result, the profile surmised, Eerdmans had been "the largest and most active publishing house of books in the Holland language, or for the Hollanders in America," but "the sales of the firm are now as high as ninety per cent in English." Commenting on its shift in 1923, William Eerdmans explained that "the influence of church, school and business is for the Americanization of the Hollanders who came to this country to make it their home." Described at the time as a "book dealer and importer," Eerdmans remarked that "persons advanced in years may cling to the language of their youth, but young Hollanders coming over and Hollanders of the second generation learn English."[29] Speaking for themselves, younger Dutch Americans attributed their use of English to more than generational change. Writing about his childhood as a Dutch kid in Grand Rapids, David De Jong explained that he and his peers were ridiculed for being "Dutchy looking," and they accordingly tried "terribly hard not to be Dutch." The World War I era exacerbated such feelings, due both to an emphasis on loyalty to the United States and to restrictions on immigration passed between 1917 and 1924. Worried about "Americanization," denominational leaders regularly encouraged members to remember their covenantal status and to avoid recreational activities that undermined their separation from the world.[30]

As a shift toward English decoupled Dutch identity and Reformed identity, many members of the Reformed community claimed a Kuyperian logic for leaving Dutch behind. Their hope was that the use of English might enable their young people to remain loyal to the Reformed tradition and to engage the wider world from that perspective. Abraham Kuyper himself had made this suggestion. Visiting the United States in 1898—just a few years before becoming prime minister of the Netherlands—Kuyper had traveled to western Michigan and addressed crowds in Grand Rapids and its environs. Against expectations, he had encouraged Reformed communities to educate their children in English. Only by doing so, Kuyper argued, could successive generations become faithful members of the church and full members of American society. Together, that dual status would enable Reformed Christians to help the United States bring common grace to the entire world.[31] Modeling that public engagement, William Eerdmans unsuccessfully attempted to secure the Republican nomination for election to the state legislature in 1922. Following his loss, Eerdmans abandoned his partnership with Brant Sevensma and focused more intently on cultivating Reformed identity through English-language publishing, under the brand name of William B. Eerdmans rather than Eerdmans-Sevensma.[32]

Christian Reformed leaders ultimately praised Eerdmans's English-language efforts. Noting that Dutch readers previously had been able to "slake their thirst for sound Biblical knowledge" by reading Calvinist literature in the Dutch language, H. J. Kuiper reminded his magazine's readers that "there is but a small and rapidly diminishing number which is able to read Dutch books with profit and pleasure." Recognizing that "a wonderfully rich literature on Calvinism and of a Calvinistic stamp is gradually becoming inaccessible to our people because it is written in a language which is gradually but surely dying out among us." Kuiper insisted that the Reformed needed comparable literature in English, of the sort that Eerdmans regularly published. He warned that "denominations which do not at all indoctrinate their members suffer heavy losses due to sectarian propaganda." And if more books did not offer competing Reformed propaganda, "the decadent, moribund Protestantism of America, with all its fatal weaknesses, will lay its clammy hand of death on our Church also unless we make strong and persistent efforts to inculcate our distinctive beliefs in the minds and hearts of each new generation of people."[33]

Addressing the problem that Kuiper put in such cataclysmic terms, the Eerdmans Company's advertisements offered consumers "the type of books we used to read in the Holland language." Its books were "distinctive." But they also were "exclusive"—that is, Eerdmans claimed to publish "books which cannot be had in any other place."[34] Through the combination of these qualities, Eerdmans simultaneously solicited support not just from the Christian Reformed but also from consumers who found the notion of theological and cultural distinctiveness compelling. Avowed fundamentalists ranked high among those potential consumers.

CURATING CONTACT

The same impulse that led Christian Reformed leaders to call for more Dutch Reformed literature in English also led them to become more comfortable with Christian literature written by people outside their community. But not any literature would do. Eerdmans accordingly wielded its brand identity in service of curating books, ideas, and authors that Reformed ministers and laypeople might find acceptable and appealing. By pursuing this curatorial task, Eerdmans helped knit cultural connections between the Reformed community and a broader fundamentalist network. Presented and perceived as a service to the Reformed community, this task also provided an opportunity for Eerdmans to expand its commercial market.

Long before William Eerdmans's legendary encounter with Billy Sunday, self-consciously Dutch and Reformed Protestants had been evaluating their community's relationship with other traditions of Protestantism. In 1915 Billy Sunday himself had been an index of that evaluative process. Visiting Grand Rapids at the height of his popularity, Sunday drew the attention of Christian Reformed pundits, who sought to assess his mode of Christianity. Discussing Sunday in a Dutch-language book published by Eerdmans-Sevensma, for example, the author John Van Lonkhuyzen dismissed Sunday's teachings as "superficial." Van Lonkhuyzen claimed that Sunday was "good for America but bad for Christianity," and he asserted that Sunday "made Christianity a laughingstock." Seeking to highlight the relative merits of Reformed Christianity, Van Lonkhuyzen lamented that Sunday preached far less about inherited human depravity than about individuals' sins.[35]

But many Christian Reformed leaders and laypeople were willing to view Billy Sunday and other ostensibly conservative Protestants with less opposition. Although the Christian Reformed minister and editor Henry Beets initially shared Van Lonkhuyzen's critical opposition to Sunday, for instance, Beets began supporting Sunday in 1916 on the logic that he preached a generally orthodox message and attacked sin on a scale that few others could.[36] Beets reasoned that friendship with leaders like Sunday might allow the Reformed to bear witness to misguided American Protestants. And yet Beets also joined Reformed critics in labeling Sunday a "Methodist"— a label they used to describe an array of perspectives that included a penchant for innovation, an indifference to doctrine among the laity, a preference for Sunday school instead of catechism, and a view of church as entertainment. As the minister Barend K. Kuiper explained in 1911, "Methodism leaves the door open to Modernism."[37] But Beets pragmatically recognized some "Methodists" as more friend than foe.

In their fight against the specter of modernism, the Christian Reformed found potential allies especially among Protestants known as fundamentalists, an ecumenical coalition defined by the sense that doctrinal and hermeneutical precision offered a primary solution to theological and social disorder they associated above all with "modernists" and "modernism."[38] With the mythology behind the Reformed secession from the national church of the Netherlands and subsequent emigration highlighting that pioneering generation's opposition to theological and social disorder, the Dutch Reformed in America identified other antimodernists as kindred spirits. "MODERNISM is now having its heyday in the churches of the United States," the *Banner* reported in 1930, "as it was rampant in the Netherlands about fifty years ago. Practically all of the larger denominations and many of the smaller ones are capitulating to the spirit of 'liberalism.'" Henry Beets appreciated what he saw as fundamentalists' efforts to purge liberalism from their denominations and public schools, and Beets found himself agreeing with most of the "fundamental" teachings enshrined in *The Fundamentals* (1910–1915)—a series of booklets dedicated to articulating the doctrines that fundamentalists saw themselves conserving. Intended to serve as a sort of recipe for society's coherence, the booklets featured doctrines such as the inspiration of the Bible, the deity of Christ, the substitutionary atonement, and the Virgin Birth.[39]

Yet criticisms of fundamentalism abounded. Reformed leaders regularly disparaged fundamentalist teachings and presumptions during the 1920s and 1930s. In 1932, for instance, Rienk B. Kuiper published a series of articles in the *Banner* about "the attitude of our Christian Reformed churches" to the "two opposing camps" of American Protestantism. While modernists composed one camp, he explained, "the adherents of Orthodoxy in our land are commonly called Fundamentalists."[40] The president of Calvin College from 1930 to 1933, Kuiper claimed that "the atmosphere in the Fundamentalist camp strikes us as being somewhat oppressive, not altogether pure." That oppressive atmosphere stemmed in part from fundamentalists' "Biblicism," which Kuiper described as a "widespread error of present-day Fundamentalists." Noting that "the Biblicist . . . is frequently heard to say with emphasis that he accepts the Bible from cover to cover as the very Word of God," Kuiper argued that such "Bible-only" notions were naïve and devalued other forms of Christian teaching far too easily. Lamenting that fundamentalist biblicists often took a "rather scornful" attitude toward "the great Creeds of Christendom," Kuiper insisted that "we of the Reformed faith think not a whit less of the Bible than does the most ardent Biblicist." The fundamentalists might view creeds as human accretions to the divine revelation found in the Bible, Kuiper said, but such disdain fails to acknowledge that God historically had provided the church with "highly enlightened leaders," who had devised creeds that can be seen as "a most important work of the Spirit of God."[41] The value of creeds lay partially in their corrective function. Louis Berkhof, an Eerdmans author and esteemed professor of Calvin Seminary, criticized fundamentalists for endorsing teachings that creeds such as the Heidelberg Catechism and the Belgic Confession implicitly and explicitly condemned; those teachings included fundamentalists' emphasis on "accepting Jesus"—which deemphasized the sovereign authority of God to determine individual election—as well as premillennial and dispensationalist teachings—which failed to recognize Christ's reign over the church today by focusing so much on his future advent.[42]

Through these criticisms of modernism and fundamentalism, the CRC consistently pursued a brand identity of its own. Its brand rested above all on the ideal of strict Calvinism, firm confessional standards, and bounded communities. That is what distinguished the Christian Reformed Church—in theory if not in practice—from the Reformed Church in America (RCA), as well as other Protestant bodies that stood in the Calvinist tradition. Many of the most public and persistent critics of fundamentalism were not ordinary Christian Reformed ministers but instead the leading lights of the denomination itself. While R. B. Kuiper and Louis Berkhof both served tenures as president of Calvin Theological Seminary, Henry Beets and Henry Kuiper both served as editors of the *Banner,* the denomination's English-language magazine. Their desire to defend their denomination's identity and distill its brand derived in part from their fear that Christian Reformed laypeople increasingly found the distance between Reformed and fundamentalist Christianity difficult to discern. "Toward Fundamentalism," R. B. Kuiper admitted, "we are, to put it very mildly, sympathetic." Insofar as the Christian Reformed joined fundamentalists in clinging "tenaciously to the basic doctrines of the Christian religion," he insisted that "we of the Reformed faith are Fundamentalists, and strong ones at that." But Kuiper also realized that this sympathy endangered Reformed distinctiveness.

Many Christian Reformed laypeople were less committed than their leaders to making sure that they continued to affirm Reformed principles as they endorsed fundamentalist sensibilities. Kuiper noted that "a considerable number of individuals and families have severed their connection with our churches in order to become affiliated with this or that Fundamentalist Group."[43] By the end of the 1920s, both individuals and whole congregations had decided to leave the RCA and the CRC in order to join the "undenominational" movement, a strain of fundamentalism that presaged what later became known as "nondenominational" evangelicalism. In Grand Rapids, the undenominational movement was associated above all with the minister and broadcaster M. R. DeHaan. The son of Dutch immigrants, DeHaan became minister of the Calvary Reformed Church of Grand Rapids—an RCA congregation—in 1925. A dramatic preacher in the exuberant mold of Billy Sunday, DeHaan drew a large following to his church. Yet he also began espousing teachings that conflicted with conventional Reformed doctrine, and the RCA ultimately charged him in 1929 with teaching such erroneous ideas as adult baptism and dispensational eschatology. The following year DeHaan founded Calvary Undenominational Church, emphasizing the need for individual conversion and criticizing Reformed creedalism. In 1930 he even had Calvary Undenominational host a national convention of independent fundamentalist churches.[44]

Responding both to the perceived threat of modernism and to lay sympathy for fundamentalism, Christian Reformed leaders redoubled their dedication to the ideal of indoctrination. Reflecting upon potential responses to the undenominational movement in 1930, H. J. Kuiper acknowledged that "some may shake their heads in vigorous dissent and say: 'We have too much doctrine already; if we had less, fewer members would probably have left us.'" But he insisted that members had not left because of too much doctrine; instead, he argued, they never had fully learned how to embrace the doctrine that they had received. "If our doctrine chases certain members away, it is either because they want *other* doctrines, . . . or because doctrine is preached in a stale, dry-as-dust *fashion*—in sermons which are devoid of spiritual warmth and of the application of Christian doctrine to modern errors and practical life." Kuiper called for *"a better indoctrination of our members."* And yet he also underlined the need for Reformed ministers and teachers to be more mindful of "the *necessity of striking the evangelical note* and striking it more strongly than perhaps we have been doing it." Using "evangelical" to denote a straightforward gospel message, stripped of doctrinal intellectualism, Kuiper insisted that "this does not mean that the covenant idea should be 'soft-pedaled.'"[45]

Viewing books as instruments of indoctrination as well as "evangelical" spirit, Reformed leaders argued that books provided readers with knowledge that the Bible alone could not. Commenting on a bible-reading marathon conducted at a Grand Rapids meeting of Christian Endeavor—a fundamentalist youth organization led at the time by the minister and magazine editor Daniel Poling—one Christian Reformed critic discredited the devotional value of such an event. "The books of the Bible should be studied, not simply read," the critic remarked. Arguing that Christians should read the Bible for quality of understanding rather than for mere quantity of consumption, the critic urged readers not to preoccupy themselves with reading as much of the Bible as possible. Instead, readers also should seek out books that complement their bible reading by providing "information about the various books of the Bible which one needs to be able to read its chapters with much profit."[46]

Although books could not stand in for the Bible, they substantially enhanced biblical study by helping a reader to connect passages to Christian teachings, traditions, and current events. As one Eerdmans advertisement illustrated in 1932, books like Nicholas J. Monsma's *The Trial of Denominationalism* not only promised to help readers appreciate the "problem of denominationalism" and its divisive sectarianism but also offered to help readers understand the countervailing value of denominational attachment in an era of "increasing agitation for Church Unity" among both ecumenical liberals and undenominational fundamentalists.[47] Echoing the notion that books enhanced readers' understanding of the Bible, H. J. Kuiper argued that "those servants of Christ who surpass others in the knowledge of the Word have both the right and the duty to instruct their brethren, either orally *or in writing.*" Kuiper presented this claim as "the origin and justification of the production of Christian literature." Rather than disparage either creeds or religious books as nothing more than man-made teaching, Kuiper insisted, Christians should recognize "the good which can be derived from the study of those Christian writings which are the fruit of the work of the Holy Spirit in the minds of superior persons among those who are regenerated by that Spirit." To fail to do otherwise was to display "a type of religious individualism for which we have very little sympathy."[48]

But this emphasis on books required people to read them. "We appeal to our readers to develop a taste for good religious literature," H. J. Kuiper announced to readers of the *Banner.* "*So few Christians read good books!*" he exclaimed. "They will find it less exciting perhaps, but more, far more satisfying and beneficial than hearing or reading the extravagances and religious offices of the many would-be spiritual leaders of our day who make a good deal of noise, but whose knowledge of the Scriptures is pathetically insufficient."[49] Commercially invested in supporting Kuiper's call, Eerdmans offered its own explanations for diminished devotion to reading. Acknowledging trade publishers' recent efforts to publish lower-cost paperback books, an Eerdmans advertisement from 1932 lamented that consumers had been trained to buy "books to read and toss away." Suggesting that the "present so-called business depression is doing one very good thing," the Eerdmans ad remarked the Great Depression had inspired consumers to "think twice before buying." To engage consumers trained to disregard books that did not capture their immediate interest or seem to justify the expense of purchase, Eerdmans claimed to operate with the understanding that "a book to sell must be of enduring interest."[50]

Affirming the notion that an abundance of choice undermined interest in religious literature, an article in the *Banner* reiterated this problem. "What Shall I Read?" the article's title asked. Although the writer recognized that "there are so many books that you could read only a small part of them," he also urged Christian readers to bear in mind that "many, many books are trash; many are worse than that—really harmful!" Reminding readers that they were "probably very particular about the food [they] eat," the writer asked: "Shouldn't you be much more particular about the food that is given to your mind and your soul?" To cultivate discriminating reading tastes, the writer advised readers to "make a list of the books you read, the date when finished, and just a word or two saying what you think of them." Ideally this practice would allow a reader to develop the habit of "talking over what you read, and telling it to the younger children, or to your folks at home."[51]

In addition to speculating that an abundance of books constrained reader demand, leaders lamented that this abundance nevertheless included too few books of the sort of quality that might generate reader interest and effect indoctrination. "We have not much hope for the preservation and intensification of the Calvinistic character of our group," H. J. Kuiper insisted, "unless our leaders produce more, many more, books . . . and unless our people can be prevailed upon to read them." This concern became sufficiently strong that Kuiper and other Christian Reformed leaders began to endorse books that were "not specifically Calvinistic." While it sounds odd for someone like Kuiper to treat such books as instruments of Calvinistic character, he argued that certain titles "are conservative and can very well be used by those of our people who can read with discrimination."[52] True: countless authors and books claimed "conservative" and "orthodox" labels, and not all of them passed muster with advocates of Reformed distinctiveness. As a result, this meant that readers' engagement with conservative literature required gatekeepers, who could help determine and monitor the threshold of books' acceptability. The Eerdmans Company embraced this role, claiming curatorial authority.

To pursue the mandate of producing books that reflected either Reformed or complementary perspectives, Eerdmans turned to at least two sources. First, the company recruited authors from outside the Christian Reformed tradition who were known for Reformed convictions. Chief among these authors were conservative northern Presbyterians, the most prominent of whom had become known for Reformed theology no less than fundamentalist identity. These Reformed fundamentalists included the Princeton professors B. B. Warfield and J. Gresham Machen. Both possessed impeccable fundamentalist credentials. A decade before he died in 1921, for example, Warfield had authored an article in the first volume of *The Fundamentals*. As for Machen, he famously left Princeton Theological Seminary in 1929 after concluding that it had become a bastion of modernism. Machen subsequently led an "Orthodox Presbyterian" emigration from Princeton and helped found Westminster Theological Seminary, which the Christian Reformed supported with money and personnel. The Dutch Reformed theologians Cornelius Van Til and R. B. Kuiper became early members of the faculty at Westminster, where they trained students in an extreme form of Kuyperian thinking known as "presuppositionalism"—the idea that Christians should view the world with Christian principles in mind, rather than principles based on "worldly" evidence.[53] Due to his reputation for insisting that Reformed fundamentalists were truer intellectuals than their critics, Machen himself regularly received attention in Christian Reformed periodicals.[54] As the example of "the Established Church in the Netherlands" evidences, one Christian Reformed editorial explained, churches "seldom, if ever, return to their original purity." For this reason, the writer praised Machen for spurning "all compromises with Modernism," refusing to be "drawn into the vortex of so-called Liberalism."[55]

Branding itself during the 1920s as "The Reformed Press," Eerdmans published books by both Machen and Warfield. In 1930 Eerdmans published Warfield's sermon collection *The Power of God unto Salvation,* which a reviewer from Calvin Seminary urged readers of the *Banner* to digest "book in hand at their fireside this winter." Acknowledging that many lay-people might find the book too academic, the reviewer remarked: "You ask, should the general public be urged to read these scholarly sermons? By all means! And it is *hereby* urged to do so." Explaining that the book demanded that readers "take their time and pour [*sic*] over these happy pages," the review suggested reading each sermon multiple times, with increasing levels of concentration. Through that method, readers might avoid bypassing "acres of diamonds."[56]

By publishing books by people like Machen and Warfield, the Eerdmans Company simultaneously supported Christian Reformed dreams of doctrinal distinctiveness while also broadening the conception of Reformed identity that they served. Although Reformed in principle, authors like Machen and Warfield took an approach to Reformed doctrine that the Dutch Reformed had not originally shared. While Reformed conservatives like Warfield focused on defining and defending an understanding of Reformed faith as a repository of truths that could not change, many Christian Reformed followed Kuyper's emphasis on transforming Reformed doctrine into a "life system" that applied religious principles to "all areas of life." Rather than treat this contrast as an opportunity to endorse one approach over another, Eerdmans embraced the variety, thereby expanding the range of consumers it might address.[57]

A second source of books expanded Eerdmans's market even more than Reformed fundamentalists. Eerdmans tapped into this source of books due to opportunity no less than admiration. In 1928 the Eerdmans Company acquired a large collection of reference works that the English publisher Hodder & Stoughton originally published in the late nineteenth century. Early in the twentieth century, the editor and entrepreneur George Doran had secured the American rights to the titles and published them through the George H. Doran Company—a firm he created after leaving the Fleming H. Revell Company, where he had come to know Hodder & Stoughton's executives. When Doran's company merged in 1927 with Doubleday and created Doubleday, Doran and Company—the largest publisher in the English-speaking world at the time—the merged firm joined other trade publishers of the era in abandoning conservative religious titles and focusing more on what the historian Matthew Hedstrom describes as "the imagined spiritual center."[58] Conveniently looking to broaden his conservative market, William Eerdmans purchased the abandoned printing plates, available copyrights, and surplus inventory. His acquired titles included a variety of standard biblical reference works, such as three sets of books by the Scottish Free Church minister William Robertson Nicoll: the six-volume *Expositor's Bible;* the five-volume *Expositor's Greek Testament;* and the two-volume *Expositor's Dictionary of Texts.*

For both Doran and Eerdmans, the appeal of these volumes lay largely in their tendency to defend a high view of the Bible's authority, yet with a British emphasis on affective piety rather than doctrinal polemicism. This approach allowed the titles to transcend disputes and divisions that wracked sectarian fundamentalists in the United States. To be sure, as in the United States, British evangelicals regularly disagreed and divided over distinctions between what they sometimes termed Modernism and Traditionalism. Yet at the same time, British evangelicals continually found greater common cause in their status as "nonconformists" to the Anglican establishment. Having adopted an emphasis on personal and congregational revival following Dwight Moody's tour of Scotland in the early 1870s, for example, Nicoll had become known not just for his staunch defense of Calvinist doctrine and biblical inspiration but also for his opposition to Presbyterian secessionism. Consistently, he attempted to appeal to as broad a cross-section of British nonconformists as possible.[59] Although Nicolls's ecumenism reflected his own status as senior editor at Hodder & Stoughton, which sought to cultivate its reputation as Britain's premier evangelical publisher, his volumes appealed to conservative biblicists not only due to Nicolls's emphasis on helping readers "to feel, and to be elevated by" the inspiration of the Bible but also due to the exhaustive scope of his work. With dispensationalist teachings demanding that fundamentalists examine, compare, and cross-reference every verse of the Bible, detailed yet conservative commentaries proved invaluable aids.[60]

Other examples from Eerdmans's acquisition shared Nicolls's emphasis on pious biblicism. When Eerdmans released its new edition of *Maclaren's Expositions of the Holy Scripture,* for instance, the *Banner* praised its ability to enhance virtually any reader's devotion to and understanding of the Bible. Beginning by announcing that "the enterprising Wm. B. Eerdmans Publishing Company has again made a mark for itself in the world of religious publications," the review reported that the multivolume collection complemented two different methods of bible reading. For ministers, the collection's benefit "does not lie in the ideas which it offers so much as in its function to clarify and elicit the preacher's own thoughts." For laypeople, by contrast, the reviewer hypothesized that the collection could help them discover "a precious gem in obscure corners of the Bible."[61]

Following the acquisition of these books, the Eerdmans Company increasingly branded itself as an advocate for a tradition that exceeded the Dutch Reformed. William Eerdmans would come to describe the Doran collection of books as the Eerdmans Company's "patrimony"—a phrase that held at least two meanings. First, it presented the books as cornerstones of the firm's financial foundation. Because the company did not have to pay royalties to authors of books in the patrimony, the steady sales and high prices of those books generated large profit margins and financial sustenance. Reprinting older books had become particularly helpful during the Depression, when money saved by avoiding royalty payments helped publishers subsist on small profit margins, which had fallen as publishers dropped prices to foster consumer demand.[62] Second, the idea of "patrimony" presented the volumes as part of an ancestral inheritance. As their books, their advertisements, and others' perceptions all suggested, Eerdmans cultivated a brand premised upon the notion that they served a Christian tradition within which Reformed Protestants and other antimodernist Protestants stood as allies.

One benefit of this approach was that Eerdmans could share explicitly Reformed teachings with its broader audience. As early as 1926, for example, Eerdmans published a revised version of a Reformed catechism that Henry Beets first published in 1912. Originally titled *Primer of Reformed Doctrine,* the new edition bore the title *Elementary Christian Doctrine for Bible Classes.* Although not exactly snappy, the new title sought "to reach wider circles which often do not understand, much less appreciate the word 'Reformed' in its historical and doctrinal sense. . . . We hope and pray that under its new name it may find doors open which hitherto were closed for it."[63] Yet even if this brand identity allowed Eerdmans to circulate Reformed ideas more widely, it also gave the company license to build a network of authorship, marketing, and distribution that capitalized upon the opportunities that its "distinctive" brand enabled.

EXTENDING THE BRAND

By his own admission, William Eerdmans did not become a "major publisher" until the 1930s. Encouraged by his Reformed community not just to publish Reformed literature but also to curate literature that represented what the company viewed as complementary perspectives, the Eerdmans

Company set about cultivating commercial relationships with a wide range of authors, institutions, and booksellers. As historians of fundamentalism regularly have recounted, the 1930s became an era of proliferating fundamentalist institutions and expanding networks, both within and across discrete geographic regions and denominational traditions.[64] Groups of evangelical businessmen—such as the Christian Business Men's Committee (CBMC), the Christian Laymen's Crusade, and the Gideons—contributed significantly to developing a national network of evangelical businessmen who previously had operated through more regional relationships.[65] Eerdmans and the company's competitors contributed to this process by redeveloping their brand identities and book businesses in the 1930s, which provided fundamentalists and other "distinctive" Protestants with a common commercial and cultural infrastructure.

To see this infrastructural initiative at work, consider the relationship between Reformed publishers and the Winona Lake Bible Conference (WLBC). Although the town of Winona Lake, Indiana, does not rank today among well-known centers of evangelical activity, it functioned in the 1930s as a nexus of conservative white Protestant cultures. Founded in the 1890s as a sort of independent and conservative expression of the Chautauqua movement, the WLBC went on to become the most prominent stop on a national Bible conference circuit that grew from 27 sites and 88 sessions in 1930 to more than 50 sites and over 200 sessions in 1941.[66] Billing itself as the "World's Largest Bible Conference," the WLBC also spawned a long list of associated meetings at Winona Lake—including the Winona Lake Prophetic Conference, an "Annual Old-Fashioned Camp Meeting," the Rodeheaver Sacred Music Conference, and the Winona Lake School of Theology, which hosted pastors and Bible teachers for fifteen-day "semesters" through which they earned credit toward a theological degree.[67] In 1937 many of these meetings began operating under the corporate umbrella of the newly established Winona Lake Christian Assembly (WLCA), which made its fundamentalist orientation clear not only by writing fundamentalist doctrinal standards into its corporate charter but also by mandating that its "declaration of purpose shall never be amended, modified, altered, or changed." Recognizing the heart of Protestant modernism as a dedication to what one historian describes as "the process of redefining Christianity," this WLCA charter sought to forestall process of any kind.[68] Around 1930, William Eerdmans laid a commercial claim upon the authors, ministers, and laypeople who passed through Winona Lake and its varied meetings. In addition to spending time at Winona Lake and building relationships with its leaders and speakers, Eerdmans began serving on the WLBC's board of directors.[69]

Why had a small town in Indiana become so prominent? Its proximity to Chicago contributed to its success. A relatively short ride on the interurban train, Winona Lake became an easily accessible destination for midwestern Christian families. Like most Bible conferences, the WLBC served as more than a place to receive religious instruction and inspiration. Following the model of such camp meetings as the Methodist-affiliated Ocean Grove in New Jersey, they also served as modest resorts, where visitors could enjoy inexpensive summer vacations.[70] "Combine Profit with Pleasure," the camp's slogan suggested in 1944.[71] Throughout the 1930s, members of Christian Reformed communities in Chicago and Grand Rapids spent their summers at Winona Lake. As early as 1931, the WLBC attracted a group of eighty Christian Reformed members, including seventeen clergy. And in 1930, R. B. Kuiper featured among the conference's speakers. His sermon focused on the "common grace of God," which ensured that "all men in a general way are looking for the truth."[72]

Yet Winona Lake attained prominence due to more than geography; above all, its success reflected its own brand identity. Beginning in 1910 the Winona Lake brand drew heavily on the celebrity of Billy Sunday. He had begun visiting the town a few years before his revival career blossomed in 1904, to spend time with his friend J. Wilbur Chapman. A friend and supporter of Dwight Moody, Chapman had become the best-known evangelist in the United States following Moody's death in 1899. Before and after receiving a call in 1895 to become minister of John Wanamaker's Bethany Presbyterian Church in Philadelphia, Chapman held regular revivals in midwestern cities, and he tutored Billy Sunday in revival methods. Appointed director of the WLBC after being nominated for the job by Dwight Moody, Chapman served as a tireless booster on its behalf. Due in part to Chapman's influence, in 1904 Winona Lake became home to the International Association of Evangelists, an organization that served as a forum for professional revivalists to discuss everything from preaching techniques to what can only be described as branding strategies.[73] Many of its best-known members spent time teaching at Winona Lake every summer. Billy Sunday bought at house near the lake in 1910, and he became a celebrity mascot for the institution. The main meeting space on the conference grounds was named the Billy Sunday Tabernacle.

Sunday made a fitting mascot for the conference and the town alike, as Winona Lake represented his ideal Christian community. Throughout his sermons, Sunday regularly portrayed the ethnic, economic, and religious diversity of cities as corruptive influences on individual Christian conviction and morality. Drawing a distinction between his view of contemporary society and his hope for a future potentially transformed by "fighting saints," he predicted that "the civilization of the future will center in the cities." Sunday argued that "what is enthroned in the city will give tone to the country," and he insisted that "Christianity creates civilization."[74] Although Sunday did not claim any affiliation with Ku Klux Klan, his admixture of xenophobia, religion, and nationalism bore close similarity to the white nationalism espoused far more explicitly by the Klan, which drew strong support in Indiana.[75] Implicitly, at least, Winona Lake's branding reflected its idealized status as a bastion of middle-class whiteness, where both family and true faith could thrive.

The WLBC pursued its branding efforts through circulations of media, including everything from advertising circulars to newsletters to books. Every year, fundamentalist conference centers and camp meetings printed circulars that they distributed to congregations and individuals. In addition to providing details about conference costs, recreational activities, lodging options, and daily schedules, circulars touted the speakers who would be in residence for any given conference's summer sessions. More than mere descriptions of an institution's offerings, these circulars served as portraits of institutional self-understanding and comparative clout. By naming prominent names and displaying famous faces, a conference presented itself as the kind of place such figures valued and sought to spend their time. No conference circulars named more names or displayed more faces than the Winona Lake Bible Conference. In 1940, for instance, the WLBC circular advertised more than forty speakers, with names and faces splayed across six pages, arranged in descending order of renown. "Nothing like this program is to be found elsewhere," the circular boasted, without much hyperbole. Famous figures featured on the first two adjacent pages included Harry Ironside, the pastor of Moody Memorial Church; R. G. LeTourneau, described on the circular as "American's Christian Layman No. 1"; W. A. Sunday, the widow otherwise known as "Ma" Sunday; V. Raymond Edman, the president of Wheaton College; and Lewis Sperry Chafer, the president of Dallas Theological Seminary. The circular promised: "Here are assembled a host of the leading preachers, Bible teachers and missionaries of the world. You will be thrilled, inspired and mightily strengthened in your faith."[76]

Circulars mediated a claim to authority that readers evidently accepted. In 1943, for instance, Harold J. Ockenga—then the minister of Boston's Park Street Church and a founding leader of the nascent National Association of Evangelicals—received a letter from someone in England inquiring about Ockenga's participation in the previous year's conference. "I have just been reading through the programme of last year's Winona Lake Conference," Frederick Flavell explained, "so I thought I would take this extremely

As these 1956 leaflets illustrate, the Winona Lake Bible Conference cultivated nostalgia for the past and branded itself as a paradise for white, middle-class Christian families.

welcome opportunity of writing to you. I was greatly impressed to see you were to speak on 'The Modern Merry-Go-Round or Rock', and the title is so attractive and unusual that I thought I might take the liberty of asking whether it has been published in printed form."[77] As Flavell's letter suggests, conference circulars trained readers across the United States and the wider world to view conference speakers as members of a coherent interdenominational fundamentalist network that possessed its own economy of authority. Selection as a conference speaker simultaneously confirmed and cultivated an evangelist's status. That status in turn boosted the conference's brand.

By serving on the WLBC's board of directors, William Eerdmans not only secured access to potential authors and their consumers but also gained sway within the fundamentalist network. When Flavell asked Ockenga if his lecture had appeared in print, he likely knew that the answer was yes, because the WLBC annually published previous years' addresses in volumes entitled *Winona Echoes*. And while conferences allowed publishers to develop relationships with established speakers and authors, they also served as proverbial minor-league systems, where publishers could identify speakers whose ideas or personalities seemed likely to generate interest. At Winona Lake, Eerdmans could observe and meet lesser-known speakers who might not yet feature at the WLBC but who might have served as featured evangelists at smaller conferences. Viewing publishing as a method of ascending the loose hierarchy of fundamentalist celebrity, evangelists themselves often sought out the opportunity to publish books. The biographies of the more prominent evangelists on the WLBC's 1940 roster typically mentioned their books, whereas the lesser-known speakers were identified merely as "evangelist" or "missionary."

Books helped boost an evangelists' prominence, due in part to their ability to circulate long before and after evangelists physically spent time in any given location. When traveling to conferences or other speaking opportunities, evangelists often carried their books with them or asked their publishers to send books to places they would be visiting. Evangelists also used books to cultivate their own brands from a distance. When an aspiring minister from Los Angeles wrote in 1946 to the prominent Chicago minister Harry Ironside to praise one of Ironside's books and ask for other recommendations, Ironside offered to start sending him a book every month, "in the way I often do with young ministers."[78] Ironside received a steady stream of such requests, and he regularly sent complimentary copies of his books or forwarded orders to his publishers. To maximize the opportunity that their books offered, some evangelists devised extensive publicity strategies for themselves. When the evangelist and Eerdmans author Paul Hutchens set out in 1934 to sell his first book, he not only managed to have Moody Bible Institute's bookstore agree to sell the book but even allowed fundamentalist periodicals around the country to sell and republish it serially. "You might try to sell 50 to 100 copies to Defender Publishers, Wichita, Kans.," Hutchens wrote to William Eerdmans in 1934. Hutchens encouraged Eerdmans to "Stress the fact that the book is FUNDAMENTAL AND A REAL DEFENDER OF THE FAITH. I know they will get behind it if they approve of it." Hutchens even had the English evangelist and Zondervan author Herbert Lockyer agree to sell the book and arrange its serial publication in England.[79]

Throughout the 1930s, many of Eerdmans's most profitable authors were regulars on the conference circuit and at Winona Lake. Through his connection to Winona, Eerdmans secured William Biederwolf as an author. A prominent revivalist who served as president of the International Association of Evangelists, Biederwolf succeeded J. Wilbur Chapman as director of the WLBC. A fixture at Winona Lake during the 1930s, Harry Rimmer also became an Eerdmans author. In many ways Rimmer was Eerdmans's ideal author. Recognized as fundamentalism's foremost scientist and archaeologist, he espoused a scientism that supported antimodernist fundamentalists' conviction that their own ideas were no less well-founded than those they scorned. Such ideas allowed Rimmer to appeal to fundamentalists as well as allied antimodernists. With the Reformed increasingly embracing fundamentalists on the basis of such antimodernist concerns as opposition to teaching evolution in public schools, Rimmer suited Eerdmans's desire to cater to multiple conservative constituencies. One of the most popular opponents of evolution in the 1930s, he developed a following in Grand Rapids among the Reformed and other conservative Protestants by visiting the town regularly.[80] Rimmer's constant itinerancy also allowed him to sell books wherever he traveled, which elevated his sales and his stature as an Eerdmans Company author.

His success notwithstanding, Rimmer had no formal scientific training. Without the ability to lend credence to his teachings by citing educational credentials, both publishers and conference organizers evidenced his expertise in other ways.[81] To justify his archaeological arguments, for example, a conference circular for a Bible conference in Charleston, West Virginia, boasted that Rimmer had "spent months at the tomb of King Tut." And to support Rimmer's general scientific trustworthiness, his biographical descriptions typically noted his status as president of the "Research Science Bureau"—an organization he founded in 1929.[82] Dedicated to using science to promote "research in such sciences as have direct bearing on the inspiration and infallible nature of the Holy Bible," the Bureau accepted new members either for making scientific contributions or for contributing $5, which bought a year's worth of Rimmer's booklets. Eerdmans published those booklets, as well as Rimmer's books and booklet collections such as *Harmony of Science and Scripture* (1936), which Eerdmans reportedly produced due to extraordinary reader demand for more permanent and comprehensive versions of his booklets. *Harmony* alone went through seventeen editions between 1936 and 1958, and Rimmer received prime placement in the Eerdmans catalog. Regularly receiving praise from dozens of prominent fundamentalist periodicals and their readers, Rimmer became such an emblem of antimodern scientism that at least one reader in Baltimore deemed his life story "the finest presentation of Christ" that she had read. Acting on that conviction, she reported buying copies of Rimmer's books and sending those copies to prominent cultural figures, whom she had identified through prayer.[83]

By developing relationships with fundamentalist evangelists and institutions, Eerdmans became known as a publishing outlet for aspiring authors. Paul Hutchens, for example, began publishing with the Eerdmans Company in 1934 after sending Eerdmans an unsolicited letter to inquire about possibly publishing his first novel, *Romance of Fire*. Hutchens already had tried and failed to secure a contract with three other companies, each of which proved uninterested for one reason or another. One publisher reportedly had explained that "fiction with a purpose is the hardest for us to market," while another encouraged Hutchens to pursue "factual writing rather than fiction."[84] When he reached out to the Eerdmans Company, Hutchens made sure to include evidence of his status as an evangelist and his potential audience—or, to use contemporary publishing jargon, evidence of his "platform." Hutchens's evidence consisted of a broadsheet advertisement for an upcoming fifteen-day revival that he would be leading at a Methodist church in Endicott, New York, outside Binghamton. Hutchens also noted that he was an alumnus of Moody Bible Institute. "Our list of perspective [*sic*] buyers," Hutchens explained, "should include every former student as well as every present student, also the faculty." Hutchens became confident that "if the book gets started right, 'THE FUNDAMENTALISTS' are going to get back of it strongly." All of this persuaded Eerdmans. Yet the company still shrewdly demanded that Hutchens purchase half of the initial print run of 2,000 copies.[85]

Through its relationship with evangelists on the conference circuit, Eerdmans achieved substantial commercial success. *Romance of Fire* would go through seven editions in one year; by 1945 Hutchens's books collectively sold more than a million copies, making him what Eerdmans described as "the most popular American author of Christian fiction."[86] Encouraged by such success, Eerdmans created a formal program that encouraged authors to submit unsolicited manuscripts. "If you are in a position where publishing will aid your career," an advertisement in Eerdmans's 1940 book catalog explained, "you will need this type of service." Deemphasizing any specific doctrinal standards, the advertisement emphasized the company's ability to "bring your book before the public at a minimum of expense and with the maximum opportunity for success."[87]

Both conferences and publishers branded themselves not just by circulating advertisements or by giving evangelists their own books but also by devising marketing strategies and retail experiences that complemented their branding strategies. Seeking a broad fundamentalist audience for its books, for instance, William Eerdmans asked Hutchens to remove any ethnic particularity from the manuscript of *Romance of Fire*. Eerdmans complained about the "Irish vernacular which you introduce into the conversation." Eerdmans also encouraged Hutchens's attempt to insert "certain things . . . to exalt the school," in order to help Moody Bible Institute's administrators view the book as "good advertising."[88] Recognizing that books could advertise and disseminate ideas and preferences only to the extent that people either purchased or otherwise handled them, conferences and camp meetings often sold books to their attendees. But bookstores also provided conference attendees with places to spend their recreational and devotional time. And through retail experiences, consumers could become familiar with the brands that both conferences and publishers sought to cultivate.

Insofar as conferences sold the fantasy of personal transformation and enhanced Christian living, they used bookselling to serve those ideals. "One of the most far-reaching ministries of these Victorious Life Conferences," a circular for "America's Keswick" in Keswick Grove, New Jersey, explained in 1941, "is that of the books and pamphlets in the Conference bookstore. Many a life, in homeland and foreign field has been revolutionized through the sending of a leaflet or book." Describing the bookstore at the Lake Whatcom Bible and Missionary Conference, in Bellingham, Washington, an article in the conference's newsletter boasted that it carried "books for every age" and offered brief descriptions of several new books. They included a devotional book by Herbert Lockyer, which featured the practical benefit of offering daily readings for each week that focus on "some vital theme, making the book a real guide to God's great precepts." And the Winona Lake Bible Conference's circulars advertised the Winona Book Store, which offered "a choice supply of safe, sound literature."[89]

IMITATION AND INNOVATION

To be sure, the Winona Lake Bible Conference did not exhaust the William B. Eerdmans Company's retail or branding activities in the 1930s. It draws so much attention here, however, for two reasons. First, Eerdmans's relationship with the WLBC, its evangelists, and its attendees distills the company's attempt to build markets that allowed it to engage multiple publics. But a second reason for focusing on the WLBC involves the view it offers of the imitation and competition that Eerdmans's overall strategy generated. No company imitated Eerdmans more completely than Zondervan Publishing House.

Before founding their own company in 1931, Pat and Bernard "Bernie" Zondervan had worked for William Eerdmans, their uncle. Pat Zondervan even lived with William Eerdmans and his family beginning in 1924. He was fifteen at the time. Writing to a friend in 1943, William Eerdmans would recount that his sister had "brought the boy [Pat] with tears and begged us to take him in." After working his way from maintenance to a warehouse to a job in the shipping department, Zondervan had begun working as a local book salesman. Bernie started working for Eerdmans in 1928. By 1930 the Zondervan brothers regularly took sales and acquisition trips with their uncle, including trips to Britain, where Eerdmans trained his nephews to identify potentially lucrative titles and to negotiate book rights.

As the story goes, however, Eerdmans fired his nephews after returning from a solo trip to England in 1931. Eerdmans discovered that Pat Zondervan had been selling Eerdmans books and keeping sales proceeds for himself. Having already granted Pat a series of second chances for other offenses, Eerdmans fired him. "Most people would have sent him away much sooner," Eerdmans later explained, "I kept it up for seven long years, until I simply could not keep him any longer."[90] Bernie departed soon after his brother. To make peace, Eerdmans claimed to have offered his nephews a line of credit and invited them to work for him as "jobbers"—the term for wholesalers who buy large quantities from a publisher and resell their inventory to sales outlets. Having already sought ownership status, however, by asking their uncle unsuccessfully to make them partners in his company, the Zondervans decided instead to go into business for themselves. Almost immediately, they set about imitating their uncle's commercial strategies. That imitation included a campaign to wrest commercial control over the Winona Lake Bible Conference away from Eerdmans.

The Zondervans imitated Eerdmans in at least three general ways. First, they focused initially on Reformed books. They began by buying heavily discounted remainder copies of Reformed books, such as J. Gresham

Machen's *The Virgin Birth* from Harper & Brothers in New York, and re-selling them in Grand Rapids and by mail, using mailing lists culled from denominational yearbooks and business contacts made through Eerdmans. But the Zondervans quickly moved from mere bookselling to book publishing. Beginning with the Grand Rapids market in mind, they identified an out-of-copyright Abraham Kuyper book titled *Women of the Bible* that had not appeared in English, and they paid a Calvin Seminary student to translate it. Zondervan published Kuyper's book as two separate books, *Women of the Old Testament* (1933) and *Women of the New Testament* (1934).

A second form of imitation was Zondervan's emphasis on out-of-print theological texts, including their own version of books from the Eerdmans "patrimony." Looking back in 1957 on the 1930s, William Eerdmans boasted that he had generated tremendous profits by acquiring "more standard sets of books than any other publisher in the United States—standards which are used in seminaries and Bible schools of all denominations."[91] Well aware of this fact, the Zondervan brothers created their own version of sets like the *Jamieson, Fausset and Brown Commentary Critical and Explanatory on the Whole Bible,* also known more simply as the *Jamieson, Fausset and Brown Commentary.* First published in 1871 in Britain, the commentary was esteemed by figures like William Bell Riley and Harry Ironside as a reliable and accessible multivolume reference. Eerdmans had made it available to Americans as a single volume for the first time, and the Zondervans quickly created their own version.

Other competitors joined Zondervan in imitating these first two aspects of its business model. In 1939, for example, Herman Baker set up a used-books store in Grand Rapids, and began publishing reprints and original books the following year. Baker was the nephew of the Dutch immigrant Louis Kregel, who had sold used theological books in Grand Rapids since 1909. Contemporary company mythology at both Baker Publishing Group and Eerdmans Publishing Company suggests that Herman decided to begin his own publishing enterprise after working during the 1930s alongside both Kregel and William Eerdmans. Before beginning his own company, Baker had accompanied Eerdmans on trips to Britain, where they often would buy the libraries of retired or deceased ministers. Baker then would sell the imported books at Kregel's bookstore, and Eerdmans would reprint whichever books sold best. By 1939, the stories go, Baker decided to step out on his own as a bookseller and, soon thereafter, a publisher.

Yet if other companies competed with the Eerdmans Company in similar ways, the Zondervan brothers competed with the benefit of knowledge they had gleaned by working for Eerdmans. The Zondervans reprinted the

The catalog entry for the William B. Eerdmans Company's one-volume edition of the *Jamieson, Fausset and Brown* biblical commentary, a lucrative title that Zondervan began copying.

Used with permission from the William B. Eerdmans Publishing Company. *Catalog and List of Publications, 1939–1940.*

Jamieson, Fausset and Brown commentary, for example, knowing that customers occasionally had complained about the print quality of Eerdmans's version, which relied on the old, worn printing plates the company had purchased from Doubleday Doran. To distinguish their own version, the Zondervans reproduced the text of an original copy using the cutting-edge technique of photo offset reproduction, which replaced metal plates with inked rubber sheets, produced through a negative photograph of an original. Herman Baker began using this technique after World War II, when his company set out to supply the demand for reprinted books that had fallen out of print during the war due to paper rationing.[92]

But Zondervan's third area of imitation involved Eerdmans's network of authors and distributors—including the network around the Winona Lake Bible Conference. Having worked for William Eerdmans as his company began its relationship with the WLBC, the Zondervans had become familiar with the individuals and institutions affiliated with it. And so they sought to capitalize upon those connections. Beginning around 1931 the brothers began spending significant portions of their summers at Winona Lake, and they used that time to acquire authors and to develop contractual relationships with other fundamentalist institutions. Pat Zondervan won his legendary prayer battle with Eerdmans in 1934, the year before Billy Sunday died. A few years later, in 1937, Zondervan Publishing House published Sunday's book as *Billy Sunday Speaks!*, a collection of Sunday's aphorisms, which Zondervan described as "sentence sermons." In addition to Sunday, Zondervan conscripted a variety of Winona Lake speakers as authors. Many of them previously had published with other presses. "I have taken your advice concerning the matter of Revell," the revivalist Hyman Appelman assured Pat Zondervan in 1942. "They are to publish one more book for me, but that is all." Following a discussion at Winona Lake in 1941 with Harry Ironside, an author who had published previously with Revell and the Brethren firm Louizeax Brothers, Pat Zondervan wrote: "We appreciated the privilege that we had of conversing with you and your family at Winona Lake." They soon agreed on terms for a new book contract.[93] In addition to publishing books by individual Winona evangelists, Zondervan began publishing *Winona Echoes,* WLBC's annual collection of sermons, in the late 1930s. In its 1941 book list, Zondervan listed every edition of *Winona Echoes* published since 1920 in its popular "Bargains" section, offering the volumes for 75 cents each. Visitors to Winona Lake could buy copies of *Winona Echoes* or books by any conference speaker at the conference's bookstore, which the Zondervans began managing in 1937.[94]

Although Eerdmans never had operated a bookstore at Winona Lake, Zondervan's retailing activity took to its initial apogee the company's campaign to siphon influence away from Eerdmans. The Zondervan brothers helped finance the construction of a building to serve as the bookstore, and they also financed a subsequent expansion in 1958. In return for a modest lease payment and a small percentage of sales revenue (1 percent in 1958), they secured exclusive rights to sell and distribute books at any events associated with the Winona Lake Christian Assembly.[95] Cherishing this monopoly, Zondervan guarded it closely. When Zondervan executives learned in 1963, for instance, that members of the organization Youth for Christ had been selling books during one of their weeklong conferences, Zondervan began issuing strong complaints, insisting that they alone possessed "the right to sell books here at Winona Lake."[96] When Youth for Christ persisted, Zondervan's general retail manager announced that Zondervan's lease had been violated. "I trust that your office realizes how serious this is to Zondervan Book Store," William F. Moore explained. "The loss in sales that has resulted is not a small item with us."[97] A few years later the WLCA rented space to a local seminary student to sell some antiques, gifts, furniture, and thirty to fifty books—mostly related to topics like woodworking,

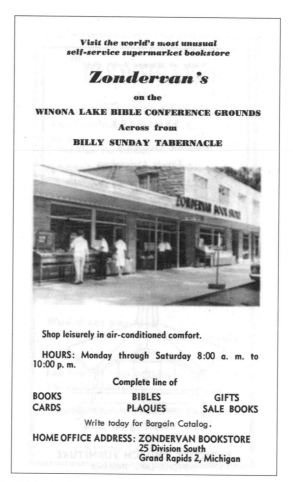

Visit the world's most unusual
self-service supermarket bookstore

Zondervan's

on the

WINONA LAKE BIBLE CONFERENCE GROUNDS

Across from

BILLY SUNDAY TABERNACLE

Shop leisurely in air-conditioned comfort.

HOURS: Monday through Saturday 8:00 a. m. to 10:00 p. m.

Complete line of

| BOOKS | BIBLES | GIFTS |
| CARDS | PLAQUES | SALE BOOKS |

Write today for Bargain Catalog.

HOME OFFICE ADDRESS: ZONDERVAN BOOKSTORE
25 Division South
Grand Rapids 2, Michigan

A Winona Lake Bible Conference circular for 1965, advertising Zondervan's bookstore as one of the conference's attractions.

Used with permission from Archives & Special Collections, Morgan Library, Grace College & Seminary, Winona Lake, Indiana. Winona Lake Christian Assembly collection, box 43.

metal working, and other manual arts. When Pat Zondervan heard about this, he wrote to the WLCA's business manager and complained: "This really is contrary to the arrangement that the Assembly has with us."[98]

Zondervan did not defend its bookselling arrangement purely to maximize revenue for the store itself. Although the store generated significant revenue from large songbook orders and by selling books to the "outside, fundamental, evangelical organizations" to whom the WLCA increasingly rented the grounds in the 1960s and 1970s, the value of the store lay largely in branding Zondervan Publishing House as the commercial face of the global evangelical network that the WLCA manifested.[99] During the 1970s, attendees increasingly included groups of Korean evangelicals, whom the WLCA viewed as a sufficiently lucrative constituency that they provided Korean delegations with a 10 percent discount in 1979.[100] After an era of depressed sales due to falling attendance throughout the 1970s, the Zondervan bookstore achieved its greatest revenue figures in the late 1970s and early 1980s, as the rise of the New Christian Right inspired renewed evangelical mobilization and conference attendance. Between 1974 and 1981, annual sales rose by more than 23 percent, from $158,503 to $195,679.[101]

Personally aggrieved and commercially threatened by what he perceived as his nephews' betrayal, William Eerdmans sought continually to undermine the Zondervan brand by discrediting its reputation among fundamentalist institutions, distribution outlets, and authors. With WLBC under the commercial control of the Zondervans, for instance, Eerdmans developed a close relationship with the Pinebrook Bible Conference in Pennsylvania, a smaller, regional fundamentalist conference. Founded by the radio evangelist Percy Crawford, Pinebrook ran the Pinebrook Book Club, which described itself in advertisements as the "world's largest fundamental book-of-the-month club."[102] Throughout the late 1930s and early 1940s, William Eerdmans demanded that Pinebrook agree not to work with the Zondervans.

Constantly discussing the personal disrespect he felt that his nephews had shown him, Eerdmans regularly accused the Zondervans of disreputable business practices. "They are just 'SINISTER,'" Eerdmans explained in 1945 to Norman Kellow, Pinebrook's club manager. Describing a Zondervan book that Eerdmans deemed "packed with stolen goods," Eerdmans explained, "We pay a goodly royalty for this material, and they just take it, and don't pay anybody a cent. Is not that taking undue advantage. Is that honest and ethical? I think it is criminal." As his comment to Kellow suggests, much of Eerdmans's evidence involved copyright infringement. "There is not a single religious publisher in the country," Eerdmans wrote to an associate in the book business in 1944, "which so arbitrarily fathers material from all kinds of copyrighted and existing and good selling sources, and publishes this in reprint form and then has it copyrighted."[103] Eerdmans complained in particular about Zondervan's new periodical, *Christian Digest.* Designed to serve as a Christian version of *Reader's Digest,* it offered extracts from a variety of evangelical books. But Zondervan did not secure permission to include many of its selections.

In addition to accusing Zondervan of stealing actual text, Eerdmans accused the Zondervans of stealing business ideas. Remarking in 1949 on an out-of-copyright title that Zondervan published after Eerdmans already had done the same, William Eerdmans explained to the Bible teacher and evangelical leader Wilbur Smith that "the Z. boys KNEW that this book was on our list before they ever dreamed of it. They acknowledged the list, and, yes, as you said in your letter They certainly 'slipped something over on us.'"[104] After hearing Eerdmans besmirch the Zondervans' reputation for years, Norman Kellow urged Eerdmans to be more forgiving with his nephews. But Eerdmans insisted, "I don't care how anyone soft-soapes [sic] and Uncle Billy's me. Sin remains sin. If you have a wallet on your hip pocket, with a hundred dollar bill in it, and I, as a pickpocket, succeed in lifting that, what am I?"[105] To convince Kellow that he should abandon any relationship with Zondervan, Eerdmans even resorted to threats. In 1945, for example, he casually noted that he had stopped working with the Wheaton Book Club because it had continued to work with Zondervan.[106]

But fundamentalist institutions continued to welcome and work with Zondervan Publishing House despite Eerdmans's protests. By the end of the 1930s the Zondervans simply had situated their brand so firmly within the fundamentalist economy of authority that their company proved too strong for Eerdmans to defeat. After Eerdmans's repeated requests that Pinebrook abandon all relations with Zondervan, Norman Kellow eventually responded that Zondervan deserved the business it received. "You know as well as I, that some Z books are excellent, all that a Christian book should be. . . . I personally believe that the Lord Himself inspires some writers who may have Z publish a book. I believe that the Lord moves me to accept some books, down others." Despite their apparent sins, Kellow explained, Zondervan often published more appealing books. "In dollars and cents, we could make out better with Z's," he speculated.[107]

Noting that his club's readers preferred Zondervan books, Kellow urged Eerdmans to take stock of his own company's brand. "You just have not been publishing the type of books we need," he explained to William Eerdmans in 1945. "You just haven't the titles. Should you take on a program of good evangelical authors, . . . I do not think the Z question would crop up—at least it wouldn't worry you." Because Zondervan had succeeded in cultivating a brand that drew such respect from evangelicals, Kellow explained, "even Moody will not consent to stop selling and stop featuring Z books altogether." Yet Kellow did agree not to feature Zondervan books. Comparing his book club and conference bookstore with Moody Bible Institute's book business, Kellow boasted that he had "cut Z's out a lot more than Moody has. There [sic] magazine is full of Z from cover to cover. Their store reeks with the stuff."[108]

Rather than hurting its brand, Zondervan's aggressive imitation of Eerdmans ultimately had enhanced Zondervan's stature. Citing other booksellers' policies as support for their own, the Sword Book Club—a division of the company that produced the popular fundamentalist periodical *Sword of the Lord*—responded to Eerdmans's criticism of Zondervan by noting that Pinebrook Book Club sold Zondervan selections.[109] From the Sword Book Club's perspective, close competition seemed to evidence the two companies' common conviction. Just as Eerdmans had translated the Dutch emphasis on "distinctiveness" into a way of describing an antimodernist emphasis on "distinctive" features of fundamentalist faith, so had Zondervan. Well into the 1960s, Zondervan branded itself as "Publishers of Distinctive Religious Books."

The two companies even shared some of the same traveling booksellers. Like general publishers of small and moderate size, evangelical publishers relied partly on traveling salespeople to sell their books in new sales territories and to new bookstores. Essentially serving as brand ambassadors, salespeople typically endorsed a publisher's brand in order to secure a sales contract. In 1937, for instance, William Eerdmans received a letter from F. J. Wiens, then manager of the Mennonite Book Concern. Lamenting that the small size of his denomination made his business "almost a missionary enterprise," and explaining that he desired "somewhat more remunerative" work, Wiens told Eerdmans that he had "learned to think a great deal of your firm." Boasting that a decade of sales experience had earned him "contacts that should be of inestimable value to me if I should enter your organization and spend part of my time traveling with your line of books," Wiens also noted that he did not endorse all publishers equally. "You have definite Christian principles," he explained, "and that is more than I can say for certain religious publishing houses."[110] Yet even though Wiens claimed to give Eerdmans preference, he carried with him materials representing at least one other firm's books.[111] For smaller publishers, this practice generated authority for new books and authors by associating them with books, authors, and companies that consumers already trusted.

Despite the Eerdmans Company's disdain for Zondervan, Eerdmans contributed to the appearance of alignment between the two firms and their brands. In 1938, for example, Zondervan ordered 500 copies from Eerdmans of the novel *Rachel*, Agnes Scott Kent's novel about a Jewish housewife who studies the Bible with a female missionary and converts to Christianity over her family's wrathful objections.[112] Eerdmans allowed Zondervan to buy and resell its books because Eerdmans acknowledged that its own consumers also belonged to Zondervan's market. But there were limits to collaboration between competing companies. When Bertha Moore, an author of some of Eerdmans's most popular children's fiction, sought in 1952 to publish a work of historical fiction with the firm Moody Press, William Eerdmans refused to let her publish under the Bertha Moore name.[113]

During the 1940s the Zondervan and Eerdmans catalogs displayed far more similarity than difference. Both companies focused on common book genres. In addition to publishing a variety of older reference works, both companies published a substantial amount of Christian fiction for both children and adults. Billing itself as the leader in Christian fiction, Eerdmans explained in its 1946 catalog that its novels were "written from a distinctly Christian viewpoint, with wholesome and inspiring motivation." Best-selling books included the titles in Bertha Moore's "The Triplets" series, which claimed to provide Christians with "wholesome, character-building books for their boys and girls." In 1948 Eerdmans would release Argye M. Briggs's *Root Out of Dry Ground*, a book for both juvenile and adult readers that illustrates how people can discover a vibrant faith in Christ through difficult circumstances. Zondervan's 1946 catalog meanwhile marketed its "choice fiction" for children by quoting Proverbs 22:6, which suggests that children "will not depart" from the path in which their parents train them.

But the two companies also began to develop distinct approaches to the genres of doctrinal and devotional literature. Having premised his company's commercial embrace of fundamentalism upon a "distinctive" theological posture, Eerdmans presented robust ideology and theology as the path toward a vital Christian life. "A GREATER WAR HAS JUST BEGUN," an Eerdmans ad trumpeted in 1945, "it is the war of ideas. And not even an atomic bomb can kill or destroy an idea." And so the Eerdmans Company emphasized the notion that its books could equip readers to fend off the ideological seductions of "modernism, humanism and scepticism on the one hand, and a tendency to ignore norm and precept on the other hand."[114] Pursuing these priorities, Eerdmans became known during the 1940s for publishing books by leading evangelical intellectuals—including many faculty members from the influential Fuller Theological Seminary.[115] Those authors include Edward J. Carnell and Carl Henry, who lamented in *The Uneasy Conscience of Modern Fundamentalism* (1947) that fundamentalists had failed to pursue social justice because they too often had backed themselves into theological corners, often compelling themselves to take up positions "so extreme that only a mental incompetent would subscribe to it." Calling for fundamentalists to abandon what he sometimes termed "fundamentalist phariseeism," Henry encouraged fundamentalists to address their theological limitations by developing "competent literature in every field of study."

These suggestions drew defensive criticisms from more conservative fundamentalists, whom Henry accused of trying to discredit his work.[116]

Expressing the Eerdmans Company's emphasis on girding Christian faith with robust theology, the company's logo in the early 1940s depicted a middle-aged man seated next to a collection of books, quietly and earnestly reading. The seated figure could be a layperson interested in theology, or it could be a pastor preparing a sermon. Eerdmans continued to prioritize both of those constituencies throughout the second half of the twentieth century and into the twenty-first. Today Eerdmans is a brand known for substantive theology, Christian history, and biblical studies. Although that brand identity allowed the company to engage consumers beyond the orbit of evangelicalism, it also hurt its claim upon popular evangelical devotional culture. In 1964, for instance, William Eerdmans wrote to Billy Graham and asked for the opportunity to publish a book that he recently had heard Graham describe. "In the 54 years I have been in the Religious Publishing Business I have never published a book . . . which was in violation or denial of revealed Scripture," Eerdmans assured Graham. "To publish a book by Billy Graham certainly would be the crowning effort of a blessed career of Fifty Five Years." Despite this praise, Graham turned Eerdmans down; just a few years later, however, Graham chose Zondervan to publish *The Jesus Generation* (1971). Focusing on the notion that a new generation of Christians increasingly had recognized "the vertical relationship of man with God" as the only recourse in a "darkening world," Graham began his best-selling book by thanking its publishers. "The Zondervans," he notes in the book's preface, "have been my personal friends and supporters since the beginning of my ministry."[117] Unlike Billy Sunday, Graham saw no need to have Eerdmans and Zondervan pray competitively for his book. Zondervan won without a fight.

Zondervan raised its profile and popularity by focusing on making and selling books that nurtured lay piety. As a company executive surmised a few decades later, their books became "experience-oriented, life-centered and Bible-based."[118] Its 1946 catalog featured a variety of daily devotionals, as well as several books about personal prayer. Examples included Theodore Engstrom's pocket-size *My Daily Guide*, Rosalind Goforth's *How I Know God Answers Prayer,* and John R. Rice's *Prayer—Asking and Receiving*. By focusing on individual devotion, Zondervan not only provided a wide range of sectarian fundamentalists with something to appreciate but also shifted the company's commercial focus toward women. Encouraging women to see the company's books as tools for transforming their own lives and their families', Zondervan's catalog also included products for the home. Those products included an assortment of Christian knick-knacks,

WM. B. EERDMANS PUBLISHING CO.
234 PEARL ST., N.W.   GRAND RAPIDS 2, MICHIGAN

—3—

One of the William B. Eerdmans Company's logos in 1945 depicted a middle-aged man deeply reading and reflecting on the company's books.
Used with permission from the William B. Eerdmans Publishing Company. *Complete Catalog and List of Publications, 1945–1946.*

including dozens of wall plaques impressed with bible passages and Christian slogans such as "Love Never Faileth."

To be sure, Eerdmans did not ignore female authors and consumers. Throughout the 1940s the company featured Christian fiction in its catalogs, focusing especially on stories with female protagonists who experience crises of faith or lead their families through difficult experiences. Examples include Sara Elizabeth Gosselink's *Roofs over Strawtown* (1945) and Clara Bernhardt's *Song of Zion* (1944). But as Eerdmans's logo visually indicated, that emphasis was not central to the company's brand.

The Zondervan brothers cultivated their company's brand of ecumenical piety throughout their everyday affairs. In addition to serving on the board of the Winona Lake Bible Conference, the Zondervans participated in a variety of other organizations dedicated to infusing varied corners of American society with versions of their devotional brand. As early as 1938 the Zondervans began participating in Gideons International and the Christian Business Men's Committee. Founded in 1899 as a sort of Christian fraternity for Christian salesmen interested in proselytization, the Gideons spawned the CBMC in the early 1930s as an association of local committees of businessmen devoted to inspiring revivalism, biblicism, and business authority in their respective locales. Pat Zondervan reportedly joined the Gideons after Charles Trumbull, editor of the *Sunday School Times,* asked Pat about his devotional life. "It was then," Zondervan later explained to James Ruark, Zondervan's company historian, "that I realized that I had been operating from my head but not from my heart." A year after joining the Gideons, Pat began a three-year stint as president of the Grand Rapids Gideons Camp; in 1956 he began the first of three one-year terms as international president of the entire Gideons organization.[119] As president of the

Grand Rapids Camp and as founding president of the city's CBMC chapter, Pat Zondervan regularly organized revivals in his city, bringing prominent evangelists to Grand Rapids.

Through organizational events and board memberships, Pat and Bernie Zondervan created and encountered countless opportunities to promote Zondervan books. When the Zondervans brought Hyman Appelman to Grand Rapids in 1944, for instance, Pat Zondervan wrote personally to 150 community leaders and sent each of them a copy of Appelman's *Ye Must Be Born Again* (1939). By circulating the book, Zondervan simultaneously testified to Appelman's prominence, cultivated his company's brand, and proclaimed his own piety.[120] To drive home this latter point, Pat Zondervan concluded virtually every letter he wrote during the 1950s and 1960s with a sign-off ostensibly drawn from his own morning bible study. "This morning," Zondervan wrote right above his signature in one archetypal letter from 1969, "after I read the first four words of the eleventh verse of Romans chapter twelve, I thought . . . I won't be." Through this habit of offering citations and mini-reflections in his business letters, Zondervan continually branded himself as someone who braided pious biblicism together with the spirit of initiative described in the four words he cited from the King James Version's translation of Romans: "not slothful in business."

CONCLUSION

If, as some scholars argue, brands and branding give religions meaning, then evangelicalism is an exemplary instance of this fact.[121] Evangelical media firms consistently have amplified the significance of brands. Well before and after institutions like the National Association of Evangelicals or the Moral Majority developed brand identities premised upon the notion that they spoke for a national evangelical public, evangelical media firms cultivated brands that gave consumers the opportunity to embrace distinct forms of transdenominational identity through acts of purchase. Companies such as Eerdmans, Zondervan, Moody, and others manifested divergent evangelical sensibilities through their branding strategies and practices.

Capitalizing on their brands, evangelical corporations not only have pursued commercial advantages over their competitors but also have bestowed celebrity upon countless evangelical authors. Evangelical firms have valued celebrity status because it valorizes independent authority. Whereas older categories of status—such as "renown"—recognized people especially for serving well in esteemed social institutions and offices, the phenomenon of celebrity has directed admiration and imitation away from institutions and toward particular people for merit that they have seemed to deserve as individuals.[122] That apparent independence has led evangelical media firms to treat celebrity as a quality that can compel consumers to purchase products by people who possess celebrity status. But perceptions of independent authority always have depended upon successful branding, and evangelical celebrities accordingly have needed evangelical media firms to help substantiate their authority through advertisements, marketing, sales, publications, and stories. Although the Billy Sunday story seems to invest the aging revivalist with far more power than William Eerdmans or Pat Zondervan possessed, Sunday's celebrity brand depended upon those publishers and the economy of authority they oversaw just as much as those firms depended commercially upon him.

To William Eerdmans's dismay, Zondervan received a reward in 1945 for its investment in evangelical celebrity. After more than a decade of conflict with Eerdmans, the Zondervan brothers had achieved sufficient commercial and cultural stature that they felt free to resolve past disagreements. Toward that end, they arranged a meeting with their uncle and several "impartial" judges. The judges all were preeminent evangelical celebrities who held positions that reflected their status. Not coincidentally, all of the judges also were prominent Zondervan authors. Will Houghton was president of Moody Bible Institute. E. Schuyler English was editor of *Revelation* magazine and president of the Philadelphia School of the Bible. And J. Palmer Muntz was Biederwolf's successor as director of the Winona Lake Bible Conference.

The judges cleared the Zondervans of all wrongdoing. Summarizing their judgment in a letter that they sent to William Eerdmans, the judges explained that the Zondervans "admitted having erred in the past." The judges acknowledged that "the Zondervan brothers had in times past performed and followed certain practices which we would not deny as having been doubtful and unethical." But they insisted that "there will be no repetition of them in the future, and no reason for complaint."

The penalty might have been stiffer if William Eerdmans had explained his side of the story. Yet he had refused to attend the meeting. In the decade since Billy Sunday had challenged Eerdmans to pray competitively, the brand of distinction that Eerdmans pioneered had bestowed immense value upon Zondervan Publishing House and its evangelical ecumenism. By 1946, not even Eerdmans could challenge the economy of authority that he and his nephews had created.[123]

3

Trade Associating

EVANGELICAL ALLEGIANCE
IN THE MASS MARKET

IN THE SPRING OF 1956, representatives from the Christian Booksellers Association (CBA) visited the White House. They had come to donate an assortment of books to the White House library. Writing a letter of thanks the day after the booksellers' visit, President Dwight Eisenhower remarked that "the range of spiritual wealth covered by your selection is wide and deep." Eisenhower predicted that the CBA's books "will be the source of strength to me and to others in the days and years ahead."[1] Repeating this ritual eight years later, a delegation of Christian booksellers would deliver fifty books to Lyndon Johnson. In addition to a few bibles, Johnson's delivery included such titles as Amy Bolding's collection of "ready-made devotions" *Please Give a Devotion* (Baker, 1963), Richard C. Halverson's *The Quiet Men: The Secret to Personal Success and Effectiveness by Men Who Practice It* (Cowman, 1963; Zondervan, 1965), and Eugenia Price's *Woman to Woman* (Zondervan, 1959), which explores "the difference Christ makes" for various aspects of a woman's life.

What was the point of this new White House ritual? One objective lay in the booksellers' hope that each president might become more familiar with the religious cultures that their books reflected, including the books' perspectives on the social opportunities and obligations that men and women possessed. Although Eisenhower regularly spoke in an evangelical idiom as president, he had not been especially devout before becoming a candidate in 1952, when supporters like the conservative media magnate Henry Luce urged him to view Christian identity as a key to national unity in an era of Cold War with a supposedly godless Soviet Union.[2] Convinced like so many other evangelical booksellers that books could and should somehow transform whomever they reached, the members of the CBA delegation delivered their books to Eisenhower just three years after he received baptism and made a confession of faith to the ruling elders of the Presbyterian Church in the United States of America.[3] Displaying similar intent during Lyndon Johnson's presidency, the CBA delegation made a point of donating the books to Johnson's personal library, as opposed to the White House library.[4]

But a second and equally important objective had less to do with presidential piety than with the mission of the organization that the booksellers represented. Founded in 1950, the Christian Booksellers Association drew its membership from evangelical bookstores, distributors, and independent booksellers throughout the United States. With the word "Christian" signaling their expansive ambition as well as their self-understanding as advocates for what they saw as true Christian faith, the founders and leaders of the CBA treated their visit to the White House not just as an expression of their hope for evangelicalism's claim upon American society but also as a symbol of their industry's claim upon evangelicalism. Reporting in 1964 that the CBA had compiled its White House donation "by means of a poll of bookstore owners and operators who are members," the magazine *Christianity Today* noted that some evangelicals had criticized this strategy. Critics complained that the selections "are not representative enough of the best in evangelical literature," and they lamented that the CBA had "introduced the commercial element into the selection process so conspicuously."[5] Understanding themselves as custodians of book culture, evangelical librarians especially objected to the notion that commercial success should serve as the basis for a book's selection.

Yet from the CBA's perspective, commercial booksellers and bookstores represented evangelical ideals far more than libraries did. By the 1960s, evangelicals had spent decades nurturing antiliberal suspicion of the government, and libraries not only depended upon public funding but also operated in cooperation with liberal cultural institutions and filled their shelves with books selected by librarians rather than consumers.[6] According to the CBA, neither evangelical literature nor evangelicalism itself could exist apart from its commercial element, which offered foundational freedom and choice to the American mass market. By delivering books to the leader of the United States, the CBA did more than announce its ambitious claim to represent evangelical booksellers and their commercial interests; the CBA also presented the book industry as a primary advocate for a way of life that its members sought to situate at the heart of American society.

The CBA made these ambitious claims in its capacity as a trade association, a type of organization designed for the "mutual benefit" of independent businesses in a particular industry.[7] Like most trade associations, the CBA advocated above all for policies that benefited their members' businesses. But trade associations also channeled their members' social preferences and prejudices, which included normative understandings of racial and gender inequalities. On these issues and others, the CBA's associative efforts drew inspiration not just from other trade associations but especially from earlier evangelical initiatives, which had championed renewed confidence in an avowedly "evangelical" movement.

Institutional models for the CBA included publishing companies like Eerdmans and Zondervan as well as organizations like the National Association of Evangelicals (NAE). In addition to heralding ecumenical alliance, those institutions had served as engines of evangelical allegiance. They had this effect by cultivating shared ideas, practices, and priorities, which the CBA and its trade associates sought to circulate among mass markets of American consumers. Through their efforts, the industry's sales figures became evidence of evangelicalism's social stature and its potential growth.

SEEKING MASS MARKETS

Although scholars often have described evangelicals as members of a religious "subculture" that has maintained distance from and tension with an American mainstream, that separatist notion has not always reflected the way that avowed evangelicals have idealized evangelical association and ambition.[8] Throughout the first half of the twentieth century, evangelical leaders, executives, and allied institutions typically proclaimed a desire to saturate American society with their "distinctive" brand of Protestantism. To maximize the circulation and reception of that brand, they oriented themselves toward a mass market.

The idea of the mass market took shape around the turn of the twentieth century, as improvements in transportation and communication increasingly allowed companies to broaden the geographic boundaries of their market and to increase the scale of their supply. To capitalize on that potential while also reducing production costs through economies of scale, companies often standardized their products and used mass media to advertise their limited product range to markets that they imagined as a homogeneous mass.[9] With a mass market in mind, companies relied on a strategy known as "product differentiation" to secure sales. As one market theorist explained in 1966, product differentiation begins "with the implication that any particular market consists of a homogenous or a *typical* group of buyers." Assuming that some portion of the mass market's total demand would converge upon virtually any product that displayed unique and desirable qualities, product differentiation strategy led companies to focus on "the promotion of product differences, whether they are actual or imagined." When successful, such promotion was understood to secure what the marketing pioneer Wendell Smith described in 1956 as "a horizontal share of a broad and generalized market," or "a layer of the market cake."[10] Smith's metaphorical layer cake encapsulates the concept of the mass market: unified despite internal variations.

In this commercial context, religious publishers presented their products as commodities that could and should appeal to portions of the mass market. Consider the case of the publishing initiative known as *The Fundamentals,* a series of volumes containing essays meant to articulate the "fundamental" principles of true Christian faith. Published between 1910 and 1915, the project received financial support from Lyman Stewart, an oil magnate from Los Angeles who sought to counteract what he saw as the threat of theological modernism. He saw his business fortune as a resource for counterbalancing the financial support that the oil baron and industrialist John D. Rockefeller had lent to such modernist bastions as the University of Chicago. Before financing *The Fundamentals* project with a gift of $300,000, Stewart had tried distributing other religious literature, including bibles, copies of the dispensationalist periodical *Our Hope,* and thousands of copies of William Blackstone's *Jesus Is Coming.* But Stewart and his collaborators ultimately concluded that they could codify their own orthodoxies more effectively and circulate them more widely by creating their own product and overseeing its systematic distribution. To provide their product with the broadest possible appeal, they avoided issues that they deemed especially divisive, such as the meaning of baptism and communion. By distributing their palatable product to as many ministers, seminary students and teachers, Sunday school leaders, missionaries, librarians, publishers, and periodical publishers as their financing allowed, the creators of *The Fundamentals* hoped that their version of orthodoxy might saturate American society, conjuring an expansive public devoted to "pure religion."[11]

Similarly seeking to avoid controversy in the hope of engaging as much of a mass market as possible, William Eerdmans regularly criticized authors and their books for teachings that might inspire disagreement. Writing in

1944, for instance, Eerdmans censured an author for presuming that all readers opposed drinking alcohol. "It is certainly a controversial point," Eerdmans explained, "and we always try to avoid such things in the books we publish. Millions of people such as all Episcopalians, practically all Lutherans, Presbyterians, Reformed, and people of many other denominations would take exception to such a statement and the result would be that one would have endless criticism and polemicks [*sic*] on his hand."[12] Reflecting upon his editorial approach, Eerdmans explained that his "attitude always has been the positive and constructive one. . . . I always tried to stay away from the negative and the controversial, telling the theologians to discuss and settle those things in their Synods etc." Eerdmans's remarks remind us that religious liberals were far from alone in seeking to liberate Christianity from what one historian describes as "sectarian captivity."[13]

In addition to arguing that doctrinaire moralism unhelpfully threatened to alienate potential consumers, Eerdmans asked authors to avoid ethnic, racial, or regional particularity. Offering his thoughts on a manuscript in 1944, Eerdmans suggested that the author remove any language written in a distinct dialect. "Sometime ago we published a Negro story with a lot of Negro dialect," he remarked, "and we have also published a book or two which contained a lot of mountain dialect. In the sale of these books, we discovered that the reading public does not take kindly to dialects or provincial vernacular."[14] For most of the twentieth century, evangelical publishers created relatively few books written by or intended for nonwhite consumers, and even fewer books that drew explicit attention to ethnicity and race. Publishers worried that significant attention to those issues might alienate members of the mass market that their companies prioritized.

This mass-market orientation was more than a commercial strategy; it was a commercial and cultural aspiration. And as Eerdmans's comments indicate, part of that aspiration was the persistent power of normative whiteness. Of course, Eerdmans was not alone in treating whiteness as a default identity. That assumption proved fundamental to the notion of the mass market itself. It pervaded such popular mass-market media as the magazine *Reader's Digest*.[15] First published in 1922, *Reader's Digest* kept subscribers up-to-date on current affairs, foreign policy, and literature by providing selections from books and articles that its editors presented as "impartial" reflections of reader interest and authorial merit. The magazine epitomized what scholars often describe as "middlebrow" culture, which found its animating principle in the notion that middle-class Americans should treat the mass market's cultural production as a means of cultivating a common set of intellectual, moral, and spiritual resources.[16]

The historian Joanne Sharp notes that the production of a common American character seemed especially important during World War II and the protracted struggles of the Cold War. Through the selections it reprinted, *Reader's Digest* served that unifying objective not only by taking for granted that its readers belonged to white, Christian families but also by contrasting American democracy with the undifferentiated specter of communism and fascism. By the end of the twentieth century, the magazine had 16 million monthly subscribers.[17]

Dreaming of similar circulation and cultural saturation, both Eerdmans and Zondervan developed Christian alternatives to *Reader's Digest* during the 1930s. Eerdmans began publishing its *Religious Digest* in 1935. Zondervan followed Eerdmans's lead in 1939 by acquiring a small Omaha-based magazine called *Christian Digest*. Both digests appeared monthly and reprinted what they described as the best of current Christian writing. Although fundamentalist magazines and newspapers like *Christian Life and Times* and *Moody Monthly* often had reprinted articles from like-minded periodicals, these two digests stood out for their deliberate attempt to serve a sensibility that the *Religious Digest* described as not "narrow or sectarian." The periodical would "be positive in our approach," its editorial policies claimed, "and seek to present the best from the whole field of religion per se." Elaborating upon its expansive orientation in January 1936, the editor of Eerdmans's *Religious Digest* lamented that the world had not changed significantly in the seventeen years since the end of the First World War. "We cannot build a new world out of men with old dispositions," the editor proclaimed. "New years are for new men, with new heart and spirit. It is through new thinking and feeling and living that the new light will break on the horizon."[18] Two decades later a similar impulse animated the evangelical magazine *Christianity Today,* which achieved far greater circulation due to the free distribution made possible by the financial support of J. Howard Pew.[19] Zondervan appealed to a sense of common Christian purpose as a way of justifying its unauthorized reprinting of texts to which other companies claimed copyright.

But these attempted alternatives to *Reader's Digest* never achieved even a fraction of their model's circulation, and the root of their relative failure had everything to do with what made *Reader's Digest* a commercial success. Middle-class Americans subscribed to *Reader's Digest* because it provided them with an easy method of consuming what the magazine presented as the essence of middlebrow culture—an ideal in which its readers were invested. Although Eerdmans and Zondervan shared many of *Reader's Digest*'s assumptions regarding their public's social profile, both companies struggled to provide potential consumers with the posture upon which they should predicate their purchase. Potential consumers might have asked: What could a "Religious" or "Christian" digest offer, when *Reader's Digest* already offered religious edification?

To communicate the premise of their aspirational commercialism, Eerdmans and Zondervan both began presenting their products in the early 1940s as "evangelical" in orientation. "It is our desire," Zondervan explained in a catalog from the mid-1940s, "to circulate only those books with a distinctly evangelical flavor."[20] The term "evangelical" had been used for centuries to conjure Protestant ecumenism, and it also pointed toward an alignment between a white ecumenical ideal and a broader national interest.[21] To help draw a national audience, Eerdmans soon launched a book competition for the "Evangelical Book Award," which it promised to "the author of a book in the field of Evangelical Christianity. . . . Long a leader among evangelical publishers, Eerdmans is seeking to encourage writers, both old and new, to produce volumes which will make a real contribution to the field." The contest rules explained that "all unpublished manuscripts in accord with the spirit and great doctrines of Evangelical Christianity are eligible for the award." In February 1948 the firm announced that the Fuller Seminary professor E. J. Carnell had won the $5,000 prize with his *Introduction to Christian Apologetics*, which Carnell originally had titled, more narrowly, *The Logic of Conservative Christianity*.[22]

Even as Eerdmans and Zondervan sought to cultivate their evangelical brands, many of their primary consumers remained confused about what merited the "evangelical" label.[23] Writing in the official magazine of the National Association of Evangelicals in 1945, Rutherford L. Decker, a Baptist minister and soon-to-be president of the NAE, acknowledged that the word "was not exactly a house-hold term among Bible-believing Christians." Boasting that "the term is certainly more widely used than ever before," Decker highlighted its etymological emphasis on the Gospel and boasted that contemporary evangelicals had taken "a doctrinal stand which is consistent with the etymological and historical significance of the term."[24] Reformed leaders in Grand Rapids also puzzled over the term's imprecision. Writing an editorial about one of Eerdmans's book contests, H. J. Kuiper pointed out that the rules required submissions to "be evangelical in doctrine and spirit." Noting that "the word 'evangelical' can be interpreted in various ways," Kuiper asked "whether the Wm. B. Eerdmans Company intended this qualification to express the minimum or the maximum of Christianity which the novels that will be submitted should contain." Kuiper hoped that "evangelical" identity might reflect "our Calvinistic approach to life." To answer his own question, Kuiper had asked William Eerdmans himself. "Yes," Eerdmans responded, "what we say . . . is the very minimum. An 'evangelical story of a definitely Calvinistic type' is the very thing we hope we will get, and I hope it will win the prize."[25]

As Eerdmans's earlier history evidences, its branding strategies had prioritized capacious concepts, which allowed consumers and supporters to associate the firm with whatever strain of Protestantism they valued most. Those phrases included terms like "constructive," "Calvinistic," or even "distinctive." By using the label "evangelical" to denote their mass-market ecumenism, publishers like Eerdmans helped animate the unified evangelical brand that institutions like the National Association of Evangelicals and the Christian Booksellers Association would champion. Those organizations also would address a mass market by attempting to conjure evangelical allegiance.

ASSOCIATING EVANGELICALS

Founded in 1942, the National Association of Evangelicals was nominally unrelated to any particular industry. And yet it served as a sort of trade association. Like trade associations, the NAE focused not only on conjuring a sense of common cause but also on encouraging industrial and business endeavors that complemented that sense. Those endeavors included broadcasting and publishing initiatives.

For centuries, members of varied industries have formed organizations dedicated to providing practical support to practitioners of their particular trade. Such organizations have seemed necessary especially in the wake of economic crises or changes, including economic depressions and wars.[26] Whenever they have appeared, trade associations have appealed particularly to businesses in complex areas of economic activity, such as those using technologies that perpetually change, or those that rely upon cooperation and collaboration across elaborate chains of production and distribution. Due to the complexity of the book industry and the trades it comprises, book publishers and booksellers consistently have established trade associations. As early as 1801 the "booksellers of the town of Boston" established the Association of the Boston Booksellers in order to address what their rules and regulations described as "a want of system in business." Their association sought to "cultivate a good correspondence between ourselves," in the hope that their "trade should be carried on under proper regulations." Chief among the practices that demanded proper regulation were matters of pricing, including guidelines for discounts that members could provide their customers. "On American publications," the regulations explained, "no discount shall be made from the retail price established by the publisher, for any single copy sold to a transient person, or retail customer."[27]

With such mutual dependencies in mind, trade associations have focused not merely on establishing trade agreements that benefit their members but also on cultivating cooperation, fair competition, and common priorities.[28] Founded in 1900, the American Publishers Association (APA) and the American Booksellers Association (ABA) both emerged out of a desire to secure "mutual benefit" among their members. To protect booksellers from what they perceived as "unfair competition," the APA agreed that its members would not do business with booksellers who cut prices without permission; meanwhile, the ABA agreed that its members would only sell books published by members of the APA, and it would price books as publishers determined.[29] The agreement ultimately fell apart in 1913, when the U.S. Supreme Court ruled in favor of the department store magnate R. H. Macy, who had sued the APA in 1902 on the grounds that its pricing policy violated the Sherman Antitrust Act of 1890.[30] But even as the courts enforced that Act by prohibiting what they saw as the restraint of trade through the suppression of competition, the government welcomed cooperation and controlled competition that seemed to promote or sustain trade. During World War I the government even invited trade associations to regulate wartime production.[31]

This notion of promoting trade encouraged trade associations to pursue practices that inspired common purpose within particular industries. As inexpensive mass-market paperbacks became commonplace after World War II, for example, the American Booksellers Association asked publishers to shift attention back to hardback books, on the logic that hardbacks provided both booksellers and publishers with the larger profit margins they needed to survive. The ABA also encouraged bookstores to cultivate standard retail cultures. In addition to encouraging bookstores to stock high-margin items such as toys and music recordings, the ABA trained its members in techniques related to better store operation, training, stock control, and merchandising. Beginning in 1948 the ABA also offered prospective bookstore owners standardized store plans, stock lists, estimates, and display fixtures. These "packaged bookstore" assemblies embraced functional, modern, colorful design, as opposed to the patrician, library-like atmosphere of earlier bookstores.[32] Through product selection, store design, and more, trade associations trained booksellers to see themselves as partners with shared commercial and cultural goals.

This emphasis on cultivating common purpose is what the National Association of Evangelicals shared most with trade associations, as opposed to the interdenominational religious associations that the NAE's founders often cited as their primary preoccupation. Reporting on the new association's initial 1942 meeting in Chicago, the *Christian Century* described the NAE as "a rival organization which will parallel the Federal Council of Churches in every one of its activities."[33] At the heart of that supposed rivalry lay the each organization's claim to represent large constituencies of American Protestants. But the NAE and the Federal Council of Churches (FCC) did not represent their constituencies in similar ways, and that dissimilarity defined their respective associational strategies.

The NAE deviated especially from the FCC's approach to denominational distinctions. Founded in 1908, the FCC took "federal" partnership as its primary principle. An outgrowth of decades of more limited ecumenical efforts to establish cooperation among Protestants, the FCC accepted only denominations as members, rather than individuals or individual churches. This provided denominations with authority to speak for their churches and to effect authority through their respective modes of governance. Insisting that the Council "shall have no authority over the constituent bodies adhering to it," the organization's constitution limited its scope to "the expression of its counsel and the recommending of a course of action in matters of common interest."[34] In order to respect the theological and ecclesiastical authority of its constituents, the Council avoided theological pronouncements that might divide its members. To be sure, the FCC made implicit theological pronouncements by supporting an array of initiatives that its leaders viewed as manifestations of a truly "social gospel." But the Council also remained deferential toward denominational distinctions, and the NAE's founders disparaged the FCC's reluctance to espouse theological claims. According to a NAE mission statement in 1942, "The Federal Council, because of its lack of a positive stand on the essential doctrines of the Christian faith, . . . does not represent the evangelicals of America."[35]

Just as trade associations encouraged their members to see themselves as united "booksellers" or "publishers," the NAE cultivated shared self-understanding among its members. It did so by downplaying the identity and authority of individual denominations, proposing other categories of allegiance. Instead of limiting membership to denominations, the NAE invited individual churches to become members, so that "churches which are affiliated, through denominational agencies over which they have no control, with organizations which have betrayed the Gospel, can join the National Association of Evangelicals, thus repudiating as individual churches their connection with unsound organizations."[36] This meant that the NAE could not cite the sum of several denominations' membership figures as its own membership figures, as the Federal Council did. But the NAE's membership model presented it as a safe haven for individuals and churches that sat unhappily within FCC-affiliated denominations. Although the NAE's leaders did not fully appreciate many evangelicals' persistent loyalty to their denominations, the NAE's approach to membership proved especially appealing to Baptists and other Protestants whose polity prioritized congregational autonomy.[37]

This membership model also appealed to congregations in the North and South that objected to the Federal Council's efforts to transform relations between black and white people. Although the FCC had not condemned racism or segregation consistently, the Council had included the four largest African American denominations from its founding, and the FCC allowed black leaders, such as the sociologist George Hayes, to help steer its Department of Race Relations, which began in 1921 as the Commission on the Church and Race Relations.[38] By contrast, the NAE's founding constitution make no reference to race or inequalities of any kind. Instead, the organization initially known as "the National Association of Evangelicals for United Action" identified its actionable items as broadcasting, missions, evangelism, education, and the separation of church and state.[39] The historian Tisa Wenger notes that white supremacists regularly appealed to religious freedom during the 1940s and 1950s as a way of defending segregation in schools, businesses, and churches.[40] With that context in view, a reference to "separation of church and state" in the NAE's constitution can be seen as a metonym for the organization's presumed whiteness. In 1943 the association's executive committee underlined that presumption by voting to remove the question "White? Colored?" from its membership application.[41]

To articulate the organization's principle of union, the NAE's leaders encouraged members to view themselves above all as "evangelicals." The term itself explicitly recalled nineteenth-century evangelical ecumenism, and Harold John Ockenga highlighted that reference to revivification by describing himself and his allies as "neo-evangelicals."[42] United behind a common category, the NAE privileged an ecumenical ideal of "cooperation without compromise," encouraging members to reconsider taken-for-granted theological divisions that might undermine cooperation.[43] In that spirit, one representative for InterVarsity admitted that he had "always had a dislike and distrust of Holiness and Pentecostal people but I think this conference has done more to right my attitude toward them and to help me to discover in them real Christian brethren than anything I know."[44] Considering that many holiness and pentecostal communities were relatively racially diverse, this InterVarsity representative's remark reflected a tendency for white fundamentalists to use theological criticisms as euphemisms for racist contempt.[45] By encouraging potential members to embrace the "evangelical" label, the NAE accordingly cultivated a new method of naming white, conservative Protestant identity beyond conventional denominational and theological categories.

Like a trade association, the NAE also identified and advocated for policies and trade objectives that benefited its members. While trade associations such as the American Publishers Association and American Booksellers Association had taken shape through efforts to set book pricing policies, the NAE initially mobilized around radio broadcasting policies. As a number of historians have shown, religious broadcasts began almost as soon as the first radio transmissions aired in 1920. Within four years, religious organizations controlled about 10 percent of the 600 radio stations in the United States.[46] Beginning with Radio Act of 1927, the federal government sought to bring order to the emerging radio landscape by creating the Federal Radio Commission (renamed the Federal Communications Commission in 1934). In addition to granting and renewing station licenses, the FRC assigned particular broadcasts to categories that determined their access to airtime. The FRC insisted that radio stations should offer free noncommercial airtime to religious broadcasters as a service to the public. To determine which religious broadcasters merited access to this free "sustaining time," the FRC heeded the advice of the organizations recognized as representatives of the largest religious constituencies.[47] Representing Protestants, the Federal Council of Churches insisted that the FRC should provide sustaining time only to religious programs that were "non-sectarian and non-denominational in appeal," offering "constructive ministry of religion" and interpreting "religion at its highest and best."

Excluded under those criteria, fundamentalist broadcasters responded by purchasing airtime; but the Federal Council subsequently encouraged radio networks to stop selling airtime to religious broadcasters. Viewing the Federal Council's authority as the root of their problems, fundamentalists like Ockenga encouraged radio companies such as NBC to modify their policies "so as to include Protestants of a different opinion from the liberal Federal Council." Claiming in 1940 that current policies created a situation in which a "large group of religious minded people are not being represented upon the air," Ockenga insisted that "a representative organization of this second group could easily be formed."[48] Channeling the spirit of the Christian libertarianism that had become pervasive among fundamentalists in the wake of the New Deal, William Ward Ayer complained not just that the government had become an agent of "regimentation and classification in religion" but also that it regimented and classified on the basis of the wrong people's advice. "The government," Ayer lamented, "gladly does business with the Federal Council as representing Protestantism." But the Federal Council "does not represent me in many of its programs and pronouncements."[49] Promising to offer Ayer, Ockenga, and other potential members the representation they claimed to lack, the NAE predicated that promise upon potential members' willingness to embrace an ecumenical and "evangelical" posture.

BELIEVING IN BOOKS

Although increasingly restrictive policies led evangelicals to fixate upon radio during the early 1940s, the NAE and its leaders simultaneously identified publishing and bookselling as trades that not only required advocates but also had the power to enhance evangelical allegiance. In an address to the NAE's 1946 annual convention, for example, the Moody Bible Institute professor Wilbur Smith drew attention to what he portrayed as a "wave of soul-destroying, agnostic, God-denying books and periodicals." Listing what he saw as signs that such books threatened to saturate American society, Smith noted that the Army had selected liberal titles such as Bruce Barton's *The Book Nobody Knows* (1926) to distribute to soldiers. Smith also lamented that books by the "modernist" minister Harry Emerson Fosdick had experienced "a phenomenal sale." In Smith's view, part of the problem was that "the official religious lists of books put out by the various national library associations, reading clubs, etc., are made up for the most part of modernistic titles." He also pointed out that "our religious book stores are advertising and hanging up for display charts supposedly sketching the development of religion from the earliest times, and show our faith to be ultimately descended from the mythological conceptions of savages." Beyond these particular examples, Smith undoubtedly had in mind the longstanding book industry campaign to cultivate liberal religious sensibilities.[50]

Beginning in the 1920s, a variety of institutions had labored to amplify the production, distribution, and consumption of liberal religious literature. In addition to the Religious Book Weeks of the 1920s, institutions included the Council on Books in Wartime, its Religious Book Committee, and the National Conference of Christian and Jews. Founded in February 1942, the Council on Books in Wartime had popularized the notion that books and reading are essential to democratic societies. "Books are weapons in the war of ideas," the Council insisted. Noting that "religious books are becoming recognized as important to a sustained total war effort," the chairman of the Council's influential Religious Book Committee added that "a trend in this direction is expected in a democracy where religious freedom is considered worth fighting for."[51] While this Committee provided soldiers with the kinds of books that Smith criticized, the interfaith National Conference of Christians and Jews (NCCJ) supplemented the Committee's work by encouraging Americans to see the idea of "Judeo-Christianity" as the cornerstone of American democracy.[52] During the 1940s the NCCJ organized new Religious Book Weeks dedicated to promoting books that expressed a tolerant and forward-thinking faith. The NCCJ also distributed lists of books that it endorsed. Overseeing the NCCJ's book activities was Henry Seidel Canby, who also oversaw the book selection committee of the Book-of-the-Month Club.[53] These close relationships between prominent initiatives and individuals inspired Wilbur Smith and his colleagues to diagnose what they saw as a liberal monopoly over religious literature. Smith complained that the mainstream book industry threatened to "deceive many people into thinking they are reading something that is religious truth."[54]

Recognizing the potential cultural sway of these initiatives, Smith insisted that evangelicals could not respond to the preponderance of liberal religious literature merely by avoiding it. "Let us not be guilty of repeating," Smith cautioned, "what many people think is such a smart statement, but is really a dangerously erroneous one, that all we need to do is to put the Bible in the hands of men and women, and it will suffice." A wide range of fundamentalists and evangelicals had expressed versions of that "erroneous" sentiment. In 1939, for example, Moody Bible Institute's president Will Houghton had championed the idea in his book *Let's Go Back to the Bible*. The book's title encapsulates his message. "You can get along without other books," he insisted, but "this one you ignore at your peril." Reflecting in one chapter upon the relationship between the Bible and other books, Houghton recalled sitting alone in his office and speaking out loud to his bookshelves and the books that filled them. "Some of you have been my companions for many years," he had told his books. Describing each book as "a bottle of pure spring water," he reportedly took a bible in his hand and insisted: "But, books, this is more than a bottle of spring water, this is the spring itself, and if you have anything of truth in your pages, that truth was first in embryo here."[55]

Although Wilbur Smith never would deny fundamentalist confidence in the Bible's all-sufficiency, he had become convinced that modernistic authors, publishers, and publications increasingly misrepresented the Bible's teachings, thereby preventing ordinary Americans from discovering the Bible's truths for themselves. To listeners who insisted upon a "Bible only" policy, Smith inveighed, "the Bible *is* in the hands of thousands of people today who are lying about it."[56] Smith accordingly announced: "*It is time that we begin the production of some literature that can powerfully and triumphantly, let us pray God, meet this mounting tide of faith-destroying* literature." The NAE's founding had helped to make the time seem right.[57] Dreaming about how the NAE might reinvigorate evangelical publishing and reading, Smith insisted: "An *evangelical Christian church can do it.*" In addition to recruiting authors and convincing them to write, Smith suggested that the NAE could "aid in underwriting the cost of such compositions." With both spiritual and financial support, "from their pens may come pages, and chapters, and books, that will stir our indifferent laodicean age, and make young men and women realize once again that Jesus of Nazareth is none other than the only begotten Son of God."[58]

Idealistic and ambitious, this vision for evangelical books called for cooperation between ministers, churches, and authors no less than businesses and financiers. According to Carl F. H. Henry—who served as literary editor of *United Evangelical Action* before becoming a founding professor at Fuller Theological Seminary and an editor of *Christianity Today*—practical constraints always had suppressed the scale of evangelical book production. Published with Zondervan and originally written as a thesis for the masters of divinity degree he received from Northern Baptist Theological Seminary in 1942, Henry's *Successful Church Publicity: A Guidebook for Christian Publicists* (1943) retold Christian history as a history of print publicity. It cast the authors of the Bible, Reformation leaders, and American founders as the publicists of their respective eras. Throughout Christian history, Henry explained, Protestants historically relied upon print to publicize and shape their movement. Primarily because of financial constraints, however, books had made up a relatively small percentage of Christian publications.[59]

With sufficient financial and logistical investment, Henry later argued in *The Uneasy Conscience of Modern Fundamentalism* (Eerdmans, 1947), fundamentalists could develop "competent literature in every field of study," which would allow evangelicals to address the theological shallowness that limited their ability to unite and mobilize collectively. Only by organizing could evangelicals "project a solution for the most pressing world problems," and only by developing such solutions could evangelicals could honor their best intentions and draw more Christians into the evangelical public.[60] "The world of religious books is a propaganda world," Henry explained in 1950. Although some propaganda "tends to be either false or deficient," he pointed out that "the Christian message came into the world as *news*, indeed as *the good news*. Christianity from its beginnings has involved a literature which has been set apart from all other world writings as the written revelation of God."[61] Hoping to set evangelicals apart by generating robust book propaganda, Henry and his allies sought to address the industry's practical constraints.

Evangelical leaders argued that "Faithful & Loyal" books could rout "False Philosophy," "Science So-Called," and other rebellious books.

Used with permission from First Covenant Church, Minneapolis, Minn. Reproduced from microfilm. *United Evangelical Action*, March 15, 1950, 4.

The late 1940s seemed like a good time for evangelical publishing not only because "an evangelical Christian church could do it" but also because the end of World War II allowed the book industry to align evangelical ambition with commercial capacity. Throughout the first half of the 1940s, severe wartime paper quotas had constrained publishers' potential production, and business strategies had adapted to those restrictions. As the president of the publishing firm Little, Brown and Company explained in 1947, publishers took "drastic steps" to save on paper and manufacturing costs. By the summer of 1945, "all possible economies had been made." Throughout the industry, publishers restricted new titles. The minister Harold Ockenga felt the sting of those restrictions even in 1947, when Revell's president William Barbour rejected one manuscript and asked Ockenga to drastically shorten another.[62] Barbour explained to Ockenga in an apologetic letter: "Of course, you realize that we are facing unbeliev-able production problems and indications are that conditions will be worse, rather than better." Barbour noted that publishers had reduced their output so dramatically that the National Arts Club struggled to solicit enough books in the fall of 1945 to organize the fair it typically held for new books.[63] In addition to focusing on publishing books from their back-lists, publishers adopted a variety of strategies to use their quotas more ef-ficiently. They printed in smaller type, reduced margins, cut words, used thinner paper, dropped entire sections from books, and raised sale prices to meet higher production costs. Occasionally publishers tried to deal with their constraints by cooperating among themselves.[64] For some pub-lishers, the war created a financial windfall when the government granted higher paper quotas and lucrative purchase contracts for books to dis-tribute to members of the armed services.[65] But intense competition made those contracts difficult to secure.

As evangelical publishers attempted to increase their offerings, the NAE began creating lists of book recommendations for booksellers and their con-sumers. With the NAE itself seeking to conjure a common evangelical identity beyond attachment to other denominational or interdenomina-tional agencies, the NAE's book list served that objective by cultivating ideas and concerns outside the influence of the federal government and its auxiliaries. The NAE's list of recommendations served as counterparts to lists that the American Library Association (ALA) and the National Con-ference on Christians and Jews shared annually with national newspapers and libraries across the United States. The ALA had compiled lists of rec-ommended religious reading since the 1920s. In June 1943, for instance, the ALA touted a list of fifty books composed by a committee of "five distinguished theologians, educators in the fields of philosophy and reli-gion."[66] During the 1940s the NCCJ's list became even more prominent, due to its release as part of a broader Religious Book Week initiative.

In contradistinction with organizations like the ALA and the NCCJ, which worked in close cooperation with the government and its political and cultural leaders, the NAE cast itself as an advocate for ideas and indi-viduals that the government had shielded from view. For more than a de-cade, fundamentalists had criticized the expanding power and political lib-eralism of the federal government. Applying a premillennial eschatology to the New Deal state, some fundamentalists even viewed President Roose-velt and his initiatives as signs of the impending apocalypse.[67] Setting out to challenge liberal book lists, the NAE's Board of Administration voted in 1944 to request representation on the board of the committee that created the American Library Association's list of recommended religious books.[68]

But when the ALA failed to provide the representation they desired, the NAE's board determined to create a list of their own. In announcing the NAE's competing list, the Free Methodist bishop Leslie Marston made a point to note that it "is intended to supplement the American Library Association's general list of outstanding religious books, and it is hoped will serve Christian America as a guide to the best in current evangelical thought." Under the oversight of Carl Henry, the first "N.A.E. Book List" appeared in June 1945.[69] In 1946, *United Evangelical Action* began dedicating an entire issue to books, with its "Annual Book Number"; by 1950, book numbers appeared in both the fall and the spring. Special issues devoted to books subsequently became a regular feature of prominent evangelical periodicals, including *Christianity Today.*

The NAE's book initiative sought to transform evangelical reading habits and business practices alike. Styling himself as an evangelical intellectual rather than as an evangelist, Henry viewed books not as tools of evangelism but instead as means by which evangelicals could and should strengthen their own conviction and devotion. Only by doing so could evangelicals evangelize effectively. He predicted that the book initiative would encourage evangelicals to read more and would "remind secular publishing houses of the vast demand for evangelical publications which is now largely overlooked." By encouraging evangelicals to read, Henry hoped, the initiative also would "stimulate the publication of a higher quality of evangelical literature by evangelical publishing houses." Through better books, evangelicals could "make historic Christianity relevant to peculiar contemporary problems." Lamenting that "non-evangelical thought continues to speak definitely in numerous crisis areas because no orthodox treatment appears," Henry proclaimed that "better days are ahead for the evangelical movement."[70]

By 1950 Henry began to criticize evangelical books and attack what he saw as the cause of their inferiority. In his view, publishers' penchant for reprinting older books had become a primary impediment to evangelicalism's intellectual advance. "A word must also be said about the reissuance of choice evangelical volumes which have been long out of print," Henry began, "a program for which the William B. Eerdmans Publishing Company especially provided impetus." After acknowledging that such reprints had done a "substantial service to the evangelical cause" by providing "older classics, tried and true" at a time when evangelicals lacked "contemporary volumes of similar merit," Henry meanwhile decried reprinting as a practice that would "result only in embarrassment to the evangelical cause" if not "paralleled by contemporary evangelical effort." Escalating his critique over the course of the next year, Henry condemned publishers like Eerdmans for spearheading "the increasing flow of last-generation and even last-century material." Noting that "a primary consideration seems to be an opportunity to reissue volumes on which a publisher's royalty need no longer be paid," Henry called upon publishers to recognize that "rather acceptable substitute volumes are available."[71] Only if publishers produced new books and booksellers circulated them, Henry believed, could the evangelical public continue to grow.

The NAE's leaders became sufficiently enchanted with books' potential power that the NAE itself attempted to purchase a publishing company in the 1950s. The purchase plan began in 1952 when the owners of Cincinnati's Standard Publishing Company decided to sell it. Privately owned but closely connected to the Disciples of Christ since its founding in 1866, the company had cultivated a "non-denominational inter-faith" brand since 1947 in order to "expand the scope of the business."[72] The leading advocate for the NAE's potential purchase of the company became James DeForest Murch, the editor of *United Evangelical Action* and former editorial secretary of Standard's *Christian Standard* newspaper. Emphasizing sympathy between the NAE's mission and the core convictions of the Disciples, Murch explained that Standard Publishing had "for close to a hundred years produced religious journals, books, Sunday School supplies, religious art subjects, . . . [and] materials for some thirty Protestant denominations."[73]

But the company would not come cheaply. Valued at nearly $6 million, with an estimated annual revenue of $1.5 million, protracted negotiations set a purchase price just over $4 million.[74] Such a purchase would have been out of the question if not for the variety of wealthy businessmen who had been supporting evangelical initiatives with both time and money. They included Charles Fuller, R. G. LeTourneau, Herbert Taylor, and John Bolten, all of whom Murch described as "large-visioned." The owner of Bolta Rubber Company, Bolten viewed investment in evangelical initiatives as an opportunity to redress a problem recently diagnosed in a *Harvard Business Review* article, which had argued that the industrialization of the economy had left American businesses and workers without the sense of "God manifesting Himself in His creatures."[75] Among the several businessmen whom Murch initially contacted about the purchase opportunity, Bolten had expressed the most interest in acquiring Standard. Bolten had become convinced that if he helped the NAE purchase the company, the NAE's non-profit status would allow Standard to avoid paying federal taxes on its profits. But the Internal Revenue Service ultimately balked at this assumption, and Bolten accordingly created a "non-profit and non-sectarian organization" to serve as a shelter for the company. The purchase was completed in 1955, with rumors circulating that Billy Graham had contributed some of the funds.[76]

The investment potential of figures like Bolten helped fuel excitement among book boosters like Smith and Henry, who believed that investments would enhance the book industry's infrastructure. By 1952 businessmen already had been funding other evangelical initiatives.[77] Boasting to Billy Graham about the impending purchase of Standard, Murch had insisted that "it would be difficult to envision the vast possibilities for the evangelical cause which could grow out of such a purchase." Eventually hired as a consultant to the firm, Murch proclaimed his hope that "Standard can be a spokesman" for the "New Evangelical Movement." He imagined that it could furnish "strategy, literature, promotion," linking together disparate evangelical organizations and producing an "orthodox journal" analogous to the *Christian Century*.[78] This latter goal ultimately produced the magazine *Christianity Today*, which Standard printed but did not own.

"The book business has a potential far beyond that which is being developed," Murch would foretell in 1955.[79] To realize that potential, however, evangelical leaders had to generate a shared vision of common cause. From the beginning, they recognized the production and distribution of evangelical media not only as a primary field of evangelical initiative but also as an engine of evangelical identity. The evangelical book trade accordingly became both an effect and a cause of evangelical allegiance.

INDUSTRIAL IDENTITIES

When representatives from the Christian Booksellers Association visited the White House and delivered books to the president in 1956, they modeled that practice as well as their organization's overall purpose on what they saw as analogous initiatives, institutions, and ideas. Drawing inspiration and institutional support from organizations like the NAE, the CBA also sought to cultivate common evangelical purpose. Toward that end, they treated selling and purchasing as a primary means by which consumers could be incorporated into an evangelical movement. As a formal trade association, the CBA built upon earlier efforts to associate evangelicals through trade.

Although it drew inspiration from the NAE and its leaders, the CBA modeled itself above all on the American Booksellers Association, which had made its own deliveries to the White House for more than two decades. The ABA delivered its first donation to the White House in 1930. That initiative had begun the previous year, when a bookseller from San Francisco heard a rumor that President Herbert Hoover and his family had found virtually no books available in the White House following his inauguration. Already committed to the notion that every home should possess an edifying collection of books, the ABA organized a committee of ten reputed book experts to select suitable titles for the White House "home library." After the committee compiled its list, booksellers around the country were invited to donate money to purchase a book, on the promise that their name would appear inside the book itself.[80] The ABA updated the collection every few years. In 1934, 1937, and 1941, the organization presented batches of 200 books, selected again by committee.

The ABA's ritual took shape around the conviction that books could provide a fracturing American society with what the historian Matthew Hedstrom describes as "a common set of widely accepted religious ideas, practices, and presuppositions." More than a decade before this aspiration produced the White House library campaign, it produced such initiatives as Religious Book Week, which married "cutting-edge business practices with a liberal religious outlook," in the name of cultivating a "modernized faith" that might provide American culture with a "spiritual center."[81] In addition to sharing objectives, the White House library and Religious Book Week initiatives shared leadership. Their leaders included prominent companies—including religious publishers such as the Fleming H. Revell Company—as well as particular individuals, such as Frederic Melcher. During the 1920s, Melcher led Religious Book Week and served as the chairman of the committee that selected books for the White House. Functioning as the initiative's administrator, Melcher even collected the funds that booksellers sent to purchase books from the committee's list.[82] At that time Melcher also served as editor of *Publishers Weekly*—a magazine published by the R. R. Bowker Company, which appointed Melcher as president in 1934. Before then Melcher had served stints as secretary of the ABA, executive secretary of the National Association of Book Publishers, and president of the Booksellers League of New York. A practicing Unitarian, Melcher did not have a religious posture that the leaders of the CBA recognized as their own.

Although trade associations like the CBA and ABA have concerned themselves with shaping society and generating common cause, they also have connected those initiatives to more practical matters. Note, for example, that individual publishers and individual booksellers always have been inclined to seek a commercial advantage over their competitors by setting comparably low prices. But as the book historian James West explains, "if prices are not stable, no one can pay the bills."[83] When individual booksellers receive large discounts from publishers and pass low prices on to their retail consumers, competing booksellers must either secure their own discounts to match competing prices or reduce their retail prices without a discount on their inventory, which causes their profit margins to shrink. Lower profits in turn limit a bookseller's ability to acquire new stock, to set competitive prices going forward, or to pay their bills. These kinds of tensions ultimately generate financial uncertainty, cultivate resentment, and undermine an industry's sociality. To avoid such problems, the CBA began dealing with pricing issues not long after its founding in 1950. CBA officials urged booksellers not to discount books substantially. "There were so few good Christian books and publishers anyway," former president Jerry Jenkins later explained, "by discounting what *is* available to sell, stores would be cutting into their own profits."[84]

Behind these efforts to conjure industry-wide cooperation lay the general book industry's desire to increase "standardization," which an influential 1931 report had identified as the primary problem faced by publishers and booksellers. Approaching the nadir of the Great Depression, members of the book trade had become increasingly worried that the economic crisis would destroy their businesses. The National Association of Book Publishers accordingly commissioned a report "to study the economic structure of the industry and to suggest practical means for strengthening it." It received financial support from such allied trade groups as the American Booksellers Association, the International Council of Religious Education, the American Library Association, and the American Association for Adult Education. Publishing luminaries like W. W. Norton and Alfred A. Knopf served on the survey committee. The responsibility for directing the survey and authoring a report based on its findings rested primarily with Oliver H. Cheney, a New York banker who claimed to have "taken a special interest in publishing facts and figures" as vice president of Irving Trust Company.[85]

Among his findings, Cheney concluded that haphazard communication systems and management strategies weakened the distribution chain by introducing significant "hazards and wastes," which forced publishers and booksellers to compensate for higher costs by selling books at higher prices. Those prices made books less desirable for consumers and less profitable for active booksellers as well as potential booksellers, who accordingly possessed little incentive to create the new bookstores that the industry required. Even though the general book industry relied primarily upon bookstores for distribution, Cheney found that two-thirds of all counties in the United States, and more than 50 percent of the rural population, possessed no place to buy books. That statistic included not just bookstores but also drugstores or gift shops, which often sold books.[86]

Although Cheney viewed these problems as endemic to the entire book industry, he noted that some segments of the book industry could implement his solutions to especially great effect. "The church is beginning to discover," he explained, "that it needs more than three books, the Bible, the prayer-book and the hymn book." Reporting that religious people read more than average, Cheney suggested that a greater variety of religious books not only would find eager consumers but also could reach those consumers through unique distribution pathways. Despite its denominational and ecclesial division, Cheney surmised, "the church has probably the most widespread and highly organized machinery for stimulating adult reading of books—potentially." In addition to communication channels within and between religious groups, that machinery included religious bookstores. Due to that machinery, the religious book industry possessed "a group of buyers of established loyalty." Nevertheless, Cheney remarked, "this advantage is not utilized as much as it should be."[87]

Seeking to utilize its supposed advantage, the CBA began standardization initiatives in the 1950s. At the time, one of the CBA's founders later recalled, "the Christian bookstore industry was in a sorry state." He imagined that many bookstores "were operated by people who had a desire for ministry but very little business experience."[88] The CBA accordingly began offering correspondence courses and selling to members short handbooks that offered guidance on bookstore ownership. In books such as *The Christian Book Store*, authors John Bass and Robert DeVries offered advice on issues that included typical costs, ideal locations, lease negotiations, arranging in-store displays, and how to choose nonbook "sidelines."[89] Reflecting in 1968 on eighteen years as a book salesman, Moody Press's Sid Zullinger testified to the effectiveness of these training campaigns. "I can recall the appearance of the majority of the Christian bookstores, the types of displays, and the appearance of the merchandise . . . left much to be desired," he explained with reference to his early days in bookselling. "Now I can truthfully say that I, as well as the majority of other salesmen that I talk to, are very proud of the attractive new [book] jackets, the new racks and displays, the attractive lighting, and the new fronts on many of the stores. One very significant factor is the better trained and sharper sales personnel in the stores." During the 1970s the CBA would boast that its training initiatives and systems of member support ensured that the CBA's member stores consistently had a lower rate of failure than general bookstores.[90]

Through shared priorities and practices, the book trade's associations cultivated collective identity among their members. In addition to committing American booksellers to common commercial strategies, products, and physical store layouts, the trade's associations drew members together by organizing regular meetings and conventions. In 1946, for example, the

ABA set up one annual convention and six regional meetings to reconnect an industry whose contacts had frayed during the war. On that model, the CBA began holding its own annual conventions in 1950.[91] "Christian booksellers know very little if anything about the existence of each other," one bookseller complained after the inaugural convention. Praising the CBA for redressing that problem, the bookseller admitted that "booksellers as a rule are individuals here and there who felt they should sell Christian literature, and their scope of operation varies from an agent with a set of samples to a store stocked with a complete line." In the name of addressing the division that this bookseller bemoaned, the CBA's leaders compiled what it described as "a master list of some 5,000 religious booksellers and supply dealers," inviting everyone on the list to attend its annual meetings. The CBA also invited publishers, touting the meetings as "your BEST OPPORTUNITY TO REACH BOOKSELLERS at a minimum of cost and with a far greater opportunity to display more merchandise."[92]

By inviting publishers, the CBA affirmed an alignment of interests across the book industry's sectors that consumers often presumed. During the 1970s the Fleming H. Revell Company received a steady stream of letters in which readers heaped their scorn for certain books they disliked upon bookstores as well as those books' publishers. Referring to William Proctor's *The Commune Kidnapping* (1975), for example, one reader complained about "the emphasis he put on sex and the way he went into detail." In this scandalized reader's view, "this is the type of book one would expect to find on a paperback rack in a drugstore, secular bookstore, etc. Certainly not in a Christian Bookstore."[93] Criticizing the author Anita Bryant for claiming in *The Total Woman* (1973) "to have a Christian home when she says she's lived '20 years of hell' with her husband," another reader announced that Bryant's book had ruined her interest in Christian books. "I'm not sure how many books I'll be buying from now on," the reader remarked, adding: "I just cancelled my subscription to a Christian book store."[94] As these complaints indicate, consumers often have viewed booksellers and publishers as united in both business and mission. But their interests never have aligned completely. Although publishers often have relied upon booksellers to circulate the goods that they produce, that reliance has presupposed not just that booksellers can circulate products more effectively and efficiently than publishers can themselves, but also that publishers and booksellers agree broadly on who ultimately might buy the product. Both of those presuppositions have proven uncertain because distribution paradigms, evangelical self-understandings, and consumer desires recurrently have changed. Although online bookselling has decimated many bookstore businesses in the twenty-first century, publishers sometimes have praised companies like Amazon for delivering books more efficiently than bookstores ever have.[95]

Even as the CBA sought to strengthen a sense of common concern between publishers and booksellers, the CBA's associative efforts inspired publishers to create a trade association of their own. In 1953 William Eerdmans began a conversation with the CBA about bringing together "the Evangelical Publishers who are not denominationally related." Eerdmans explained that "if the independent Christian publishers were united, we no doubt could exert some wholesome influence on the American Christian people. Now and then we could issue statements supporting Christian movements and give all good movement, especially those that bear on Christian literature, our full and moral support." Eerdmans believed that such a group might prove especially helpful in cases where a publisher sought to publish a book that seemed unlikely to make much money, yet had the potential to "render a definite and valuable contribution to some cause or issue or problem might be worthy of support." In such a case, Eerdmans suggested, members of a trade association might share expenses. Two decades later these preliminary efforts developed into the Evangelical Christian Publishers Association, whose members agreed in 1974 not just to serve "the purpose of exalting the Lord Jesus Christ" but also to "promote professional excellence through training, research, sharing of strategy, and initiating programs for the solving of common problems."[96]

In order to enhance a sense of common purpose through shared information and strategies, evangelical trade associations attempted to shape how their members understood their trade. To reinforce an understanding of bookselling as a spiritual vocation rather as mere business, for example, the CBA taught members to see their businesses as the primary means through which they might achieve their shared cultural priorities. Annual meeting attendees were encouraged to view themselves as more than merchants who trafficked in Christian literature; attendees shared an identity as "Christian booksellers"—a label that emphasized commercial and cultural distinctiveness. "Make this Convention and the Association a real means of increasing the distribution of religious books and Bibles," the CBA exhorted.[97] Training its members to recognize that new evangelical priorities and possibilities required effective advocates, the CBA insisted that booksellers were ideally suited to the task. "We have a product that is needed for every age," one CBA leader explained, "for every circumstance life brings. We are the only business in the world that can give the rich what he can not obtain with his riches or the poor what he needs to become a child of the King."[98] Although grandiose, this comment expresses the industrial confidence that the CBA helped inspire during the first decades following its founding. By cultivating common cause among publishers, booksellers, authors, and even consumers, the CBA presented the book trade not just as an engine of evangelical culture but also as the primary means by which evangelicals might realize their mass-market aspirations.

THE YEAR OF THE EVANGELICAL

"Born Again!" announced the cover of the *Newsweek* magazine when it hit newsstands in October 1976, the week before the 1976 election. This brief exclamation served not only as the title of the issue's cover story but also as a two-word portrait of "The Evangelicals," whom the magazine described as "the most significant—and overlooked—religious phenomenon of the '70s."[99] Why did these evangelicals seem so significant? In an age when polling about religious identity remained in its relative infancy, George Gallup Jr. had organized the first survey that quantified with proclaimed precision the number of American evangelicals.[100] Summarizing Gallup's findings and methodology, *Newsweek* writer Kenneth Woodward explained that "half of all Protestants—and a third of all Americans—say that they have been 'born again.' That figure comes to nearly 50 million adult Americans who claim to have experienced a turning point in their lives by making a personal commitment to Jesus Christ as their Saviour."[101] Those figures had led Gallup to describe 1976 as the "year of the evangelical," an assessment that Woodward helped popularize.[102]

Yet if Gallup's survey figures convinced Woodward and others of evangelicalism's social stature, the evangelical book trade's mass-market success already had endowed Gallup's findings with plausibility. As the leaders of the NAE and CBA long had hoped, evangelicals had achieved recognition as a constituency with a claim on the future of American society, and the evangelical book trade served as corroboration for that claim. Attempting to chronicle evidence of evangelicalism that pundits had overlooked, Woodward highlighted the "booming evangelical book market." During the first half of the 1970s that market had produced a number of standout best sellers. They included Kenneth Taylor's *The Living Bible* (Tyndale House and Doubleday, 1971), which ranked as the best-selling book nationwide in 1972 and 1973; Hal Lindsay's *The Late Great Planet Earth* (Zondervan, 1970), which went on to become the best-selling title of the 1970s; and Marabel Morgan's *The Total Woman,* the best-selling nonfiction book of 1974.[103] All of these books were published by evangelical publishers, and their best-selling sales figures linked Gallup's percentages to tangible consumers.[104]

Between 1970 and 1976, journalists regularly took the evangelical market's growth as evidence of a correspondingly substantial public. As early as 1970, a reporter from the *New York Times,* McCandlish Phillips, set out to explain the seemingly conjoined rise of the evangelical book industry and evangelicalism. Phillips explained that "a new kind of piety that stresses immediate personal experience and encounter—encounter with other humans and with the divine—and that deemphasizes doctrinal formulations has given Protestant religious publishers a big new surge in sales." Reporting that those books generated "book sales sometimes as great as, and sometimes greater than, those of the regular trade" despite circulating "through channels that only rarely coincide with those of the regular trade," Phillips asked Zondervan's vice president of publications, Robert DeVries, to explain how this could be. DeVries answered by claiming that the U.S. population included "26 million evangelical Christians," and that those people constituted the "main audience" for his company and its competitors.[105] Five years later, the nationally syndicated religion journalist Russell Chandler reported that "the demand for books that appeal to religious needs has been soaring." Chandler noted that a recent survey had found that "42 percent of American families bought bibles or other religious books last year." While the general publishing field had grown at a rate of less than 10 percent between 1967 and 1975, Chandler explained, "religious book sales volume has increased 16.6%." He also noted that most of those sales reflected an "evangelical view."[106]

The evangelical market's success allowed evangelicalism to appear socially coherent and limitless in its potential for growth. Noting in 1975 that "the 'big five' religious publishers" all focused primarily on evangelical consumers, Chandler described that market's primary consumer constituency as "middle-of-the-road evangelicalism."[107] Throughout the 1970s, journalists recurrently attempted to describe and define that evangelical center. In 1975, for instance, *Forbes* magazine suggested that evangelical media responded to "post-Watergate morality" and capitalized upon a social drift toward "nonsectarianism" in both religion and politics by avoiding divisive ideas and teachings, focusing instead on broadly inspirational literature. As an example, the magazine cited the country singer Johnny Cash's autobiography and "spiritual odyssey" *Man in Black* (Zondervan, 1975). Beginning with Cash's decision at age twelve to "accept Christ" and become born again, the book traced Cash's rise to fame and his history of drug and alcohol abuse, before arriving at his decision in 1971 to "try harder to live my life as God wants."[108] Surprised not just to see Cash's book achieve bestseller status (selling 225,000 copies in its first eleven months on sale) but even to see Cash write a religious book at all, *Forbes*'s reporter incredulously asked: "Johnny Cash a religious writer?"

But the reporter made sense of the apparent incongruity between Cash's persona and religious authorship by reflecting on what an "evangelical" designation demanded. The reporter surmised that it required little more than an "inspirational personal witness story" or a self-help strategy, which might focus on anything from dieting to financial advice. "Religion is not so much dying in the U.S.," *Forbes* concluded, "as it is becoming more personal and less formal." It was a commercial religion made for the mass market.

CONCLUSION

Not all evangelicals portrayed the mass market as a welcoming realm. Although evangelical books had achieved best-sellers status, many individuals and institutions insisted throughout the 1970s and 1980s that "there is a tendency to keep Christian thinking out of the mainstream."[109] They noted that evangelical books often had outsold other books without receiving recognition on mainstream best-seller lists.[110] Responding in 1983 to what participants described as the mainstream book industry's "silent censorship," one CBA-supported initiative parodied a recent "banned books week" campaign organized by the American Booksellers Association. While the ABA's campaign had focused on ninety-three titles that moralizing Americans often had chosen to censor, the CBA initiative presented evangelical books in general as "banned books."[111]

This campaign drew inspiration from the recent publication of Cal Thomas's *Book Burning*, which argued that secular bias against Christian views kept Christianity out of the public sphere. A speechwriter for the Southern Baptist conservative polemicist Jerry Falwell, Thomas posited a parallel between racial segregation in baseball and the supposed exclusion of conservative Christians from the mainstream book market. "The reasoning goes like this," Thomas claimed, "Sure, you can publish your books/play baseball, but not in 'our' industry/ballpark." Thomas described that exclusion as a "'separate but equal' approach" that "assures we [conservative Christians] are kept on the fringes."[112] Through his argument, Thomas drew a parallel between the supposed exclusion of conservative Christians from the mass market and the exclusion of people of color from white social spaces before the U.S. Supreme Court declared "separate" as "unequal" in the *Brown v. Board of Education of Topeka* decision of 1954. Although Thomas's racist reasoning grossly minimized the violence of segregation and structural racism by equating it with the perceived pain of insufficient market access, his remarks testified to the close relationship that members of the New Christian Right saw between presence within the mass market and power over American society.[113]

Uniting both "middle-of-the-road" evangelicalism and the evangelicalism of the New Christian Right, however, lay a belief that evangelicalism's continued growth depended in part on the expansion of the evangelical market. Everyone agreed, and evangelical publishers supported this idea wholeheartedly. Asked in 1980 to explain why the evangelical book market continued to experience an "upsurge in sales," Peter Kladder noted that "the need is permanent." But he also argued that new business tactics had allowed evangelical media companies not only to engage people who already saw themselves as evangelical consumers but also to reach new consumers by addressing those "permanent" spiritual needs.

Surmising that evangelicals had operated "more from tradition instead of from results" for too long, Kladder insisted that his company and others had "learned to sell." Whereas conventional explanations often had presented evangelicalism as a kind of product that had supplied Americans' existential demand, Kladder argued that companies like his had expanded the evangelical market by developing their supply.[114] Through these comments, Kladder testified to the associative power of trade. It was exactly what the members of the CBA's White House delegation had envisioned.

4

Righteous Retail

WOMEN, FAMILY, AND
THE SOCIAL POWER OF SELLING

Do publishers pray, really pray, I mean—
For unknown patrons, sight unseen?
Do they think of the book-folk here and there—
And carry their names to the Lord in prayer?
                                I WONDER!

Do publishers pray, really pray for ME—
an unknown quantity—no identity?
Do they take time off from a busy day
To pray for a lady down Dixie-way?
                                I WONDER!

Daisy Moody, 1947
Christian Book and Supply Store
Meridian, Mississippi

"DO PUBLISHERS PRAY?" It was not a rhetorical question. Writing to the William B. Eerdmans Company's credit manager in 1947, Daisy L. Moody sought to remind Eerdmans that both of their book businesses had religious as well as commercial obligations. Moody, the owner and operator of the Christian Book and Supply Store in Meridian, Mississippi, recalled that another publisher recently had told her that it was "praying for your success."[1] But that remark had led her to wonder: What kind of success did that company have in mind? Viewing the task of selling books as a field of ministry too often reduced to financial revenue, Moody used her initial question as the title of a poem that encouraged publishers to pray not just for booksellers but also for their consumers' spiritual well-being.

Moody's exchange with Eerdmans belongs to a long tradition in which Christians have invested commercial activity with religious significance.[2] Both before and after the 1940s, booksellers have been especially strong participants in this tradition. In 1969, for instance, the bookselling consultant Frances Gardner asked the readers of her column a question: "What is the real purpose of a Christian bookstore?" Gardner offered two possible answers. One purpose, she explained, was "to make a fortune for the owner." But she presented that purpose as an adjunct to a larger purpose. Every Christian bookstore, she insisted, should be understood above all as "a LIFE SAVING STATION."[3] Reiterating the spirit of Gardner's remark, the editors of a bookselling trade journal reminded readers that Christian bookstores represent "more than just a place of business." Above all, the editors argued, Christian bookstores should concern themselves with cultivating "a way of believing, thinking and behaving." Their purpose lay in producing "a way of life."[4]

As scholars have sought to interpret these kinds of claims, they often have treated commercial practices and paradigms as instruments of religious life, which avowedly religious practitioners have "used" in service of their theological and cultural values. This instrumental approach often has served as the premise for debate over whether the commercial or religious spirit of particular activities or behaviors has reigned supreme. Some scholars have seemed to lament that religious practitioners often accommodate rather than condemn the commercial priorities or neoliberal sensibilities that they have encountered.[5] This mode of critique typically implies that religion should resist capitalism rather than sanctify it. Yet even if one reading of Frances Gardner's question about the "real purpose of a Christian bookstore" casts her question and answer merely as an effort to authorize commercial endeavor, an alternate interpretation of her question adopts a less instrumental approach. Rather than asking whether and how Gardner's understanding of Christianity shaped her understanding of Christian bookstores, in this chapter I ask how forms of bookselling have animated interpretations of Christianity.[6]

Examining infrastructures of bookselling can help us see how retail settings and strategies have nurtured a "way of life" for both retailers and consumers.[7] Early in the twentieth century, retailing featured door-to-door bookselling, a sales strategy through which evangelical women extended authority from the domestic sphere to address the consumer needs of other families and children. Especially during the second half of the twentieth century, however, a larger proportion of evangelical books were sold through evangelical bookstores. Between 1950 and 1984 alone, the number of stores affiliated with the Christian Booksellers Association swelled from 102 to more than 3,000.[8] Designed like supermarkets and increasingly built in suburban shopping centers across the United States during and after the 1960s, evangelical bookstores braided ideals of individual choice and personal responsibility together with traditionalist family values. Capitalizing on women's expertise while also providing space for women to negotiate gender roles that economic changes reoriented, evangelical bookstores expanded opportunities for American consumers to encounter the commercial religion that evangelical employees, managers, owners, and suppliers valued.[9] It was in this spirit of righteous retail that Daisy Moody poetically prayed for the right ideals and aspirations to reign over the hearts and minds of William B. Eerdmans and his employees.

BOOK MISSIONARIES

While virtually all participants in the evangelical book industry have portrayed their work as "ministry," booksellers often have received the more specific mantle of "missionary." In 1922, for example, the fundamentalist magazine *Moody Monthly* encouraged schoolteachers to spend their summers "in a much needed and appreciated Christian service sometimes called 'book missionary' work—the carrying of the gospel message, together with inspiring books for the saints of God—directly into the homes of people."[10] A half century later, the evangelical trade magazine *Bookstore Journal* recommended viewing "the bookstore manager as a missionary," grounding that recommendation on an anecdote about a Christian bookstore manager who led a customer toward conversion by simply recommending a Christian get-well card.[11] At the heart of the missionary metaphor lies an emphasis on booksellers' dedication to disseminating faithful ideas and objects. Yet an emphasis on the fact of outreach tends to collapse the varied motives and methods through which book missionaries have understood and undertaken their work. Gendered obligations and opportunities always have oriented missionary outreach and its legacies.

Etymologically, the terms "mission" and "missionary" emphasize the act of sending. Both terms derive from the Latin word *missus,* or "being sent." The terms became common during the colonization of the Americas in the sixteenth century, as Europeans sent Christianity and its emissaries to new worlds. Before then, a more common way to describe the distribution of Christian people and teachings to distant locations involved variations on the Latin word *propaganda,* or "that which is to be propagated."[12] In the eighteenth and nineteenth centuries, the latter term helped denominate missionizing institutions such as the Church of England's Society for the Propagation of the Gospel in Foreign Parts (1701), which sent both clerics and religious literature throughout the world.[13]

If we consider the history of missions as a history of sending, the process of outreach comes more fully into view. This process merits attention

An advertisement for the Bible Institute Colportage Association, asking school teachers to considering serving as book missionaries during school breaks. Reproduced from a copy in Google Books. *Moody Monthly,* July 1922, 1127.

because missionaries often have invested just as much meaning in the process and practice of missionizing as in the ostensible goals of their effort. In the seventeenth century, for example, Franciscan missionaries viewed the number of conversions achieved as far less important than the missionary's personal adherence to standards of personal faith and devotion. The historian Amy DeRogatis notes that nineteenth-century Protestant missionaries to the American western frontier often sought to follow the model of such legendary missionaries as David Brainerd, whose popular diary and biography chronicled his failure to inspire many conversions. With that failure evidencing his disinterested benevolence, Brainerd portrayed missionary activity as the prototypical act of self-sacrificial piety, self-reflection, and personal devotion. Reflecting in interviews on their reasons for undertaking an onerous two-year mission commitment, Mormon missionaries have highlighted such incentives as the opportunity to live away from home, to grow personally, and to develop friendships.[14] Although many missionaries undoubtedly have undertaken their work due to a desire to serve others or to share the gospel, other personal desires and constraints invariably have shaped how and why missionaries have pursued their work. The same maxim applies to evangelical booksellers, who continually have highlighted, in one bookseller's words, "the sense of mission that drives their owners and employees."[15]

For centuries, evangelical women have been prominent as missionaries and book missionaries, partly because missions have provided them opportunities for Christian service despite patriarchal constraints on women's religious activity. "Denied the opportunity to be priests, preachers, and ordained clerics throughout most of the history of Christianity," the historian Dana Robert writes, "women missionaries have concentrated largely on lifestyles of service and personal relationships as the way to spread the gospel."[16] Female church members in eighteenth-century New England, for example, took primary responsibility for sharing Christian faith with unconverted people living on their towns' outskirts, due in part to their lack of formal authority within their churches.[17]

Especially in the nineteenth century, women embraced missionary and book missionary activities as expressions of gendered domestic ideals. As the historian Sally Gallagher notes, "The ideal of women's domesticity eventually set in motion its antithesis: a wave of women's leadership in religious and social reform."[18] During the antebellum era, a growing industrial economy increasingly consigned men and women to dissimilar modes of work. With wage labor drawing men out of the home economy and distancing them from its affairs, women took primary responsibility for domestic life. To be sure, men and women never operated in strictly "separate" spheres. But that idealized division generated corresponding cultural conceptions of male and female character. Femininity became associated with homebound purity, piety, domesticity, and Christian nurture.[19] Historians such as Tracy Fessenden and Amy DeRogatis have noted that these gender ideals always served not simply as expressions of religious culture but also as a means through which evangelicals have tethered religion to class and race. By tasking women with Christian nurture, white, middle-class evangelicals often have used "an allegedly universal vocabulary of gender" to distance themselves from other social groups, including African American Protestants as well as Catholic immigrants.[20] For all of these reasons, evangelicals portrayed the home as an engine of true religion, where mothers could mold their children into pious, virtuous, and useful citizens.[21] "Natural" female strengths seemed to suit missionary activity.

As missionary efforts boomed in the nineteenth century, the family and the home became primary sites of outreach, which relied upon the labor of women and mothers.[22] When the first male missionaries were sent to India in 1812 by the Congregational Church's American Board, for instance, the missionaries' wives relocated with them and subsequently became responsible for ministering to the women and children they encountered. Because preaching and formal religious teaching remained privileges that only men received, throughout the nineteenth century missionary women focused their efforts on showing hospitality in their own homes and on visiting others' homes. By the end of the century, this domestic emphasis blossomed into a mission strategy that identified the conversion of family matriarchs as the key to Christianizing foreign societies. With such strategies reinforcing women's dedication to missionary work, women formalized their leadership by creating a wide array of women's missionary societies, many of which originated as auxiliaries to or offshoots of male-led denominations or missionary organizations. Examples include the Woman's Foreign Missionary Society of New York, founded in 1868 in cooperation with the Congregationalist American Board, and the Woman's Foreign Missionary Society of the Methodist Episcopal Church (1869).[23]

Although a patriarchal ethic of women's subordination historically had shaped the domestic orientation of women's missionizing, missionary societies also developed specifically in response to the continued reluctance of Protestant denominations to grant missionary appointments to unmarried women, a demographic that mushroomed as the Civil War made many wives into widows. Often focusing their evangelization efforts less on preaching Christian doctrine than on teaching home economics, caring for children, and generally diffusing "civilization," women's missionary societies presented their labor as "Woman's Work for Woman," lending organizational and ideological inspiration to first-wave feminism. Before early fundamentalists began attempting to restrain women's enthusiastic service by calling for an assertively masculine faith and undermining the perfectionist theology that empowered teachers such as the Methodist evangelist Phoebe Palmer, more women than men were enrolled at institutions such as Moody Bible Institute. The largest proportion of those women focused their studies on foreign missions.[24]

Especially toward the end of the nineteenth century, book distribution became one way in which evangelical women sought to share Christian civilization and cultivate domestic reformations. As Victorian evangelicals had come to privilege the domestic nurture of family piety, books increasingly had featured as means of cultivating Christian values. At home, women not only turned to religious fiction to reinforce their own piety but also read books to their children, often preferring to teach through pious stories rather than doctrinal catechisms. Aware that their books had this domestic use, female evangelical authors treated the writing of magazine articles and books as acts of missionary service, through which they could reach into readers' homes.[25]

A woman
can do as
well as a
man in the
city, work-
ing in her
own or
adjacent
neighbor-
hoods

A manual for book missionaries explained that "a woman can do as well as a man."

Courtesy of Crowell Archives, Moody Bible Institute, Chicago. *A Primer on "Book Missionary" Work,* undated, folder: BICA Promo Materials, 11, MBI-ED.

Braiding this emphasis on books together with the home-centered orientation of women's broader missionary activity, women increasingly took up work as colporteurs.[26] "A woman can do as well as a man," the Bible Institute Colportage Association (BICA) insisted inside the front cover of its *Primer on "Book Missionary" Work,* alongside a photograph of a woman showing a small book to another woman. Throughout this primer and other booklets, such as one that offered "confidential instructions" to authorized BICA agents, the colportage elaborated upon why women made ideal colporteurs. Above all, women seemed to understand how to engage with and appeal to the wives and mothers whom colporteurs would encounter while traveling door-to-door.

By contrast, when men recounted their book distribution efforts, they often depicted distribution through churches or among church members. One male colporteur's account described a church that purchased "an assortment of very choice religious books on a table in front of the pulpit to loan to the people." Another minister recalled going "out among my parishioners a couple of afternoons," in the hope of having "every home supplied with literature that is in keeping with the sort of preaching I have given my people here." He described the books as an "antidote," available "in case they should every be cursed with modernistic preaching."[27] As these examples illustrate, men often portrayed their book distribution as extensions of church-based ministry.

Meanwhile, female colporteurs became seen as salespeople who could develop intimate rapport with housewives and mothers. "Endeavor, if possible," a booklet of advice for colporteurs suggested, "to meet the people where they are at the time of your call. A housewife working in the rear of the home will not feel especially pleased to have you call her away to the front door." The booklet also suggested asking to be admitted inside the door of the homes they visited. "Few good sales are made upon the doorstep," BICA cautioned, while acknowledging that not all colporteurs could gain access to homes with equal ease. Offering "book evangelists" ideas for placing books in potential consumers' lives, one article in *Moody Monthly* suggested in 1925 that colporteurs encourage women to buy books in order to "lay them on the parlor table that callers may read them while waiting." These callers included "the milk man, the grocer, the postman." With knowledge of the domestic domain serving as a source of sales expertise, women especially could carry "the Gospel into thousands of homes where pastors or other Christian workers do not usually or cannot go."[28]

Credited with the ability to develop rapport with housewives and mothers, female colporteurs also seemed to possess intimate understanding of the needs of children. Children were important not just due to logic of Christian nurture, which predicted that faithful children would ensure a faithful future, but also due to the hope that children would develop habits of reading and purchase that would lead them to buy books in years ahead. These priorities lay behind BICA's constant call for schoolteachers to serve as colporteurs. "Do not such persons know the needs of the children and of the home?" asked BICA's secretary, William Norton. "Are they not themselves intelligent and well read? Do they not usually have the confidence of the parents, as well as the children? A rich spiritual blessing awaits the endeavorer in these lines."[29] BICA's *Primer* explained that "school teachers have an opportunity to do a great work for the Master through their intimacy with the children. Try to secure their co-operation." The *Primer* also suggested that colporteurs seek the assistance of Sunday school teachers, who were another source of knowledge about and access to students.[30]

Women were seen as especially adept at reaching other consumer constituencies that Anglo-American Protestants long had prioritized. For much of the nineteenth century, for example, Catholic immigrants figured in Protestant imaginations as ideal candidates for conversion and reform. Partly because Protestants so often understood women as custodians of family faith, Protestants often viewed Catholic women in particular as people who especially needed to buy and read evangelical literature. And Protestant women took it upon themselves to attempt, as the historian Monica Mercado explains, "to fill Catholic women's homes with bibles, tracts, and other religious publications."[31] To enable such outreach, publishers like BICA encouraged colporteurs to prepare themselves for encounters across language barriers by carrying "a supply of our foreign numbers if there are Germans or Scandinavians in the locality where you are working." In addition to outreach among Catholics and Catholic women, colporteurs for BICA identified "negro schools of the South" as "a ripe mission field." A version of general outreach to schoolteachers and Sunday school teachers, distribution to African American schools was presented as a way to fight back against "propagandists of error." One BICA flyer presented the colportage's books as "the only message that can bring them true freedom and really solve the racial problem."[32]

Despite outreach toward Catholic and African American constituencies, guidebooks for colporteurs often assumed that female colporteurs would be selling books largely to women whose desires mirrored their own. Familiarity abetted trust, which enabled sales. BICA's *Primer* taught that the first step to securing a sale was to earn a customer's trust. BICA attempted to assist colporteurs with this step by branding the colportage's books as "trustworthy," but the production of trust became easier when salespeople seemed trustworthy themselves. Trustworthiness allowed colporteurs to accomplish another bookselling task: the creation of desire. According to BICA's *Primer,* potential colporteurs should "keep in mind the fact that people can usually buy any low-priced article that they feel they really want and should have," and that "the canvasser's aim, then, is to create the desire for the book or books." Gendered cultural obligations and experiences made female colporteurs more trustworthy and more attuned to their consumers' potential desires.[33] And by attuning themselves to consumer desire, colporteurs became more likely to secure sales that would continue in the colporteur's absence. Both missionaries and book missionaries sought above all to cultivate behaviors that would persist beyond the missionary's visit.

As colporteurs, women also helped allay publishers' long-standing anxieties about profit. Throughout the nineteenth century, publishing firms had fretted about how much to compensate colporteurs for their evangelistic labor. When the American Tract Society developed the first American colportage system in 1841, for example, the Society emphasized the spiritual benefit of serving as a colporteur. The Society encouraged colporteurs to view themselves as "self-denying, devoted and spiritual men," who would "visit the more destitute counties; carry the books among the people; summon the friends of Christ to cooperation."[34] Although the Society paid its colporteurs modest salaries and covered their travel expenses, its leaders worried that significant "pecuniary gain" from sales would lead colporteurs to become "secularized and rendered spiritless in their work."[35] Other publishers shared this anxiety about encouraging colporteurs to prioritize monetary compensation. In 1905, BICA's superintendent dourly reported that higher postal rates had forced BICA to "establish depots and agencies in various points," in order to make distribution less expensive and more efficient. This change had led BICA's sales agents to operate more independently. Fearing that more independent agents might allow pecuniary gain to motivate their efforts, the superintendent suggested reemphasizing agents' work as "missionaries," who would travel "from house to house, selling books wherever possible, all under our direct supervision." BICA's subsequent advertisements continually sought to balance monetary and missionary motive. An advertisement in 1921 explained, for example, that "many kinds of service are not so remunerative financially," while emphasizing that remuneration was not the point. "No employment could have a higher purpose," the advertisement insisted.[36]

Amid this anxiety about remuneration, some female colporteurs did not portray modest compensation as a problem. As BICA's leaders hoped, modest compensation encouraged some women to highlight the devotional payoff of colportage work. "I am a poor woman," one colporteur testified, "and it is my only desire to do something for my blessed Savior. I know of nothing better than distributing these little books. They have been such a blessing to me."[37] BICA also encouraged colporteurs not to view their work as their primary means of employment. Promising that anyone could take up colportage in their spare time with "the smallest outlay of money and the least possible risk of failure or loss," one set of instructions explained that "the remuneration offered is in proportion to amount of time and energy expended." Careful to acknowledge that this work was unlikely to bring colporteurs great wealth, the instructions assured colporteurs that diligent employees would at least "make all expenses and enough more to provide a reserve fund."[38] Such modest remuneration made the work ideal, they suggested, for homemakers who sought income to supplement their husbands', or for schoolteachers who sought income to supplement their ordinary salary. In addition to presenting modest remuneration as supplementary income for colporteurs' families, BICA justified low wages by suggesting that multiple colporteurs might pool their modest revenue and devote it toward such a cause as their church's staff salaries.

Capitalizing on gendered understandings of women's social responsibilities and opportunities, evangelical publishing initiatives often have turned to women as primary consumers and laborers. Although much of that labor has been conceived and performed as missionary work, the "missionary" label not only tends to obscure the social disparities that have helped make that ideal especially appealing to and empowering for women but also transforms those disparities, their effects, and their beneficiaries into aspects of service to God. Throughout the twentieth century, gendered family ideals constituted the foundation upon which the evangelical book industry would boom. At the same time, however, that industry would draw other ideals into its service, fusing conceptions of family and gender together with ideals of individual choice and personal responsibility.

THE FREEDOM OF SELF-SERVICE

During the second half of the twentieth century, women dominated the realm of evangelical retail. The majority of evangelical consumers were women, and women increasingly outnumbered men as employees in retail settings. By the late 1960s, trade periodicals and manuals tended to take it for granted that stores had a gendered profile.[39] In 1969, for example, a representative of Moody Press suggested that salesclerks could generate more sales by showing interest in customers' "children, their clothing, or their hairdo." The trade consultant Ruth Hackman similarly had women in mind when she suggested in 1970 that retailers should cultivate book knowledge and recommendations for customers by keeping "a book handy in the kitchen and read while fixing dinner." In its handbook for new book-store owners, the Christian Booksellers Association suggested hiring sales-people with such qualities as "orderliness for housekeeping."[40] Throughout these remarks and countless others, women's domestic responsibilities and capacities figured as forms of expertise that seemed suited to evangelical retail.

Although this gendered understanding of retail drew upon some of the same traditionalist gender ideologies that had animated women's work as book missionaries, the domestic aura of evangelical retail received reinforce-ment from new infrastructures of consumerism. Preeminent among those infrastructures was the form of the "self-service" supermarket, which pri-oritized the ideal of individual consumer choice. Just as Anita Bryant and other leaders of the New Christian Right later would elevate women's po-litical stature by presenting women's political authority as an extension of their domestic authority, self-service shopping presented women's consumer choices as extensions of the choices they made at home.[41] As bastions of religious consumerism, evangelical bookstores became significant sites of evangelical culture.

Evangelical bookstores proliferated throughout the United States beginning especially in the 1960s. Granted, consumers long had been able to find evangelical books in general bookstores; as early as 1913, the Fleming H. Revell Company reported selling most of its books through general bookstores.[42] Yet Revell's retail access reflected the esteemed status it had earned over decades of business as a prominent New York publisher, as well as its tendency to avoid more sectarian books due to their seemingly limited appeal. Well into the 1960s as much as 85 percent of all religious books had reached consumers through mail delivery, which included direct sales from evangelical publishers as well as religious book clubs. By 1975, however, more than 60 percent of evangelicals reported purchasing religious books, and they made most of their purchases through evangelical bookstores. In 1984 a more comprehensive survey found that evangelicals purchased 54 percent of their religious literature through evangelical bookstores.[43]

With evangelical bookstores appearing everywhere, industry analysts and survey organizations searched for explanations. Some pointed out that evangelical bookstores and their sales both had risen over the same period when church affiliation had been declining. "While church membership is dropping," one industry observer noted, "the demand for books that appeal to religious needs is soaring."[44] Evangelical bookstores seemed like physical manifestations of that religious revival. Through bookstores, American Protestants could encounter and examine religious concerns outside the orbit of either churchly contexts or affiliates of the state, such as public libraries. Bookstores seemed able not only to nourish evangelical communities but also to reverse a decline in religious affiliation.

As bookstores became a primary mode of evangelical book distribution, their design emphasized consumers' responsibility to choose for themselves. Earlier distribution paradigms had not prioritized choice. For much of the nineteenth century, bookstores generally operated like dry goods shops and grocers, in which customers approached a counter, interacted with a salesclerk, and asked the clerk to retrieve selections from a storage area that customers could not access. As publishers sold more books through department stores, however, bookstores aspired to follow a department store paradigm. During the 1940s, bookselling trade periodicals encouraged bookstores to follow department stores in creating attractive window displays, developing informative mail advertising, and offering elaborate training for staff, so that salesclerks might help consumers identify and appease their desires through acts of purchase.[45] Through these practices, the department store model pursued lower prices through high sales volume and encouraged consumers to see shopping as a

With turnstiles located at the entrances and exits, this self-service Piggly Wiggly in Memphis, Tennessee, guided consumers in 1918 through a circuit of aisles and invited them to choose products for themselves.
Courtesy of Library of Congress.

therapeutic leisure activity.[46] Yet even as these practices capitalized on consumer desire, they did not present consumer choice as the practical priority.

Bookstores began to prioritize choice and choosing during the 1950s, as they embraced a supermarket model. Developed during the 1920s and 1930s, the supermarket took shape around at least three main principles. First, supermarkets emphasized "self-service." Pioneered in 1916 at a Piggly Wiggly store in Memphis, Tennessee, and patented by its owner, self-service stores forced customers to enter through a turnstile, guided them through a circuit of stocked shelves, and invited customers to select whichever goods they desired. Customers then paid at a checkout counter near the exit.[47] Second, because self-service stores required fewer salesclerks, they offered lower prices than their competitors. As low prices became even more important during the economic depression of the 1930s, stores elaborated upon the self-service model by creating larger stores with large parking lots, often located outside the city centers where stores typically had been located. These strategies lowered operating costs by enabling stores to purchase goods in greater volume and to pay lower rent than they would have in the city. Stores once sought proximity to consumers, but automobiles made proximity far less important.

Finally, supermarkets encouraged consumers to imagine a tight relationship between their home and their store. Although initially built as spartan warehouses, self-service stores quickly adopted an array of physical features meant to conjure a spirit of domesticity, such as imitation windows and pleasing pictures. Focusing especially on capturing the patronage of suburban housewives, supermarkets invited women to view shopping as a pleasurable and gratifying experience. Reducing the role of salesclerks and sales counters as intermediaries between the consumer and the product, a self-service model minimized delay and allowed the store to serve as a sort of fully stocked pantry. As one store designer explained in 1930: "The properly arranged store . . . lets women and merchandise meet." It was, the commercial historian Kate Bowlby surmises, "a fantasy experience for women." With in-store advertisements and displays reminding consumers which products seemed especially important or affordable, many consumers reportedly abandoned the practice of creating shopping lists. With only the store's offerings and her own intuition as a guide, a woman could select whichever affordable items she deemed important for her family. Although supermarkets initially sold only food, they quickly began selling nonfood items, such as housewares, toiletries, and books. In this way, supermarkets engaged and enhanced women's authority over purchasing decisions for their families.[48]

When supermarkets began accounting for a growing share of book sales during the 1950s, bookstores responded by becoming what one industry observer described in 1957 as "a kind of supermarket."[49] Urban bookstores increasingly began experimenting with the model in the early 1950s. "Supermarket type of bookselling was tried with great success at Snellenburgs, Philadelphia, recently," *Publishers Weekly* reported in 1952. "In true supermarket style, there were no clerks, but plenty of signs showing mark-down prices and original prices, cashiers and check writers and wire supermarket baskets. The baskets were piled high with books by the customers and wheeled to the cashiers."[50] As this account suggests, the supermarket model emphasized discount pricing and sales volume. Of course, those priorities did not appeal only to women and families. College bookstores also adopted the supermarket paradigm as they sought to address the mushrooming consumer demand created by the G. I. Bill.[51] But the ability to purchase as much as needed, at low prices, enhanced women's ability to treat bookstores as spaces with fewer limitations on the imagined effects that book purchases might have on their households and families.

Even more than low prices and high volume, the self-service supermarket paradigm prioritized choice. Profiling the Super Book Mart on Wabash Avenue in Chicago in 1955, for example, a trade magazine noted that the self-service store's more densely packed shelves and steadier sales allowed it to stock a much higher proportion of each publishers' complete line—including more books from publishers' backlists. The reporter in turn attributed the store's volume to "the huge variety of books displayed and because of the suggestion to buy that is implied in the freedom of self-service." More choice inspired more choosing.[52]

Evangelical bookstores embraced the "freedom of self-service" early in the paradigm's history. In 1959 *Publishers Weekly* profiled a new bookstore that Zondervan Publishing House had opened in Grand Rapids. Zondervan's Super-Market Book Center took its design cues from Zondervan's only other store at the time—its bookstore in Winona Lake, Indiana. Located on the grounds of the Winona Lake Christian Assembly, the Winona Lake store had been redesigned on a supermarket model the previous year. Both stores featured "wide, roomy aisles, with all merchandise displayed on open racks to inspire browsing and impulse buying," and the new store located checkout counters in both the front and back of the store. Zondervan reported using its supermarket stores as laboratories, where they could "test public response to titles, merchandising and advertising methods."

Whereas the supermarket model generally reduced the number of sales-clerks required in any store, evangelical manifestations of that model actually increased bookstores' reliance on women as customer consultants. Women became more prominent because they not only helped reduce bookstore costs by accepting lower wages than men but also helped guide customers in choosing products that would nurture both family and faith. Comparing sales at the new store and the former store in Grand Rapids, which had been located across the street from the new location, Zondervan learned that the supermarket store generated more than twice the sales volume of its predecessor.[53]

Not all evangelical bookstores embraced self-service so swiftly. In 1963 the Christian Booksellers Association's "model store" for the association's annual convention still featured a design that emphasized function, minimized clutter, and utilized sales counters throughout.[54] By the end of the 1960s, however, the supermarket model became so prevalent that small supermarkets occasionally transformed in whole or part into evangelical bookstores. At one supermarket in Bakersfield, California, the owners

Opening in 1959, Zondervan's new supermarket-style bookstore reportedly generated twice as much revenue as its predecessor.

Used with permission from *Publishers Weekly.* "Zondervan's New Store Geared for Self-Service," *Publishers Weekly,* January 5, 1959, 69.

decided to replace their store's liquor section with evangelical books and bibles. "The Lord spoke to my heart and reminded me that we have thirty to thirty-five thousand people throughout our market every month and only a small percentage know Him," co-owner Anita Hashim explained. By providing those thousands with the opportunity to choose evangelical books and bibles alongside groceries, Hashim explained, she and her co-owner husband sought to put "God's Word into homes that knew Him not." Enshrining the ideal of choice in the slogan for its 1969 annual conference, the Christian Booksellers Association announced: "Choice, Not Chance, Determines Our Destiny."[55]

Just as the early supermarkets of the 1930s presented themselves as low-cost sources of sustenance for communities wracked by an economic depression, evangelical booksellers presented their stores as retail resources for their own communities and families. "The future of the community and the church," the bookseller and writer Edith Jones explained, "may very well depend on what we as booksellers do."[56] For Jones, for Anita Hashim, and for countless other women, merchandizing was a mode of missionizing.

Although evangelical bookstores manifested the ideal of choice and the freedom of self-service, booksellers such as Jones and Hashim made themselves responsible for helping consumers make the right kinds of choices.

WOMEN'S BUSINESS

Economic and political changes successively have reoriented the concerns of evangelical consumers and the means by which evangelical retailers have responded to those concerns. Beginning especially in the 1930s, New Deal policies based on the ideal of "the white middle-class nuclear family headed by a patriotic and heterosexual male" cultivated what the historian Robert Self describes as "breadwinner liberalism," which put renewed emphasis on the notion that women should devote themselves primarily to the domestic realm.[57] The supermarket retail model complemented that ideal and invigorated evangelical retail. But the bookselling business would receive an additional boost during the economic and political transformations of the late 1960s, which inspired widespread anxiety that the ideal family would dissolve. Those transformations created new opportunities and obligations for evangelical women who worked and shopped in evangelical retail settings.

Retailers had asked women to treat domestic experience as professional expertise since early in the twentieth century. As the historian Susan Porter Benson explains, male department store retail managers urged women during the 1920s to "transfer skills from their domestic to their work lives." Benson argues that women had spent a century cultivating skills that aided the task of selling. Those skills included "adeptness at manipulating people, sympathetic ways of responding to the needs of others, and familiarity with things domestic."[58] Despite the Victorian view that women's retail employment was "undignified and improper," one sociological study found as early as 1912 that "mercantile establishments employ a large proportion of the women wage-earners of this country."[59] And as a growing consumer economy made businesses more reliant on consumer revenue while also increasing competition for that revenue, sales managers sought to draw consumer interest away from competitors by providing deferential service. Retail corporations continued viewing women as a source of deferential service throughout the twentieth century. According to the historian Bethany Moreton, Wal-Mart used the labor of women to saturate its stores during the 1970s with an ethos of intimate and caring service, making "mass consumption safe for the white Protestant heartland." Because married white women with young children had not entered the labor force in mass numbers until the second half of the twentieth century, women also were undervalued and cheap employees.[60]

Before evangelical women worked for Wal-Mart, they worked in evangelical bookstores, where ideas about essential gender differences between men and women shaped the scope and style of evangelical women's retail employment throughout 1960s. Committed to what they saw as the divinely ordained authority of men over women and the ideal of the breadwinning husband and the stay-at-home mother, evangelical bookselling experts championed those ideas. "Your husband is so lucky to have a stand-by clerk available at any time of the day or night!" exclaimed Ruth Hackman in a 1968 article "For the Manager's Wife Only." By suggesting that a bookstore manager's wife might fill in for the "main salesgirl" during her lunch hour, Hackman clearly acknowledged that women worked as salesclerks. But she also suggested that women ideally would serve simply to "lighten the load for our busy husbands." Hewing tightly to a domestic ideal, Hackman concluded her article with a recipe for peanut butter ham, noting that "a woman's column should have a recipe."[61]

Other suggestions encouraged female retailers to treat customers like guests in the salesperson's home. As with any guest, the bookselling expert Frances Gardner suggested, retailers should "STAY AWAY FROM DOCTRINE" when greeting Christian consumers. Instead of discussing doctrine, women should share cheery quips like "Praise the Lord," leaving consumers to spend time in the store and select products that suited their own needs and desires. Trade journals did not encourage men to infuse their retailing with a spirit of domesticity. The editor of *Bookstore Journal* described the ideal Christian bookseller as "a man of high moral and ethical values—he works, he sweats, he plans, he worries . . . and he prays."[62]

In underlining the primary authority of men over retail spaces, evangelical trade journals displayed the same patriarchal perspectives that long had saturated the evangelical book industry's stance toward women. Evangelical publishers such as Zondervan always had created products designed specifically for women. But most of the earliest examples focused on using female characters of the Bible to identify what their male authors saw as women's essential strengths and limitations. The first book Zondervan ever published was Abraham Kuyper's *Women of the Old Testament* (1933). In this and a subsequent New Testament volume, Kuyper presented women in the Bible as models of piety or sin. In the book's second chapter, Kuyper focused on the figures Ada and Zillah, who appear briefly in four verses from the book of Genesis. Using that account, Kuyper explained that the two women "degraded the dignity of womanhood" by accepting a polygamous marriage, and Kuyper defined the Hebrew meaning of the name "Ada" as "a gorgeously adorned woman" in order to caution women against allowing "external adornment" to obscure their "inner beauty." Kuyper also used their example to insist that women are not "naturally more pious than man."[63] Similarly designed to offer a typology of good and evil women, Harold John Ockenga's *Have You Met These Women?* (1940) explains that a woman "may lead a man to heaven or to hell." Marketed throughout the early 1940s as one of Zondervan's "Books of Special Interest for Women," Ockenga's book described "evil women" as "temptresses" and "good women" as "full of virtue." Only through careful nurture of virtue, Ockenga argued, could women acquire "power over man."[64]

Yet even as male publishers and retailers underlined what they understood as the superior piety of men, they also recognized that women were the primary consumers of evangelical products in most evangelical families. When Zondervan reprinted Kuyper's book, Pat Zondervan inserted study questions at the end of each chapter "to spark its use among women's study groups."[65] Evangelical women also wrote to publishers and authors with feedback more regularly than men did, testifying to their use of books to cultivate personal virtue. "To me it is the most wonderful book I've ever read (barring none) and I've read quite a lot," Mrs. Ray E. Busch of Chicago wrote to the Eerdmans fiction author Paul Hutchens in 1935. Attempting to account for her appreciation, Busch explained: "I'm a young married woman, just beginning to realize how important it is to live one's life for God, yet not knowing quite how to go about it, until your book came along. It actually explained everything I most needed to know relative to Christianity."[66] This sort of comment encouraged publishers like Zondervan to see both nonfiction and fiction as important means of cultivating what their executives, editors, and authors understood as ideal womanhood.

Testimonials from readers eventually received support from social-scientific industry research. In 1972, for instance, Tyndale House Publishers and the communication department of Wheaton College Graduate School sought to gather information that might aid the marketing of Kenneth Taylor's *The Living Bible*. Through personal interviews with 300 housewives in the suburb of Elmhurst, Illinois, they concluded that the mother "was directly involved in need recognition and actual purchase" in 88 percent of households.[67] Later studies reached similar conclusions. In 1997 a survey of 12,347 Christian bookstore customers revealed that 77 percent were women. Most of those women were between the ages of 30 and 49, and 85 percent were white. The proportion of white, female readers exceeded figures from the general population and general book industry.[68]

Already committed to traditionalist understandings of the family, evangelicals intensified those commitments during the late 1960s and 1970s, when economic and political changes generated widespread anxiety about the future of the family. The historian Natasha Zaretsky has argued that a variety of factors threatened the traditionalist family ideal. Those factors included a rising divorce rate, revelations about the confused objectives and high human costs of the war in Vietnam, growing uncertainty about the ability of the Cold War's containment policy to protect American families, and forced desegregation of public and private institutions following the *Brown v. Board of Education* decision of 1954 and the Civil Rights Act of 1964. During the early 1970s, another factor was the economic recession, which not only diminished expectations for rising standards of living but also required more women to help earn income for their families. The U.S. Senate responded to this perceived family crisis by organizing a committee to assess the pressures families were experiencing, and media outlets like PBS addressed the crisis by producing new television documentaries about the family.[69]

Evangelicals responded, in part, by writing, publishing, selling, and buying tens of millions of books that offered advice about the state of the family and its future.[70] Women sold, bought, and wrote many of those books. Committed to rejecting feminism, opposing abortion and homosexuality, and offering resources for saving troubled marriages, best-selling authors included Marabel Morgan, Anita Bryant, Dale Evans Rogers, Phyllis Schlafly, Vicki Frost, Beverly LaHaye, and James Dobson.[71] Publishing companies invested in their cause. In 1969 the Revell Company even established a new imprint, entitled Hewitt House, which it described as "a new publishing concept" that would prioritize "the American family, its interests and activities, its problems and pleasures."[72] The Zondervan Corporation even began renaming its bookstores in 1964. Previously known as Zondervan Book Stores, they became Family Bookstores, which Zondervan held in a newly formed retail corporation, Family Stores of America.[73] Zondervan's new name for its retail division exemplified one historian's remark that evangelicals "made the family, rather than the individual, the irreducible unit of social organization."[74]

Even as economic and political changes led evangelicals to obsess over the family and its future, evangelical women increasingly entered the workplace during the 1970s, supplementing their families' incomes during an economic recession.[75] Adapting to those material conditions, some evangelical leaders began to focus less on the primacy of men's authority, shifting pragmatically toward an emphasis on cooperation between men and women, who possessed different but complementary skills and capabilities.[76]

The scale of economic change had made any number of theological and practical changes seem more warranted than they might have seemed a decade earlier. In 1974 the Christian Booksellers Association held a "Future of the Industry Meeting" that focused largely on sharing strategies of response to "the current paper shortage and energy crisis." Speakers noted that the crisis had limited consumers' ability to purchase, which reduced revenue, and constrained bookstores' ability to pay sales representatives as much as they had earned before the crisis.[77] The CBA had already counseled bookstores to secure their survival by paying low wages and using "part time help when possible," and the economic crisis of the 1970s provided additional cause to give low-wage retail jobs to women.[78]

Before long, the logic of pragmatic "complementarianism" allowed evangelical executives to affirm women's bookselling supremacy by allowing women to ascend into managerial ranks within bookstores. Some women had held managerial positions before the 1970s. Reporting on a sales tour he had conducted throughout the Pacific Northwest in 1937, the traveling book salesman F. J. Wiens noted that one of the five bookstores he visited around Portland, Oregon, had a woman as its manager. By comparison with most male managers, Wiens noted, she possessed an exceptional desire "to keep abreast of religious books," which helped her to identify books that might draw consumer interest.[79] For much of the 1930s, a woman also managed wholesale sales to and from Moody Bible Institute's bookstore. Writing to an Eerdmans author in 1934, E. A. Thompson boasted that she possessed "latitude in wholesale selling which is my department." But she also made sure to qualify that claim by subordinating her authority over business decisions to her male superior, William Norton.[80]

By the turn of the twenty-first century, many more women were managing evangelical bookstores. "Retail managers are mostly women," Sue Smith told me in 2016. Smith spoke not just as the manager of the bookstore Baker Book House in Grand Rapids, Michigan, but also as the chairman of the board of directors of the organization formerly known as the Christian Booksellers Association—known since 1996 simply as CBA (with the subtitle "The Association for Christian Retail").[81] Acknowledging a variety of gender imbalances across portions the evangelical book industry more broadly, Smith noted that women had acquired far more authority in retail than in other areas of commercial and corporate initiative. Very few women held executive positions in publishing companies or trade groups, she explained. More than sixty years after the CBA's founding, she was the first woman to serve as the head of its board. Smith also had remarked "to any publisher that will listen to me" that virtually every book in the "Leadership and Administration" category was written by a man. "There are a couple by women about being leaders in churches. But not in business. It's still about how the man should be the leader." In practice, at least, complementarian gender ideals invested evangelical women with far more authority in retail than executive leadership.[82]

During the second half of the twentieth century, evangelical bookstores were not alone in serving as retail spaces that provided women with authority within particular communities and constituencies. The education scholar Maisha Fisher has demonstrated that since the 1970s African American women and mothers have turned to black-owned and black-operated bookstores as "alternative and supplementary knowledge spaces" to public schools and universities, where common curricula have tended to devalue or omit histories and experiences of people of African descent.[83] Even more closely related to evangelical consumers and culture, "patriotic bookstores" blossomed in Southern California during the 1960s. Like evangelical bookstores, patriotic bookstores became sites where conservative women practiced consumerism and retail as forms of activism. As the historian Michelle Nickerson explains in her study of conservative women and the postwar Right, prevailing ideas about women's responsibilities had changed substantially after the Great Depression of the 1930s, which "radically reconfigured female political ideology by devaluing maternal uplift and reform while elevating the importance of maternal protection and community-building." Linking their activist inclinations to their domestic ideals, avowedly conservative women developed subcultural institutions such as home-based study groups, speaker's circuits, churches, as well as patriotic bookstores. Those bookstores became sites through which conservative women promoted what Nickerson describes as "a conjoining system of economic, social, and religious values taking shape in their political consciousness while nurturing their own ambition and creativity." Conceiving Christianity as a core component of the conservative culture they sought to cultivate, patriotic bookstores sold books on themes that overlapped with evangelical interests. Examples included Verna M. Hall's *Christian History of the Constitution* (1960), which presented Christianity as the bedrock of "political freedom and happiness." Judging by the stores' names, some patriotic bookstores even doubled as evangelical bookstores, such as the Good Word Book Stop in Santa Monica.[84]

In evangelical bookstores and patriotic bookstores alike, women negotiated what they understood as their domestic responsibilities by sharing ideas, building community, and selecting which books to purchase and share with their families. Acts of recommendation, sale, selection, and purchase served as expressions of individual responsibility for a woman's faith, her family's, and their common future. As the historian Emily Johnson notes, evangelical publishing executives recognized the commercial value of these intersecting conservative subcultures. Former executives of the Fleming H. Revell Company attributed the outsized success of Marabel Morgan's *The Total Woman,* for example, to the conservative women who already had built a market for books on issues relating to gender, family, and sexuality.[85] Evangelical literature served conservative constituencies especially well because religious themes aided the broader conservative effort to recast concerns born of racial or ideological prejudice as matters of faith, family, and individual responsibility.[86]

Both evangelical bookstores and patriotic bookstores addressed conservative consumers not just by offering books about Christian womanhood but also by focusing especially on Christian motherhood. Using retail to address debates regarding urban unrest, public education, countercultural movements, and shifting attitudes about sex, patriotic and evangelical bookstores specialized not just in literature for parents but especially in wholesome or edifying literature for children. By addressing this specialty, authors like James Dobson developed reputations as evangelical experts and nurtured sufficient authority to establish prominent parachurch institutions, such as Dobson's Focus on the Family.[87] Books on motherhood and parenting proved especially popular by tapping into the longer history of evangelical effort to develop and distribute products for children.

THE YOUTH MARKET

Responsibility for cultivating faithful families and children extended evangelical women's domestic authority not just to the realm of retail but also to other contexts beyond the home, including and especially those involved in the education and spiritual formation of children. Since the nineteenth century, evangelicals had focused on ensuring that educational institutions—including public schools and Sunday schools—possessed the right sort of devotional orientation. Examples of this educational obsession included conflicts during the 1870s over the use of the King James Bible in public schools, debates over Sunday school curricula, antievolution activism before the Scopes trial of 1925, and efforts to expose liberal "brainwashing" of children during the 1950s.[88] Throughout these and other instances, the production and purchase of books served as practices of Christian nurture. Evangelical publishers, booksellers, and interdenominational institutions all cultivated and capitalized upon this fact.

The evangelical book industry amplified its investment in children especially in the late 1930s. By the 1940s, publishers such as Eerdmans focused a significant proportion of their offerings on literature for young people, including a large proportion of fiction. "The children may not always understand what they read," an editorial in an Eerdmans Company newsletter explained. But the editorial also noted: "If we place good books in the hands of children, we will cultivate for them the desire for only the best types of literature."[89] Putting that principle into practice, the Eerdmans Company published a range of books by the author Bertha Moore, which sought to offer "a definite Christian message adapted to the mental grasp of the preschool child."[90] During the same period, Zondervan published an array of novels by the authors Ken Anderson and Basil Miller, describing the volumes as "Character building Fiction."

In addition to publishing more fiction for children, evangelical publishers sought to overhaul Sunday school materials, which could be sold in large quantities to churches around the country. One revision campaign focused on a curricular system known as the "International Sunday School Lessons." A product of the sort of nineteenth-century international evangelical ecumenism associated above all with organizations such as the YMCA, that curriculum sought to have all English-speaking Protestant Sunday schools examine the same passages of the bible every week.[91] Yet even though many different Protestant denominations used the system, they often disagreed about how to teach each week's bible selections. Publishers accordingly offered a variety of commentaries on the International System's selections; fundamentalists produced several competing commentaries.[92]

Following the founding of the National Association of Evangelicals, evangelical leaders criticized what they saw as the control of modernists over the International System and other ecumenical initiatives.[93] In April 1944 a group of evangelical publishers met to discuss the creation of a new lesson system, arguing that it was "impossible to combine the modernistic ideas of the social gospel with truly evangelical literature." The Fleming H. Revell Company cautioned against such a project, suggesting that a new system of lessons would create chaos.[94] But other publishers threw support behind a new lesson system, recognizing the sustained sales potential that new Sunday school materials promised. Firms such as Zondervan went out of their way to ingratiate themselves with the initiative's leaders.[95] Although no single curriculum ultimately emerged from these discussions, the initiative inspired the formation of the National Sunday School Association as an affiliate of the NAE.[96]

During the 1940s, commercial emphasis on the youth market also drew support from organizations like Youth for Christ (YFC), which treated children as both the object and the index of evangelical success in saturating American society.[97] Founded in 1944 under the leadership of the pastor

Torrey Johnson, the businessman Herbert Taylor, and the young evangelist Billy Graham, YFC organized large youth rallies throughout the country, depicting such gatherings not just as an alternative to secular amusements but also as an opportunity for young people to be part of something larger than themselves.[98] Reflecting on the movement in a 1945 Zondervan book, the YFC leader Merv Rosell explained: "Youth demands a challenge! It will accept nothing less. It hungers for victory, conquest, warfare, faith!" Toward that ambitious end, Rosell argued that "books are the best means of preserving and transmitting truth in its integrity." Rosell insisted that books like his own were necessary to "challenge the youth I cannot reach personally."[99]

Although the influence of organizations like the NAE and YFC helped turn renewed commercial attention toward children, publishers also focused on the youth market due to new industry research. In his industry-funded *Economic Survey of the Book Industry* (1931), Oliver Cheney argued that publishers and booksellers could benefit significantly by making more products for children. "The educational processes which create new readers," Cheney lamented, "are weakened at a number of dangerous points." Noting that children often fail to "carry-over" reading habits as they age, Cheney encouraged the book industry to focus on retaining children as consumers as they cross "the break between school and 'life.'" Investment in children could prove especially fruitful because they had not yet become quite as "advertising-conscious" as adults, which meant that children's consumption depended more on what book outlets provided than on what advertisements instructed them to desire. As a result, the industry could generate more consumer demand among children by directing the supply of books toward them. But Cheney also argued that publishers and booksellers could not reach children or other readers efficiently without revolutionizing distribution pathways that had remained plagued by significant "hazards and wastes"; this criticism inspired the creation of the Christian Booksellers Association.[100]

The CBA was the brainchild of Kenneth N. Taylor, who became best known as the creator of *The Living Bible* and the founder of Tyndale House Publishers. Earlier in his career Taylor worked as the director of Moody Press, which he joined in 1947. Later reflecting on his early career, Taylor remarked that "the Christian bookstore industry was in a sorry state" during the 1940s. In addition to arguing that many Christian bookstores could have benefited from standardization and professionalization, Taylor suggested that additional bookstores could dramatically enhance the scale at which publishers could create books. Without sufficient distribution capacity, he explained, Moody Press not only had struggled to sell the books it printed but also had found itself unable to publish as many new books as it hypothetically could have. "There was a large stack of perhaps a hundred manuscripts piled in a corner of my office," Taylor explained, "but we didn't have the capital to carry out such an aggressive publication program."[101]

Having concluded that the industry needed a way of selling books more efficiently and effectively, Taylor and his assistant director, Bill Moore, created the CBA as an evangelical counterpart to the American Booksellers Association.[102] As Moody Press's wholesale manager and director of its retail sales, Moore reportedly had spent several hours of every day answering letters from people who had little "money to start a store" yet "felt 'called' to serve God in this way and were anxious to get started." Although Moore had managed to double Moody Press's retail sales between Decembers 1945 and 1946, he and Taylor set out to make new bookstores easier to create.[103] Toward that end, he and a dozen other store managers met in 1950 to discuss "mutual problems in retailing."[104] In addition to creating the CBA, they decided to hold a convention in the fall of 1950. A decade later, Taylor used the annual CBA convention to drum up interest in his new bible.

One way that Taylor conjured consumer interest in his bible was by emphasizing the product's benefits for women, families, and children. Educated during the 1930s and early 1940s at such bastions of fundamentalism as Wheaton College, Dallas Theological Seminary, and Northern Baptist Theological Seminary, Taylor devoted much of his professional life to crafting books and periodicals that might cultivate young people's engagement with the Bible.[105] The story he later told about the creation of *The Living Bible* featured his frustration with his ability to retain his children's interest in the Bible's language. After his frustration led him to paraphrase some passages for his children, Taylor reportedly "was elated to note that . . . they had understood."[106] This origin story ultimately became the basis for some of the advertisements for Taylor's bible. "Their future lies in your hands," a print ad trumpeted in the early 1970s. Those cautionary words appeared alongside an image of two children playing dress-up in a woman's clothes, including purses and frilled scarves. Addressing mothers above all, the ad explained: "Your children are depending on you and you can depend on the Living Bible."[107]

As Kenneth Taylor evidenced through his own career, the faithful nurture of children provided publishers and booksellers with a commercial rationale. The CBA and other evangelical organizations invested in that youth market, helping to standardize bookselling practices and cultivate common purpose across the evangelical book industry. Up through the

1970s, however, evangelical companies continued to lament that too few evangelical consumers had access to booksellers and their stores. Suburbs and shopping malls would help solve this problem by becoming preeminent places for evangelicals to cultivate white, middle-class Christian families through practices of religious consumerism.

SHOPPING CENTERS AND SUBURBAN SOCIETY

During the 1970s many American consumers continued to see traditional bookstores as intimidating and elitist spaces. Although self-service bookstores had helped change that view, the aura of bookstores and bookselling would be revolutionized by the rise of bookstore chains in new suburban "shopping centers"—the name for a group of stores with a shared parking lot overseen by a development company. A "shopping mall" is an enclosed shopping center. As the historian Laura Miller explains, shopping-center bookstores brought "the bookstore down to the level of the supermarket across the parking lot or the teen jeans outlet next door." With property developers encouraging consumers to view shopping centers as safe commercial spaces, those commercial contexts presented general bookstores and evangelical bookstores alike as "just another place to shop" for suburban women and families.[108]

Whereas mail delivery allowed booksellers and publishers to address consumers scattered throughout the country, shopping-center bookstores focused especially on local suburban communities. The Zondervan Corporation reported in its 1980 annual report that their chain of Family Bookstores sought to "dynamically meet the needs of families, teachers, and pastors."[109] Family Bookstores set out to be what one Zondervan executive described as "the store of choice for Christian families."[110] The shopping-center setting aided that objective not simply because shopping centers and malls served as what one historian described as "a new kind of consumption-oriented community center" for white, middle-class families but also because those spaces transformed how consumers understood the products that were sold within them.[111]

When modern suburbanization began in the 1940s, new suburban developments took shape as homogeneous communities of white, middle-class families. The earlier suburbs of the Victorian era had proven more socioeconomically diverse. As train and trolley transportation allowed new residential clusters to proliferate on the outskirts of urban centers at the end of the nineteenth century, Victorian suburbs became home not just to the wealthy but also to diverse working-class families. During the middle decades of the twentieth century, however, pervasive auto ownership, abundant highways, and mass-produced construction detached new suburbs from their connections to particular cities and their ethnic and racial communities. In contrast with an understanding of place that prioritized attachment and obligation, suburbs championed the idea that consumers could and should choose places to live that suited their own taste, class status, and self-understanding.[112]

Meanwhile, local, state, and federal governmental authorities fueled suburban homogeneity by denying mortgage assistance to working-class applicants and people of color. Authorities also created zoning restrictions that distinguished between communities of renters and buyers. Municipalities and mortgage programs justified these policies by citing the need to protect "property values" on behalf of mortgage holders as well as local governments, which tied property taxes to property valuations.[113] By arguing that undesirable populations undermined property value, that mode of valuation became an ostensibly neutral metric by which homeowners, governments, and businesses all justified racist segregation. Arguments about school quality and children's education similarly served as euphemistic vehicles for racism and classism. All of this allowed midcentury suburbs to present cities and older suburbs as inhospitable places for white, middle-class families to live, by contrast with new suburban settlements. Portraying the suburban home as an ideal site of family nurture, where parents and children could retreat from the world and its perils, new home production rose from 142,000 to nearly 2 million between 1944 and 1950 alone.[114] By 1990 less than a third of Americans lived in urban areas and half of the U.S. population lived in suburbs.[115]

With suburbs drawing families to migrate away from urban communities and the institutions that anchored them, suburbs generated new institutions that suited their social setting. Shopping centers and large, enclosed shopping malls served this purpose. Federal tax policy encouraged developers to build shopping centers in suburbs. In 1954 the federal government began allowing real estate developers to dramatically accelerate the rate of depreciation they claimed on new real estate construction. Suddenly able to use tax write-offs to offset the burden of real estate taxes, shopping-center developers realized that they could keep a larger share of their tenants' rental income as profit. Because investors accordingly came to see shopping centers as lucrative investment opportunities, developers set about finding new tracts of cheap land outside urban areas for shopping centers and shopping malls. Land near suburban developments proved especially ideal. With the number of shopping centers tripling annually between 1953 and 1956, their overall new square footage grew from an annual average of 6 million square feet in the early 1950s to an average of 30 million square feet in 1956. Between 1949 and 1967, the number of regional shopping centers with more than 300,000 square feet grew from one to forty five.[116]

Shopping centers and malls took shape in response to their ideal consumer markets, while they also helped transform those imagined markets into social communities. Modeled partially on the collections of shops in downtown business districts, shopping centers were designed to serve simultaneously as commercial and social centers. Their purpose as a community center even helped determine the array of stores within them, insofar as shopping-center developers selected retail tenants on the basis of what those businesses contributed to the commercial whole and the community it ostensibly served. "Unlike downtown emporia," the historian Vicki Howard explains, "shopping centers and their branch department stores catered specifically to the needs and preferences of a more homogenized group—middle-class, white suburban customers." Acknowledging those customers' emphasis on the priority of family, shopping malls sought to appeal specifically to families, even by attempting to transform fathers and husbands into more active shoppers.[117]

Evangelical bookstores became fixtures within shopping malls, but they did not migrate immediately. Throughout the 1950s about half of general book sales occurred in downtown department stores; well into the 1960s evangelical trade periodicals continued to suggest that bookstores also did best in downtown locations.[118] In their Christian bookstore handbook John Bass and Robert DeVries devoted an entire section to guidance on choosing a location for a store. While encouraging potential bookstore owners to select high-traffic locations, they also acknowledged that retail space in high-traffic downtown locations came at a premium. As a result, they advised "finding a vacant store on the ground floor one to three blocks from the main street." Bass and DeVries noted that "a number of Christian bookstores are now located in some of the numerous shopping centers springing up across the country." But they also claimed that "these stores have special problems of their own," reporting that "thirty eight percent of all bookstores located in shopping centers were losing money." The authors advised that "the operation of a store in most shopping centers must be done on a skilled, professional basis, and we have found that few are qualified to start there with their store first."[119] During the 1960s one of the premier evangelical bookstores in the United States was the Logos Bookstore, in Ann Arbor, Michigan. But in a series of articles in *Bookstore Journal* in 1971, founder Jim Carlson essentially admitted that his store had achieved success in a uniquely appealing location. Describing his store's downtown location, he boasted that its proximity to the University of Michigan provided his store not only with abundant foot traffic but also with a proven population of readers willing to invest in books. Although Carlson's store eventually generated a successful chain of Logos Bookstores, that success reflected Carlson's own genius as a wholesale buyer and distributor.[120]

Zondervan Publishing House pioneered a shift toward the shopping center. When it set out in 1962 to find a location for its first bookstore outside Grand Rapids and Winona Lake, Zondervan selected a suburb south of Grand Rapids, near the first large shopping mall in the region. By 1980 Zondervan Family Bookstores had sixty stores, almost all of which were located within what the company's annual report described as "high-traffic malls."[121] As a chain with standardized commercial practices and internal communication, Zondervan's bookstores addressed some of the distribution problems that Oliver Cheney had highlighted in 1931. By 1994, with 153 stores in twenty-seven states, Zondervan possessed one of the largest bookstore chains in the United States, just behind such ubiquitous mass-market bookstore chains as Waldenbooks, B. Dalton, and Crown. These shopping-mall chains far outnumbered traditional chains such as Brentano's and Doubleday, which respectively possessed fourteen and thirty-three locations in 1960.[122] Zondervan's chain reportedly generated more than $110 million in annual revenue in 1993—more than its publishing division.[123]

By relocating to shopping malls, Zondervan's bookstores shifted attention away from some of the consumer strategies that evangelical bookstores traditionally had emphasized, including mail-order sales. Although publishers had delivered books by mail for decades, the practice had become even more profitable after 1939, when the parcel post rate fell to 1.5 cents per pound.[124] Evangelical bookstores sold both new and used books by mail. Because used books were inexpensive for bookstores to acquire, and because demand often proved strong for rare and out-of-print classics, some of the best-known bookstores even had prioritized used books over new books. Prominent used-books stores included Baker Book House in Grand Rapids, Chicago's Blessings Book Store, and New York's Schulte's Book Store, all of which distributed sales catalogs across the United States. Each of these stores built their business models on offering the most comprehensive selection imaginable. On every piece of its promotional literature, for example, Blessings Book Store offered a simple slogan: "If It's a Religious Book, Try Blessings." The typical Blessings catalog from the early 1940s presented potential customers with more than 1,000 choices and encouraged them to write in with requests for any books that they did not see on the list. "If the Book you are seeking is not listed please write us," the store's 1941 Summer Book News mailer announced, "this list contains only a small portion of our huge stock of Religious Books." Baker Book Store, by comparison, offered a more curated selection of books, offering fewer options with longer descriptions. On the final page of its catalog, Baker offered a list of the books that the store sought to purchase.[125]

In addition to revising long-standing bookselling strategies, shopping-center bookstores sought to dramatically expand the markets that evangelical companies addressed through their stores, moving beyond narrower evangelical aspirations. For decades, figures like Wilbur Smith had emphasized the notion that evangelicals composed a subculture or counterpublic that functioned in opposition to a dominant liberal culture and public. Smith and other midcentury "neo-evangelicals" dreamed of a day when the evangelical book industry would be able to produce and circulate literature on such a broad scale that it would overwhelm liberal religious literature and its proponents. Their oppositional ideal drew support in the second half of the twentieth century through the work of figures such as Francis Schaeffer, who challenged readers to oppose what he portrayed as the decline of a Western culture that had lost its intellectual and moral moorings. He called upon evangelicals to build a society in which everyone embraced "presuppositions" that they viewed as absolute and antithetical to others. Describing loyalty to such presuppositions as the essence of a distinct evangelical "worldview," Schaeffer argued that an evangelical worldview comprised particular understandings about the Bible and theology no less than particular convictions about gender roles, sexuality, and abortion. As the historian Neil J. Young explains, for Schaeffer and his allies, "secular humanism and feminism were cited as Satan's attack on the traditional family." Schaeffer became especially well known for drawing a close connection between the defense of the family and opposition to abortion.[126]

By establishing a presence in shopping centers, evangelical bookstores conjured a far less oppositional mode of evangelicalism than people like Smith and Schaeffer had championed. To be sure, evangelicals often had paired a subcultural priority of opposition with the hope that evangelical ideals might saturate the American mass market. Capturing this idea, Heather Hendershot has argued that "if evangelical media producers and consumers constitute a 'subculture,' it is one that aspires to lose its 'sub' status."[127] Even Francis Schaeffer expressed a version of this inclination, insofar as he hoped that a subculture grounded on Christian presuppositions might eventually produce "a monolithic culture."[128] But in shopping centers and shopping malls, evangelical bookstores served as subcultural spaces that sought mass-market recognition more deliberately. The ideal of the mass market always has prioritized white, middle-class consumers, and suburban shopping centers took shape as nothing less than manifestations of the mass-market principle.

Situated within the mass market, shopping-center bookstores conjured what can be seen as an "ambient" evangelicalism. As the anthropologist Matthew Engelke argues, evangelical organizations often have sought not simply to enhance the private devotional lives of people they reach but especially to create "a world in which there is nothing to be gained by referring to religion as public or private in the first place." Just as ambient musical styles are designed to serve as forms of background music that saturate listeners' senses without demanding their focused attention, "ambient faith" describes religious forms that publics accept without question, but not without interest. By establishing a presence in people's worlds without seeking deliberate or conscious commitment, ambient faiths not only enable deliberate participation for some people but also allow even more people to develop a general awareness of and sympathy for the ambience around them.[129]

Ambience served as an evangelical market strategy. The commercial theory was that visitors to shopping centers might begin an evangelical experience by encountering and acknowledging the presence of an evangelical store. Next, their initial attention and interest might lead them to venture into a store. Already participating in a broad evangelical public through their attention and presence, suburban consumers might then become more active participants by finding, purchasing, and consuming a particular bible, novel, daily devotional, parenting handbook, or home decor item. Recognizing the effectiveness of this process, industry leaders acknowledged that "non-churchgoing and nominal Christians" increasingly engaged with evangelical products during the 1970s.[130]

To encourage consumers to translate their ambient awareness of evangelicalism into acts of purchase, the evangelical book industry cultivated a variety of subsidiary consumer and media industries beginning especially in the 1970s. As early as 1941 Zondervan had been producing both songbooks and recordings. As the official distributor for the Singspiration line of songbooks and recordings, Zondervan helped popularize such well-known songs as "This Little Light of Mine" and "Fishers of Men."[131] But in the age of shopping-center stores, evangelical bookstores also provided the contemporary Christian music industry with the distribution pathways it required to develop, which ultimately allowed it to break away from books during 1970s. Although contemporary Christian music drew musical styles and popularity from such sources as the Jesus Movement of the 1970s, it fundamentally "grew out of the established evangelical publishing business," the communications scholar Quentin Schultze argues, "using religious bookstores for retail outlets."[132] In the 1990s, breakout artists like as DC Talk and Jars of Clay exemplified the ambient objectives of evangelical retail. Those acts neither remained bounded by subcultural opposition to secular society nor constituted the "uniform culture" that Frances Schaeffer had in mind. Wherever their music was sold and played, it circulated an ambient evangelicalism.[133]

CONCLUSION

While evangelical media industries have sought to pervade popular culture, transforming evangelicalism from "subculture" to dominant culture, or from counterpublic to dominant public, those ambitions have been constrained by the same infrastructures and settings that allowed those industries to grow in the first place. "My job is to serve the community, to come alongside the church," an evangelical bookstore manager explained to me in 2016. Although that mandate sounds generic, the "church" and "community" in this formulation extend only as far as the store's consumer market. In suburban shopping centers, evangelical bookstores addressed a market constituted predominantly by white, middle-class families. As a result, the "community" they served shared that profile. "Do you see a particular market for your books among black readers?" a reporter from *Publishers Weekly* asked the president of Revell, William Barbour Jr., in 1977. Barbour responded by claiming colorblindness. "I don't see blacks as a single market," he explained, "rather, I see *all* evangelicals as potential readers of our books." But potential readers became actual readers only when given the opportunity, and evangelical bookstores never made that a priority. Appeals to colorblindness invariably exacerbate discrimination and segregation by denying or ignoring the structural conditions of racial inequality.[134]

In recent decades, even as shopping malls have lost the commercial power they had during the second half of the twentieth century, and as shopping-center bookstores steadily have shuttered, evangelical booksellers have continued to address a white, middle-class, suburban consumer constituency. In 2016, for example, the CBA announced a new retail strategy, which it hoped would secure revenue for stores that had been experiencing steady declines in profit. The plan was to "bring high-margin exclusive releases to Christian stores," the trade magazine *Christian Market* reported, "driving traffic and helping reestablish the channel as a key vehicle for reaching the faith-based community."[135] To enhance this strategy's effectiveness, the CBA welcomed new stores as members. Chief among them were the 745 branches of Hobby Lobby, the chain of craft stores that drew attention and infamy in 2014 through the U.S. Supreme Court case *Burwell v. Hobby Lobby Stores, Inc.*, in which the company sued for exemption from federal requirements to provide its employees with contraception coverage. Citing a conflict between certain forms of contraception and their evangelical principles, the company's owners successfully claimed that for-profit corporations deserved the same religious freedoms as individuals and nonprofit corporations.[136]

With stores located almost exclusively in suburban locations and known as an avowedly evangelical company, Hobby Lobby addressed the same market that evangelical bookstores historically had. The trade magazine *Publishers Weekly* made that legacy explicit in 2017. Not long after reporting that Family Christian Stores (the name that Family Bookstores adopted after 1997) would be closing its remaining 240 stores, the magazine suggested that the closure might boost Hobby Lobby's evangelical retail efforts.[137] Whether located in suburban shopping malls or strip malls, Family Christian Stores no longer were the primary means by which consumers could experience, engage with, and purchase an evangelical "way of life." Highlighting this shift, the CBA's president accounted for Family Christian's closure by citing "changing consumer behavior and declining sales."[138] But consumers still could experience evangelical ambience by other means. To practice Family Christian's eponymous investment in the Christian family, consumers could turn not just to Hobby Lobby but also to other fixtures of suburban religious consumerism, including but not limited to the fast-food restaurant Chick-Fil-A.[139]

For a time, shopping centers provided the sort of distributive standardization that Oliver Cheney had called for in 1931. Through the imbrication of tax policy, suburbanization, anxiety about the future of family, traditionalist gender systems, and more, evangelical bookstores made social sense as a vehicle for evangelical media, culture, and the way of life they sought to circulate. But even during the heyday of shopping-center bookstores, other modes of distribution had standardized practices and priorities that helped generate the shift in consumer behavior that contributed to Family Christian's collapse. Those distribution pathways included catalog sellers like Christian Book Distributors, which joined evangelical book clubs and other catalog-based retailers in delivering commodities by mail, helping evangelical books and music reach individuals and churches who preferred not to visit or could not access suburban retail outlets. Catalog sales appealed especially to what one historian describes as "dispersed countercultural lifestyle communities." Those communities included people described by the historian Axel Schäfer as "countercultural conservatives."[140]

In addition to distributors that focused on individuals and churches, wholesale companies like Spring Arbor helped funnel evangelical media to larger retailers such as Barnes and Noble and Wal-Mart.[141] More recently, online retailers like Amazon have imposed standardization upon the book industry by offering prices and choices that physical stores have struggled to match.

But if these latter distribution infrastructures have supplanted the evangelical bookstore, which in turn supplanted the colporteur and her home visits, those paradigms nevertheless have continued to allow circulations of cultural commodities to function as engines of evangelicalism. As retail outlets such as Hobby Lobby show, that commercialism has continued to cultivate evangelical understandings of gender and family, which have helped to heap righteousness upon retail. When the bookseller Edith Jones remarked in 1968 that the future of her Christian community depended on "what we as booksellers do," she was prescient.[142] Yet Daisy Moody had come to the same conclusion even earlier, which is why she took it upon herself to pray for her publishers and patrons alike.

5

Financial Faith

CORPORATE FINANCE AND THE SACRED TRADITION OF GROWTH

I tell you, Open your eyes and look at the fields!
They are ripe for harvest.

John 4:35 (NIV)

THESE WORDS serve as a caption for the only image that adorns the cover of the Zondervan Corporation's 1985 annual report. The image depicts a field of golden-hued stalks of wheat, stretching to the horizon. The wheat appears to rustle in the breeze beneath a brilliant blue sky. Considering that Zondervan's corporate activity had nothing to do with wheat, a reader might ask what sort of harvest Zondervan's executives hoped the image and its caption would bring to mind.[1] Of course, evangelical interpreters of the Bible traditionally have viewed the passage as a call to see the proverbial fields of the world as ripe territories for harvests of souls. Given its appearance on an annual report of financial performance, however, readers might have reached a different interpretation. From an alternate angle, the harvest is not just metaphysical; it also is financial.

Thumbing through this annual report at Zondervan's annual meeting in April 1986, shareholders undoubtedly hoped that the company would experience an abundant financial harvest. During the past two years, the company not only had announced large financial losses but even had signed an agreement with the Securities and Exchange Commission to stop misstating its financial performance, as it had in 1984.[2] By early 1986 some shareholders began threatening to fix the company's problems themselves. "We are coming to the conclusion that perhaps it would be best if the company is put into other hands," explained James Apostalakis, an investor from New York. At the time Apostalakis owned 7 percent of Zondervan's shares. Acknowledging that Zondervan's leaders understood their business as a mode of ministry, Apostalakis quipped: "I don't believe God's mission will be any worse served by having the company run in a profitable manner." In his view and that of many other investors, money mattered most. "They can believe whatever they want," he insisted, "but they are a public company and they have public shareholders."[3] Whatever interpretation of John 4:35 Zondervan's graphic designers intended or inspired, the company's leaders hoped that shareholders would open their eyes and see that Zondervan's proverbial fields remained ripe.

Although Apostalakis's comments sound cynical, he could insist that Zondervan should prioritize profit because the company already had proclaimed faith in financial structures that maximized growth. In this chapter I explore the company's pursuit of growth, focusing especially on how Zondervan and its competitors cultivated a sacred tradition that conjoined their monetary and metaphysical objectives. In order to expand the evangelical market and public, evangelical firms sanctified a variety of corporate financial strategies—including mergers, conglomerate structures, and public offerings of corporate stock. While Zondervan pioneered many of these techniques, most of the evangelical book industry embraced them during the final decades of the twentieth century.

The industry's embrace of corporate finance illustrates how evangelicals continually have authorized new social practices and priorities through the ongoing creation of sacred tradition. Based etymologically on the notion of "transmission," the concept of tradition can be understood as a living deposit of teachings that are developed and passed down over time.[4] While Catholic and Orthodox forms of Christianity typically view tradition and the Bible as complementary forms of divinely inspired revelation, Protestants often have expressed disdain for tradition. Evangelicals especially have insisted instead on the need for Christians to focus exclusively on the teachings canonized in the Bible.[5] Yet as biblical and theological scholars have acknowledged, evangelicals undoubtedly have developed and upheld their own deposits of tradition. The evangelical theologian Stanley Grenz admits, for example, that evangelicals' emphasis on "believing the Bible" fundamentally has entailed "believing the doctrines that evangelical theologians concluded the Bible itself teaches."[6] Just as the Roman Catholic Church's Second Vatican Council claimed that "sacred tradition takes the word of God entrusted by Christ the Lord and the Holy Spirit to the Apostles, and hands it on to their successors in its full purity," evangelical leaders and laypeople commonly have presented their principles and practices as the authentic legacy of Jesus and his apostles.[7] Evangelical deposits of sacred tradition always have included principles and presumptions associated with varied social formations, including race, gender, class, and economy.

With this understanding of tradition in mind, I focus in this chapter especially on how evangelicals within the publishing and bookselling industries cultivated religious rationales that helped authorize the financial revolution that swept through U.S. society beginning in the 1960s.[8] These rationales built upon earlier advocacy for "free enterprise," the notion that social stability and prosperity depended upon profit-seeking businesses rather than the state and its redistributionist policies. While the economic collapse of the 1930s had convinced many policymakers and ordinary Americans to question the assumption that capitalists and free markets could and would create a better world, advocates of free enterprise insisted for decades that businesses uniquely respected "the sacredness of the individual" and provided a bulwark against social transformations that undermined individual responsibility and the traditional Christian family.[9] Similarly viewing new financial markets and strategies as means of expanding Christian society and nurturing individual choice, the evangelical publishing industry put faith in corporate finance as the best way to reap ever more abundant metaphysical and financial harvests.

FINANCING GROWTH

Beginning especially in the 1930s, champions of Christian free enterprise treated corporate growth not just as a means of enhancing society's devotion to Jesus but also as evidence of spiritual success. As the historian Sarah Hammond has shown, industrialists such as R. G. LeTourneau transformed the mantra that "God needs business men as well as preachers and missionaries" into a call for Americans to recognize that "spiritual authority hinged on success in a marketplace in which earthly and heavenly dividends were one." In a similar spirit, the Zondervan editor and manager Ted W. Engstrom—who would go on to lead the evangelical organizations Youth for Christ and World Vision International—claimed in 1947 to speak for all evangelical businessmen in boasting that "they are successful not *in spite of* their being Christians but *because of* their acceptance of Jesus Christ as Savior."[10] Convinced that God needed businessmen and business needed God, evangelical businessmen sought new opportunities to invest in that partnership.

In the book industry, new opportunities for growth loomed especially large beginning in the early 1960s, as avowedly secular and religious publishers, booksellers, and investors all turned renewed attention to the challenge of easing the industry's long-standing limitations. Before then the industry persistently had endured—and earned—a reputation for operating far behind the commercial cutting-edge. Business-minded critics charged publishers with an inability to produce a product of consistent quality or to distribute their books reliably on a mass scale. The book business generally remained—as the sociologist Laura J. Miller explains—"impervious to attempts to rationalize its distribution sector."[11] This imperviousness rested, in part, on a tendency for industry critics and participants alike to perceive commercial inefficiency as a kind of virtue. The book industry's antiquarian ethos allowed publishers and booksellers to appear blessedly resistant to crude commercialism and seemingly persistent in their dedication to the life of the mind.[12] Reconsideration of that traditionalism became more alluring as both secular and religious publishers and booksellers developed and embraced aspirations of expansion.

The broader book industry's sudden expansionist ambitions and modernizing sensibilities reflected a wide range of causes. Virtually all publishers and booksellers sought, for example, to supply the consumer demand that rose in response to the additional leisure time, rising disposable income, and enhanced reading habits of the growing postwar middle-class. Reading habits had developed for a variety of reasons, including the federal government's efforts to cultivate reading among both soldiers and citizens during World War II. Following the war, the government worked to develop elementary education, raise high school graduation rates, expand higher education, and even build new suburban homes with shelving for books.[13] Religious books in particular appeared to both liberal and conservative business leaders as means of asserting cultural influence.[14] In the spirit of reformulating the landscape of American religious identity, evangelical advocates of free enterprise encouraged evangelicals to see culture industries as sites of unrestricted growth potential.

Book industries also seemed poised for growth because rising book sales had allowed book publishing to appear as "big business," which made book publishing corporations seem suited to the same financial strategies that other large corporations had adopted. Between 1952 and 1959, general book sales had risen by as much as 72 percent. As a result, book publishers became swept up in the "merger mania" of the 1960s. Mergers appealed to corporate executives and managers not just as a way for particular corporations to capture larger markets and profits but also because a corporation's size became recognized as an index of its prestige and power as a social institution. While virtually every industry saw a dramatic increase in corporate mergers, publishing companies merged at a rate that more than doubled and almost quadrupled that of other comparable industries; between 1965 and 1969, at least twenty-three publishing mergers occurred annually, with forty-seven mergers in 1968 and forty-four in 1969.[15]

Throughout the 1960s, publishing companies most frequently merged "horizontally," which means that they combined with companies that sold similar products to similar markets. Horizontal mergers served a variety of practical purposes. Until the late 1950s many publishing firms remained family-owned enterprises, often directed by members of the same families from which the companies derived their names. Responding to growing investor interest in the publishing industry, many of those companies' aging founders and owners decided to sell their firms to competitors, both to enhance the size of their financial estates and to ensure that their companies would not dissolve in posthumous estate settlements. Beyond matters of inheritance, horizontal mergers allowed competing companies to combine their rosters of authors and their copyright holdings, to cover wider swaths of particular consumer markets, and to take advantage of economies of scale with regard to staffing, production, and distribution. Similar objectives had inspired an earlier wave of publishing mergers in the nineteenth century, when mergers produced such large firms as the American Book Company, which famously took control of more than 90 percent of the American textbook business.[16] Mergers also offered financial benefits. An acquiring company could treat its acquisition's corporate debt as a tax deduction; and merged companies could combine their capital, using their collective assets to justify greater investment from banks. Publishing firms had become prime candidates for mergers partly because many remained "undercapitalized"—they possessed less capital than they needed to achieve their goals or to meet demand. And so mergers allowed undercapitalized firms to secure funds that allowed them to repay existing debts or to develop and deploy more elaborate production strategies and distribution systems. In short: horizontal mergers simultaneously created larger companies and enabled additional growth.

By 1970 the magazine *Business Week* reported that "the big story in books is financial," and evangelical executives often portrayed themselves as that story's primary protagonists.[17] For evangelical firms, horizontal mergers had both practical and metaphysical effects. Practically, mergers allowed evangelical publishers to enlarge the scale and scope of their activities. In 1966, for example, Zondervan acquired Harper & Row's bible department for $1 million. Providing Zondervan with printing plates, inventory, and publishing rights for versions of the King James Bible, the Revised Standard Version, and Harold Lindsell's *Harper Study Bible,* this acquisition increased the variety and volume of bibles that Zondervan could publish. Meanwhile, in 1968 Baker Book House announced its purchase of the book publishing division of W. A. Wilde Company of Boston, a hundred-year-old publisher of religious books. The acquisition allowed

Baker to expand is nascent book publishing program, having focused previously on book reprinting and reselling.[18] And in the fall of 1969, Word, Inc., expanded its music publishing by acquiring the Rodeheaver Company, founded in 1910 by Homer Rodeheaver, who had achieved renown as Billy Sunday's music leader.[19] Attempting to cash in on the corporate obsession with mergers, some smaller publishers prominently advertised themselves as acquisition targets. In 1972 Five Star Publishers of Tupelo, Mississippi, published a stark full-page ad in *Bookstore Journal,* the trade magazine of the Christian Booksellers Association. "WANTED: MAJOR PUBLISHER," the ad trumpeted in large capital letters. Below that announcement, the ad explained that a major publisher was desired to take over the press's current books and to publish future books. "We have six books which have sold over 50,000 copies in two years," the ad boasted, "this despite very limited distribution and promotion. Sales potential for these books, with proper promotion and distribution, is tops!"[20]

These mergers allowed acquiring firms to produce new products and to engage new consumers. Following Zondervan's acquisition of Harper & Row's bible department, for example, company founder and president Pat Zondervan prepared himself for his company's annual sales and strategy meeting by studying and annotating the 1965–1966 Harper bible catalog. Throughout the catalog, he made note of potential market opportunities, which Harper & Row might have overlooked due to less familiarity with Christian cultures. On a page dedicated to the *Harper New Pocket Reference Bible,* Zondervan drew a circle around the word "concordance" and identified denominations whose techniques of Bible study relied heavily on concordances, suggesting that this bible's "Best customers" might be "Nazarene & Church of Christ." Zondervan also scrawled his assessment that the Churches of Christ were "large and fast growing." On a page dedicated to the *Harper Imperial Pica Text Bible,* Zondervan described it as "the one Christian Science uses," and he noted that the *Harper New Testaments and Psalms*—the so-called Tiny testament—sold best in New Jersey. Pat Zondervan also identified bibles that typically appeared in denominational book catalogs.[21] To help sell Zondervan's newly acquired bibles through bookstores, the company developed and invested in a new initiative designed to give bookstores free sales training—focused especially on Zondervan products. Appointing a new full-time bible representative in 1968, Zondervan announced that this representative would "give help to the dealers in inventory control, salesclerk training and merchandising of Bibles."[22] Due both to growing demand and publishers' efforts to address and generate demand, the editor of *Decision* magazine declared in 1969 that "religious book publishers in America have just had the greatest year in their history, both in cloth and paperback."[23]

Less obvious but no less important than these practical effects, horizontal mergers encouraged cultural and theological realignments. In 1964, for example, Zondervan acquired Dunham Publishing Company, an Ohio-based company with strong ties to Dallas Theological Seminary. The acquisition granted Zondervan the rights to books by Lewis Sperry Chafer, president of Dallas Theological Seminary between 1924 and 1952. The year after acquiring Dunham, Zondervan purchased Cowman Publishing Company, publisher of *Streams in the Desert*, a daily devotional book written by Mrs. Charles A. Cowman.[24] Zondervan's 1965–1966 trade catalog included books from both of these acquisitions. Acknowledging that the book dealers and booksellers who read their trade catalog might associate many of the titles with their original publishers, Zondervan identified the acquired books with the letters *D* for Dunham and *C* for Cowman. At first glance, many of the designated titles appear to fit easily alongside Zondervan's prior books. But a more sustained analysis reveals that many of the titles were clustered around themes with which Zondervan had not regularly engaged. A significant number of the Dunham volumes emphasized dispensational theology, with such titles as *Revelation: Clear and Plain,* Cyrus Scofield's *Rightly Dividing the Word of Truth,* and *Satan.* Meanwhile, many of the Cowman titles strongly enhanced Zondervan's nascent emphasis on inspirational literature, with such titles as *Consolation, Traveling toward Sunrise,* and *Handfuls of Purpose.*[25]

Although both the Dunham and the Cowman books emphasized themes that theoretically could have appeared in a Zondervan catalog before their publishers' acquisitions, those publishers' mergers with Zondervan amplified those themes and incorporated them into a common theological culture. Whereas authors like Lewis Sperry Chafer and Mrs. Charles Cowman previously represented regional evangelical cultures, their appearance alongside each other worked against that distinctiveness. A similar phenomenon occurred through the many cooperative efforts that other firms undertook during the 1960s, many of which eventually blossomed into mergers. In 1968 Bethany Fellowship of Minneapolis began distributing books for Baker Book House, and the Presbyterian publishers John Knox and Westminster joined their sales forces the following year; Bethany ultimately became a Baker imprint, and John Knox and Westminster eventually integrated, collapsing distinctions that previously had separated the Presbyterian imprints.[26] Taking together all of these collapsed distinctions and collaborations, the "middle-of-the-road" evangelicalism that journalists often identified during the 1970s took shape in catalogs, in bookstores, and on consumers' bookshelves. This same process also helped the charismatic movement to saturate evangelical cultures during the 1980s and 1990s, when larger evangelical companies began acquiring or partnering with firms that specialized in books that presumed the miraculous power of the Holy Spirit in the contemporary world.[27]

With mergers expanding both the scale of production and the scope of the potential evangelical audience, evangelical publishers remained optimistic about the industry's growth potential well into the 1970s—even as a relative gloom overcame the book industry more broadly. The general book market became depressed in the early 1970s in part because the "merger mania" of the previous decade had produced an oversupply, which was exacerbated by a recession that stunted the growing consumer demand that mergers had sought to address.[28] As early as 1971, secular publishers reported that the previous decade's rising profits had stalled, relative to investment. "Five years after books sales in America reached the $2-billion mark and publishing became big business," the New York Times reported in 1971, "the industry is facing a time of trouble and soul-searching even though more books are being bought than ever before." Describing it as a time of "belt-tightening," editors admitted that they excitedly had expected a constant supply of best sellers and their attendant revenue; but more modest expectations now required them to "produce fewer but better trade books."[29]

Meanwhile, evangelical publishers boasted that they continued to benefit from the industry's expansion without comparable decline. As Robert DeVries—Zondervan's director of publications and former editor in chief of Moody Press—admitted in an article written for the evangelical book trade in 1970, that confidence might have seemed unwarranted to someone unfamiliar with his industry. After all, many observers had identified a "drop in U.S. church membership" as well as an "accompanying plunge in the part religion plays in influencing the average American life." Those factors alone might be expected to inspire what DeVries described as a "crisis in religious publishing." But he pointed out that "the evangelical book editor . . . can be relatively sure of the success of his product because of the character of his public." DeVries insisted that the evangelical public did not take shape through "adherence to the rigid strictures of the institutional church." He claimed that evangelicals even possessed "a greater sense of identity with one another in spite of ecclesiastical association." Rather than developing within the walls of churches, DeVries explained, evangelicalism took shape largely through the efforts of the book industry, which conjured shared sensibilities among its consumers. Noting that evangelicals valued a "sense of personal faith" and "need to be comforted, encouraged, and assured of God's grace and compassion—especially in an age of activism, change, and discomfort," DeVries predicted that Christian literature should remain increasingly in demand.[30]

Optimism pervaded the industry because sustained expansion had led the growth of the industry and its audience to appear as the will of the God whom the industry ostensibly served. During the early 1970s the first pages of virtually every issue of the trade magazine *Bookstore Journal* featured news updates about the industry's unrelenting growth. One report in 1971 highlighted a recent story by Velma Clyde, a reporter for *Oregonian Staff*. The report described Clyde's assessment of monthly evangelical book sales for 1971 as "a source of amazement," noting that Clyde's interviews with members of the Christian book industry "further mystified the reporter." Sharing his view of the industry's growth with Clyde, a book distributor from the firm West Coast Distributors explained: "We aren't in total control. You watch the phenomenon but it is nothing you have worked out."[31] This faith in God's commercial provision increasingly inspired the creation of new firms, such as Chosen Books in 1971.

LEARNING TO LOVE THE SECULAR CONGLOMERATE

When evangelical companies eventually faced their own financial challenges during the 1970s, evangelical entrepreneurs treated those challenges as opportunities to embrace new corporate strategies—including new merger strategies. Chief among those challenges was economic inflation, which began toward the end of the 1960s. As inflation rose, production costs rose. And as the government raised interest rates to slow inflation, loans to finance production or expansion costs became more costly.[32] These phenomena ushered in an era of financial belt-tightening, leading companies to consider how they might protect themselves if and when their primary products generated less profit than expected. Media corporations began solving this problem by undertaking vertical and conglomerate mergers. But this raised a question: could Christian companies remain Christian if a secular conglomerate acquired them? Sacred tradition enabled evangelical corporations to answer: yes.

During the 1960s, publishing companies experienced depressed revenue, in part because horizontal mergers had produced a glut of products. Combining companies that produced similar products for similar markets, horizontally merged corporations had produced larger quantities of new publications due to the theory that more books increased the likelihood that one product might become a best seller. Horizontal acquisitions also had allowed acquiring firms to capitalize upon access to their acquisitions' "active backlists"—that is, books published previously and still in print. In response to what one publishing historian describes as a "clogged distribution system," media corporations increasingly pursued mergers that allowed them to utilize varied distribution pathways and to engage diverse consumer constituencies.[33]

To diversify their markets, vertical mergers combined companies that represented different steps in chains of production and distribution, and conglomerate mergers combined companies devoted to different products and markets. A corporation's "degree of conglomerateness" depended upon how distinct its subsidiaries' production processes operated or its markets remained. By 1970 conglomerate mergers became increasingly popular as companies navigated tighter governmental oversight that had developed since 1950, when the Celler-Kefauver Amendment to Section 7 of the Clayton Antitrust Act began scrutinizing mergers more closely for anticompetitiveness. In comparison with horizontal and vertical mergers, conglomerate mergers seemed less likely to draw regulatory ire. Although a secular publishing corporation's acquisition of an evangelical publishing company could be viewed as a kind of horizontal merger, the perceived dissimilarity of their markets bestowed a conglomerate quality upon such mergers.[34]

While mergers of any kind enabled economies of scale and scope with regard to aspects of staffing, distribution, and production, conglomerate mergers allowed companies to diversify their activities, investments, and sources of revenue. Fueled by the notion that similar business principles could apply to virtually any business setting, conglomerate corporations sought to create businesses that would complement each other both practically and especially financially. Ideally, dissimilar subsidiaries would prevent dramatic fluctuations in the conglomerate's overall corporate profit and prosperity by generating revenue streams that would flow independently. This emphasis on complementarity began to become popular as early as the 1960s, as the U.S. government increased its financial support for education. That potential funding inspired many corporations to see books and their publishing firms as reliable sources of revenue. In 1966, for example, the Radio Corporation of America acquired Pantheon Books and Alfred A. Knopf, in the hope that books and broadcasting might work together. To maximize collaborative activity, conglomerate corporations heralded new production and distribution paradigms, including mass-market paperback publishing, distribution through outlets like newsstands and drug stores, and television marketing and cross-promotion.[35]

Leading evangelical firms welcomed conglomeration as a technique of expansion. Whereas horizontal mergers had allowed evangelical companies to expand their scale in the name of reaching more people, conglomerates enabled media companies to expand their scope in the name of engaging a greater variety of consumers, with diverse interests and media consumption habits. In addition to generating other sources of revenue to supplement the book publishing business, conglomerate structures allowed Zondervan and other firms to present diversification as an attempt to mediate God's message beyond books. Although Zondervan had started publishing music in the 1960s, the company reorganized itself in 1970 in order to give corporate structure to its distinct, but aligned, areas of commercial activity. As a new "holding company" (which "holds" a variety of subsidiary companies), the Zondervan Corporation included Zondervan Publishing House; Family Bookstores; the music publisher Singspiration; the recording division of Singcord; and the Zondervan Broadcasting Corporation, which operated several radio stations in the Midwest.[36] "Our objective," Zondervan president Peter Kladder explained to the company's employees in his 1973 Christmas message, "is distribution to the glory of God, . . . and by His grace and the efforts of everyone one of our employees, we have significantly increased distribution this year and trust God we'll do the same in 1974."[37] Although the evangelical book industry long had portrayed greater circulation of religious literature as a method of giving greater glory to God, Kladder's comment illustrates how conglomerated diversification became seen as a natural method of generating that glory.

An emphasis on financial complementarity continued well into the 1990s and beyond. In 1992, for instance, the book and bible publishing firm Thomas Nelson acquired Word, Inc., for approximately $72 million. Although Word published books, it long had specialized in music. "As a result of the acquisition of Word," Thomas Nelson's annual report explained in 1995, "there has been a shift in [Thomas Nelson's] product revenue mix with each of music and book products contributing a larger percentage of the Company's net revenues than Bible products." The report noted that "this shift in sales mix and distribution channels has positively impacted the Company's gross profit, as a percentage of net revenues."[38] The allure of complementary revenue streams not only led evangelical firms to diversify the modes of media that they produced and sold but also inspired secular media conglomerates to become interested in acquiring evangelical firms as a way of diversifying their own businesses. Beginning around 1990 virtually every major multinational media conglomerate created or acquired an evangelical publishing firm.

While newly created firms have included Warner Faith (founded in 2001) and Amazon's Waterfall Press (2013), conglomerates have tended to acquire evangelical companies even more often than they have created new ones. After the French media conglomerate Lagardère and its Hachette Book Group acquired Warner Faith in 2006, it became FaithWords. That same year, CBS Corporation's Simon & Schuster acquired Howard Publishing, and the evangelical firm Multnomah became part of German conglomerate Bertelsmann's Random House. Multnomah joined Random House alongside WaterBrook Press (1996), and the two firms together formed the new WaterBrook Multnomah Publishing Group.[39]

Originally founded in Oregon in 1969, Multnomah became seen as a cautionary tale within the evangelical media industry, underlining the importance of complementary revenue. The company had achieved outsized success early in the 2000s with Bruce Wilkinson's *The Prayer of Jabez,* a book that taught readers to use a prayer from 1 Chronicles 4:10 of the Hebrew Bible to petition God for spiritual and material riches. Building on the commercial success of inspirational books about the power of prayer and positive thinking, Wilkinson's book debuted in 2000 and became the best-selling nonfiction title in the United States in 2001. By the end of that year, it had sold more than 8.3 million copies.[40] To meet the incredible demand for Wilkinson's book, Multnomah devoted large amounts of its capital to building new infrastructure and hiring almost twenty new staff members. When interest in Wilkinson's book waned and no comparable best sellers followed, however, the company's resultant financial troubles led it to reduce its new titles by half and lay off employees.[41] Without other significant revenue streams to support its declining publishing revenue, Multnomah's owners felt compelled to sell.

In 2012, HarperCollins—a subsidiary of Rupert Murdoch's conglomerate News Corporation—deepened its position in evangelical media by acquiring Thomas Nelson. Having already acquired Zondervan in 1988, HarperCollins bundled Zondervan and Thomas Nelson together as independent "publishing programs" within the newly created HarperCollins Christian, which described itself as "a world leading Christian content provider."[42] After their merger, Zondervan and Thomas Nelson controlled as much as 50 percent of the Christian market and 75 percent of the bible market.[43] In 1988 no less than 2012, these acquisitions made sense to evangelical companies largely because mergers of all kinds had appeared as necessary features of growth in service to the kingdom of God.

To be sure, from the outside an observer might expect the dominance of secular multinational corporations over evangelical media industries to draw evangelical opposition. In 2016 the chairman of the Evangelical Christian Publishers Association estimated conservatively that secular multinationals accounted for as much as 70 percent of the evangelical market's sales.[44] But evangelical entrepreneurs continually have been able to invest markets with meaning. Writing in 2016, Dwight Baker—the president of the family-owned Baker Publishing Group—explained that he had "learned to love media conglomerates." Why? Secular media conglomerates possess financial resources that independent companies do not. As a result, Baker explained, "the major publishers invested in the religion category because the independents were unable or unwilling to accept the full burden of that task directly."[45] Recognizing large media corporations' financial power as a resource for creating evangelical constituencies and for circulating God's grace, Baker had come to see secular conglomerates' dominance as "God's hand investing in this category through the general market."[46] This rationale wrapped theological thinking around an idea that investors and corporate consultants had cultivated since the 1970s: namely, that large but lean conglomerate corporations would enable smaller and less efficient firms to realize their true potential.[47]

As evangelical firms cultivated a tradition that sanctified conglomerate structures and corporate strategies, that same tradition inspired them to deny that those structures and strategies undermined their proclaimed missions. Even though it may seem inevitable that an independent company would change some of its preferences and practices after being acquired by another corporation, both evangelical executives and employees often have challenged that conventional wisdom. They have insisted that acquired firms have remained true to their original spirit, retaining similar employees and publishing similar titles. And some scholars and journalists have affirmed aspects of this perspective.[48] These claims do not stem solely from wishful thinking; a shift of sensibility simply can prove difficult to perceive, either inside or outside an organization. In the decades since Zondervan's acquisition, its employees have claimed that News Corporation's executives have not imposed their will on Zondervan's own editorial vision. "Although [Rupert] Murdoch became famous for his lurid tabloid newspapers and also controls the Fox movie and television empire," one report explained in 1992, "Zondervan officials have said that they have been unhindered as publishers of evangelical Christian materials."[49]

Yet as studies of general media industries have shown, the "cultural effects of merger" lie more subtly in the language and ideas through which companies interpret themselves and their activities. Examining the 1966 merger of the independent art book publisher Harry N. Abrams, Inc., with the communications conglomerate Times Mirror, one study tracked both quantitative and qualitative changes among employees and in the company's publications between 1966 and 1984. In partial support of those who disavow change following an acquisition, researchers found that Times Mirror did not "imperiously assert its managerial prerogatives." But the study ultimately found that Abrams employees gradually adopted the rationale through which Times Mirror measured success. While Abrams initially calculated success "in terms of the professional recognition and the public acclaim engendered by his publications," Times Mirror "measured success in fiscal language." Abrams slowly adopted more bureaucratic control and stressed the Times Mirror priorities of "profit making, managerial efficiency, and collective decision making."[50] Because conglomerates are created in order to generate stable streams of complementary revenue, conglomerate ownership leads companies to systematically minimize risk through greater coordination, bureaucracy, and more systematic control of financial concerns. Even as conglomerate structures made possible new forms of multimedia integration and provided companies access to larger pools of capital, such possibilities ultimately incentivized greater focus on identifying authors, titles, and institutions with evident sales potential, bureaucratically weeding out more speculative options.[51]

To see this reorientation at work, consider Zondervan's decision-making process for selecting books to publish in the 1990s. Speaking to me in 2016, former Zondervan president and chief executive (1984–1993) James Buick explained that Zondervan's acquisition ultimately required that every potential book "make [financial] sense by itself." Buick contrasted this with a hypothetical evangelical firm that operated in pursuit of "pure ministry," rather than steady corporate profit. Companies that pursued pure ministry, he explained, likely would publish many books that "probably aren't going to sell a lot that you should [publish] anyhow." Buick admitted that Zondervan's acquisition forced the company to abandon that ideal. "We had a whole formula," he remarked, and "if it doesn't pay out in reasonable period, with a reasonable degree of confidence, you didn't go with it."[52] Of course, executives and editors recognized that this formula could lead the firm beyond the bounds of what either they or their critics might consider ministry of any sort. And so they developed what executives described as a theologically oriented "publishing philosophy." But any application of that philosophy had its limits. "I told my editorial staff to think of themselves as mutual fund managers," a former Zondervan executive explained to me. Just as a mutual fund manager must generate the most revenue possible from whatever capital clients provide, editors and executives had to use the content available to them to generate the best possible return.[53]

Insofar as the conglomerate form privileged predictable financial returns, it also led Zondervan to hire executives primarily based on their managerial expertise rather than their familiarity with evangelical theology, ministry, or publishing. When Buick initially arrived at the company in 1984, for example, he came to publishing from a career in executive positions at Ford Motor Company and, most recently, the Brunswick Corporation, which manufactured bowling equipment and owned a chain of bowling alleys.[54] Granted, Buick had been an active layperson in his denomination. Raised a Free Methodist, he had helped develop the denomination's pension plan, and he had served as chairman of a fundraising campaign for missionaries. Beyond that work, however, his experience connecting faith to work had occurred primarily through his efforts to curb the moral indiscretions of the bowling-alley managers who had worked for him. Hired by a headhunter who appreciated Buick's success leading Brunswick's bowling alleys, Buick focused his efforts at Zondervan on reducing corporate expenses and raising revenues.[55] One of Buick's successors, Maureen Girkins, became the company's first female CEO in 2008, after converting from Roman Catholicism just five years earlier. A former executive at AT&T and Motorola, Girkins received the position due to her knowledge of digital media. This led Zondervan's board to see her as a leader with proven reliability, who could generate financial predictability despite the uncertainty that the digital transition had inspired.[56]

As Zondervan developed a tradition that assessed religious expertise and evaluated the religious merit of potential products in new ways, the company's application of that tradition defined the contours of its evangelical public. While the company's pursuit of financial growth had led it to focus less on questions of theological appropriateness, Zondervan set firmer limits on cultural appropriateness. This process of creating new boundaries exemplifies Karl Marx's observation that capitalism continually overcomes limits on production before reestablishing more compatible limits. Applying Marx's observation to the history of "family values" since the 1970s, the historian Melinda Cooper reveals how neoliberal advocates of free enterprise defended the ideal of the white, heterosexual, male-breadwinner family as the "linchpin" of the modern capitalist order.[57] The evangelical book industry similarly has tended to treat liberationist stances on issues of racial inequality and sexuality as perspectives most firmly beyond the bounds of evangelical tradition. Regarding sexuality, for instance, a prominent trade group severely censured the firm WaterBrook Multnomah in 2014 following the release of Matthew Vines's *God and the Gay Christian,* a deeply biblicist defense of same-sex relationships by an avowed evangelical. WaterBrook Multnomah had not actually published the book; but its publisher also belonged to Penguin Random House, and critics faulted WaterBrook Multnomah for assisting with the book's creation.[58]

On matters of both sexuality and race, executives and editors regularly have navigated the limits of evangelical tradition by relying largely on feeling and affect. In 1985, for example, the company published an autobiography of John DeLorean, the engineer and entrepreneur who designed the car made famous in the *Back to the Future* films. Recently acquitted on charges of cocaine trafficking, DeLorean claimed to have become a born-again Christian during his ten-day stay in prison in 1982. Although Zondervan's executives and editors worried that DeLorean did not possess a form of faith that the company's readers would find convincing, they recruited him and offered him a nearly $1 million advance.[59] To gauge DeLorean's worthiness as a Zondervan author, James Buick traveled to California to spend a weekend with DeLorean. By the time the two men parted, Buick reported feeling that DeLorean "wanted to serve the Lord." In contrast with that decision, Zondervan's executives made a similar trip during the early 1990s to assess an African American pop star. Although that potential author was more famous than DeLorean and had a more extensive history of Christian commitment, editors ultimately decided that the singer was not "credible as a Christian."[60]

Why did Zondervan's executives decide not to publish that African American celebrity's book? We do not know all of the details of what transpired over the course of the time that Zondervan's representatives spent with their potential author. But even if we did, the primary lesson here is that the company's representatives conducted their visits and assessed potential authors' Christian devotion by prioritizing their own feelings. Although the company's leaders could present their decisions as theological or devotional, their explanations complemented calculations that depended inherently upon their emotional sympathies, prejudices, biases, and empathetic sensibilities. This phenomenon exemplifies the anthropologist Andrea Muehlebach's finding that liberal and neoliberal economic activity has cultivated subjects that "trafficked in, bartered, and exchanged virtues and passions as much as they did money and commodities."[61] In order to put their sacred tradition into practice, Zondervan's executives drew upon their own feelings to identify authors who might generate reliable revenue for the conglomerate. And they ultimately prioritized authors who felt potentially "credible" to the cultures of faith and family they found familiar.

GOING PUBLIC

As shifts in policy and practice suggest, evangelical media executives, editors, and authors continually have transformed newly popular structures of financial capitalism into principles of sacred tradition. Even more than mergers, however, the stock market brought the ascendance of finance to its apogee. That high point came into view beginning in 1976, when Zondervan became a public company.

What is a public company? Fundamentally, public companies are not private companies, owned by private individuals or groups. Private proprietorships belong to a single owner; private partnerships distribute ownership and liability between partners; and private corporations divide companies into any number of shares. Although companies have incorporated for centuries, the process became available to ordinary businesses in the United States only in the second half of the nineteenth century, when "general incorporation" replaced an earlier paradigm that required legislatures to grant all corporate charters.[62] By incorporating, companies become independent entities, protecting both companies and their shareholders from each other's legal liabilities and debts. Incorporation also allows a company to raise money by selling its shares, essentially trading portions of ownership for shareholders' money, which serves as investment capital. While private corporations sell or allocate their shares privately, public corporations offer shares to the public. Offering investors a promise to seek financial return on their investment, public companies do not demand in return that investors share the company's avowed principles. This fact is what James Apostalakis had in mind when he noted that Zondervan is "a public company and they have public shareholders," no matter what they believe.[63]

But if one definition of a public company emphasizes forms of ownership, another definition highlights the logic at the heart of public ownership. Insofar as public companies trust public shareholders to operate not only in their own best interests but also in the best interests of the company in which they share ownership, public companies manifest faith in the market. As the economic historian Ron Harris explains, England became in 1844 the first country to adopt general incorporation, due in part to a free market ideology whose "underlying principle was to replace the discretion exercised by state officials with one exercised by investors."[64] This ideology reached back at least to the eighteenth century. "Every individual necessarily labours to render the annual revenue of the society as great as he can," Adam Smith explained in The Wealth of Nations (1776), adding that each individual serves society unwittingly, by "pursuing his own interest." In this way, Smith famously suggested, an individual is "led by an invisible hand to promote an end which was no part of his intention."[65] This notion that general social benefit flows from activity that expresses an individual's perceived self-interest became a founding principle of classical economic liberalism. In the twentieth century, neoclassical thinkers repurposed classical theories of self-interest, replacing Smith's ideal of the individual owner with the individual shareholder, whose self-interest has stood theoretically in alignment with the corporation's interest.[66]

The ideal of the supportive yet self-interested shareholder became a central theme of business manuals from around 1960 that encouraged corporations to consider public financing. A manual from 1959 begins by acknowledging that the owners of closely held private companies often feared losing control over their firms. Written by Maxwell Mangold, the head of the management consultancy Corporate Growth Consultants, Inc., the manual addressed owners' anxiety by claiming that public ownership of corporate shares actually protects majority owners insofar as it weakens the power of any particular minority interest. "In actual practice," Mangold explained, "control is more uncertain if a large minority interest is sold to one or two or even a small group of individuals rather than if shares are sold to the public."[67] Public stock supposedly had this effect by generating the support of diverse investors who offered their financial support for their own self-interested reasons.

In the model of the public company that Mangold championed, shareholders pursued financial self-interest that aligned neatly with the corporation's own interest. Mangold described the strength of that alignment as "public confidence."[68] In this way public companies essentially trusted shareholders to have confidence in long-term growth, even potentially despite evidence in the short-term. And public companies actively asked shareholders to see their investment as an expression of self-interest, which also served the corporation's interest. To transform a private company into a public company is to believe that public shareholders, through the open market, naturally would resolve any tension between self-interest and corporate interest. They would do so by expressing or withholding confidence on the basis of growth. What is good for the company is good for an investor, and what is good for an investor is good the company.

Although Zondervan's executives may not have read Max Mangold's particular manual, the sort of belief that Mangold describes is what propelled Zondervan's own decision to become a public company in 1976. "We believed that, over the long term," Zondervan CEO Peter Kladder explained following the public offering, "the majority of our stock will be in the hands of people who can relate to us personally." Speaking for the board of directors, Kladder explained: "We felt that there were many people who were investment-minded, but who were also like-minded spiritually and would be eager to see their money working two ways: first, to grow in an investment situation, and second, to be supportive of a kingdom cause."[69] By inviting public investors, Kladder suggested, Zondervan expected the market not just to effect the company's mission but to do so through profit-seeking investors, who could proverbially eat their financial cake and still have it spiritually.

So it was that Kladder had begun meeting with underwriting companies in the early 1970s to "tell the Zondervan story." The 1973 prospectus described Zondervan as a company that pursued all of its activities "with an evangelical Christian perspective." Explaining that "the Company attributes a measure of its growth in the past several years to a reawakening of evangelical Christianity in the United States," it also admitted that its growth had resulted from "the Company's expanded distribution capability."[70] Zondervan's annual financial reports from the early 1980s emphasized this elision of spiritual and financial investment. As a 1982 profile of Ruth Peale (the wife of the prosperity preacher and free enterprise advocate Norman Vincent Peale) explained, "Ruth believes so deeply in the ministry of publishing that when Zondervan offered the public a chance to participate in its publishing ministry by becoming a shareholder, she jumped at the opportunity." The report added: "Ruth Peale is a fine example of the kind of investors that the Zondervan Corporation attracts. Many of them share with the company a desire to strengthen the ministry."[71] In a way, these remarks illustrate how Zondervan continued to prioritize its ministry mission at a time when public corporations increasingly acknowledged an obligation to maximize shareholder value.[72] Yet in another way, the remarks reveal how Zondervan committed itself to a tradition that made its religious mission and its shareholder value inextricable.

UNLIMITED MARKETS

Consistently, evangelical media corporations have insisted that their embrace of finance has not changed how they have understood their religious mission or audience. In 1984 Peter Kladder predicted that the company could "double current sales within five years yet retain the same religious tone that has marked Zondervan from the beginning."[73] Financial growth and commercial expansion could even enhance the company's ability to broadcast its religious tone. But what is a "religious tone"? The phrase's ambiguity neither articulates any particular doctrinal perspective nor identifies any specific denominational constituency. The historical gesture toward "the beginning" adds little specificity. "We're basically open to all sorts of approaches," Kladder remarked in 1985, "although the background of the company is Protestant evangelical."[74] As these remarks suggest, the boundaries of the company's corporate address appeared limitless.

Capitalizing on the malleability of Zondervan's commercial religion, the company had worked since 1980 to overhaul what spokespeople described as its "lackadaisical" business practices. "There's only one way to go," Kladder had insisted in 1980, "and that's up." Boasting that "we are becoming more sophisticated," Kladder had remarked that "we have been inbred for too long, operating more from tradition instead of from results." New practices included a formal budget-making process, the hiring of a head of marketing, and the use of headhunting firms to identify potential new executives.[75] According to one profile of the company in 1984, executives had hoped that the 1980s would become "a time . . . to double—perhaps even quadruple—the firm's size."

Whether evaluating "size" with reference to sales, products, or its portfolio of subsidiaries, Zondervan arguably succeeded by the middle of the 1985.[76] Between 1976 and 1985 the company's new revenue streams allowed it to acquire several music and book publishers. In 1980, for example, Zondervan purchased a majority stake in Benson Company, a Nashville-based producer and distributor of religious music and recordings. The purchase brought Zondervan an additional $5.2 million of revenue in 1980 and $15.7 in 1981. By 1983 Zondervan traded some of its stock for complete ownership of both Benson and Marshall Pickering, a British publisher of Christian literature.[77] The firm acquired Chosen Books in 1981 and Fleming H. Revell Company in 1983. An acquisition announcement described the Revell Company as "the house of best sellers" and touted its connection to Dwight Moody. These two acquisitions brought Zondervan such leading evangelical authors as Joyce Landorf, Helen Steiner Rice, James Dobson, John Stott, J. I. Packer, and Charles Colson. Zondervan also bought a New Jersey–based company that specialized in fine leather bookbinding, enhancing its bible publishing capabilities. And Zondervan dramatically multiplied the number of its retail stores. From thirty-nine stores in seventeen states at the time of its public offering in 1976, Zondervan established eighty-nine by the summer of 1984, making it one of the largest bookstore chains in the United States.[78]

Throughout this era of expansion, Zondervan was not the only company to nurture faith in finance. The company Thomas Nelson provides another example. The Lebanese immigrant and entrepreneur Sam Moore purchased Thomas Nelson from its English owners in 1969. Founded in 1844 and focused primarily on bible publishing, the firm had possessed exclusive rights to the American Standard Version (until 1928) and the Revised Standard Version (until 1962). But after losing its hold on the RSV, sales fell from $10 million in 1962 to just $1.4 million in 1968. Moore acquired the firm in that financially depressed state.[79] Born in 1930 as Salim Ziady in Beirut, Moore had come to the United States in 1950 to attend Columbia Bible College in South Carolina, on the recommendation of an American missionary. After discovering a knack for selling books and bibles door-to-door, Moore created National Book Company in 1957 and then Royal Publishers in 1962. Both companies focused mostly on bibles. Moore subsequently purchased Thomas Nelson for $2.6 million with cash generated by selling shares in Royal; Billy Graham's mother reportedly purchased one hundred shares. Combining his firms under the Thomas Nelson name, Moore listed Thomas Nelson on the NASDAQ and then the New York Stock Exchange (NYSE) in 1995. Moore later described the day of the company's NYSE listing as "one of the most exciting days of my life." He explained that the NYSE provided "the greatest exposure for its companies in the worldwide markets," and he also argued that worldwide markets allowed the company to pursue its mission most effectively.[80]

Moore's comments illustrate how public ownership led both Thomas Nelson and Zondervan to reimagine their expansive markets and publics. In 1984 a newsletter produced by and for Zondervan's employees asked them to answer a simple question: "Who are our customers?" Virtually every response published in the newsletter avoided bounded theological interpretations of Zondervan's market, focusing instead on the supremacy of any potential consumer. Bruce Ryskamp, president of company's bible division, answered the question by quoting a passage from Earl Nightingale's *The Customer*: "The Customer is the one person who pays everyone's salary and who decides whether a business is going to succeed or fail." Ryskamp added, "The people who ultimately will pay our salaries and determine the future success of Zondervan's are not our distributors, our dealers, our salesmen, our advertising, our executives, etc. These people are all important as vehicles in helping us reach the final decision maker with our product—*the consumer.*" Meanwhile, other employees emphasized a strategically vague understanding of those consumers. "Zondervan's customers are *every living person*," Dave Kok, an employee in the print shop, explained, "whether rich or poor, healthy or sick. From the baby who can only look at pictures to the elderly who can only read large-print. . . . Zondervan customers are *unlimited.*"[81]

In a way, an "unlimited" understanding of its audience aligns with common understandings of evangelicalism. It even accords with definitions of evangelicalism that emphasize such characteristics as "conversionism" and "activism," which together gesture toward an active pursuit of "unlimited" conversions to Christianity.[82] Citing Jesus's injunction in Matthew 28:19 to "make disciples of all nations," an employee in the book sales department remarked, "Our customers are the entire world—if we believe the *Great Commission.*" Seemingly enacting this Commission, the company even reached beyond Christian readers. Discussing the company's turn toward "modern packaging and marketing techniques," for example, one profile from 1980 explains how Zondervan planned to capitalize on the Jewish Feast of Purim to market one of its lead books for that fall, a fictional story based on the Hebrew Bible book of Esther by the author Gini Andrews, entitled *Esther: The Star and Sceptre.* "Zondervan will market the book heavily in New York," the *Grand Rapids Press* reported, "in search of strong sales in the large Jewish population."[83] Yet even if this plan to transform Jewish readers into customers arguably expressed the soteriological objective of leading Jews to accept the Christian messiah, the plan also reflected an effort to shift away from more bounded conceptions of its market.[84]

Had Zondervan's business model and stock revenue enabled the company to heed the Great Commission on a scale it had not previously? Or, by contrast, had conversionist ideology and rhetoric allowed the company to justify its desire to raise revenue and secure the price of its stock, in the name of feeding the confidence of public shareholders? The question is impossible to answer, because Zondervan executives themselves would have answered both questions affirmatively. More to the point, the impulse to reduce Zondervan's motivation to principle or profit obscures the company's fundamental elision of religion and results. Sacred tradition had enabled that financial faith.

Plainly, Zondervan's "religious tone" did not alienate investors who had no particular interest in explicit evangelical intonations; to the contrary, investors found the tone appealing, not least because they recognized the expansionist objectives and market principles that it carried. Due to the dramatic growth of its corporate size and objectives, Zondervan's public status drew attention from financial analysts and investors, who increasingly became confident that Zondervan and its evangelical audience would continue to grow. Since the 1970s both surveys and media attention had suggested the same. Writing for *Barron's National Business and Financial Weekly* in 1983, Nanine Alexander praised the firm's 50 percent increase in profit between 1976 and 1979, as well as the 25 percent increase between the first nine months of 1981 and 1982. Market analysts increasingly touted this "'excellent' growth potential," praising the company's recent reorganization into five divisions, each led by its own manager. The financial analyst Robert Stovall, who dispensed investment advice regularly on PBS's "Wall Street Week," reportedly described Zondervan as "the best stock buy of 1983." That year Zondervan reported sales of $92.8 million; by comparison, the firm's closest competitor—Thomas Nelson—had sales of just $61 million. Citing a study of twenty-nine book publishers, produced by a private investment firm in New York, *Business Week* reported in 1984 that Zondervan's earnings had increased at a rate that consistently outperformed the general publishing industry.[85]

But as investor attention translated into further capital investment, which in turn fueled additional expansion, which in turn created new debts that required further capital investment, Zondervan found itself in a circular cycle that weakened its self-direction. Eventually Zondervan's financialization generated a corporate crisis. In October 1984, after a few years in which the company experienced what the *Wall Street Journal* described as "a considerable following on Wall Street," Zondervan announced a large loss. The company lost more than $400,000 in the third financial quarter of 1984, due to unexpected taxes on inventory that its bookstore chain had lost.[86] Zondervan also announced that it would reduce or "write-down" its pretax value by $1 million. Because financial investors learned of the loss before the public, the stock price declined by 21 percent, and the Securities and Exchange Commission subsequently launched an investigation into the disclosure as well as the public's seemingly mistaken understanding of the company's financial condition.[87] The SEC had an obligation to protect those public shareholders because most of Zondervan's shares belonged to the public.

Zondervan also launched an internal investigation into the inventory loss. By the spring of 1985 at least one cause appeared: the computerized inventory system that the company had touted as a pillar of corporate expansion had failed. Designed to keep track of sales and inventory in the company's rapidly proliferating bookstores, neither the system and nor its human users could keep of track stores' growing transactions. Before announcing this discovery, however, Zondervan followed its initial write-down with an additional $4 million in December 1984, citing inventory loss, royalty advances that would not be recouped through sales, and other debt obligations.[88] Although a bookkeeping error reportedly lit the proverbial fuse of Zondervan's crisis, the crisis took shape through a tradition of financial faith, which had sanctified an ambitious corporate expansion, performed in the name of continued growth, all of which the company financed through public stock offerings and the rising sales that those offerings made possible.

A CRISIS OF FAITH

The notion of faith or belief helps explain why any company or person might pursue practices that in hindsight seem inconsistent. In its colloquial sense, "faith" typically is a thing that people possess, often after accepting specific propositions self-consciously. Yet as the ritual theorist Catherine Bell has suggested, faith can be seen more productively as a continual process, through which people struggle to embrace particular understandings of the present or future despite inconsistent and even contradictory ideas, actions, and evidence.[89] Configured by sacred tradition, this sort of faith is what enabled Zondervan to remain confident that investors would support its avowed mission despite the real possibility that public ownership would weaken their control over their company or even reduce it to little more than a set of disenchanted legal contracts.[90]

Historically, owners and managers of larger corporations have tended to cede control of a corporation as it grows. This has been the case since the end of the nineteenth century, when large corporations began proliferating and financing their growth through securities and stock. After all, a share of corporate stock is a liquid asset, designed to be traded fluidly and maximized in value.[91] Control accordingly has attenuated, the economic historian Naomi Lamoreaux explains, precisely because tradable assets enable and encourage investors to pursue their financial interests above all else—even at the expense of the corporation or its employees.[92] Highlighting the distinction between a "corporate capitalism" focused on a company's success and a "financial capitalism" focused on investment in those companies, the historian Ranald Michie adds that public corporations make "investment . . . center stage, with everything directed towards maximizing the returns obtained." For this reason, Michie argues, public corporations "have been found not to be ideal where a strong and continuous bond between owners and managers was necessary for success."[93] As a public company, Zondervan's stockholders essentially became its owners, and the bond between those owners and its managers became less strong and continuous. But Zondervan's executives had believed in that bond, even as that belief created an opportunity for shareholders to attack the firm.

The firm came under attack in 1986. Responding to the company's depressed stock value, a group of uneasy shareholders began plotting a takeover. In Zondervan's view the chief villain became a British investor named Christopher Moran. Early in 1986 Moran began buying Zondervan shares. Described as "hard-nosed and litigious," Moran purchased 5.4 percent of Zondervan's public shares by February 1986, and he acquired almost 10 percent by August.[94] Moran also established a contractual agreement with other shareholders that placed almost 30 percent of Zondervan's shares under his formal control. Between this formal agreement, his own shares, and informal agreements with shareholders who owned additional 22 percent, Moran controlled more than half of the firm's shares. With this majority support, Moran offered to purchase the company for $23.50 per share, and he demanded representation on the company's board of directors. "We will consider any and all steps to protect shareholder interest," one of Moran's supporters insisted, "and prevent any waste of corporate assets." Hostile shareholders advocated for Zondervan to sell some of the companies it recently had acquired, including Fleming H. Revell Company.[95]

In the end, Zondervan dodged Moran's takeover attempt by agreeing in October 1986 to seek a buyer. When news of that decision broke, the firm's stock price accordingly rose, and Moran relented. Zondervan ultimately found a buyer in the publishing company Harper & Row (renamed HarperCollins in 1990), a division of the conglomerate News Corporation, which purchased Zondervan for $56.7 million, or $13.50 per share. But why, if willing to sell itself, did Zondervan heed Moran's request to sell the corporation but turn down his offer to buy it?

Zondervan had rebuffed Moran by citing a conflict between the company's principles and Moran's personality. Executives claimed that they disapproved of Moran's past behavior as well as his ideas for the future. Reportedly ousted from a British insurance firm due to "discreditable acts" and later investigated for insider trading, Moran also had floated a number of ideas that Zondervan employees abhorred, including the possibility of opening Zondervan's bookstores on Sunday. As a result Zondervan cast itself as the victim of a disreputable individual and his associates. Throughout 1986, employees organized prayer meetings at the company's headquarters, to seek divine protection from what they perceived as an attack on the company.[96] At a summer rally, the Christian recording star Phil Driscoll led 150 employees through a hopeful session of singing and prayer. Reading from a story in 2 Chronicles of the Hebrew Bible, in which foreign armies wage war against King Jehoshaphat, Driscoll likened Moran to Jehoshaphat's enemies. "Do not be afraid or discouraged because of this vast army," Driscoll insisted. A couple months before this rally, two dozen employees in the printing department had met to pray that Christopher Moran would come "to understand the mission of the company."[97]

Yet even if these employees were right to note that Moran's understanding of the company seemed to conflict with their own, their prayers did not acknowledge that Moran understood part of the company's mission very clearly. Above all, Moran understood that Zondervan had prioritized both expansion and profit, and he insisted that the company had not fully honored that aspect of its tradition. Speaking from that tradition in his Christmas message to employees for 1987, James Buick did not attribute the previous years' turmoil to any fundamental flaw in the company's business practices. "While uncertainty is a characteristic of life on this earth," he remarked, "we do have the certainty that God is in charge and will see us through the difficult as well as the good times."[98] Instead of suggesting that the company revise its financial strategies and corporate structures, Buick simply attributed Zondervan's crisis to the inscrutable ways of a loving but unknowable God. Although initially uneasy with News Corporation's acquisition, financial faith even allowed Zondervan's employees to find themselves comfortable in their conglomerate's embrace.

At first, many employees feared that Harper & Row would change their company's structure and culture, in the name of maximizing profit. "Will the two sales forces be consolidated?" one employee asked George Craig, the president and CEO of Harper & Row, when he visited Grand Rapids in August 1988. Another asked: "Will you sell Family Bookstores?" Although HarperCollins went on to lay off dozens of workers in 1992 and deemed the bookstore division a "noncompatible venture" in 1994, Craig initially denied any desire for change. But some Zondervan employees worried even more that their company's religious culture would change than they did about structural changes. "Will there be any change in the publishing mission of the company?" one employee asked Craig. "In no way," Craig responded, "will we interfere in your publishing mission." Repeating the same question, more specifically, another employee asked: "Will we soften our Christian view when selling books and music?" Craig replied, "This company was built on solid principles and a good foundation. . . . We will not interfere with that." Craig insisted that he had not come to Grand Rapids "as a bureaucrat, thinking of just numbers. I'm here to encourage the executives and the management teams to get actively involved in this joining of forces. . . . I look at this as a good opportunity for both businesses, a start of a new *partnership* utilizing the strengths of both Harper & Row and Zondervan."[99]

But Craig's assurances also stood in contrast with public statements that Harper & Row already had made regarding its acquisition of Zondervan and its understanding of the company's ministry. Addressing the acquisition in the *Wall Street Journal*, Harper & Row announced that the consolidated company would combine its diverse consumer constituencies. The article explained that "Harper publishes some 130 new religious books a year, ranging from Catholic to New Age"; meanwhile, "Zondervan's publishing division is targeted toward the narrower evangelical Christian market." Moving forward, one of Harper & Row's vice presidents explained, "We think Zondervan can take parts of our list into their market, and we'll do the same with their list in our market." Craig described the opportunity to reimagine Harper & Row's market as "the most exciting aspect of the whole acquisition." Within months, Zondervan had accepted almost 400 books, including such varied titles as *Harper's Bible Commentary* and Shel Silverstein's *The Giving Tree*.[100]

Unease within Zondervan even inspired an effort in 1992 to purchase the company back from News Corporation. "The motivation is to return the direction and control of the company into the Christian community," Buick explained. Insisting that HarperCollins had shown "an incredible level of support," Buick justified the move by noting that "corporate structures can change." By purchasing Zondervan, Buick and his associates hoped to "put it in a secure position for the long term." Ultimately, however, the buyout failed for at least one simple reason: the price was too high. George Craig justified a high price by pointing out that HarperCollins had assumed Zondervan's debts in the 1988 acquisition; and since then, Zondervan had become much more profitable.

Despite all of this unease, financial faith allowed Zondervan and its employees to overcome their anxiety about being accountable to News Corporation. Tranquility already had started to appear in 1991, the year that Zondervan celebrated its sixtieth anniversary. For that occasion, the company put together a booklet describing its history and activity. The first pages featured testimonials from a variety of evangelical leaders, executives, authors, and even politicians. Billy Graham remarked that "the great contribution that Zondervan has made in the field of religious literature is as great as any publishing house in the world." A former president of the United States, Gerald Ford, insisted that Zondervan had advanced "the great American principle of Freedom of Religion," insofar as that principle "implies, among other things, the wide dissemination of religious books and publications." Senator Mark O. Hatfield praised Zondervan for managing "to keep its eyes on the goal of serving Christ and glorifying God while engaged in a business enterprise."[101] Following these quotations, an overview of Zondervan's history and ownership status assured readers that HarperCollins Publishers had allowed Zondervan to maintain "its editorial independence and evangelical integrity" while also providing the company with "an avenue into the general market." A less explicit endorsement of HarperCollins's support appeared later in the booklet, in a timeline of Zondervan's achievements. Listing the years between 1931 and 1991, most entries before 1988 included three to five bullet points. But the years 1989 and 1990 featured thirteen and then twenty-one. The message of this list was clear: if the company's history before 1988 had seen it become "as great as any publishing house in the world," the acquisition had allowed it to become even greater.

Buick and his associates undoubtedly held this narrative in mind in 1992 when their campaign to extract Zondervan from News Corporation overlapped with a competing campaign. During the fall of 1992 Thomas Nelson completed its acquisition of Word, Inc., a merger that united Zondervan's two largest competitors. Insofar as that merger dramatically increased Thomas Nelson's financial resources and publishing clout, News Corporation's financial resources suddenly held more appeal. One executive remarked, "It's like having a bank built-in."[102] That appeal only grew in succeeding years, as private equity firms and public conglomerates increased their stakes in evangelical publishing. The solution to Zondervan's crisis ultimately demanded more financial faith rather than less.

CONCLUSION

Although Buick and his associates dreamed briefly about returning Zondervan to "the Christian community," the ideal of closely held private ownership became the exception rather than the rule in the evangelical book industry. Seeking to maximize growth, evangelical corporations increasingly treated conglomerate ownership and sales of stock as necessary conditions of service to God. The problem with this sacred tradition, however, was that the ascendance of shareholder value limited the ability of corporations to do anything that might depress potential profits. By 1980, the historian Gerald Davis argues, corporations that tried to retain tight managerial control over their priorities and principles inspired critics of "managerialism" to conclude that "those that viewed the corporation as a social institution were deluding themselves."[103] While the concept of "delusion" provides one way of denoting an attempt to confront and overcome perceived contradictions, I offer "faith" as a more empathetic way of describing evangelical efforts to navigate the contradictions of financial capitalism.

Sometimes, however, faith abides delusion. In 2016, for example, when Thomas Nelson joined Zondervan as part of HarperCollins Christian Publishing, evangelical executives from a variety of evangelical publishing companies expressed surprise about the news. "I just did not see that coming," a senior executive at the publishing firm Crossway told me.[104] For years evangelical firms in Grand Rapids and beyond often had ridiculed Thomas Nelson. Considering that Thomas Nelson had overtaken Zondervan in the 1990s as the largest religious publisher in the United States, that ridicule undoubtedly reflected some jealousy.[105] But critics of Thomas Nelson also accused the company of pure commercialism. Although Zondervan continually had expanded the variety of theological ideas and devotional practices that its books engaged with, it always had proved unwilling or unable to capture the market for books by authors associated with the prosperity gospel, a catchall term for teachings that focus on what the historian Kate Bowler describes as "spiritual, physical, and financial mastery." Meanwhile, Thomas Nelson regularly had published titles by internationally preeminent prosperity preachers, such as Benny Hinn and T. D. Jakes.[106] These and other books and authors came up in conversations I had with Zondervan's employees before the merger, when the mention of Thomas Nelson regularly elicited the exclamation: "They'll publish anything!" In the end, however, it was a delusion to imagine such a strong distinction between the two companies. For decades, Zondervan and Thomas Nelson both had championed financial faith, and their merger simply manifested the sacred tradition that shaped their shared convictions.

The Spirit of Market Segmentation

MAKING SOMETHING FOR EVERYONE

CELEBRATING A RECENT BUSINESS deal in February 1990, the conservative Australian media tycoon Rupert Murdoch hosted a dinner party at his apartment in New York. The guest of honor was the former Marine Corps lieutenant colonel Oliver North, who had become famous—and also infamous—for his leading role in what became known as the Iran-Contra scandal. While serving on the staff of the National Security Council under Ronald Reagan, North coordinated the sale of weapons to Iran, in order to secure the release of American hostages and raise funds to support to Nicaraguan rebels who opposed their country's socialist government. Through his unapologetic testimony before a televised congressional inquest, North became an icon of Reagan-era conservatism, embodying the conjunctive cause of anticommunism, patriotism, and militarism. Following his conviction in May 1989 for obstructing a congressional investigation of the entire operation, many political conservatives in the United States came to see North as a kind of martyr. That status provided him a ready-made audience—what is often described by media executives as a commercial "platform."

And so, just a few months after being sentenced to a suspended prison term, North had decided to take advantage of his newfound platform by writing a memoir. Initiating contractual conversations in secrecy, for fear of jeopardizing the ongoing appeal of his conviction, North reportedly contacted Harper & Row before any other publisher, due in part to his interest in its recent acquisition of the Zondervan Corporation. One of North's editors at Zondervan later explained, "North wanted access to the evangelical Christian market through Zondervan."[1] In the eyes of executives at both Harper & Row and News Corporation, North's book presented an opportunity to attempt collaborative co-publishing with their new corporate possession. A publishing agreement between North, Harper & Row, and Zondervan occasioned the dinner party. Murdoch hosted it as founder, CEO, and leading shareholder of News Corporation, which had acquired Harper & Row in 1987.[2]

But not everyone at the party had initially supported the agreement. Skeptical Zondervan editors identified two primary problems. First, some feared that North would not be able to give sufficient "evidence of his Christian faith" to make his story "suitable for the CBA market." The company had abandoned other deals for similar reasons, but Zondervan's editors felt sufficient commercial cause to baptize North with suitability. To generate material for the book, they met with North and his co-writer, William Novak, to "grill" North about his "spiritual journey." They also amended and annotated Novak's notes on their eight-hour interview.[3] Drawing on those interviews, Novak's writing evidenced North's faith through frequent remarks about North's perceptions of divine providence, anecdotes about his prayer habits, and descriptions of North's interest in both the Bible and books by authoritative evangelical authors like James Dobson.[4]

By remaking North in their own image, Zondervan's editors had addressed the first problem. Yet the second problem was harder to resolve. Recognizing that the general public knew North not for any kind of religious devotion but instead for his willingness to pursue illegal activities in the name of conservative political loyalties, Zondervan's editors had feared that a relationship with North would create the impression that Zondervan viewed political conservatism as a defining feature of their corporate identity. Even though they recognized that many in "the Christian market" undoubtedly appreciated North and his politics, some editors worried about giving potential consumers cause to conclude that Zondervan was "captive to political conservatives and fundamentalist activists."[5] And despite their best efforts to address this problem, North's book ultimately tethered conservatism to Christianity exactly as some of Zondervan's editors had feared it would. The majority of *Under Fire: An American Story* focuses on detailing North's secret activities, recounting his testimony and trial, and conveying his overall message: "With our history and our ideals," North argues near the end of his book, "the United States should never have allowed revolution and change to become the exclusive domain of the left." Conservatives can and should, North goes on to insist, "abandon our old tendency to support the status quo."[6] In short: North called for a politically active conservatism, which aligned with the orientation of the New Christian Right.

This second problem proved more difficult because it involved an ongoing shift in how evangelical companies understood and addressed their audiences. At the heart of this shift lay the principle of market segmentation, according to which a company approaches its potential consumer constituency not as a unitary market but rather as an amalgam of subgroups, segments, or niches. During the final decades of the twentieth century, evangelical companies came to treat segmentation as a key strategy of commercial expansion. Insofar as evangelicals often had viewed evangelicalism and the evangelical market as a constituency that operated in contradistinction with mainline Protestantism and the general consumer market, evangelicals long had been sympathetic to market segmentation's logic. But as the anxiety about Oliver North's authorship illustrates, the evangelical ideal of unified opposition to a liberal religious mainstream also had led companies like Zondervan to envision the evangelical market with a focus more on the power of its collective whole rather than its potential parts. As a result, cultures of evangelicalism accommodated politically moderate and even liberal sensibilities well into the 1980s.[7] Yet as segmentation strategy encouraged evangelical companies to break their mass markets into submarkets, dissimilarity and disagreement increasingly defined evangelical publics, which became legible only when they served as useful market segments. Among evangelicalism's market segments, a socially and politically conservative segment achieved social prominence and significant success.

More than just a means by which evangelical companies sought to raise revenue, segmentation strategy oriented how ostensible evangelicals and outside observers came to understand and experience evangelicalism itself. The same market research that fueled domestic "Church Growth" initiatives, which called for churches to cater to people's unique perspectives and needs, inspired the creation of new bibles and bible translations for distinct market segments. After encountering success niching the Bible, evangelical institutions also began cultivating African American and Latino consumer segments. Although those commercial efforts challenged evangelicalism's whiteness, segmentation strategy simultaneously licensed the creation of an evangelical public that endorsed a strident mode of conservatism.

As the saga of Oliver North's authorship illustrates, a conservative constituency did not possess the full support of Zondervan's editors in 1990. Yet the ongoing salience of "family values" already had led Harper & Row to recognize the commercial potential of a market focused on that preoccupation. Toward the end of the twentieth century and into the twenty-first, some of News Corporation's other subsidiaries also would build businesses around a conservative segment. Those media outlets included the conglomerate's Fox News Channel, which would help braid a form of evangelical identity together with devotion to the political and social agenda of the Republican Party.

SEGMENTING THE WHOLE

A feature of commercial common sense today, market segmentation achieved ascendance through the effort of ostensibly secular and avowedly religious interpreters. As a formal marketing technique, segmentation strategy appeared during the 1960s. It developed as a response to commercial emphasis on the notion of the mass market, which treated consumers as members of "a broad and generalized" unit.[8] Although mass-market strategy had allowed companies to achieve economies of scale by addressing large sets of consumers, marketing strategists increasingly had come to see the mass market as a "myth" that served few products well. "The concept of segmentation is based on the proposition that *consumers are different*," a team of marketing consultants explained in 1971. Segmentation strategy accordingly called for companies to adapt their "product or service to suit the distinct wants of selected groups of buyers."[9]

Aspects of segmentation strategy began taking shape long before marketing professionals codified its principles. As one historian of marketing remarks, turn-of-the-century producers of consumer goods "knew very well that a single product did not satisfy everyone."[10] Relatively early in the nineteenth century, evangelical bible and tract societies started designing products that might appeal to different aesthetic tastes and social classes. In its 1834 annual report, for example, the American Bible Society announced the creation of two new bibles, each a different size. Both bibles were printed "on fine paper and bound in embossed calf, and yet are furnished at a moderate price."[11] During the first half of the twentieth century, evangelical publishers continued offering multiple design options. In its fall 1943–spring 1944 catalog, Zondervan offered bibles with optional features that included genuine or imitation leather covers, thin "India paper," and a concordance. In addition to touting the interpretive assistance or aesthetic options of any given bible, publishers also suggested which consumers might find particular features most appealing. In 1834 the American Bible Society suggested that its new small reference bible might "be found highly convenient and useful among Sunday-school teachers and Bible-class scholars." Similarly, Zondervan suggested in 1944 that its concordance bible's light weight and small size made it ideal for people in the military. The company also suggested that a larger bible with large type might serve well for the elderly, for schools, and for pulpits.[12] Although these and countless other potential examples demonstrate that commercial publishers and commodity producers became sensitive to diverse consumer preferences over a century before the advent of market segmentation strategy, this attention to consumer preferences had continued to presume a mass-market orientation. In almost every case, companies bundled features on the hunch that significant proportions of a mass market might find particular bundles appealing.

By contrast, the heart of market segmentation lay not just in a general awareness of diverse consumer preferences but especially in the practice of identifying distinct consumer constituencies and creating products tailored to those idealized groups. This process often claimed a scientific rationale and drew upon social scientific research methods. Describing how a company might gain a better understanding of its groups of buyers, one marketing consultant suggested undertaking a "market-dissection process," which would reveal useful "statistical facts about consumers," such as age, income level, and family size; "behavior traits," such as "social-class membership or "ethnic origin"; and "psychological characteristics of consumers." By paying attention to such criteria, the consultant explained by way of an example, a rice company had decided to focus on people who had never cooked rice, and a coffee company had realized that "certain religious groups represent much higher volume potentials per capita than do other groups." Only by dissecting their markets through consumer research had these companies fragmented their previously undifferentiated markets.[13]

This sort of market-dissection strategy relied upon social scientific methodologies that took shape during the 1920s and 1930s. As early as 1911, institutions such as the Harvard Bureau of Business Research had begun aggregating sales figures and reporting profits for varied industries and locations, thereby inaugurating modern market research. But consumer research subsequently came to rely especially upon sampling techniques and interview protocols that sought to measure with greater precision American identities and desires.[14] George Gallup, the best-known champion of these methods, became a pioneer of public opinion polling after founding his American Institute of Public Opinion in 1935. Correlating respondents' political and cultural preferences with their education, class, gender, and age, Gallup sought not just to quantify respondents' differences but also to create a comprehensive portrait of "the people's voice," which Americans supposedly shared despite their apparent differences.[15] Almost from the start, Gallup offered his services to companies that hoped to learn more about their potential consumer constituencies.

Although Gallup developed a reputation for accurate sampling methods and adaptable survey designs, his obsession with measuring social differences and unities had found earlier advocates in a variety of religious institutions. Beginning especially in the 1880s, Protestant church leaders and philanthropists had organized "sociological canvasses" of urban neighborhoods in order to identify social problems that constrained church attendance and depressed standards of living. Following World War I those ecumenical initiatives inspired the creation of institutions such as the Interchurch World Movement, which used funding from John D. Rockefeller Jr. to compile and correlate statistics regarding labor unrest, divorce, migration, race relations, and church attendance. After the IWM disbanded in 1920, Rockefeller funded the Institute for Social and Religious Research (ISRR), which used both statistical research and canvassing to determine why rates of church affiliation seemingly grew more slowly than the general population.[16]

Typically focused on a particular city or region, the ISRR's research studies paid volunteers to canvas thousands of households, seeking detailed information about their religious and social lives.[17] Its most well-known study became the basis for the sociological classic *Middletown: A Study in Contemporary American Culture* (1929), written by Helen Lynd and her husband, Robert—an amateur social scientist and seminary graduate whom ISRR recruited for the project in 1922. Originally approaching the study as an analysis of church affiliation and attendance in a typical small city, the Lynds ultimately broadened it beyond church life by exploring social, cultural, and political activity in Muncie, Indiana—a "representative" American city with a "homogeneous" white population. Although many critics censured the Lynds for their inattention to racial and ethnic diversity, marketing professionals praised the book as a helpful portrait of American consumer preferences and consumption habits.[18]

While marketing professionals drew inspiration from the ISRR's study of Muncie, other ISRR studies of religious life also nurtured the spirit of segmentation strategy. In 1928, for instance, the ISRR provided financial support, strategic advice, and logistical support to a study organized in India by the National Christian Council of India, Burma, and Ceylon. Determined to identify social problems or concerns that prevented Indians from joining Christian churches, lead investigator and American Methodist missionary J. Waskom Pickett and a team of researchers used detailed interview schedules to canvas households throughout several regions of India. They found that Indians were far more "group-conscious" than "in the individualistic West," and Pickett accordingly concluded that missionaries should encourage "mass movements" or group conversions as "the most natural way of approach to Christ." This ISRR study incited subsequent Christian social scientists in India and elsewhere to ask how to best protect potential converts from experiencing what Pickett described as "social dislocation."[19] During the late 1930s and 1940s, the missionary and missiologist Donald McGavran pursued follow-up studies and evangelism campaigns in rural India that elaborated upon Pickett's conclusions. The leader of what became known as the "Church Growth" approach to missions, McGavran taught that missionaries should not waste precious resources attempting to convert people unlikely to embrace Christianity.

To describe McGavran's approach in commercial terms, he encouraged missionaries not to treat potential converts as members of a mass market. Instead, missionaries should focus on engaging coherent social groups or "homogeneous units," so that members of those units could convert more easily, without experiencing social dislocation. Distilling the rationale behind this strategy, McGavran explained that "people like to become Christians without crossing racial, linguistic, or class barriers."[20] Conversion, in short, should feel convenient. Just as segmentation strategy required market dissection, Church Growth strategy required missionaries to circumscribe the market that they sought to address. Missionaries defined the supposed homogeneity of particular social units on the basis of social characteristics such as caste, primary language, and what they recognized as racial differences.[21]

This emphasis on positing sociological divisions drew scorn from a variety of avowed evangelicals. The Ecuadorian theologian and missiologist C. René Padilla insisted that Christians constitute a "unit" based above all on faith in Jesus, "in which membership is in no way dependent upon race, social status, or sex." Padilla condemned Church Growth not only for prioritizing conversion over social action but also for highlighting markers of supposed difference and division between Christians, rather than "breaking down of the barriers that separate people in the world."[22] Responding to critics who insisted that South African supporters of apartheid and other racist segregationists had seen the homogeneous unit principle as a "seal of approval," proponents of Church Growth suggested that racially and ethnically homogeneous churches could and should establish "heterogeneous associations" of congregations.[23]

As Church Growth transformed during the 1970s from a mode for missiology used outside the United States into a mode of ecclesiology applied within the United States, the creation of homogeneous units relied even more on apparent social divisions based on categories of race, gender, and political allegiance. This transformation occurred in part through the efforts of C. Peter Wagner, one of McGavran's colleagues at Fuller Theological Seminary. Wagner distilled his interpretation of Church Growth theory in the title of his 1979 book, *Our Kind of People*. Lamenting that evangelicals had developed a "Christian guilt complex arising from the civil rights movement," the jacket for Wagner's book suggested that evangelicals transform the de facto segregation of evangelical churches "from a millstone around Christian necks into a dynamic tool for assuring Christian growth."[24] Wagner explained in 1986 that church leaders could pursue evangelism more efficiently and effectively by recognizing that "American ethnics are under-evangelized, compared especially to Anglos and blacks." He accordingly encouraged evangelists to develop approaches tailored specifically to each ethnic and racial constituency.[25] As the historian Molly Worthen surmises, the homogeneous-unit principle allowed its advocates to treat ostensible divisions of race and class as matters of cultural preference, which "seeker-sensitive" ministries and megachurches could treat as primary concerns.[26]

Recounting his experience implementing this approach at his own church in the guidebook *The Purpose Driven Church* (1995), Rick Warren detailed his church's focus on a niche associated with a "composite profile" that Warren named "Saddleback Sam." In one of his book's images, Warren depicted this ideal congregant. The image presents a forty-something white man wearing an oxford shirt and pleated chinos, with an accompanying caption that describes Saddleback Sam as someone who is well educated, likes his job, prioritizes health and fitness, and is "self-satisfied, even smug, about his station in life."[27] This fixation on identifying homogeneous "targets" based on race and class drew support from new research firms that used social scientific methodology to discern seeker preferences, such as Barna Research Group, which George Barna founded in 1984.[28]

For creators of evangelical media, homogeneous units functioned as productive market segments, and productive market segments served as ideal homogeneous units. To be sure, an emphasis on difference complemented the rhetoric that evangelical publishers long had used to describe their industry's rationale. While Dutch Reformed publishers had proclaimed "distinctiveness" as a watchword meant to appeal to both Reformed and fundamentalist consumers, neo-evangelical leaders like Wilbur Smith and Carl Henry championed difference in the 1940s by attacking what they had seen as the tyranny of middlebrow culture. All along, however, evangelical publishers had labored to reach a mass market. The appeal of segmentation strategy accordingly lay in its ability to champion cultural distinctiveness while also enabling unlimited expansion through the continual cultivation of new products for new or distinct consumer constituencies.

Inspired by the call to reduce the barriers over which potential converts must hurdle, bible translators and publishers set about developing countless bibles targeted to particular homogeneous units. Translation theorists such as Eugene Nida urged bible translators to focus not on capturing the "formal correspondence" between the original biblical languages and the target languages but instead on facilitating potential readers' understanding by using what he termed "dynamic equivalence."[29] The concept of dynamic equivalence gave translators permission to predicate their translation of any biblical passage upon what they saw as the passage's main point and the readers' ability to understand that point. This principle inspired a boom in "vernacular" or "colloquial" translations or paraphrases of the Bible. Some of these bibles appealed to the mass market. Examples include *The Living Bible,* a paraphrased version that Kenneth N. Taylor released in 1971 after publishing portions throughout the previous decade, as well as Today's English Version, a translation the American Bible Society released as the *Good News Bible* in 1976, a decade after releasing its New Testament as *Good News for Modern Man.* The creators of these bibles emphasized their broad accessibility, while noting that they might appeal most to young people, families, and people who read English as second language.[30]

But the alignment of segmentation strategy and the homogeneous unit principle also led evangelical publishers to consider the creation of bibles designed by and for avowed evangelicals. A prominent result of this effort became the New International Version (NIV) of the Bible. With portions of the New Testament appearing in 1973 and the entire bible released in 1978, the NIV took shape through two decades of evangelical effort. In the NIV no less than more thematically niched bibles, an idealized identity became a market category, which in turn nurtured the ideal identity from which it derived.

"THE VOICE OF GOD IN YOUR OWN WORDS"

Reporting the release of the New International Version of the Bible in the fall of 1978, an article in the *Washington Post* described the bible's target market in its title: "Newest Bible Said to Appeal to Evangelicals." The report elaborated by explaining that the NIV was "expected to appeal to conservative evangelicals."[31] A decade earlier, however, when the translation initiative had begun, its leaders preemptively had denied this claim. The translators insisted that they were not attempting to "produce a partisan 'evangelical' version," and they disavowed an "'evangelical club' mentality." Instead, they explained, the translation committee and its supporters simply wanted to let the Bible "speak as it wants to speak."[32] Denying that their bible translation was either "evangelical" or "partisan," they insisted that it was neutrally "biblical." But as the *Washington Post*'s profile recognized, that supposed neutrality belied the translators' commitment to what they described as the Bible's "full authority" as well as their claim that "no existing English translation of the Bible" had managed to honor that authority.[33] Their claim to the contrary notwithstanding, the NIV reflected the translators' evangelical sensibilities and evidenced their desire to create a bible by and for an evangelical niche. This approach allowed the NIV to sell out its initial print run of 1.2 million before its release in October 1978. By 1986, with 100 million copies in print, the NIV became the best-selling bible translation in the United States. Although King James Version (KJV) bibles always remained more prevalent due to that much older translation's lack of copyright restrictions, the NIV became recognized as the "most popular English-language bible," with an approximately 45 percent share of the bible market.[34]

Among the bibles that the NIV's translators deemed inadequate for "churches and individuals having similar viewpoint," the Revised Standard Version (RSV) reigned supreme.[35] Published in 1952 under the auspices of the National Council of Churches, the RSV drew a wide range of criticisms.[36] Accusing the NCC of commercialism, the executive committee of the National Association of Evangelicals faulted "certain features of advertising and promotion that appear to have been designed primarily to stimulate sales." More significantly, the NAE condemned some of the RSV translators' decisions, such as their decision to address God with a casual "you" rather than the more formal "thee" and "thou," as well as their decision to interpret the Hebrew word *almah* in Isaiah 7:14 as "young woman" rather than the KJV's "virgin."[37] Evangelicals claimed that the RSV's translation of *almah* undermined the passage's traditional status as a prophecy that referred to the virginal status of Jesus's mother.[38] Summarizing and intensifying criticisms of the RSV, the editor of the NAE's official magazine argued in 1953 that *"the RSV in many instances weakens the fundamentals of the Christian faith."* The editor claimed that the RSV's translators were *"practically all 'modernists'"* and insisted that "evangelicals should be roused to action," dedicating themselves to "the production of a new, universally-acceptable translation of the Holy Scriptures in the English vernacular."[39]

Viewing the RSV as a product that served its mass market well, several high-profile evangelical leaders and teachers refused to condemn it. They included senior professors at Fuller Theological Seminary, such as George Eldon Ladd, E. J. Carnell, Wilbur Smith, Carl Henry, and Harold Lindsell. In 1946 Carl Henry's Evangelical Book List had recommended the RSV's New Testament to evangelicals as "a translation that makes for pleasurable reading." Lindsell gave the RSV such strong support that he used the translation as the basis for his *Harper Study Bible* (1964).[40] Although Lindsell acknowledged that a distinctly evangelical translation theoretically could help gird evangelical faith, he also portrayed the attack on the RSV as a diversion. Pointing out that the King James language "still commands the affections of millions who do not understand what it means half the time, but who swear by it anyway," Lindsell remarked that evangelicals should focus above all on helping nonbelievers to encounter and understand the Bible.[41] Initially some evangelical publishers affirmed Lindsell's view. After 1965, when Zondervan Publishing House began publishing the RSV as well as Lindsell's study bible, Pat Zondervan became a vocal opponent of a new translation. And when the 1966 Synod of the Christian Reformed Church rejected a proposal to participate formally in a new translation initiative, Zondervan described the decision as a "great step forward."[42]

But Pat Zondervan would change his mind in 1971, when exclusive commercial rights to the new evangelical translation became available. The NIV initiative had begun in 1962, when committees from Calvin Theological Seminary and the National Association of Evangelicals first met together. After merging in 1964, the committees reorganized in 1966 as the fifteen-member Committee on Bible Translation (CBT).[43] Initially the CBT relied entirely on the financial backing of the New York Bible Society (NYBS). Founded in 1809, the NYBS became and has remained NIV's copyright holder. Not long after the CBT began its work, however, the NYBS's funding faltered, and news of the shortfall reached Pat Zondervan through Edwin H. Palmer, the pastor of a prominent Christian Reformed Church in Grand Rapids who also served as the CBT's executive secretary. Zondervan agreed to meet the CBT's financial needs in exchange for thirty years of exclusive copyright privileges to the translation. In 1995, the former NYBS—known by then as the International Bible Society (IBS)—extended those privileges for twenty-eight more years.[44]

How did the NIV's translators and publishers tailor their bible to evangelical sensibilities? It complemented a variety of particular theological claims, devotional practices, and social sensibilities. With respect to theology, the translators avoided phrases that conveyed unclear or ambiguous meanings. Some critics of the NIV lamented this fact, insisting that ambiguity was an essential feature of the text.[45] But ambiguity merited avoidance due in part to an evangelical emphasis on presuppositionalism, an idea that took shape through the teachings of figures like Abraham Kuyper and Francis Schaeffer. Defining presuppositions as "the basic way an individual looks at life, his basic world view," Schaeffer explained that presuppositions in turn drew authority from "that which a person considers to be the truth of what exists."[46] Although presuppositions ideally would enable readers to interpret ambiguous bible passages in ways that complement their presuppositions, the worry was that ambiguous passages also could undermine the textual cohesion that made presuppositions seem true. Presuppositionalist orientations accordingly have led evangelicals to prefer bibles that contain what the anthropologist James Bielo describes as "a cohesive story about the nature of God and humanity, the purpose of history, and the unfolding of time."[47] Cohesive texts allow readers to invest authority in biblical passages such as supposed prophecies, including the reference in Isaiah 7:14 to the messiah's mother—described in the RSV as a "young woman," yet known in the NIV (and the King James) as a "virgin." To undergird the NIV's claim to reliability, advertisements touted the scholarly credentials of its translators as well as the translation's "mature" quality. One ad boasted that its "top-level transdenominational team" included "more than 100 noted scholars from five countries." Those translators were required to affirm that "the Bible alone, and the Bible in its entirety, is the Word of God written, and is therefore inerrant in the autographs."[48]

The NIV also complemented devotional practices that prevailed within Zondervan's evangelical market, including an emphasis on cultivating intimacy with God. Locating evangelical identity largely in "an intense desire to experience personally a God who is as present as when Christ walked among his followers," the anthropologist Tanya Luhrmann argues that evangelicals develop a sense of intimacy by spending time immersed in evangelical media, such as books like *The Purpose Driven Life* and the Bible itself. Luhrmann notes that evangelicals accordingly have prioritized translations that have seemed more direct.[49] Putting special emphasis on training children to read the bible and develop their own spiritual intimacy, the NIV's translators supported a research study conducted in 1976 that measured how well schoolchildren between grades four and eight could comprehend passages and vocabulary from the NIV, KJV, and New American Standard translations. Among those translations, the NIV "proved superior in communicating to this age group," and Zondervan ultimately reprinted the study as marketing material.[50]

Overall, the NIV offered consumers a translation that managed to be authoritative while also catering explicitly to the consumer's own needs and desires. This set it apart from other biblical translations and paraphrases that had merely sought to make the language of the King James translation easier for ordinary readers to understand. Two years before the launch of the full NIV in 1978, Zondervan initiated an elaborate marketing campaign to cultivate demand for its upcoming release. Whereas previous bibles might have been described as vessels for God's own words, the campaign described the NIV as a product that offered "The Voice of God in Your Own Words." In addition to tailoring its language to its customers' own, Zondervan promised that it would provide "a Bible for every individual need."[51]

To see the peculiarity of this approach to the Bible, consider how Reuben A. Torrey, the first superintendent of the school that became Moody Bible Institute and a founder of the Bible Institute of Los Angeles, described a method of bible study in 1896, in *How to Study the Bible for Greatest Profit.* Published with Fleming H. Revell Company, the book depicted bible reading as difficult work. Insisting that bible reading typically generated reward only through exhaustive effort, Torrey explained that readers must sift through the Bible's layers of textual sediment just as someone might sift soil in search of gold. Torrey even suggested that a reader might have to read through the same book "again, and then again, say a dozen times in all, at a single sitting" before the Bible "begins to open up."[52] Throughout these and Torrey's other suggestions, an understanding of the Bible depended upon a reader's effort and discipline. In contrast, the NIV offered consumers a bible that complemented their own convictions.

In addition to treating a broad evangelical public as a large niche, Zondervan also produced a torrent of bible editions and related products that catered to more specific niches. The company had begun experimenting with so-called "niche bibles" after 1983, when Bruce Ryskamp arrived from a previous position working for the Yellow Pages and became head of the bible division. "When Bruce arrived," one report explained, "he brought a mindset that the Bible could and should be marketed to meet the needs of specific people."[53] Marketing plans accordingly proposed placing "an NIV Bible in the hands of 'Larry lunch box and Dottie do-it-all' at each stage of their life that will help them understand the Bible and 'take it personally.'"[54] Examples of Zondervan's most prominent niche bibles included the *Student Bible, Women's Devotional Bible, Adventure Bible, Teen Study Bible,* and *Men's Devotional Bible,* each of which sold well more than one million copies as of 1999.

But other bibles catered to even narrower consumer segments, often in response to surveys that evidenced the existence of previously unacknowledged constituencies. In 1994, for example, the Gallup organization reported that 72 percent of Americans believed in angels. The organization had asked the same question in 1978, when only 54 percent of Americans answered affirmatively. While many people might have recognized that statistical shift as nothing more than a curiosity, the entrepreneur Doris Rikkers saw a market opportunity. Her company, World Bible Publishers, responded by publishing *The Angel Bible,* which a company vice president described in 1997 as a product for "people out there who seem to want to know what the Bible has to say about angels."[55] Rikkers's company published a wide range of other niche bibles, which addressed particular market segments. They included bibles for children, several bibles for African Americans and Latinos *(Original African Heritage Study Bible, Women of Color Study Bible, Latino Heritage Bible)*, bibles for mothers and fathers *(A Mother's Bible, Dad's Bible)*, bibles for graduates *(Graduation Bible)*, and much more. Before founding her own company, Rikkers had worked for almost two decades as an editor at Zondervan, where she had helped not only to create the popular *Women's Devotional Bible* but also to make Zondervan a pioneer in the realm of niche bible publishing. Alongside new niche bibles, Zondervan and other companies were able to create a steady stream of high-margin "add-ons" to their texts, such as study guides and other paraphernalia.[56]

But even as the practice of niching the Bible created a variety of commercial advantages, the logic of segmentation also undermined the authority of particular niched products. By training evangelical consumers to recognize bibles as products beholden to their own needs and desires, evangelical companies simultaneously trained consumers to shift their commercial allegiances when they perceived a lack of alignment between their priorities and their products. Although the practice of market segmentation allowed evangelical media companies to address diverse segments within the general evangelical public, some products tested that logic's limits. Zondervan learned this lesson beginning in 1997, when prominent evangelical leaders objected to the company's decision to revise the NIV with "gender-inclusive language."

Talk of revision had developed in part as a response to the publication of the New Revised Standard Version (NRSV) in 1989. Released by the National Council of Churches, the NRSV featured more colloquial language than the RSV, and it had abandoned the practice of using masculine nouns and pronouns as a default. Instead, the NRSV used gender-neutral nouns and pronouns when appropriate. Due in part to feedback that the NIV's publishers received about their bible, they became anxious that it might lose market dominance to the NRSV. After the NIV received an update in 1984, one Fuller Seminary professor disparaged it for remaining "male-biased." He cautioned: "'If I were an *NIV* publisher, I would start to realize that I'm going to begin losing my market within the next decade."[57] The NIV's publishers also believed that a new NIV could serve as a platform for an array of new niched bibles that could appeal to new consumer segments, especially spiritual "seekers."[58] For these reasons, Zondervan and its partners began planning a revision of the NIV around 1993.[59]

Yet even if some potential evangelical consumers appreciated gender-inclusive language, a substantial evangelical segment abhorred such a revision. They valued the original NIV's language, which not only complemented traditionalist gender ideals but also enabled readers who valued those ideals to view the Bible as relevant to their own lives.[60] As the historian Emily Johnson explains, conservative evangelical women in the New Christian Right often treated the idea that men and women possessed different yet complementary strengths and patterns of thought as the premise for opposing feminism and championing women's domestic roles.[61] Opposition to gender egalitarianism was the bedrock of their "conservative" subcultural self-understandings. As a result, the NIV's revision inspired what one report described as "accusations of being driven by the feminist or liberal agenda."[62] Heeding these criticisms, one editor cautioned against removing "traditional" language, such as revising the command in Matthew 4:19 to be "fishers of men" by adding "and women." The same editor also noted that the inclusive practice of changing single pronouns to plural pronouns ultimately "seems to de-personalize the scripture," undermining the intimacy that its readers valued.[63] Yet as the revision proceeded, gender-inclusive language quietly appeared during 1990s in an NIV version for children known as the New International Reader's Version (NIrV). An inclusive-language version of the NIV also was released in Great Britain, where the idea of a "gender-accurate" edition of the Bible drew far more interest than opposition among English evangelicals.

Decrying gender-inclusive language as a symptom of compromised theology as well as a lack of concern for evangelical consumers, a variety of periodicals and publishers in the United States transformed the NIV's revision into both a controversy and a market opportunity. In March 1997 the evangelical magazine *WORLD* published a scathing exposé-style report entitled "The Stealth Bible," which accused Zondervan and the IBS of "feminizing" the NIV and cultivating "egalitarian" gender ideology and "unisex" language. The report captured the attention of a wide range of evangelical leaders and institutions, including James Dobson and his Focus on the Family, as well as Albert Mohler and the Southern Baptist Convention. The Southern Baptist leader Paige Patterson described the NIV's revision as a "feminist effort to re-engineer society and abandon God's parameters for the home and for the church." The avowedly conservative Presbyterian Church in America insisted that the revision efforts were "inconsistent with the Biblical doctrine of divine inspiration."[64]

To quash the controversy, the International Bible Society promised in May 1997 to halt the revision, and Zondervan pledged to continue publishing the 1984 NIV.[65] That decision reflected the recommendation of a public relations firm that created a "damage control/crisis communications" plan entitled "When the 'Good News' Becomes Bad News."[66] The IBS also organized a series of meetings and "meet the critics" events with leading critics of any change to the NIV's patriarchal language. These critics included Jerry Falwell, Albert Mohler, Wayne Grudem, John Piper, and representatives from WORLD magazine and Focus on the Family.[67] These meetings served as opportunities for the company to rebuild the NIV's brand. "'NIV' is such a brand among evangelical Christians," one executive remarked. "It stands for quality, reliability, dignity, clarity—all the things we say in our advertising. The public actually believes us!" The same executive suggested that any changes to the NIV's "taste" might provoke "dismay and outrage, just as Coca-Cola experienced when it tampered with the taste of its product."[68] And yet even as Zondervan and the IBS sought to allay criticism, they set about nurturing the notion that the NIV could and even should be revised. One internal statement argued that critics of the revision claimed to be opposing "the radical feminist agenda running rampant in the world"; yet in "their zeal to defend against its onslaught," the statement insisted, those critics are "themselves becoming victims of the subtle Zeitgeist of political correctness—not in the secular world—but in the Church."[69]

Ultimately, the same market ambitions that had led Zondervan and its partners to initiate a revision of the NIV led them to continue their revision despite public statements to the contrary.[70] They hoped to secure the evangelical market while also engaging new consumer segments, and market research continued to justify that endeavor. One 1998 report on "NIV Strategy" revealed that almost 76 percent of consumers cited "accuracy" as the most important factor in their bible purchasing. This seemed to justify an effort to remove masculine pronouns that did not accurately reflect the original biblical languages. Of course, "accuracy" is an ambiguous concept, which people often define for themselves with reference to their own preferences. But Zondervan and the IBS meanwhile worried that failure to enhance their bible would allow their consumers to decide either in the near or long term that other translations proved more accurate. This anxiety drew strength from market research reporting that 20 percent of NIV owners planned on buying a new bible in the next year and that "there are unmistakable signs of a worldwide multi-denominational religious revival." A public relations report estimated that Christian consumers represented 39 percent of the general consumer market for books.[71]

All of this suggested that revising the NIV would enable it to retain existing consumers and to capture an impending rush of new consumers. They insisted that the "growing portion of the overall Bible market" that demanded "inclusive language" would "offset recent NIV market share declines." Marketers suggested that a revised NIV seemed well positioned to appeal especially to "seekers" and "new believers," whose weak preferences for particular bible translations made them susceptible to "influence."[72] By engaging those consumer constituencies, Zondervan expected to enhance its dominance over more than 40 percent of the overall bible market, which grew 7 percent in 1999.[73]

To engage both new and existing consumer constituencies while also acknowledging critics, Zondervan considered inventing a new brand name for the revised bible.[74] Marketing executives insisted that it "should not be tied to the NIV, in light of controversy." But the revision ultimately became known as Today's New International Version (TNIV), with the New Testament appearing in 2002 and the complete bible following in 2005.[75] To pacify criticism, a marketing plan encouraged consumers to think about the Bible not as a text with meaning that remains reliable over time but instead as a text that draws its meaning from the English language, which "has always been, and will continue to be in a state of flux." The plan noted that successive generations often understand words differently, including "generic masculine terms."[76]

Despite these and other attempts to justify the TNIV, the project provoked a response both from critics and competing companies. Questioning the "theological integrity and/or discernment of the leadership of both IBS and Zondervan," the Presbyterian Church in America removed Zondervan from its list of approved exhibitors at its annual meetings.[77] More significantly, in 2001 Crossway Books released its English Standard Version (ESV) translation, which it marketed almost explicitly as a response to the controversy surrounding the NIV's revision. Billing the ESV as a bible that offers "what God desired to reveal to us," Crossway's marketing material insisted that the ESV "doesn't improve on the original." Ridiculing the TNIV's translators for privileging "the interpretive judgment of the translator and contemporary culture," the ESV claimed to be a "word-for-word translation" that took "accuracy and readability to new levels of excellence." It drew endorsements from prominent critics of the TNIV, some of whom served on its "translation oversight committee" and "advisory council," including Wayne Grudem, Max Lucado, Albert Mohler, and John Piper.[78] The English Standard Version would go on to achieve prominence among evangelicals who emphasize what they see as its readable literalism and its translators' refusal to allow egalitarian cultural values to determine its language. But this rationale can be seen as an expression of its translators' and consumers' own cultural preferences, including complementarian views of gender.[79]

Even if the controversy over the TNIV ultimately cost Zondervan a share of dominance in some market segments, the company continued to capture new segments with new versions of the TNIV and NIV that appealed to particular niches. Crossway had claimed success with consumers who found meaning in opposition to gender-neutral language, but Zondervan continued to encourage its consumers to predicate their purchases of bibles and other books upon other indices of identity. The company sought that effect not simply by diversifying what its bibles said but also by multiplying the social constituencies that it sought to engage.

MAKING "OTHER COMMUNITIES" INTO NICHES

As early as the 1960s, evangelical companies had developed categories that could help both publishers and booksellers better understand their consumers. During that decade, Zondervan's marketing division defined their consumer constituencies not only according to their interest in such topics as scholarly material, evangelism, or "contemporary and social cultural issues" but also by way of what Zondervan recognized as their Christian identities. Categories included the "Non-Conservative Church-Oriented Layman Reader," the "Non-Christian and Unchurched Reader," and "the Christian Conservative and Church-Oriented Lay Reader." The company divided the latter category into age spectrums, including children (subteens), young teenagers (ages 13–15), older teenagers (ages 16–18), college youth, and adults. As these categories indicate, the company did not treat denominational and regional distinctions as relevant factors for predicting consumer behavior.[80] These kinds of categories took on new importance during the 1980s, as the company sought more deliberately to identify opportunities for growth.

Especially after News Corporation acquired Zondervan, growth strategies centered upon the notion of the niche, which the NIV and niche bibles already had proven effective. In public relations advertisements that Zondervan's "Corporate Identity Committee" created in 1989 to address evangelical anxiety that News Corporation would destroy the Christian ethos of its new acquisition, Zondervan president and CEO James Buick described how the company would define the success of its ministry. "Harper & Row's CEO George Craig has told me many times," Buick explained, "that to be successful, we have to build the Christian market niche." In subsequent interviews, Buick elaborated on how that niche might grow. "Now we are seeing a new market in the black community," he explained, admitting that "we have been negligent regarding the black community." Once "we get that up to where we want it," Buick announced, Zondervan would "look at the other communities," among which he counted "Hispanics and Asians."[81] These comments reveal how Zondervan came to see African American and Latino consumers as potential subsidiary segments within the "Christian market niche." Alongside its niches for evangelical mothers, dads, and angel aficionados, Zondervan created niches dedicated to evangelicals of color.

Although Buick's remarks make it easy to see Zondervan's sudden concern for black and Latino evangelicals as a decision propelled by the company's need to generate the larger revenue that its new corporate owners expected, the strategy also complemented ongoing initiatives among some evangelicals to reckon with evangelicalism's whiteness. In 1989, for example, representatives from the National Association of Evangelicals and the National Black Evangelical Association (NBEA) began what they described as a collaborative "Consultation on Racism." To begin the consultation, the two groups drafted a "Resolution on Racism and Racial Prejudice," underlining legal, institutional, and structural manifestations of racism. In addition to highlighting the long history of "prejudice based on race," the document acknowledged that "a wide range of racist structural barriers are still extant in our society today," including areas of housing, employment, education, and health services. Building on this initial effort, the two groups released a "Joint Statement on Prejudice and Racism" in 1990, in which the authors insisted that "the white evangelical church must first repent of its sin of racism" before undertaking "meaningful dialogue with black evangelical leaders."

These initiatives took shape in the early 1990s within a longer tradition of evangelical conversation about racism and racial exclusion. As historians of progressive evangelicalism have chronicled, white evangelical progressives such as Jim Wallis called throughout the 1970s for evangelicals to reckon with what they described in magazines like *Post-American* (renamed *Sojourners*) as the "social sin" of racism, which white evangelicals were obligated to address even if they did not understand themselves as racists.[82] These exhortations helped inspire more collaborative calls for mobilization, including the 1973 Chicago Declaration of Evangelical Social Concern, which emphasized the "conspicuous responsibility of the evangelical community for perpetuating the personal attitudes and institutional structures that have divided the body of Christ along color lines."[83] But even progressive evangelicals have tended to treat the issue of individual and institutional racism as one social justice problem among others. And efforts to focus evangelical attention on evangelicalism's whiteness often have taken shape largely through the efforts of black evangelicals themselves.

While drafting the 1989 "Resolution on Racism," for instance, the chairman of the NBEA's Social Action Committee, Clarence L. Hilliard, made most of the editorial suggestions that emphasized institutional and structural expressions of racial injustice. Black evangelicals had founded the NBEA in 1963 out of frustration over white evangelical leaders' relative disinterest in acknowledging and acting upon the problems and solutions to which black civil rights leaders had drawn attention.[84]

Neither in the 1970s nor in the 1990s did the good intentions of some evangelical leaders undermine the racial homogeneity of the evangelical public. Why not? To account for the low profile of black evangelicals and their concerns among white evangelicals and their congregations, scholars have emphasized two explanations. Above all, historians have noted that African Americans established their own churches and institutions during the nineteenth and early twentieth centuries, which offered black communities resources for responding to racial, economic, and political oppression. To be sure, not all of these institutions were Christian. Especially in the wake of the Great Migration of the early twentieth century, African Americans cultivated community, inspiration, and authority in new religious movements such as Father Divine's Peace Mission and the Nation of Islam.[85] Yet among Christians, institutional segregation kept black Protestants from participating in many of the theological and cultural reorientations that constituted white evangelicalism.[86] In addition to noting that black Protestants often have remained outside the churches and denominations that white evangelicals have populated, scholars have accounted for evangelicalism's whiteness by noting that white evangelicals' emphasis on the priority of the individual has depended on socioeconomic privilege that structural racism and inequality have denied to people of color.[87] The theologian Peter Heltzel argues that evangelicals' preoccupation with "a direct, personal relationship between Jesus the Lord and each individual" kept many evangelicals from developing "an adequate theological account" of racism and the need for social justice. This has meant that evangelical communities often have drawn people who have found themselves socially and culturally able to embrace an "individualistic ethos" that accounts for social inequality through a discourse of personal responsibility rather than structural oppression.[88]

Yet even though these common explanations help account for the ongoing segregation of white and black evangelicals, they also allow the evangelical book industry's relative inattention to black consumers to appear as an effect of historical and sociological patterns rather than as an additional cause of evangelicalism's whiteness. Although white evangelical publics have taken shape across denominational boundaries through circulation of commercial media, so too have black religious publics. As a rural diaspora of black urban migrants earned higher wages and salaries during the first decades of the twentieth century, phonograph recordings of popular preachers allowed many black migrants to treat commercial media markets as a means of participating in the religious cultures that took shape around popular preachers.[89] Later in the twentieth century, black televangelists offered their predominantly black audiences the ability to participate in expansive media publics, within which they could consume messages of inspiration and self-affirmation.[90] Although media companies such as Zondervan could have pursued black consumers before 1989, they generally had not recognized consumers of color as a profitable market. And in a circular way, consumers of color had not seemed worth addressing because evangelical firms had never cultivated or invested in them.

Especially before the 1980s, evangelical publishers emphasized products that seemed sure to appeal to a mass market, and they based their calculations on prior performance. Zondervan's best-selling authors were white, and many of its best-selling books focused not on racism and inequality but instead on inspirational stories. Published in 1976 with a foreword by Billy Graham, for example, Joni Eareckson Tada's *Joni* recounted how she renewed her faith by coming to see her "trials from God's point of view" after a diving accident left her paralyzed. Following the book's publication, Zondervan regularly received letters from readers testifying to how Joni's story inspired them through their own medical ailments and personal struggles.[91] The book sold approximately two million copies within two years, according to a 1978 advertisement in which Zondervan described itself as "house of the million-sellers." Of the books that joined *Joni* on the list of religious best sellers in 1977, every single one had a white evangelical author, and not one of the books addressed inequalities of any kind. Books on the list included Charles Colson's *Born Again* (Chosen/Revell), Billy Graham's *Angels* (Doubleday), and Phillip Keller's *A Shepherd Looks at Psalm 23* (Zondervan).[92] This thematic focus on devotion rather than justice complemented many white evangelicals' insistence upon prioritizing "expositional" theology rather than the "experiential" theology of black theologians like James Cone.[93]

Even as segmentation strategy inspired evangelical publishers to engage black evangelicals in the 1980s and 1990s, the industry's commercial infrastructure undermined corporate support for that cause. With evangelical bookstores serving as primary sites of circulation within white suburban communities, black Protestants had far less access to those sites than white consumers did.[94] This meant that bookstores did not concern themselves with selling books to black consumers, which meant bookstore owners did not place orders for black consumers at annual meetings of the Christian Booksellers Association, which meant that publishers did not actively recruit black authors. Consider the fact that evangelical publishing companies regularly attended and participated in annual meetings of the National Association of Evangelicals in order to use those meetings as opportunities to identify and meet with potential authors. In contrast, the annual meetings of the National Black Evangelical Association drew far less interest from evangelical firms. And white evangelical support for the NBEA continually diminished.[95] By treating commercialism as the means by which they defined evangelicalism, evangelical media companies perpetuated homogeneity that they might have theoretically and theologically opposed.

To be sure, as early as the 1960s, evangelical publishers released a variety of books by prominent black evangelicals, whose celebrity the companies helped nurture. Many of those authors wrote passionately and compellingly about the need for white evangelicals not only to open themselves to greater fellowship with black Christians but also to recognize, as the author Columbus Salley argued in the title of a 1970 book, "your God is too white." But as Salley's title suggests, these books often presumed white evangelicals as their primary audience, and many of their authors achieved prominence largely among white audiences. In *Shall We Overcome: A Challenge to Negro and White Christians* (Revell, 1966), Harold Jones primarily addressed white readers. The first black associate evangelist of Billy Graham's Evangelistic Association, Jones lamented that "within the Negro church and Christian ministry there is a spiritual apathy and deadness," and he insisted that "the Negro people require spiritual help and direction" that white evangelicals could offer—if only they could put aside their pervasive "race prejudice and bitterness."[96] Jones presented Billy Graham's crusades as examples of integration efforts, although Graham biographer Grant Wacker notes that the number of people of color at Graham's revivals remained small and "possibly extremely small" until nearly 1990.[97] William Pannell, the author of *My Friend the Enemy* (Word, 1968), served as a director of leadership training for Youth for Christ before joining the faculty of Fuller Seminary in 1974 as professor of evangelism. Criticizing white evangelicals for focusing more on "the solutions rather than the substance of the evil" of racism and segregation, Pannell offered a method by which his white evangelicals might reflect upon that substance; "The white man," he argued, "must learn to listen. . . . What you must learn is how *I* think; how I really feel."[98] Although the evangelist Tom Skinner went on to develop leadership training programs for young black Christians through his organization Tom Skinner Associates, his book *Black and Free* (Zondervan, 1968) focuses less on structural racism in society than on the notion that faith in Jesus could help both white and black individuals to surmount "the race problem" in America.[99] Typically written in the hope that white evangelicals might take their messages to heart, these books imagined a world in which white and black evangelicals might constitute a common public; in practice, however, they addressed a white evangelical market.

Recognizing the evangelical media industry's whiteness, some companies have sought to redress that problem. In 1970 the African American publishing executive Melvin E. Banks founded Urban Ministries International (UMI), which marketed Sunday school literature to African American consumers. A graduate of Moody Bible Institute, Banks began his career working in retail distribution for Scripture Press Publishers, a company based in Wheaton, Illinois.[100] Although that work familiarized Banks with the practice of selling Christian literature to general evangelical markets, he became convinced that his company "did not connect" with African American Protestants because, as he later explained, "all the writing was done from a white perspective." With the assistance of a niche marketing expert who worked for Scripture Press, Banks set out to create literature that reflected what he later described as "the culture that African Americans lived and how they worshiped."[101] Initially based at Scripture Press's headquarters in Wheaton, the company achieved commercial success and some renown as a specialist in magazines, Sunday school literature, and Christian curricula for African American Protestants. But it has not sought to publish for publics beyond its niche.[102]

Major evangelical companies made extremely modest efforts to reach beyond their primary markets and address the niche that UMI helped identify. Zondervan's efforts included creating a number of bibles intended primarily for African American consumers, including the *African American Heritage Bible,* which highlighted places and people from Africa and included pictures of people with nonwhite skin tones. The bible received the endorsement of the Congress of National Black Churches.[103] To help Zondervan overcome the inertia of its commercial habits and transform black evangelicals into an active niche, CEO James Buick hired a consultant during the 1990s to advise the firm on how to reach black authors and consumers. But as a former Zondervan marketing executive later explained to me, "they just weren't good at it."[104] And other companies proved even less adept than Zondervan. In 1993 the publisher Broadman & Holman (a division of the Southern Baptist Convention's Sunday School Board, which became known as LifeWay Christian Resources in 1997) released the book *Black Bible Chronicles,* a loose paraphrase of the Bible.[105] Writing in what she understood as the vernacular of black youth, author P. K. McCary presented the book as a "survival manual for the streets." The book begins, for example, with an account of creation that swaps the King James Version's reference to God's work "in the beginning" with a scene that begins, "When the Almighty was first down with his program." Although McCary was African American and expressed an earnest desire to engage black youth with the message of the Bible, McCary drew criticism from some black pastors for what they viewed as her misguided use of patronizing colloquialisms and narrative strategies based on caricatures of black life.[106] These books had limited commercial success.

The pockets of the evangelical media industry that successfully managed to engage both white and black consumers have been associated above all with the diverse forms of the prosperity gospel, especially charismatic and "neo-Pentecostal" ministries that have grown out of classical pentecostal movements.[107] Throughout the 1970s and 1980s, white televangelists like Jim Bakker and Oral Roberts recognized that their publics and donor rosters included large African American constituencies, and white evangelical networks like TBN began featuring black preachers such as Carlton Pearson, T. D. Jakes, and Creflo Dollar in the 1990s. Partly through their television presence, those black televangelists drew support from white consumers.[108] One sociologist traces this broad-based support for prosperity gospels to the "burgeoning consumer culture of the Reagan era," which produced an explosion of wealth and aspirations of socioeconomic ascendance. Many black prosperity teachers in particular presented their messages of prosperity as means by which their African American audiences could imagine their way beyond structural inequality or nurture their ascending class status. According to Jakes, his audience consisted largely of "upwardly mobile African-Americans" who viewed "the church as a support base."[109]

Since the 1980s the broad appeal of prosperity preachers has led some of the largest evangelical media firms to publish their books and cultivate their celebrity. T. D. Jakes has published books with firms including Baker Publishing Group's Bethany House, Thomas Nelson, and Warner Faith (renamed FaithWords in 2006). The latter company also publishes books by Creflo Dollar, Joel Osteen, and Joyce Meyer. Yet televangelists in general and black televangelists in particular have had an ambivalent relationship with media firms like Warner Faith and Zondervan.

This ambivalence reflects the way in which televangelists consistently have cultivated direct relationships with their audiences and consumers, which has made other corporate intermediaries less necessary. These direct relationships have taken shape in response to the ways that religious broadcasters have funded their activities. Because mainline Christian broadcasters monopolized access to free "sustaining time" until 1960, evangelical broadcasters were forced to purchase airtime. They accordingly became accustomed to raising audience-generated revenue to support their broadcasts.[110] As a result, successful broadcast evangelists have been adept at developing detailed lists of people who have bought their products and donated money. Such lists have provided broadcasters with demographic portraits of their commercial niches.

With these portraits in hand, evangelical broadcasters have not always needed companies like Zondervan to reach out to their primary consumers. Recognizing this fact, many leading televangelists have created their own media corporations, through which they have sold and distributed their own materials to their market segments. Examples include Jim and Tammy Faye Bakker's PTL, Creflo Dollar's World Changers Church International and his eponymous Creflo Dollar Ministries, and T. D. Jakes's T.D. Jakes Enterprises (for-profit) and T.D. Jakes Ministries (not-for-profit).[111] While leading evangelical media companies historically have shown relatively little interest in black authors due to a commercialism that has both reflected and reinforced de facto segregation, popular black authors and their consumers also have stayed away because there often has been little incentive for doing otherwise.

Note, for example, that T. D. Jakes self-financed and self-published his first and best-known book, *Woman, Thou Art Loosed!* Published in 1993, the book drew upon a series of Sunday school classes for women that Jakes had developed and taught at his church, an interracial congregation located in an affluent suburb of Charleston, West Virginia.[112] Using a mailing list that he reportedly acquired from Carlton Pearson, and arranging his own distribution agreements with retail distributors, Jakes made his book into a best seller. It ranked among the top five nonfiction evangelical books in 1995.[113] That success drew the attention of more established evangelical media firms, which sought to republish Jakes's book under their own imprints, as Bethany House did in 2003. By securing such agreements, Jakes allowed Bethany House to sell his product to their market segments without providing that company with control of his own, which he continued to cultivate through his multimedia ministries. Those ministries have included in-person conferences, videos of meetings and lectures, television broadcasts, and dozens of books published by his company or others.

Just as figures like Jakes generated large markets and publics by developing their own infrastructures of production and distribution, so too have teachers and preachers in Latin America. Beginning especially in the 1980s, evangelical media firms based in the United States sought to engage Latino niches by co-opting the commercial networks in which Latino authors and consumers participated. Focusing initially on Spanish-language literature, evangelical companies treated Latino consumers as a segment that stood largely apart from white, English-language consumers. Because Latinos have been defined with reference to language, nationality, and idealized cultural difference, their segregated segmentation from Anglo evangelical markets and publics has been able to appear more practical and less racist than the commercial segregation of African American evangelicals.

In significant ways, Anglo Protestants always have been involved with Latino evangelical media. The Reina-Valera translation of the Bible became the most popular and authoritative version among Spanish-speaking Protestants only after British and American bible societies began reprinting and distributing it. Named after the Spaniards Casiodoro de Reina and Cipriano de Valera, who respectively translated and revised the initial translation between 1569 and 1602, the Reina-Valera translation remained mostly unused before Anglo Protestant missionaries rediscovered the text in the nineteenth century and came to see its distribution as a method of undermining the political and religious authority of the Catholic Church in Latin America.[114] Anglo Protestant denominations also established new publishing initiatives in Latin America. Not long after the General Conference of the Methodist Episcopal Church began a mission to Mexico in the early 1870s, its missionaries began working to establish a Mexican analog to the Methodist Book Concern, the publishing division of the Methodist Episcopal Church in the United States. Encouraged by stories that missionaries had heard about Mexicans who had "been led to renounce Romanism by the reading of tracts and books," Methodists did not limit their publications to Methodist literature. In 1882, for example, they published a translation of Dwight Moody's *Heaven*.[115] In succeeding decades, agents of the Bible Institute Colportage Association also circulated Moody's writings throughout Latin America. "A missionary in Venezuela reports twenty-one converts in a remote mountain community resulting from a single copy of 'The Way of God,'" announced a BICA pamphlet from the early 1930s.[116]

Anglo missionaries eventually established some of the most prominent Protestant publishing companies in Latin America, and the vast majority of Spanish-language publishing programs devoted to religion adopted an evangelical orientation.[117] In 1946 missionaries from the Assemblies of God established a firm known initially as Pedro Press and subsequently as Editorial Vida. Three years later the Latin America Mission established a literature division known as Editorial Caribe in San Jose, Costa Rica. Founded in 1921 as the Latin America Evangelization Crusade by the Scottish Harry Strachan and Irish Susan Beamish Strachan, the Latin America Mission established Caribe with a grant from Moody Bible Institute. In addition to taking over the Spanish-language publication program of the American Tract Society, Caribe created an array of bible study materials and established bookstores in Costa Rica, Panama, and New York City.[118] In 1970 the American missionaries Harold and Esther Kregel established Editorial Portavoz, which became associated with Kregel Publications in Grand Rapids, the Reformed publishing house founded by Harold's brother Robert.[119] As an evangelical magazine and book publishing executive from Mexico explained to me, Latin American evangelicals sometimes have remarked that "a book is the best missionary," due to its ability to circulate among communities across both time and space.[120]

The influence of these Anglo initiatives notwithstanding, Latino evangelicalisms never have conformed neatly to the visions that Anglo missionaries have sought to cultivate. As the historian Daniel Ramírez explains, "evangelicalismo" in Latin America refers above all to the "common experience of religious dissent and marginalization" that Protestants have experienced within "contexts of hegemonic Catholicism." Despite claims that varied teachers and missionaries recurrently have made regarding the supremacy of their own theological or denominational perspectives, this common posture of dissent has cultivated a "fluid religiosity" that the notion of "evangélico" identity helps to denote.[121] Appealing especially to the proletarian and peasant classes that missionaries from historic denominations often had missed, pentecostal missionaries in particular nurtured modes of authority and devotional practice that deemphasized denominational particularity and facilitated agentive accessibility. Rather than imposing Anglo missionaries on new congregations as pastors, early pentecostal missionaries nurtured local Latino leadership. Pentecostals also have cultivated accessibility by enmeshing their practices in popular culture, including music, television, and books.[122] Responsive to the socioeconomic aspirations of people in their localities, local evangelical and pentecostal teachers often have developed ministerial regimes that have privileged the power of individual Christians to choose what the anthropologist David Smilde describes as a "forward-looking, intentional project of self- or family reform." Many Latinos, Smilde argues, have come to see *evangelicalismo* as a source of "cultural agency through which they can gain control over aspects of their personal and social contexts."[123] Complementing this concern for self-making, devotional practices have focused especially on individual bible study, moral strictures, and the pursuit of spiritual and financial "success."

Each of these emphases have preoccupied the ministries of Latin American celebrity pastors who have presented their churches as sources of both entertainment and vernacular forms of self-help. The prominent Columbian pastor César Castellanos, for example, developed a congregation in Bogotá that has drawn around 25,000 members, and an international network that claims more than 100,000 members, by implementing a method of church growth and discipleship known as the "G12," or "Government of 12." Nominally based on the motif of twelve Israelite tribes and twelve apostles of Jesus, the method calls for the successive creation of "cell groups" of twelve people who subsequently lead their own cell groups comprising twelve people from their own communities. Sometimes derided as a "pyramid scheme" designed to solicit the financial contributions of members from successive cells, the method also has made evangelical discourses and attachments more widely available through family and friend networks in Columbian society. A method of discipleship no less than a method of marketing, the G12 method has constituted networks of mediation of the sort that media companies based in the United States have sought to identify and engage.[124]

Although Anglo evangelical corporations have not been able to acquire companies like Castellanos's own G12 Editors, through which he publishes his own books and study guides, corporations from the United States have sought and secured access to Latino evangelical networks by acquiring other Latin American media companies. U.S.-based media industries began addressing Latino consumers significantly in the 1980s, a few decades after immigration from Latin America began to increase dramatically.[125] Interest in Latinos also grew especially in response to the 1980 census and related reporting, which identified "Hispanics" as a one of the largest demographic groups in the United States. As large corporations like Anheuser-Busch and Procter & Gamble launched Hispanic marketing departments, and prominent advertising agencies acquired Cuban companies, evangelical firms acquired Latin American publishers.[126] In 1991 Thomas Nelson acquired Editorial Caribe and Editorial Betania and made them part of the new Grupo Nelson. Both companies specialized in books by and for charismatic and neo-pentecostal authors and consumers. One contemporaneous analysis of those acquisitions explained that Thomas Nelson saw the purchase as a way not just to reach consumers in Latin America but also to capitalize on Thomas Nelson's sense that Latino immigrants to the United States had maintained robust ties "to the cultures and languages of their country of origin."[127]

A similar rationale led Zondervan in 1996 to acquire Editorial Vida for $11 million from Life Publishers International, which had become the foreign-language publishing unit of the Assemblies of God denomination.[128] The acquisition made sense to Zondervan especially because Vida had been licensed to publish the Spanish-language version of the NIV, and it had been marketing its bibles as products "designed specifically for Charismatic and Pentecostal believers."[129] Just as Zondervan had treated the NIV as a product that it could sell to a conservative evangelical niche, the Nueva Versión International (NVI) appeared as a product would secure the company's claim upon a Spanish-language evangelical niche. The International Bible Society's director of the NVI program, the Columbian scholar Luciano Jaramillo, has served that claim by publicly recounting the story of his decision to leave the Roman Catholic priesthood after he undertook serious study of the Bible for himself.[130] By acquiring Vida, Zondervan not only gained a backlist of books by prominent *evangélicos* but also became able to sell more translations of Anglo books through Vida's distribution pathways in Latin America. Caribe, Betania, and Vida all became part of the same media conglomerate with HarperCollins's acquisition of Thomas Nelson.

In addition to providing companies like Thomas Nelson and Zondervan with access to Latin American authors and distribution networks, these acquisitions provided the companies with editorial and marketing knowledge that enabled them to engage Latino niches in the United States. In the early 1990s just 5 percent of the CBA's 8,000 bookstore affiliates had Spanish-language sections, and even fewer had bilingual sales representatives. To bridge the apparent chasm between Anglo and Latino evangelical consumer contexts in the United States, publishers like Vida and Caribe began publishing all-English versions of their catalogs while also seeking out distribution sites that Latinos in the United States might encounter more regularly than suburban bookstores. "My market is where Spanish people buy their milk, cheese and bread, where they buy their kids' clothes," explained Caribe's director of U.S. sales and marketing. Examples of ideal locations included the variety chain store McCrory's and the big-box store Kmart.[131] The need to identify more commonplace shopping sites became even more important as subsequent generations of immigrant families adopted English rather than Spanish as a primary language, making them even less likely to seek out products in Spanish-language bookstores or Spanish-language sections of Anglo bookstores. This emphasis on helping Latinos to treat evangelical books as "impulse purchases" put evangelical firms in the avant-garde among booksellers, some of whom did not take this approach with Latino consumers until as late as the 2010s.[132]

Yet evangelical media firms have sought success not simply by adapting their distribution paradigms to the everyday lives of Latino evangelicals but also by cultivating the very notion of a common "Latino" or "Hispanic" identity. Since those identity categories began circulating in the 1970s through federal agency forms and surveys, they have collapsed varied national, ethnic, and racial identities in the name of a common Latino consciousness, or *latinidad*. This sense of *latinidad* has taken shape especially through commercial media and marketing industries. For decades, commercial media networks like Telemundo have offered programming that has claimed to represent and speak to an all-encompassing Latino audience.[133] Beginning in 1982 with the publication of a marketing handbook entitled *Reaching the Hispanic Market Effectively,* many books have offered advice about how companies might appeal more persuasively to Latino sensibilities by emphasizing the features they seem to hold in common, including the supposed preoccupation with cultural heritage that Thomas Nelson's executives affirmed.[134] As the anthropologist Arlene Dávila explains, marketing strategies often have presented the Latino ideal as "more moral, spiritual, and 'whole' than the materialistic American culture." Market analyses recurrently have repeated versions of the claim that "Spanish culture is family- and values-oriented," which has led evangelical publishers to view Latinos as ideal consumers for the family-focused literature they have produced.[135]

These ideals have helped constitute the platform for institutions like the National Latino Evangelical Coalition and the National Hispanic Christian Leadership Conference (NHCLC). Among the core components of its mission statement, the NHCLC cites the desire to "enrich the narrative of American Evangelicalism by replacing the media exacerbated image of angry white evangelicals" with an image of Latino evangelicals who "edify a multi-ethnic, trans-generational firewall against moral relativism, spiritual apathy, cultural decadence and ecclesiastical lukewarmness while simultaneously elevating biblical marriage, championing life and protecting religious liberty."[136] Founded in 2001, the NHCLC has described itself since 2014 as the "world's largest Hispanic evangelical association." Taking advantage of the expansive ambiguity of both "Hispanic" and "evangelical" to make a claim upon "millions of evangelicals," the NHCLC has presented those millions as a constituency that always has existed, yet which previously had escaped notice primarily because it had not yet grown large enough to draw attention. Recognizing that immigration from Latin America would continue and presuming that those immigrants increasingly would adopt evangelical sensibilities, the prominent pastor and NHCLC leader Wilfredo "Choco" De Jesús claimed that "Hispanics represent the growth component in American Christianity."[137] Versions of this claim have served as a commercial platform for pastors like De Jesús, whom Zondervan and Vida secured as an author in 2016.[138]

Zondervan and Vida have held up authors like De Jesús as figures with the potential to draw a crossover appeal among both Latino and Anglo publics. Prominent examples include the Guatemalan pastor Cash Luna (né Carlos Enrique Luna Arango) as well as Texas-based singer and pastor

Marcos Witt, who served for a decade as the pastor of the Spanish congregation at Lakewood Church, the megachurch in Houston, Texas, led by the televangelist Joel Osteen. All of these authors have published books with Vida, which typically has released the books simultaneously in Spanish and English. In many ways their teachings are almost indistinguishable from those of prominent Anglo evangelicals. With unmistakable echoes of Rick Warren's *Purpose Driven Life,* De Jesús's *Move into More* teaches readers to discover the "joyful contentment that comes from living passionately with a purpose."[139]

And yet even if Anglo authors have reached Latino consumers in English translation, Latino authors have proven far less successful among Anglo audiences. Why? One answer involves the tendency for Latino evangelical leaders to emphasize social policies that do not complement the priorities of American evangelicals who view themselves as social conservatives or affiliate themselves with the Republican Party. Immigration policy reform ranks high, for example, among the concerns of the NHCLC. Over the same period that companies like Zondervan have sought to engage nonwhite evangelicals around the world, the evangelical media industry simultaneously has become associated more closely with consumer niches that have expressed disinterest in multicultural Christianity. Just as concepts such as "pluralism" have enabled institutions to acknowledge diversity while simultaneously reinscribing the divisions they ostensibly address, niche segmentation has provided neither companies nor their consumers with much reason to challenge their preferred ways of being.[140]

CULTURE WAR CONSUMERS

For most of the twentieth century an orientation toward the mass market had inspired evangelical publishers and booksellers to largely avoid content that inspired division or sought to alienate potential consumers. This is why Zondervan executives remained uneasy in 1990 about recruiting Oliver North as an evangelical author, for fear that Zondervan would appear "captive to political conservatives and fundamentalist activists."[141] Yet as North's eventual recruitment ultimately demonstrates, the notion of the niche allowed the company to treat a conservative evangelical public as a consumer market that made commercial sense alongside others.

Market segmentation transformed difference and debate between consumer constituencies from a potential commercial constraint into a commercial virtue. In 1987, the virtue of difference was detailed in a report commissioned jointly by the Christian Booksellers Association, the Evangelical Christian Publishers Association, and the Protestant Church-Owned Publishers Association. "Large as the total market may be," the report found, "it is actually made up of many specific groups, each with its own characteristics." According to the report, those groups tended to share an interest in issues that acknowledged "the individual, practical, applied, problem-solving context in which these people are immersed." But the report meanwhile insisted that commercial growth flowed not just from the commercial preoccupations that united consumers but also from the concerns that divided them. Highlighting "growing debates among various Christian factions," the report concluded that "these debates are likely to generate a large publishing volume." The lesson here was that publishers and booksellers could capture "untapped potential with an interest in religion" by capitalizing on disagreement and debate between consumer constituencies. The report described this lesson as the heart of "target marketing."[142]

Granted, difference and debate always had been evangelical obsessions, which publishers and booksellers had acknowledged. The ideal of "distinction" had been the heart of the fundamentalist brand, which Eerdmans and Zondervan had embraced. That fundamentalist brand drew its meaning not just from the sets of doctrines that fundamentalists claimed in documents like *The Fundamentals* but also from the contrast that avowed fundamentalists made between themselves and "modernists." Throughout the twentieth century, this posture of distinction helped animate evangelical publics, which have taken shape successively around shared opposition to evolution, alcohol, the New Deal, communism, feminism, desegregation, abortion, same-sex marriage, and more.[143] The historian Molly Worthen argues that "uncertainties and disagreements" over both political and theological concerns is what has made evangelicalism into "a distinctive spiritual community."[144]

But this preoccupation with difference and debate became salient in a new way during the late 1970s and 1980s. Although evangelicals had been divided during the 1960s over such theological and social controversies as inerrancy, charismatic gifts, and the civil rights movement's call for desegregation, a "middle-of-the-road" evangelicalism seemed to have taken shape by the middle of the 1970s.[145] The sociologist Robert Wuthnow even describes the evangelicalism of this era as a sort of "centrist" movement, drawing both denominational Protestants and former fundamentalists. Yet even if many evangelicals continued to focus more on what they shared with other Protestants than on how they stood apart, civil rights activism and judicial decisions on issues like abortion increasingly laid bare conflicting assumptions about the relationship between individual values and public behavior.[146] Through the rise of what some historians describe as neo-fundamentalism, whose advocates prioritized both doctrinal and moral precision, a new evangelical public took division as its premise. Segmentation strategy complemented this divisive impulse.

Among the champions of division were authors and teachers such as Harold Lindsell and Francis Schaeffer, both of whom represented an older generation of evangelicals that had become anxious about what they saw as an increasingly liberal generation of younger evangelicals.[147] The editor of *Christianity Today* and a former professor, dean, and vice president at Fuller Theological Seminary, Lindsell publicly and prominently revived a smoldering debate over the inerrancy of the Bible with his book *The Battle for the Bible* (Zondervan, 1976). As the title suggests, Lindsell insisted that ostensible evangelicals had been engaged in a protracted theological battle that pit lay evangelicals who endorsed the inerrancy of the Bible against "elite" evangelicals who undermined the Bible's authority by intellectualizing and historicizing it. In Lindsell's view, only inerrantists deserved the title "evangelical." This polarizing position drew support from a wide range of evangelicals, who treated Lindsell's call to arms as an obligation to ally themselves with one side of a binary that they might not previously have drawn so starkly. Supporting what he described as Lindsell's "call for drawing a line," the Presbyterian missionary and eventual evangelical guru Francis Schaeffer agreed that "evangelicalism is not consistently evangelical unless there is a line drawn between those who take a full view of Scripture and those who do not."[148]

Both before and after endorsing Lindsell's view, Francis Schaeffer regularly urged true Christians to challenge and transform a secular society that had become hostile to biblical truth. In addition to calling on Christians to battle what he termed "secular humanism" on intellectual grounds, Schaeffer urged evangelicals to confront their perceived opponents politically.[149] This political orientation has led historians to deem figures like Schaeffer as leaders of what became known as the New Christian Right. Among its leaders, Schaeffer became known especially for fixing evangelical attention on new political priorities, which he presented as incontestable theological principles. Schaeffer preoccupied many evangelicals with opposition to abortion through his lectures, articles, and books, such as *Whatever Happened to the Human Race?* (Revell, 1979).[150]

Evangelical neo-fundamentalists inspired many of their contemporaries to see them as dogmatists who sought to revive and elaborate upon an earlier era's antagonisms; but the neo-fundamentalist posture did not simply reincarnate earlier culture wars. It popularized a new sort of culture war. Whereas earlier fundamentalist leaders had focused on compelling their audiences to adopt their own doctrinal preferences, neo-fundamentalists prioritized the ideal of intellectual and moral choice. As the historian Axel Schäfer explains, the New Christian Right "affirmed the dynamic, flexible, entrepreneurial, and self-realizing market subject." The idea was that Christians joined the transdenominational evangelical public by choice, and they could perform that choice not just through political activism and voting but also through their consumer behavior. Championing the moral virtue of what Schäfer describes as the "entrepreneurial self," neo-fundamentalists emphasized the ideal of a "self-actualizing mindset that shunned the oppressive institutions of the state in favor of the moralizing effects of the market."[151] By watching the right televangelists or buying the right books, individual evangelicals could pledge allegiance to a conservative evangelical niche through consumer choice.

Evangelical publishing companies recognized the commercial salience of neo-fundamentalist binaries and antagonisms. "Although we both understand that the book is going to become controversial," Zondervan vice-president Robert DeVries remarked to Lindsell with news that Zondervan would publish *The Battle for the Bible*, "we believe that it will serve the evangelical community in a unique way."[152] A few weeks later, DeVries elaborated upon the sentiment, admitting that Zondervan anticipated "keen interest in the book from numerous segments of the evangelical community."[153] DeVries knew that many avowed evangelicals would find Lindsell's book inflammatory, but he was clear in his conviction that the book "served" enough significant segments of the "evangelical community" to justify its publication. When the evangelical book industry's market study concluded a decade later that "growing debates" could fuel publishing volume by driving demand among conflicting market segments, the authors likely had Lindsell's high sales figures in mind.

Yet the New Christian Right did not become a dominant evangelical consumer niche immediately. As late as 1981, *Publishers Weekly* speculated openly about its dominance: "Are Christian publishers gearing their lists," a reporter asked, "to accommodate what seems to be a newly emergent militancy in the Christian marketplace?" Seeking to downplay the anxiety that inspired the question, the article insisted that most of the books at the annual Christian Booksellers Association conference seemed to reflect "a questioning rather than an accepting attitude about the Moral Majority," the right-wing political action organization. But the article also admitted that interest in books about the supposed scourges of "secular humanism," "subjectivism," and "individualism" had become increasingly abundant. Praising the spirit of the Moral Majority but criticizing its "strident" methods, figures like James Dobson explained that evangelicals had been reckoning with the same concerns that animated the Moral Majority by focusing their attention on "family problems." Reflecting on the 1988 CBA conference, the historian Randall Balmer would report that "there is a strong conservative political bias permeating the Christian Booksellers Association."[154]

By the mid-1990s, industry figures became less equivocal about the CBA's alliance with social conservatism and the Republican Party. In 1994 George H. W. Bush's vice president, Dan Quayle, addressed the annual CBA convention, as part of the publicity tour for his new Zondervan book *Standing Firm* (1994), which Quayle had hoped would help overhaul his public reputation and secure the support of evangelical voters. Chairing the conference's most anticipated panel was the conservative columnist, radio host, and author Cal Thomas, who remarked during the panel that it was "better to be a right-wing Christian than a left-wing pagan." To be sure, in 1994 no less than today, many avowed evangelicals insisted that evangelical identity is not synonymous with white, Republican identity. On the same panel that Thomas chaired in 1994, Jim Wallis argued that evangelicals must be "far more open" to a variety of perspectives. Another panelist, the evangelical author Tony Campolo, insisted that "the evangelical Christian church is *not* the Republican Party at prayer." Campolo testified that "the church and faith I love are so, so much bigger than that."[155]

Yet even if Campolo was right to note that evangelical ideals theoretically exceeded the GOP's political platform, the force of his comment highlighted the perceived plausibility of the claim he sought to reject. And his disavowal became less persuasive during the late 1990s and early 2000s, as both Zondervan and other evangelical publishing companies intensified their willingness to publish partisan books, which provided consumers with a stream of opportunities to choose the moral vision that they offered. In Zondervan's case, examples include a number of books by Ronald H. Nash, who excoriated liberals in titles like *Why the Left Is Not Right: The Religious Left—Who They Are and What They Believe* (1996). Meanwhile, Thomas Nelson published books by politically active conservatives such as Ronald Reagan's son Michael, the Presbyterian pastor D. James Kennedy, and Richard Land, the Southern Baptist Convention's public policy czar.[156] Whereas HarperCollins sometimes sold its most polemical political titles through other imprints, Thomas Nelson published a variety of books that provided their evangelical consumers with explicitly partisan polemics, including books that attacked the Clinton family and Barack Obama.[157]

Why did an alignment of evangelical identity and Republican identity characterize an increasingly prominent niche within the evangelical media industry? Overall, the alignment involves what Robert Wuthnow has described as the "restructuring of American religion." Beyond the growing sense among many evangelicals that individual moral issues should be public concerns, that restructuring featured two developments: the proliferation of "special interest groups" devoted to those moral matters, and the development of a media economy that could feed those special interests. As the historian Darren Dochuk explains, special interest groups flourished especially in California. Those cultures had taken shape beginning in the 1930s when a flood of migrants began relocating from the western South in search of new economic opportunities. These migrants and their descendants included "plain-folk," preachers, and self-made entrepreneurs; but they all shared southern evangelical sensibilities that that privileged "the primacy of individualism and local community." These sensibilities became hallmarks of conservatism, and Southern Californian evangelicals manifested that social orientation through entrepreneurial initiatives and grassroots political networks oriented toward creating a "moral geography" characterized by "all of their scriptural truths about self, community, government, money, and society."[158]

An array of individuals and institutions helped develop cultural bridges between Southern California's evangelical culture warriors and evangelical publics across the country. Prominent individuals included the businessman R. G. LeTourneau, the author Hal Lindsey, as well as the revivalists Charles Fuller and Billy Graham. Institutions included Fuller's eponymous seminary, Pepperdine College, and companies like Zondervan. When Zondervan decided to build its first stores outside the Midwest, it opened several stores in Southern California. That decision responded partly to the urging of evangelical authors based there, such as the Christian psychologist and author Clyde Narramore. As Narramore sought to publicize his new Zondervan book *The Psychology of Counseling* in 1960, he wrote to Zondervan reporting that "the head of the NAE here in Southern California" had volunteered to "take fliers around to the various NAE ministeriums," due to the NAE official's conviction that the book "should be in the hands of every evangelical minister in the country." Modeled on grassroots political mobilization, this commercial strategy was necessary, Narramore explained, because "many communities do not have a bookstore, yet they do have some kind of ministerial organization." He accordingly encouraged Zondervan to develop a commercial solution to the challenge of reaching "every minister in America . . . on a local basis." Those bookstores helped constitute a media infrastructure for conservative special interest groups.[159]

The expansion of the evangelical media industry and the proliferation of evangelical bookstores occurred alongside a realignment of the conservative media economy. As the historian Nicole Hemmer explains, the first generation of conservative media activism had lost much of its authority by the end of the 1970s. Through magazines such as *Human Events* and *National Review,* figures like William F. Buckley and Henry Regnery had lent cohesion to a conservative movement, especially by cultivating "an oppositional identity that enabled conservatives to identify as outsiders."[160] But as smaller budgets and a tendency to be "contrarian rather than conservative" led those media outlets to lose sight of the populist passion that they previously had voiced, a second generation of conservative media figures developed a new media infrastructure during the 1980s.[161] Valuing the principle of ideological purity and viewing social issues like abortion and "family values" as opportunities to generate partisan opposition, this second generation found easy allies. Those allies not only included neo-fundamentalists who had become adept at demanding that their publics endorse one side of an ideological binary but also featured conservative evangelical women who long had endorsed the social priority of the traditional Christian family.

With evangelical ideas and rhetoric providing a way of presenting conservative political policies as apolitical matters of individual conviction, evangelicalism increasingly saturated the conservative political vernacular.[162] Ronald Reagan even declared 1983 as "The Year of the Bible." As the presidential proclamation for that announcement reveals, Reagan's point was primarily to underline the status of the United States as a "distinctive Nation and people." To make that claim, Reagan appealed to "the Bible and its teachings," and the evangelical media industry embraced the opportunity that his gesture provided. The Zondervan Corporation devoted several pages to this proclamation in its 1983 annual report to shareholders, alongside sales figures for the NIV, which recently had begun accounting for nearly a quarter of the company's sales.

The conservative niche's ascendance within the evangelical media industry reached new heights in 1996 with the creation of Fox News Channel. Rupert Murdoch and Roger Ailes envisioned the network as a conservative alternative to CNN. According to Nicole Hemmer, Fox News "represented the culmination of a half century of conservative hopes," insofar as it gave conservative ideology a level of prominence and legitimacy that neither the *National Review* nor radio broadcasters such as Rush Limbaugh ever attained.[163] Building upon the critique of "liberal media bias" that the first generation of conservative media had invented, Fox News adopted partisanship as its operating principle and became the crown jewel of News Corporation's political influence in the United States. News Corporation's executives eventually amplified the effect of Fox News through other conservative media properties, including the *Wall Street Journal*, the *New York Post*, and the *Weekly Standard*. These additional media outlets allowed News Corporation not only to circulate stories and opinion pieces through multiple venues but also to cultivate common markets and publics for its companies and their products. Those companies included Zondervan, which had provided News Corporation with access to an evangelical media industry that had helped nurture the conservative niche that Fox News ultimately amplified. Rupert Murdoch had recognized the salience of conservatism among evangelicals in 1989, when he suggested that Zondervan publish a book by the future Fox News commentator Oliver North. Both on television and online, Fox News and affiliated media outlets regularly have promoted socially conservative evangelical authors and products, including Zondervan books by the surgeon-turned-politician Ben Carson, Hobby Lobby owners Steve and Jackie Green, the actor Candace Cameron Bure, and a variety of evangelical marriage experts.[164]

CONCLUSION

By encouraging Zondervan to publish Oliver North's book, Rupert Murdoch intimated his understanding that conservatism and evangelicalism were both, above all, publics that took shape through identity categories that media markets circulated.[165] Evangelicalism itself was both an identity category and a media market. This fact has been borne out over the decades since Fox News' founding. In that time, Fox News has consistently framed virtually every social and political issue as a contest between binary identities. In addition to opposition between "liberals" and "conservatives" or Democrats and Republicans, examples include opposition between people who either support or oppose ideals the network's pundits endorse or disparage. While the network's pundits have endorsed ideals such as patriotism, the family, the sanctity of life, "Judeo-Christianity," and free markets, they simultaneously have disparaged political correctness, social welfare programs, condemnations of police brutality, and efforts to address structural racism.[166] Many of these binaries are oppositions that some evangelicals helped nurture, and virtually all of these binaries have been oppositions that many evangelicals have found persuasive.

So it was that a large majority of self-identified evangelicals supported the presidential candidacy and presidential policies of Donald Trump, a media celebrity who had become adept at conjuring publics through print and television. Although many of those avowed evangelicals undoubtedly have premised their evangelical identities on explicitly theological criteria, the "evangelical" category also has provided survey respondents with a method of indicating allegiance to a public that appreciates the binaries that Donald Trump has posited, and which media outlets like Fox News have nurtured.[167] Those survey respondents have not belonged to the same evangelical niche that Melvin Banks, Wilfredo "Choco" De Jesús, "liberal evangelicals" like Jim Wallis, or many evangelical seekers have recognized as their own. But it need not be, as other market segments have stood ready to serve them, too.

Throughout the first decades of the twenty-first century, avowed evangelicals like Shane Claiborne, Tony Campolo, and other "Red Letter Christians" have labored to draw attention to what they have seen as alignment between the teachings of Jesus and progressive social and political concerns. Lamenting in 2018 that "the impression of many on the evangelical left is that the good news of Jesus Christ has been taken hostage by a highly charged, toxic subculture on the evangelical right," Mark Labberton, the president of Fuller Seminary, suggested that evangelicals "reclaim evangelical witness as accountable to the righteousness, justice, and mercy of the evangel itself."[168] Yet insofar as market segmentation encourages consumers simply to hear what they find most appealing and familiar, attempts to "reclaim" evangelicalism have become exercises in preaching to proverbial choirs of consumers who already agree. In the same way that many people like to "become Christians without crossing racial, linguistic, or class barriers," they also like to purchase and consume products and information that they find familiar. Today more than ever, that principle serves as both a reason and an excuse for the world's largest media conglomerates to make something for everyone—but for some more than others.

Epilogue

BACK IN 2007, I took a trip to a rural village in Baja California, Mexico, with my grandparents. It was not my first time there. As a child I had visited the village almost every summer. On this visit, like those earlier trips, my grandparents and I stayed with their close friends, a local Baptist pastor and his family. Sitting together one morning in the family's kitchen, the pastor asked me to update him on my educational and professional path. I was in graduate school at the time, and I explained that I was studying the history of religion in North America. I also shared that I had become especially fascinated by the popularity of evangelical books, which I described as "libros evangélicos," for lack of a better way of describing the commercial culture I had in mind. With a knowing smile, the pastor ran back into his bedroom, and proudly returned with a stack of a dozen books. All were Spanish translations of English-language evangelical bestsellers, including *The Purpose Driven Life*. He told me that he read from them every night.

How did Pastor Tomás acquire these books? How did they travel to rural Mexico from the places they were published, printed, or written? Why did Tomás read them? What does his moment of display tell us about his religious attachments and how they took shape? I asked Tomás some of these questions at the time. A few of them proved relatively easy to answer. I learned, for example, that my grandmother had given him many of the books. She had bought them in the Spanish-language section of her local evangelical bookstore in Southern California. But I have continued to wonder since then about some of the other questions, and my own answers have come to focus on the notion of commercial religion.

What does commercial religion allow us to see about modern religious life? By exploring the history of the evangelical book industry, I have shown how shared ideas, practices, and sensibilities continually take shape through commercial strategies, initiatives, and institutions. This complicates some of the ways in which scholars traditionally have conceptualized religious groups, including evangelicalism. The concept of a "subculture" is a primary example. For decades scholars have used this concept to describe evangelicalism's coherence. The historian Randall Balmer argues that the evangelical subculture encompasses the "beliefs, institutions, and folkways" that fundamentalists, charismatics, and pentecostals share. Among those beliefs Balmer counts an emphasis on a "born-again" experience, a literalist approach to the Bible, and "proselytizing zeal." Subcultural institutions include places like Dallas Theological Seminary as well as the annual conventions of the Christian Booksellers Association. And the subculture's folkways include everything from church aesthetics to musical preferences.[1] Elaborating on this idea through a "subcultural identity theory," the sociologists Christian Smith and Michael Emerson argue that evangelicalism has thrived because evangelicals "possess and employ the cultural tools needed to create both clear distinction from and significant engagement and tension with other relevant outgroups."[2] Although these scholars describe cultural boundaries in different ways, they all share an emphasis on the cohesion of an evangelical subculture that operates in contrast with a dominant culture.

Throughout this book, I often have treated evangelicalism as a sort of subculture. Over more than a century of revivals, conferences, summer camps, bookstores, trade associations, study groups, and more, evangelical media companies have created infrastructures through which evangelical cultures have taken shape. Those infrastructures often have allowed evangelical companies to treat their consumers as members of a subculture. Consider the marketing plan for the evangelist Billy Graham's best-selling autobiography, which HarperCollins and Zondervan published in 1997 under the title *Just as I Am*. Acknowledging Billy Graham's popularity among a wide range of evangelicals, the authors of the marketing plan predicted that many customers would come to the conclusion that they must buy a copy. "Not to have one," the plan explained, "will be to turn their back on their Christian faith. It is similar to making sure that your family has a Bible. Even if they don't regularly read the Bible they want to have one, 'just in case.'" Having devised this plan, the marketing team developed a strategy for implementing it through what the plan termed "guilt manipulation."

Seeking to intensify the feelings that their consumers already possessed, they described the conclusion they wanted consumers to reach: "To be a committed Christian, a well-informed Christian, a Christian who stands together with his/her brothers and sisters YOU MUST PURCHASE A COPY OF JUST AS I AM by Billy Graham."[3] In order for this sort of guilt manipulation to work, the people being manipulated must share the kinds of social capital that subcultural theory attempts to identify.

But the limits of the subcultural concept come into view by considering commercial religion. To see those limits, I invite you to look between the lines of this marketing plan. Although the plan's authors presumed that members of their target market shared some understanding of what it meant to be a "committed Christian," that commitment was not the authors' primary concern. Above all, they designed their marketing plan to generate profit by conjuring and engaging a market. With that objective in sight, they treated a subcultural understanding of evangelicalism as a commercial strategy.

That strategy reminds us that marketing plans fundamentally are aspirational documents. They summon markets for consumer goods as acts of speculative imagination. As a result, the publics that markets conjure do not hew to supposed subcultural constraints. In a consumer society, social publics always are in the process of formation and re-formation, as the practice of commercialism leads companies to nurture new markets by capitalizing on the capabilities and opportunities they perceive. Throughout the twentieth century and still today, evangelicalisms have taken shape through this sort of commercialism.

Commercial religion also allows us to acknowledge that shifting modes of technology and capitalism continually reshape the processes through which companies cultivate the markets and publics that we recognize as religions. Over the years I spent writing this book, people often asked me about the impact of electronic reading and online bookselling on evangelical media industries. And I, in turn, have asked evangelical media executives, editors, and booksellers to share their own understandings of the digital revolutions that continue to reshape their commercial landscapes. Overall, I have found that evangelical executives have seemed less anxious than outsiders often assume. As many industry observers and executives point out, new media technologies suit evangelicalism well. While the pastors of large churches and the leaders of large organizations traditionally have made ideal authors due to their broad commercial platforms, the proliferation of social media, blogs, and streaming video have multiplied the means by which authors can conjure markets and address publics. Of course, this had led some custodians of evangelical subcultures to worry:

"Just as the invention of the printing press helped spark the Protestant Reformation and created a crisis of authority," an article in *Christianity Today* reported in 2017, "the advent of social media has catalyzed a new crisis in the church."[4] But evangelical companies have remained perpetually aware of and responsive to the reconfigurations of authority that technological and commercial innovations inaugurate.

To see a reconfiguration at work, let us return to Rick Warren and his best-selling book. How did *The Purpose Driven Life* reach so many consumers? Supplementing all the answers that I have explored in this book, another explanation involves the timing of Warren's best seller. When Zondervan released it in 2002, the book took advantage of both old and new evangelical media economies. At the heart of the old economy lay Christian bookstores, which continued to operate near their peak. "In a day when consumers can buy Christian books at Amazon.com, Sam's Club, and the grocery store," an article in the magazine *CBA Marketplace* asked in 2003, "are Christian stores losing their place?" Their answer: no. The same article quipped that "e-books are only slightly more common than aircraft parked in driveways."[5] Although this article might have been less dismissive just a few years later, Christian bookstores continued to account for as much as 66 percent of industry sales in 2000, when sales figures began to drop steadily. Between 2000 and 2007, sales at the Logos chain of Christian bookstores fell from a high of $1.25 million per year to just $800,000.[6] The bookstore industry did not collapse completely until the 2010s. Family Christian Stores shut down in 2017, and LifeWay Christian Resources announced in 2019 that they would close their brick-and-mortar stores to "shift resources to a dynamic digital strategy." The CBA seemed to dissolve just a few months after LifeWay's announcement.[7]

If bookstores typified the old evangelical economy, the internet has been the heart of the new economy. Although online bookselling remained embryonic in 2002, websites like Warren's pastors.com not only enabled companies to market their products to consumer markets around the globe but also enabled individual authors to engage their publics more directly than before, cultivating their personal brands. Warren's prepublication internet marketing heralded a commercial emphasis on blending "strategies old and new" with regard to distribution, branding, and market segmentation.[8] As Warren and *PyroMarketing* author Greg Stielstra both acknowledged, these strategies helped Warren generate a network of more than 6,000 churches from eighty denominations in twelve countries, which helped Zondervan sell as many as 14 million copies of Warren's book in less than three years. I do not know if Pastor Tomás counted among those initial consumers, but Warren's market included pastors and congregations throughout Mexico.

In 2017, Family Christian Stores declared that its 240 remaining stores would close, including this store in Elyria, Ohio. In 2019 LifeWay Christian Resources decided to close their 170 stores.
© Nicholas Eckhart

By one estimate, Spanish-language versions of *The Purpose Driven Life* made up as much as 10 percent of the book's global sales.[9] In the two decades since the initial publication of Warren's book, savvy digital marketing has helped it to experience renewed periods of commercial attention, as online news and social media have circulated articles and video clips featuring testimonials from prominent celebrities and athletes. In 2016, for example, a wide range of outlets reported that the swimmer Michael Phelps had credited *The Purpose Driven Life* with renewing his career and propelling his success at that summer's Olympic games in Brazil. Around the same time, the reality television star Kim Kardashian described it as one of her three favorite books.[10]

As Warren's example suggests, commercial religion reveals how commercial success has functioned as an index of religious authority. Although thousands of American ministers would have relished the opportunity to deliver the invocation at Barack Obama's January 2009 inauguration, Warren unexpectedly received the job. Attempting to make sense of Warren's selection, a variety of pundits asserted that Warren received the honor precisely because he represented the evangelical Christians of the United States. Warren was positioned, one report predicted, "to succeed Billy

Graham as the nation's pre-eminent minister." His selection reflected "the generational changes in the evangelical Christian movement." Underlining Warren's status as "America's pastor" and the new face of an evangelical Christianity commonly believed to compose a third or more of the U.S. population, a *Washington Post*–ABC News poll reported that 61 percent of Americans supported Obama's invitation to Warren.[11] Who or what had lent Warren this supposed preeminence? As evidence of Warren's stature, journalists said little about the tens of thousands who regularly attended his Southern California megachurch, about his humanitarian initiatives in Africa, or even about Warren's church having hosted a debate between John McCain and Obama in August 2008. Instead, reporters noted that Warren had written *The Purpose Driven Life*. Its sales figures testified to the scale of the evangelical population and to Warren's stature within it.[12]

Was Warren's ascendance to the presidential podium, and his place on Pastor Tomás's nightstand, an effect of the evangelical subculture or the evangelical market? By putting the question this way, am I making too much of markets? As a tide of critical scholarship on the theme of neoliberalism has argued since the 1990s, markets have come to dominate social life around the world. Neoliberalism might be understood, the historian Kathryn Lofton explains, as "the summary term for that drift toward a society determined by markets."[13] By presenting markets as means by which evangelicalisms have taken shape, I have sought to reveal the social life of markets rather than amplify their power through my narration.

But markets continue to reconfigure contemporary religious publics. In 2012 Baker Publishing Group surveyed 15,000 of its consumers to identify their religious affiliations. Thirteen percent of respondents selected the category "other" to describe their tradition, and 3 percent identified as "spiritual but not religious." Asked about these responses, one of Baker's editors explained that religious "forms" had changed, but "not the substance necessarily." Addressing his company's response to same phenomenon, an editor at Howard Books (an evangelical division of Simon & Schuster) insisted that his company is not "publishing away from the evangelical market." Instead, he explained, "we're just casting a broader net."[14] Yet how broad can that net ultimately become before it no longer catches evangelical consumers?

In this book I have argued that the business of religion perpetually has created new answers to this question. As practices of commercialism have created new evangelical markets, those markets have conjured new evangelical publics. Today, at least, we know these publics as "evangelicalism," the commercial religion of our time.

ABBREVIATIONS IN NOTES

NOTES

ACKNOWLEDGMENTS

INDEX

Abbreviations in Notes

*Archives and Special Collections of Morgan Library,
Grace College, Winona Lake, IN*

WLCA   Winona Lake Christian Assembly Papers

Baker Publishing Group Archives, Grand Rapids, MI

FHRC   Fleming H. Revell Company Records

Billy Graham Center Archives, Wheaton College, Wheaton, IL (BGC)

HJA   Ephemera of Hyman Jedidiah Appelman (Coll. 114)
HL   Harold Lindsell Papers (Coll. 192)
RMC   Records of The Moody Church (Coll. 330)
WBS   Papers of William Ashley 'Billy' Sunday and Helen Amelia
             (Thompson) Sunday (Coll. 61)

Crowell Library Archives, Moody Bible Institute, Chicago, IL

APF   Arthur P. Fitt Correspondence
BICA   Bible Institute Colportage Association Trustee Minutes
DLM-MBI   Dwight L. Moody Correspondence Collection
MBI-BF   Moody Bible Institute Biographical Folders
MBI-ED   Moody Bible Institute Education Drawers

Fuller Theological Seminary, Pasadena, CA

WS   Wilbur Smith Papers

Gordon-Conwell Theological Seminary, Hamilton, MA

HJO   Harold John Ockenga Papers

Heritage Hall, Hekman Library, Calvin College, Grand Rapids, MI

WBE-HH   William B. Eerdmans Collection, 1912–1957 (Coll. 249)
BKK   Barend Klass Kuiper Collection, 1855–1961 (Coll. 152)
HB   Henry Beets Collection, 1824–1981 (Coll. 11)

Holloway Archives at Milligan College, Milligan College, TN

JDM   James DeForest Murch Papers

Wheaton College Archives and Special Collections, Wheaton College, Wheaton, IL

CBT   Committee on Bible Translation records, 1984 (Coll. 218)
KT   Kenneth Taylor Papers (Coll. 12)

William B. Eerdmans Company, Grand Rapids, MI

WBE   William B. Eerdmans Papers
WBEC   William B. Eerdmans Company Archives

Yale Divinity School, New Haven, CT

DLM-YDS   Dwight L. Moody Papers

Zondervan Corporation, Grand Rapids, MI

ZPH-ED   Zondervan Publishing House Editorial Records
ZPH   Zondervan Publishing House Archives

Notes

Introduction

1. Although descriptions of the book frequently have added the qualifier "non-fiction" to the label "best-selling hardcover," numerous articles and books began making the larger claim as early as 2005. The claim's inaccuracy notwithstanding, it became part of the book's reputation. See Greg Stielstra, *PyroMarketing: The Four-Step Strategy to Ignite Customer Evangelists and Keep Them for Life* (New York: HarperBusiness, 2005), ix; Daren Briscoe, "The Giving Back Awards: 15 People Who Make America Great," *Newsweek*, July 2, 2006; Suzanne Strempek Shea, *Sundays in America: A Yearlong Road Trip in Search of Christian Faith* (Boston: Beacon Press, 2008), 142; Monique El-Faizy, *God and Country: How Evangelicals Have Become America's New Mainstream* (New York: Bloomsbury, 2008), 119; Jeffery L. Sheler, *Prophet of Purpose: The Life of Rick Warren* (New York: Doubleday Religion, 2009), 181; Amy Sullivan, "Rick Warren's Magazine: A Publishing Leap of Faith," *Time*, March 10, 2009.
2. One assessment describes the book as "self-help made easy," insofar as it promises that God will change a reader's life, whereas self-help books traditionally place that responsibility on the reader herself. El-Faizy, *God and Country*, 127.
3. On measuring religion through polls, and the campaign to quantify evangelicalism, see Robert Wuthnow, *Inventing American Religion: Polls, Surveys, and the Tenuous Quest for a Nation's Faith* (New York: Oxford University Press, 2015), esp. 123–126.
4. David Kinnaman, president of Barna Group, "reported that one-quarter of all American adults—and nearly two-thirds of evangelicals—had read the book by the middle of 2005." "Gauging the Impact of 'Purpose Driven Life,' 10 Years

On," November 29, 2012, http://religion.blogs.cnn.com/2012/11/29/short -takes-gauging-the-impact-of-purpose-driven-life-10-years-on/.

5. For a diagnosis of this paradigm, see François Gauthier, Linda Woodhead, and Tuomas Martikainen, "Introduction: Consumerism as the Ethos of Society," in *Religion in Consumer Society: Brands, Consumers, and Markets,* ed. François Gauthier and Tuomas Martikainen, Ashgate AHRC/ESRC Religion and Society Series (Burlington, VT: Ashgate, 2013), 1–24, e.g., 6. Many existing studies of evangelical media follow this general framework. In her pioneering book *Shaking the World for Jesus,* for example, Heather Hendershot emphasizes how people inside the "evangelical belief system" use evangelical media to guard "against secular contamination" and "sustain faith." Heather Hendershot, *Shaking the World for Jesus: Media and Conservative Evangelical Culture* (Chicago: University of Chicago Press, 2004), 8, 11.

6. N. Gregory Mankiw, *Principles of Economics,* 4th ed. (Boston: Cengage Learning, 2007), 9, 66.

7. Kathryn Lofton, *Consuming Religion* (Chicago: University of Chicago Press, 2017), 7–8, 10. See also Gauthier, Woodhead, and Martikainen, "Introduction," esp. 3, 17–18.

8. This emphasis on institutions builds on the work of a variety of scholars, many of whom are indebted to Joel A. Carpenter's pioneering "Fundamentalist Institutions and the Rise of Evangelical Protestantism, 1929–1942," *Church History* 49, no. 1 (March 1980): 62–75.

9. Darren E. Grem, *The Blessings of Business: How Corporations Shaped Conservative Christianity* (New York: Oxford University Press, 2016); Sarah Hammond, *God's Businessmen: Evangelicals in Depression and War* (Chicago: University of Chicago Press, 2017); Darren Dochuk, *From Bible Belt to Sunbelt: Plain-Folk Religion, Grassroots Politics, and the Rise of Evangelical Conservatism* (New York: W. W. Norton, 2011); Timothy Gloege, *Guaranteed Pure: The Moody Bible Institute, Business, and the Making of Modern Evangelicalism* (Chapel Hill: University of North Carolina Press, 2015); Kim Phillips-Fein, *Invisible Hands: The Businessmen's Crusade against the New Deal* (New York: W. W. Norton, 2010); Elizabeth A. Fones-Wolf, *Selling Free Enterprise: The Business Assault on Labor and Liberalism, 1945–60* (Urbana: University of Illinois Press, 1994); Kevin M. Kruse, *One Nation under God: How Corporate America Invented Christian America* (New York: Basic Books, 2015).

10. On "commercial capitalism" as a term that highlights an emphasis on "marketing goods and making money," see William R. Leach, *Land of Desire: Merchants, Power and the Rise of a New American Culture* (New York: Vintage Books, 1994), 9. Other scholars have used the term "commercial religion." Peter Edge uses the term to highlight activities that reflect an "entanglement of the commercial and the religious." He defines a "commercial religious activity" as "one which the person carrying it out sees as part of their clear structure and belief system concerning metaphysical reality, and which is also carried out in part to generate an operating profit." Although I appreciate the entanglement that Edge describes, I use this term primarily to describe

religious formations, as opposed to particular religious activities. Peter W. Edge, "Believer Beware: The Challenges of Commercial Religion," *Legal Studies* 33, no. 3 (September 2013): 382–406, quote on 383–384. The notion "commercial religion" serves as a conceptual cousin of "industrial religion," which scholars of religion have used to describe discourses that attribute "suprahuman power" to the raw materials and mechanical technologies of industrial production. Commercial ideas and technologies have acquired "suprahuman power" by giving life to religions like evangelicalism. Richard J. Callahan Jr., Kathryn E. Lofton, and Chad E. Seales, "Allegories of Progress: Industrial Religion in the United States," *Journal of the American Academy of Religion* 78, no. 1 (March 2010): 1–39, quote on 3.

11. R. Laurence Moore, *Selling God: American Religion in the Marketplace of Culture* (New York: Oxford University Press, 1994), e.g., 6, 255–256, 272; Wade Clark Roof, *Spiritual Marketplace: Baby Boomers and the Remaking of American Religion* (Princeton: Princeton University Press, 1999), e.g., 69.

12. For more on the processual creation of religion, consider how the anthropologists Charles Hirschkind and Brian Larkin define religion and its relationship to mediation: "Religions are constituted through an architecture of circulation and representation that in turn creates the pragmatic contexts for modes of practice and worship." I appreciate this definition especially for its emphasis on the continual reconstitution of religious formations, through mediation. Charles Hirschkind and Brian Larkin, "Introduction: Media and the Political Forms of Religion," *Social Text* 26, no. 3 (96) (September 2008): 1–9, quote on 2. See also Jeremy Stolow, "Religion and/as Media," *Theory, Culture & Society* 22, no. 4 (August 2005): 119–145, esp. 124–125; Matthew Engelke, "Religion and the Media Turn: A Review Essay," *American Ethnologist* 37, no. 2 (May 2010): 371–379, esp. 347.

13. On "juvenilization," see Thomas Bergler, *The Juvenilization of American Christianity* (Grand Rapids, MI: Eerdmans, 2012), e.g., 6.

14. The notion of a "field" as a network of forces that orient strategies and actions is most commonly associated with Pierre Bourdieu, who expressed the idea in such works as *The Field of Cultural Production: Essays on Art and Literature* (New York: Columbia University Press, 1993), 30. On field theory in religious studies, see Courtney Bender, "Practicing Religion," in *The Cambridge Companion to Religious Studies,* ed. Robert A. Orsi (New York: Cambridge University Press, 2012), 273–295, esp. 280–281; see also John Levi Martin, "What Is Field Theory?," *American Journal of Sociology* 109, no. 1 (July 2003): 1–49, esp. 42.

15. John B. Thompson, *Merchants of Culture: The Publishing Business in the Twenty-First Century,* 2nd ed. (New York: Plume, 2012), 10.

16. For an example of such questioning, see Harold L. Johnson, "Can the Businessman Apply Christianity?," *Harvard Business Review* 35, no. 5 (October 9, 1957): 68–76.

17. For just one example of a debate around these matters, see David A. Light, "Is Success a Sin?," *Harvard Business Review* 79, no. 8 (September 2001): 63–69.

18. Candy Gunther Brown, *The Word in the World: Evangelical Writing, Publishing, and Reading in America, 1789–1880* (Chapel Hill: University of North Carolina Press, 2004), e.g., 244.

19. In 2013, News Corporation divided into two separate, publicly traded companies: News Corporation (generally known as News Corp), which focuses on publishing, and 21st Century Fox, which focuses on television and film. But the Murdoch family retains control of both corporations. Amy Chozick, "News Corporation Board Approves Split of Company," *New York Times*, May 24, 2013, sec. Business.

20. I capitalize "Bible" in titles or to refer to the general concept, as opposed to physical "bibles" and particular "bible passages." This follows Seth Perry, in *Bible Culture and Authority in the Early United States* (Princeton: Princeton University Press, 2018), xv. Alice Payne Hackett, "Bestsellers in the Bookstores, 1900–1975," in *Bookselling in America and the World: Some Observations and Recollections in Celebration of the 75th Anniversary of the American Booksellers Association,* ed. Charles B. Anderson (New York: Quadrangle / New York Times Book Co., 1975), 136–137.

21. Stielstra, *PyroMarketing,* 5–7.

22. G. A. Marken, "Review of PyroMarketing: The Four-Step Strategy to Ignite Customer Evangelists and Keep Them for Life," *Public Relations Quarterly* 50, no. 3 (Fall 2005): 3–4.

23. Juli Cragg Hilliard, "Purpose-Driven Interference?," *Publishers Weekly* 252, no. 29 (July 25, 2005): 14–15; Juli Cragg Hilliard, "'Pyro' Goes Ahead; Warren Weighs In," *Publishers Weekly,* August 29, 2005, 9. For more on the controversy, and on Christian marketing, see Joel Coppieters, "Marketing Spirituality," *Presbyterian Record,* June 2007; "Onward, Christian Shoppers: Religion and Business," *The Economist,* December 3, 2005.

24. On selves within systems, see Lofton, *Consuming Religion,* 211.

25. "About Pastors.Com," *pastors.com,* accessed September 22, 2017, http://pastors.com/about.

26. James E. Ruark, *The House of Zondervan,* 2nd ed. (Grand Rapids, MI: Zondervan, 2006), 188–190. See also El-Faizy, *God and Country,* 128–130.

27. On evangelical readers and reading, see Amy Johnson Frykholm, *Rapture Culture: Left Behind in Evangelical America* (New York: Oxford University Press, 2004); Glenn W Shuck, *Marks of the Beast: The Left Behind Novels and the Struggle for Evangelical Identity* (New York: NYU Press, 2005); Lynn S. Neal, *Romancing God: Evangelical Women and Inspirational Fiction* (Chapel Hill: University of North Carolina Press, 2006); James S. Bielo, *Words upon the Word: An Ethnography of Evangelical Group Bible Study* (New York: NYU Press, 2009); Erin A. Smith, *What Would Jesus Read? Popular Religious Books and Everyday Life in Twentieth-Century America* (Chapel Hill: University of North Carolina Press, 2015).

28. This story is a synopsis of the story as related through a variety of newspaper accounts. See, for example, Dahleen Glanton and John Bebow, "Hostage Won Atlanta Killing Suspect's Trust," *Chicago Tribune,* March 14, 2005. See also Shayne Lee and Phillip Luke Sinitiere, *Holy Mavericks: Evangelical In-*

novators and the Spiritual Marketplace (New York: NYU Press, 2009), 129–131.

29. On the project of defining evangelicalism's boundaries, see David F. Wells and John D. Woodbridge, *The Evangelicals: What They Believe, Who They Are, Where They Are Changing* (Nashville, TN: Abingdon Press, 1975); Mark A. Noll, David W. Bebbington, and George A. Rawlyk, eds., *Evangelicalism: Comparative Studies of Popular Protestantism in North America, the British Isles, and Beyond, 1700–1900* (New York: Oxford University Press, 1994); Donald W. Dayton and Robert K. Johnston, eds., *The Variety of American Evangelicalism* (Pasadena, CA: Wipf and Stock, 1998); Leonard I. Sweet, "Wise as Serpents, Innocent as Doves: The New Evangelical Historiography," *Journal of the American Academy of Religion* 56, no. 3 (Autumn 1988): 397–416; Jon R. Stone, *On the Boundaries of American Evangelicalism: The Postwar Evangelical Coalition* (New York: St. Martin's Press, 1997); George M. Marsden, "The Evangelical Denomination," in *Evangelicalism and Modern America,* ed. George M. Marsden (Grand Rapids, MI: Eerdmans, 1984), vii–xix.

30. David W. Bebbington, *Evangelicalism in Modern Britain: A History from the 1730s to the 1980s* (London: Unwin Hyman, 1989), 2–17.

31. Douglas L. Winiarski, *Darkness Falls on the Land of Light: Experiencing Religious Awakenings in Eighteenth-Century New England* (Chapel Hill: University of North Carolina Press, 2017), 15–16.

32. As the sociologist Corwin Smidt explains, Bebbington's criteria, and surveys based on them, ultimately produce "basically a categorical, rather than a social, group." Corwin E. Smidt, *American Evangelicals Today* (Lanham, MD: Rowman and Littlefield, 2013), 51.

33. On the use of this question to quantify evangelicalism, see Wuthnow, *Inventing American Religion*, 123–126; Smidt, *American Evangelicals Today*, 52. For a recent instance, see Pew Research Center, "Chapter 1: The Changing Religious Composition of the U.S: A Note on How the Study Defines Evangelicals," in "America's Changing Religious Landscape," May 12, 2015, http://pewforum .org/2015/05/12/chapter-1-the-changing-religious-composition-of-the-u-s/.

34. Michael Warner, *Publics and Counterpublics* (New York: Zone Books, 2002), esp. 71, 87–89. Although Warner's notion of "publics" is indebted largely to the work of Jürgen Habermas, a close conceptual cousin is the notion of mediated "imagined communities," a concept associated above all with the work of Benedict R. Anderson. See Habermas, *The Structural Transformation of the Public Sphere: An Inquiry into a Category of Bourgeois Society* (Cambridge, MA: MIT Press, 1989); Anderson, *Imagined Communities: Reflections on the Origin and Spread of Nationalism,* 2nd ed. (London: Verso, 1991). But other media theorists also have proposed variations on Anderson's insights by positing broader conceptions of religious sociality. Birgit Meyer suggests that scholars of religion and media conceive of social groups not as "communities" premised upon "vertical, hierarchical relations" but instead as "formations" that take shape processually. I use "publics" here, in part, because it captures this same emphasis on continual creation. Birgit Meyer, "From

Imagined Communities to Aesthetic Formations: Religious Mediations, Sensational Forms, and Styles of Binding," in *Aesthetic Formations: Media, Religion, and the Senses,* ed. Birgit Meyer (New York: Palgrave Macmillan, 2009), 1–30.

35. For examples of how religious categories have organized social groups, see scholarship on the creation of "world religions," including Tomoko Masuzawa, *The Invention of World Religions, or, How European Universalism Was Preserved in the Language of Pluralism* (Chicago: University of Chicago Press, 2005); Nicholas B. Dirks, *Castes of Mind: Colonialism and the Making of Modern India* (Princeton: Princeton University Press, 2001); Daniel Vaca, "'Great Religions' as Peacemaker: What Unitarian Infighting Did for Comparative Religion," *History of Religions* 53, no. 2 (November 2013): 115–150. See also Shahzad Bashir, "Everlasting Doubt: Uncertainty in Islamic Representations of the Past," *Archiv für Religionsgeschichte* 20, no. 1 (March 2018): 25–44, esp. 27–28.

36. This adjectival impulse lay behind Martin Luther's notion of an "evangelische Kirche." The nineteenth-century historian of American Christianity Robert Baird famously drew up a list of "evangelical" and "unevangelical" denominations, which included almost all Protestants in the former category and consigned only Roman Catholics, Unitarians, Universalists, Swedenborgians, Jews, Shakers, Mormons, Atheists, and other free thinkers to the latter category. Robert Baird, *Religion in America; Or, An Account of the Origin, Progress, Relation to the State, and Present Condition of the Evangelical Churches in the United States* (New York: Harper and Brothers, 1844). This adjectival impulse has held true even for scholars, many of whom have sought to narrate a tradition of "evangelicalism" that represents a tradition that they identify as their own. See D. G. Hart, *Deconstructing Evangelicalism: Conservative Protestantism in the Age of Billy Graham* (Grand Rapids, MI: Baker Academic, 2004).

37. Kathryn Lofton explains that "the only test to determine whether a Christian is an evangelical is whether he or she possesses a strong Christian identity that supersedes denominational location." Lofton, *Oprah: The Gospel of an Icon* (Berkeley: University of California Press, 2011), 73.

38. Gloege, *Guaranteed Pure,* 5–7, 139.

39. On evangelicalism and markets, see Charles Grier Sellers, *The Market Revolution: Jacksonian America, 1815–1846* (New York: Oxford University Press, 1991); Daniel Walker Howe, *What Hath God Wrought: The Transformation of America, 1815–1848* (New York: Oxford University Press, 2007); David Paul Nord, *Faith in Reading: Religious Publishing and the Birth of Mass Media in America* (New York: Oxford University Press, 2004); Moore, *Selling God;* Hendershot, *Shaking the World.*

40. On the ways in which the term "evangelical" has denoted shifting social constituencies throughout American history, see Linford D. Fisher, "Evangelicals and Unevangelicals: The Contested History of a Word, 1500–1950," *Religion and American Culture: A Journal of Interpretation* 26, no. 2 (Summer 2016): 184–226.

41. See John Patrick Daly, *When Slavery Was Called Freedom: Evangelicalism, Proslavery, and the Causes of the Civil War* (Lexington: University Press of Kentucky, 2002); Matthew Avery Sutton, *American Apocalypse: A History of Modern Evangelicalism* (Cambridge, MA: Belknap Press of Harvard University Press, 2014); Seth Dowland, *Family Values and the Rise of the Christian Right* (Philadelphia: University of Pennsylvania Press, 2015); Jason C. Bivins, *Religion of Fear: The Politics of Horror in Conservative Evangelicalism* (New York: Oxford University Press, 2008).

42. "Fewer than half of those who identify as evangelicals (45 percent) strongly agree with core evangelical beliefs," reported LifeWay Research in 2017. "Many Who Call Themselves Evangelical Don't Actually Hold Evangelical Beliefs," *LifeWay Research*, December 6, 2017, http://lifewayresearch.com /2017/12/06/many-evangelicals-dont-hold-evangelical-beliefs/.

43. As one evangelical industry study found in 2017, African American Christians not only are "more likely to say they are born again (49 percent) than whites (27 percent)" and "the most likely to have evangelical beliefs (30 percent)" but also tend to view "the term 'evangelical' . . . as applying to white Christians only." "Many Who Call Themselves." On evangelical support for Donald Trump, see John Fea, *Believe Me: The Evangelical Road to Donald Trump* (Grand Rapids, MI: Eerdmans, 2018).

44. Edward Wyatt, "Spiritual Book Helped Hostage Mollify Captor," *New York Times*, March 15, 2005.

45. Gracie Bonds Staples, "Influential Author Reaches Out to Nichols," *Atlanta Journal-Constitution*, March 24, 2005.

46. "Evangelical Protestants: Religious Landscape Study," *Pew Research Center's Religion and Public Life Project*, May 11, 2015, https://www.pewforum.org /religious-landscape-study/religious-tradition/evangelical-protestant/. Consult "Trends" for data from 2007.

47. Jim Remsen, "Powerful Words: The Book That Saved the Ga. Hostage," *Philadelphia Inquirer*, March 16, 2005.

48. Mark Rice, interview by author, Grand Rapids, MI, October 13, 2016.

49. Lofton, *Oprah*, 72–74, 129–130. On viewership, see Ed Pilkington, "Ratings of Daytime Oprah Winfrey Show Are Down 7%," *The Guardian*, May 26, 2008, sec. Media, http://www.theguardian.com/media/2008/may/27/television.usa.

50. On publics and markets, see Stolow, "Religion and / as Media," esp. 133.

51. Anderson, *Imagined Communities*, 40. See also Andrew Pettegree, *Brand Luther: 1517, Printing, and the Making of the Reformation* (New York: Penguin Press, 2015).

52. Brown, *Word in the World*, 10.

53. John Lardas Modern, *Secularism in Antebellum America: With Reference to Ghosts, Protestant Subcultures, Machines, and Their Metaphors; Featuring Discussions of Mass Media, Moby-Dick, Spirituality, Phrenology, Anthropology, Sing Sing State Penitentiary, and Sex with the New Motive Power* (Chicago: University of Chicago Press, 2011), 53, 75.

54. For an overview of books and evangelical devotional life, see Michael A. Longinow, "Publishing Books for the Tribe and Beyond," in *Understanding*

Evangelical Media: The Changing Face of Christian Communication, ed. Quentin J. Schultze and Robert Woods (Downers Grove, IL: IVP Academic, 2008), 85–97. On evangelical devotion to the authority of religious texts, see Smidt, *American Evangelicals Today,* 92–95.

55. Neal, *Romancing God,* quote on 12.

56. Frykholm, *Rapture Culture,* 182–183. On prophecy fiction, see also Crawford Gribben, *Writing the Rapture: Prophecy Fiction in Evangelical America* (Oxford: Oxford University Press, 2009).

57. Todd M. Brenneman, *Homespun Gospel: The Triumph of Sentimentality in Contemporary American Evangelicalism* (New York: Oxford University Press, 2013), 13.

58. Tanya M. Luhrmann, *When God Talks Back: Understanding the American Evangelical Relationship with God* (New York: Knopf, 2012), xvi, 14.

59. See Bielo, *Words upon the Word,* esp. 15. For the notion that "speaking is believing," Bielo draws on Susan Friend Harding, *The Book of Jerry Falwell: Fundamentalist Language and Politics* (Princeton: Princeton University Press, 2000).

60. On the social infrastructure of reading, see Elizabeth Long, "Textual Interpretation as Collective Action," in *The Ethnography of Reading,* ed. Jonathan Boyarin (Berkeley: University of California Press, 1993), 180–211.

61. Brown, *Word in the World,* 118.

62. Although books are what the media theorist John Durham Peters describes as "preeminent political animals," their commodity status often remains hidden behind other aspects of their "collective dimension." John Durham Peters, *The Marvelous Clouds: Toward a Philosophy of Elemental Media* (Chicago: University of Chicago Press, 2016), 323.

63. See Pierre Bayard, *How to Talk about Books You Haven't Read* (New York: Bloomsbury, 2007), e.g., 6.

64. *Books for Ministers,* 1974, back cover, ZPH.

65. Robert Darnton, *The Business of Enlightenment: A Publishing History of the Encyclopédie, 1775–1800* (Cambridge: Belknap Press of Harvard University Press, 1979), 7, 530–531.

66. Brown, *Word in the World,* 47–48.

67. On how technological change revolutionized publishing in Britain, see Aileen Fyfe, *Steam-Powered Knowledge: William Chambers and the Business of Publishing, 1820–1860* (Chicago: University of Chicago Press, 2012).

68. See Sarah Barringer Gordon, "The First Disestablishment: Limits on Church Power and Property before the Civil War," *University of Pennsylvania Law Review* 162, no. 2 (January 2014): 307–372.

69. David Paul Nord, "Benevolent Capital: Financing Evangelical Book Publishing in Early Nineteenth-Century America," in *God and Mammon: Protestants, Money, and the Market, 1790–1860,* ed. Mark A. Noll (Oxford: Oxford University Press, 2002), 147–170, esp. 164.

70. The history of the book industry generally has focused disproportionately on the nineteenth century. See Theodore G. Striphas, *The Late Age of Print: Ev-*

eryday Book Culture from Consumerism to Control (New York: Columbia University Press, 2009), 187.

71. As Matthew Hedstrom illustrates, liberal Protestants did amass cultural power during the middle decades of the twentieth century, and publishing served as a primary field of activity. But neither Hedstrom nor other historians have explored how evangelical publishers remained active all along. Matthew S. Hedstrom, *The Rise of Liberal Religion: Book Culture and American Spirituality in the Twentieth Century* (New York: Oxford University Press, 2013).

72. Hackett, "Bestsellers in the Bookstores," 136–137; on Marabel Morgan and *The Total Woman,* see Steven P. Miller, *The Age of Evangelicalism: America's Born-Again Years* (New York: Oxford University Press, 2014), 24–25.

73. A few scholars have explored similar relationships in other commercial contexts. Examining the Orthodox Jewish publisher ArtScroll, Jeremy Stolow argues that "ArtScroll's successes can be understood as part of a broader shift that has consolidated the position of religious publishing within the global print market and has accorded new prominence to religious print commodities in various arenas of public and private life." Jeremy Stolow, *Orthodox by Design: Judaism, Print Politics, and the ArtScroll Revolution* (Berkeley: University of California Press, 2010), 22. On capitalism and evangelicalism, see William E. Connolly, "The Evangelical-Capitalist Resonance Machine," *Political Theory* 33, no. 6 (December 2005): 869–886.

74. Cynthia Crossen, "Harper & Row Says It Will Acquire Zondervan, Expand Religious Line," *Wall Street Journal,* July 14, 1988; Roger Cohen, "Birth of a Global Book Giant," *New York Times,* June 11, 1990, sec. Business.

75. Allan Fisher, "The Man Who 'Owns' the News—and the Bible: Rupert Murdoch, HarperCollins, and the Recent History of Bible Publishing" (unpublished paper delivered at the 2014 annual meeting of the Society for the History of Authorship, Reading and Publishing, Antwerp, Belgium). One report on the acquisition explained, "The size of [the religion trade and Bible] markets is notoriously difficult to estimate; books with religion content span many genres, and publishers define what is a religion book in different ways." But the same report noted that "the acquisition is estimated to capture about 70% of known sales in the category." Lynn Garrett, "Stunned Reaction to HarperCollins's Acquisition of Thomas Nelson," *Publishers Weekly,* November 7, 2011; Lynn Garrett, "Harper Brings Thomas Nelson, Zondervan into New Publishing Division," *PublishersWeekly.com,* August 1, 2012, https://www.publishersweekly .com/pw/by-topic/industry-news/religion/article/53369-new-harper-christian -division-head-schoenwald-says-everything-is-under-review.html.

76. On the evangelical culture industry and its conservative drift in the 1980s, see Randall H. Balmer, *Mine Eyes Have Seen the Glory: A Journey into the Evangelical Subculture in America,* 5th ed. (New York: Oxford University Press, 2014), chap. 10, esp. 205–206. On evangelicalism and conservatism, see also Axel R. Schäfer, *Countercultural Conservatives: American Evangelicalism from the Postwar Revival to the New Christian Right* (Madison: University of Wisconsin Press, 2011), 111, 145–147.

77. See Jonathan L. Walton, *Watch This! The Ethics and Aesthetics of Black Tel-evangelism* (New York: NYU Press, 2009), 26; see also Eileen Luhr, *Witnessing Suburbia: Conservatives and Christian Youth Culture* (Berkeley: University of California Press, 2009).

78. Miller, *The Age of Evangelicalism*, 5, 160–163.

79. Daniel Cox and Robert P. Jones, "America's Changing Religious Identity," Public Religion Research Institute, September 6, 2017, https://www.prri.org /research/american-religious-landscape-christian-religiously-unaffiliated/. PRRI defined "evangelicals" as "those who self-identify as Protestant Christians who also identify as evangelical or born again." See also Robert P. Jones, *The End of White Christian America* (New York: Simon and Schuster, 2016), 202–203.

80. On evangelical media's diffusion beyond the United States, see, for example, Melani McAlister, *The Kingdom of God Has No Borders: A Global History of American Evangelicals* (New York: Oxford University Press, 2018), 8; Marla Frederick, *Colored Television: American Religion Gone Global* (Stanford, CA: Stanford University Press, 2015); Simon Coleman, *The Globalisation of Charismatic Christianity: Spreading the Gospel of Prosperity* (New York: Cambridge University Press, 2000).

81. To see fluidity between liberal and conservative Protestantism in another media economy, see Josef Sorrett's study of Christian rap music. Josef Sorett, "'It's Not the Beat, but It's the Word That Sets the People Free': Race, Technology, and Theology in the Emergence of Christian Rap Music," *Pneuma* 33, no. 2 (2011): 200–217, esp. 204.

1. Finding Profit

1. Founded as the Chicago Bible Institute in 1889, it was renamed the Moody Bible Institute after Moody's death in 1899.

2. February 1, 1909, 146–147, book 1, BICA.

3. February 5, 1906, 87, book 1, BICA.

4. "Harpers Give Up Control," *New York Times*, November 29, 1899.

5. See John Lardas Modern, *Secularism in Antebellum America: With Reference to Ghosts, Protestant Subcultures, Machines, and Their Metaphors; Featuring Discussions of Mass Media, Moby-Dick, Spirituality, Phrenology, Anthropology, Sing Sing State Penitentiary, and Sex with the New Motive Power* (Chicago: University of Chicago Press, 2011), esp. 87.

6. Candy Gunther Brown, *The Word in the World: Evangelical Writing, Publishing, and Reading in America, 1789–1880* (Chapel Hill: University of North Carolina Press, 2004), 55.

7. February 5, 1906, book 1, BICA.

8. R. Laurence Moore, "Religion, Secularization, and the Shaping of the Culture Industry in Antebellum America," *American Quarterly* 41, no. 2 (June 1989): 216–242, esp. 222.

9. Laura J. Miller, *Reluctant Capitalists: Bookselling and the Culture of Consumption* (Chicago: University of Chicago Press, 2006), 27.

10. Dwight Baker, interview by author, Grand Rapids, MI, October 13, 2016.

11. On business activity as religious activity, see Darren E. Grem, *The Blessings of Business: How Corporations Shaped Conservative Christianity* (New York: Oxford University Press, 2016); Sarah R. Hammond, "'God Is My Partner': An Evangelical Business Man Confronts Depression and War," *Church History: Studies in Christianity and Culture* 80, no. 3 (September 2011): 498–519; Bethany Moreton, *To Serve God and Wal-Mart: The Making of Christian Free Enterprise* (Cambridge, MA: Harvard University Press, 2009). On the commodification of religion, see R. Laurence Moore, *Selling God: American Religion in the Marketplace of Culture* (New York: Oxford University Press, 1994).

12. E. T. M., "What People Are Reading," *The Advance,* April 7, 1904, 429.

13. Philip Schaff, *America* (New York: Charles Scribner, 1855), 33–34.

14. James N. Green, "The Rise of Book Publishing," in *An Extensive Republic: Print, Culture, and Society in the New Nation, 1790–1840,* ed. Robert A. Gross and Mary Kelley, vol. 2 of *A History of the Book in America* (Chapel Hill: American Antiquarian Society/University of North Carolina Press, 2010), 75–127, esp. 86–88.

15. Ronald J. Zboray, *A Fictive People: Antebellum Economic Development and the American Reading Public* (New York: Oxford University Press, 1993), 18.

16. On state support for religious societies and corporations, see Sarah Barringer Gordon, "The First Disestablishment: Limits on Church Power and Property before the Civil War," *University of Pennsylvania Law Review* 162, no. 2 (January 2014): 307–372.

17. "American Bible Society," *Religious Intelligencer,* September 2, 1820.

18. By 1838, in cities like Philadelphia, New York, Boston, Newport, Charleston, and Baltimore, at least one hundred black benevolent societies had emerged. Donald F. Joyce, *Gatekeepers of Black Culture: Black-Owned Book Publishing in the United States, 1817–1981* (Westport, CT: Greenwood Press, 1983), 7; Robert L. Harris, "Early Black Benevolent Societies, 1780–1830," *Massachusetts Review* 20, no. 3 (1979): 603–625.

19. James D. Bratt, "The Reorientation of American Protestantism, 1835–1845," *Church History* 67, no. 1 (March 1998): 52–82, esp. 61–62. While portraying Roman Catholicism and Roman Catholics as obstacles to progress, agents of Protestant benevolence also insisted that immigrants' lives would improve if they embraced Protestant religion and culture. "Roman Catholics, particularly in this part of the United States," the Congregationalist Leonard Bacon explained in 1844, "are generally foreigners—strangers in birth and lineage, strangers to our history and our religion—marked to some extent by a distinctive physiognomy, and to a greater extent by differences of language, or at least of dialect." What any American Protestant should recognize, Bacon explained, is that "to him who takes the Bible alone for his authoritative standard, the religion of Rome is polytheism." Paul S. Boyer, *Urban Masses and Moral Order in America, 1820–1920* (Cambridge, MA: Harvard University Press, 1978), 23–24; Leonard Bacon, "Romanists and the Roman Catholic Controversy," *New Englander* 2, no. 6 (April 1844): 233; see also John Wolffe, "Anti-Catholicism and Evangelical Identity in Britain and the United States, 1830–1860," in *Evangelicalism: Comparative Studies of Popular Protestantism*

in North America, the British Isles, and Beyond, 1700–1900, ed. Mark A. Noll, David W. Bebbington, and George A. Rawlyk (New York: Oxford University Press, 1994), 179–197.

20. Finbarr Curtis, *The Production of American Religious Freedom* (New York: NYU Press, 2016), 8. For a helpful synopsis of debates over the "social control thesis," see Heath W. Carter, *Union Made: Working People and the Rise of Social Christianity in Chicago* (New York: Oxford University Press, 2015), 192 n. 56.

21. "American Sunday School Union," *Boston Recorder,* November 23, 1843, 186; see also Daniel Walker Howe, *What Hath God Wrought: The Transformation of America, 1815–1848* (New York: Oxford University Press, 2007), e.g., 192; Charles I. Foster, *An Errand of Mercy: The Evangelical United Front, 1790–1837* (Chapel Hill: University of North Carolina Press, 1960).

22. "An Evangelical Literature," *New York Evangelist,* May 26, 1838, 84.

23. David Paul Nord, *Faith in Reading: Religious Publishing and the Birth of Mass Media in America* (New York: Oxford University Press, 2004), 153. On the American Bible Society's debates over providing slaves with bibles, see John Fea, *The Bible Cause: A History of the American Bible Society* (New York: Oxford University Press, 2016), esp. chap. 7.

24. *Ninth Annual Report of the American Tract Society* (Andover, MA: American Tract Society, 1823), 19–21.

25. Nord, *Faith in Reading,* 41–45, 80.

26. Ibid., 83.

27. See ibid., esp. chap. 3.

28. "Increasing Demand for Religious Books," *New York Evangelist,* June 3, 1852, 92. See also John Modern's claim that "evangelical publishers were in the business of catalyzing desire." Modern, *Secularism in Antebellum America,* 93.

29. W. S, "The Moral Influence of 'Money-Making,'" *New York Evangelist,* March 12, 1836.

30. "Cost and Value of Colportage," *The Independent,* March 17, 1859, 4.

31. Paul C. Gutjahr, "Diversification in American Religious Publishing," in *The Industrial Book, 1840–1880,* ed. Scott E. Casper et al., vol. 3 of *A History of the Book in America* (Chapel Hill: American Antiquarian Society/University of North Carolina Press, 2007), 194–202, esp. 195. For a survey of industrial changes, see John Lauritz Larson, *The Market Revolution in America: Liberty, Ambition, and the Eclipse of the Common Good* (New York: Cambridge University Press, 2010).

32. Only in the 1830s did publishers begin to experiment with lowering prices to spur sales. Green, "Rise of Book Publishing," 75–127.

33. Zboray, *A Fictive People,* chap. 4, pp. 76–80.

34. "A Measure of Economy," *The Independent,* October 24, 1861, 4.

35. Robin Klay and John Lunn, "Protestants and the American Economy in the Postcolonial Period: An Overview," in *God and Mammon: Protestants, Money, and the Market, 1790–1860,* ed. Mark A. Noll (Oxford: Oxford University Press, 2002), 30–53, esp. 36.

36. Nord, *Faith in Reading*, 151–156; *Centennial of the Methodist Book Concern and Dedication of the New Publishing and Mission Building of the Methodist Episcopal Church* (New York: Hunt and Eaton, 1890), 70.

37. *Centennial of the Methodist Book Concern*, 75. Also quoted in Brown, *Word in the World*, 55.

38. Gutjahr, "Diversification," 194–202, esp. 200.

39. John William Tebbel, *Between Covers: The Rise and Transformation of Book Publishing in America* (New York: Oxford University Press, 1987), 24–31.

40. T. J. Jackson Lears, *Fables of Abundance: A Cultural History of Advertising in America* (New York: Basic Books, 1994), 232.

41. Brendan M. Pietsch, *Dispensational Modernism* (New York: Oxford University Press, 2015), 25.

42. "Summary of Moody and Sankey's Labors in London," *New York Times*, July 14, 1875; "Home Again: Moody and Sankey's Arrival in New York Last Saturday," *Daily Inter Ocean*, August 18, 1875, sec. IV; "Messrs. Moody and Sankey," *New York Times*, July 4, 1875.

43. Timothy Gloege, *Guaranteed Pure: The Moody Bible Institute, Business, and the Making of Modern Evangelicalism* (Chapel Hill: University of North Carolina Press, 2015), 91–92; on Moody's appeal, see 34–39, 44.

44. "The Pulpit Ogre," *New York Times*, April 2, 1875.

45. Edward J. Blum, *Reforging the White Republic: Race, Religion, and American Nationalism, 1865–1898* (Baton Rouge: Louisiana State University Press, 2005), 129, 132.

46. William R. Moody, *The Life of Dwight L. Moody* (New York: Fleming H. Revell Co., 1900), 184, 191.

47. Writing in 1910, a career reporter for the *Chicago Tribune* would recall running "Moody news" as filler on days when more important stories proved unavailable. Frederick F. Cook, *Bygone Days in Chicago* (Chicago: A. C. McClurg and Co., 1910), 305–310.

48. "Messrs. Moody and Sankey."

49. Gloege, *Guaranteed Pure*, 30–33.

50. Dwight L. Moody, *Life Words*, ed. G. F. G. Royle (London: John Snow and Co., 1875), iv.

51. For unauthorized collections, see Dwight L. Moody, *Arrows and Anecdotes, with a Sketch of His Early Life and the Story of the Great Revival*, ed. John Lobb (New York: Henry Gurley, 1877); Moody, *Life Words*; Moody, *Wondrous Love* (London: Pickering and Inglis, 1876). For book of his anecdotes about children, see Moody, *D. L. Moody's Child Stories: Related by Him in His Revival Work in Europe and America*, ed. Rev. J. B. McClure (Chicago: Rhodes and McClure, 1877).

52. Simon Gilbert, "Introduction," in *D. L. Moody's Child Stories*.

53. Edward Blum, "'Paul Has Been Forgotten': Women, Gender, and Revivalism during the Gilded Age," *Journal of the Gilded Age and Progressive Era* 3, no. 3 (July 2004): 247–270, esp. 251.

54. Nancy F. Cott, *The Bonds of Womanhood: "Woman's Sphere" in New England, 1780–1835*, 2nd ed. (New Haven: Yale University Press, 1997), e.g., 136–140.

55. See Jane MacKinnon, *Recollections of 1874,* 17–26, series III, box 14, folder 1, DLM-YDS.

56. Gloege, *Guaranteed Pure,* 45–48; Margaret Lamberts Bendroth, *Fundamentalism and Gender: 1875 to the Present* (New Haven: Yale University Press, 1993), 26–29.

57. This interpretation of consumerism responds in particular to the theory of American culture's "feminization," as argued especially by Ann Douglas in *The Feminization of American Culture* (New York: Anchor Books / Doubleday, 1988 [1977]). Among Douglas's influential claims, she argued that women sought "influence" in American society by means of consumer print culture, which led women to produce and consume "unobtrusive" sentimental content that undermined substantive theology by exerting "an enormous influence on male purveyors of that culture" (8, 9, 73). Yet even as Douglas reveals how female consumers and authors shaped popular cultural production at the end of the nineteenth century, her argument dismisses much of that material as lacking serious "content." In her analysis, women's sentimental literature sought nothing more than "offhand attention" (9, 81–84). To be sure, in this chapter and the broader book, I often note how for-profit publishers avoided or elided theological ideas and emphases for the sake of broadening their markets. Rather than depict gender relations or cultural content reductively, however, I chronicle how business strategies took shape through institutional relationships and networks that reflected shifting understandings of theology, race, gender, and economy. Here and in several other chapters, I also treat new ideas and emphases as more than wan attempts to secure influence. I treat them as substantive practices of meaning-making in modernity. As this chapter later illustrates, for example, both the sentimental literature that Douglas disparaged and the premillennialist theology she might have deemed sufficiently substantial can be seen as expressions of therapeutic culture. On considering the social logic behind ostensibly feminine or "sentimental" material without disparaging its supposed intellectual merit, see Karin E. Gedge, *Without Benefit of Clergy: Women and the Pastoral Relationship in Nineteenth-Century American Culture* (New York: Oxford University Press, 2003), 198–203. On the history of home economics as an example of a response to the spirit domesticity in an era of masculinity in ministry and business, see Carolyn M. Goldstein, *Creating Consumers: Home Economists in Twentieth-Century America* (Chapel Hill: University of North Carolina Press, 2012), 22.

58. MacKinnon, *Recollections of 1874,* 144.

59. Bruce J. Evensen, *God's Man for the Gilded Age: D. L. Moody and the Rise of Modern Mass Evangelism* (Oxford: Oxford University Press, 2003), 34–37; "A Model Sunday-School," *The Christian,* January 8, 187, 1; Gloege, *Guaranteed Pure,* 34.

60. Quoted in John Charles Pollock, *Moody: A Biographical Portrait of the Pacesetter in Modern Mass Evangelism* (New York: Macmillan, 1963), 189.

61. After Moody's death, Fleming Revell would report that Moody had made $1,125,000 in royalties throughout his life, but that "none of this was used for his own personal expenses." "Relative Value of a U.S. Dollar Amount, 1774

to Present," accessed on April 1, 2019, measuringworth.com; J. A. Adams, "Dwight L. Moody," *The Advance,* January 4, 1900, 9.

62. "A Sensation Story from London; Moody and Sankey Said to Be Employed by P. T. Barnum," *San Francisco Chronicle,* May 15, 1875. Roman Catholic newspapers repeated the story most frequently, praising Barnum for doing "a service to religion" by producing such a "vivid, but terribly coarse" spectacle, revealing "all the ministers and sects of Protestantism in their true light." Quoted in "The New York Tablet," *New York Evangelist,* May 27, 1875, 2. But these accusations misrepresented both Barnum's and Moody's approaches to religion. A liberal Universalist who believed that truth could be revealed incidentally, Barnum theoretically could have embraced Moody's revivals as a form of "humbug" that might have led listeners toward the contemplation of "true religion" in spite of themselves. But Moody believed that truth lay in directness. David Walker, "The Humbug in American Religion: Ritual Theories of Nineteenth-Century Spiritualism," *Religion and American Culture: A Journal of Interpretation* 23, no. 1 (Winter 2013): 30–74, quote on 55. For a fascinating description of a theological argument between Moody, Sankey, and Barnum, see "Barnum, Moody, and Sankey," *Chicago Daily Tribune,* February 1, 1878.

63. Carter, *Union Made,* 82.

64. Quoted in Moody, *Life of Dwight L. Moody,* 226.

65. Pietsch, *Dispensational Modernism,* 25.

66. See Carter, *Union Made,* 23; Gloege, *Guaranteed Pure,* 141.

67. See John Corrigan, *Business of the Heart: Religion and Emotion in the Nineteenth Century* (Berkeley: University of California Press, 2002), quote on 165; see also Kathryn Long, *The Revival of 1857–58: Interpreting an American Religious Awakening* (New York: Oxford University Press, 1998).

68. A more popular counterpart to nineteenth-century political economists who made similar arguments, Moody championed market capitalism while also acknowledging that individuals occasionally performed condemnable acts through business activity. See Stewart Davenport, *Friends of the Unrighteous Mammon: Northern Christians and Market Capitalism, 1815–1860* (Chicago: University of Chicago Press, 2008), 59, 205.

69. Dwight L. Moody, *Twelve Select Sermons* (Chicago: F. H. Revell, 1881), 141.

70. Pietsch, *Dispensational Modernism,* 26–29. Even Moody's physical appearance conveyed his belief in business. Describing Moody just after he disembarked the *Spain,* for instance, one report remarked how his "short, cutaway, gray-mixed coat" presented him as "the model of a businessman." "Home Again."

71. George John Stevenson, *Historical Records of the Young Men's Christian Association, from 1844 to 1884* (London: "Christian Commonwealth" Office, 1884), 23–24, 31. See Corrigan, *Business of the Heart,* 192–193.

72. Gloege, *Guaranteed Pure,* 44.

73. Ibid., 54–55.

74. Pietsch, *Dispensational Modernism,* 38–40.

75. Lyle W. Dorsett, *A Passion for Souls: The Life of D. L. Moody* (Chicago: Moody Publishers, 2003), 331.

76. During his campaigns in Britain, for example, Moody developed a close working relationship with the Scottish publisher R. C. Morgan, editor of the popular newspaper *The Christian* (known originally as *The Revival*). Morgan's paper regularly publicized Moody's speaking events; in turn, Moody encouraged listeners to subscribe. During his revival tour in the early 1870s, Moody raised £2,000 from supporters to distribute the paper for three months to clergy of established and nonconformist churches throughout England. Moody, *Life of D. L. Moody*, 223; Evensen, *God's Man*, 21–39; "Moody's Farewell Address at Liverpool," *The Christian*, August 19, 1875: 8.

77. Evensen, *God's Man*, 108–110.

78. Pollock, *Moody*, 84.

79. "Revell: Seventy-Five Years of Religious Book Publishing," *Publishers Weekly*, December 9, 1944: 2232. See also Tebbel, *Between Covers*, 141.

80. Pollock, *Moody*, 20, 43–44; Moody, *Life of Dwight L. Moody*, 115–122; Long, *The Revival of 1857–58*, 88; Evensen, *God's Man*, 125–126.

81. "Thirteenth Annual Meeting of the Y.M.C.A.," *Chicago Tribune*, May 10, 1871; on Revell's traveling sales, see Dorsett, *A Passion for Souls*, 329.

82. Philip E. Howard, "Fleming H. Revell: Publisher," *Sunday School Times*, November 7, 1932.

83. "Interview with Mr. William R. Barbour, President of Fleming H. Revell Co., at Moody Bible Institute, August 22, 1957," folder: Revell, Fleming H., MBI-BF.

84. "Advertisement: Revell and Moody," *Chicago Daily Tribune*, January 13, 1877.

85. "Advertisement: F. H. Revell," *The Advance*, January 18, 1877, 367.

86. "The City in Brief," *Chicago Daily Tribune*, February 27, 1873; "The City," *Chicago Daily Tribune*, August 4, 1876; "The City: General News," *Chicago Daily Tribune*, May 11, 1876, 8.

87. "Mr. Moody's Plans for Work in Chicago during the Fair Not Determined," *Chicago Daily Tribune*, November 3, 1892; "Moody Gets a Call," *Chicago Daily Tribune*, May 31, 1893. Moody ultimately held his own meetings nearby. *Chicago Daily Tribune*, September 9, 1893.

88. "Mr. Fleming H. Revell of Chicago," *Biloxi Herald*, April 17, 1897.

89. Allan Fisher, *Fleming H. Revell Company: The First 125 Years, 1870–1995* (Grand Rapids, MI: Fleming. H. Revell, 1995), 8.

90. William P. Mackay, *Grace and Truth* (Chicago: Fleming H. Revell Co., 1876), i–vi; Dorsett, *A Passion for Souls*, 329.

91. MacKinnon, *Recollections of 1874*, 10.

92. See, for example, Thomas N. Hall and Michael Norris, "The Chrysostom Texts in Bodley 516," *Journal of Theological Studies* 62, no. 1 (April 2011): 161–175, esp. 166.

93. Denis McQuail, *McQuail's Mass Communication Theory* (London: Sage, 2010), 72.

94. MacKinnon, *Recollections of 1874*, 31.

95. Henry Ward Beecher, *The Sermons of Henry Ward Beecher: In Plymouth Church, Brooklyn*, ed. T. J. Ellinwood (New York: J. B. Ford and Co., 1869), iv.

96. Joan Shelley Rubin, "The Boundaries of American Religious Publishing in the Early Twentieth Century," *Book History* 2 (1999): 207–217, esp. 209.

97. See, for example, Moody, *Twelve Select Sermons*. The advertisement follows the preface.

98. Advertisement, *Ladies' Home Journal and Practical Housekeeper*, September 1884, 7.

99. Advertisement, *Christian Union*, March 15, 1888; "Fleming H. Revell Company," *Men*, November 7, 1896; "A First Few New Fall Books," *Men*, November 7, 1896.

100. Advertisement, *Herald of Gospel Liberty*, March 27, 1890.

101. Advertisement, *Christian Union*, March 15, 1888; "Editorial," *Baptist Missionary Magazine*, April 1889, 4–7; advertisement, *Christian Union*, December 5, 1889; "Men's Unrivaled Premium Offer," *Men*, November 7, 1896; "Bagster Bible House," *The Sunday at Home*, July 21, 1894, 603–605. On the popularity of the Bagster Bible, see Isaac Massey Haldeman's endorsement in his book *How to Study the Bible: The Second Coming and Other Expositions* (New York: Fleming H. Revell Co., 1904), 55.

102. Kathryn E. Lofton, "The Preacher Paradigm: Promotional Biographies and the Modern-Made Evangelist," *Religion and American Culture: A Journal of Interpretation* 16, no. 1 (Winter 2006): 95–123.

103. The magazine initially went by the title *Evangelistic Record*. See Gloege, *Guaranteed Pure*, 52.

104. J. H. Gilmore, "The Literary Possibilities of the Pastorate," *Baptist Quarterly Review* 10, no. 37 (January 1888): 119.

105. *Ben-Hur* sold 230,000 copies. Brown, *Word in the World*, 77–78.

106. "Books and Bookmakers," *American Bookseller: A Semi-Monthly Journal Devoted to the Interests of the Book, Stationery, News, and Music Trades* 29, no. 4 (February 14, 1891): 130.

107. William C. Wilkinson, "Dwight L. Moody as Man of Affairs," *Homiletic Review*, September 1898, 207.

108. It appears on the title page, for example, of Moody, *Twelve Select Sermons*.

109. George Henry Doran, *Chronicles of Barabbas, 1884–1934* (New York: Harcourt, Brace, 1935), 351.

110. Ibid., 24.

111. Ibid., 21–23.

112. Ibid., 7–8, 319.

113. Pietsch, *Dispensational Modernism*, 45–46.

114. Dorsett, *A Passion for Souls*, 335.

115. Fleming H. Revell to Arthur P. Fitt, November 26, 1906, folder: Revell, Fleming H., MBI-BF.

116. Gloege, *Guaranteed Pure*, 65.

117. *Premillennial Essays of the Prophetic Conference Held in the Church of the Holy Trinity, New York City* (Chicago: F. H. Revell, 1879), 7, 12; "Inquiring Friends," *Christian Union,* March 12, 1879, 246.

118. "Literature," *The Advance,* June 26, 1879, 410.

119. Charles Henry Mackintosh, *Notes on the Book of Exodus* (Chicago: Fleming H. Revell, 1873), 146, 356. On the premillennial sympathies of Moody and friends, as well as Moody's avoidance of the topic, see Gloege, *Guaranteed Pure,* esp. 29–39.

120. Mackintosh would authorize a new edition of the book in 1880. See Charles Henry Mackintosh, *Notes on the Book of Exodus* (New York: Loizeaux Bros., 1880). Before the United States agreed to the European-led Berne Convention of 1886, American publishers avoided licensing fees by reprinting without permission. Doran explained that before the establishment of "the international copyright agreement of 1891, . . . piracy—unauthorized reprinting—was perfectly reputable. Publishers on both sides of the Atlantic were on the alert to discover books which could be reprinted." English publishers received nothing, for example, from the popularity of authors like Dickens in the United States. After 1891, American publishers usually honored foreign copyrights—but only if the actual books were printed in the United States. Brown, *Word in the World,* 48. Evidence for the relatively weak status of religious book publishing up through the 1880s is that book agents remained rare before then; only after the 1880s, as book publishing became more common, did it become reasonable for literary agents to work on behalf of authors. Adolf Growoll, *A Bookseller's Library and How to Use It* (New York: Office of the Publishers' Weekly, 1891), 6; Doran, *Chronicles of Barabbas,* 92, 97. For a review of copyright law, see Michael Winship, "The Rise of a National Book Trade System in the United States," in *Print in Motion: The Expansion of Publishing and Reading in the United States, 1880–1940,* ed. Carl F. Kaestle and Janice A. Radway, vol. 4 of *A History of the Book in America* (Chapel Hill: American Antiquarian Society / University of North Carolina Press, 2009), 71.

121. *Premillennial Essays of the Prophetic Conference,* Advertisement for "Pre-Millennial Publications."

122. William E. Blackstone, *Jesus Is Coming* (New York: Fleming H. Revell Co., 1908), "Appreciative Comments" and "Testimonials."

123. Matthew Avery Sutton, *American Apocalypse: A History of Modern Evangelicalism* (Cambridge, MA: Belknap Press of Harvard University Press, 2014), 26–27.

124. Timothy Richard Aubry and Trysh Travis, eds., *Rethinking Therapeutic Culture* (Chicago: University of Chicago Press, 2015), 5. On therapeutic culture as the pursuit of "relief from feelings of unreality," see also T. J. Jackson Lears, "From Salvation to Self-Realization: Advertising and the Therapeutic Roots of the Consumer Culture, 1880–1930," in *The Culture of Consumption: Critical Essays in American History, 1880–1980,* ed. Richard Wightman Fox and T. J. Jackson Lears (New York: Pantheon Books, 1983), 1–38, esp. 6 and 21.

125. On plain interpretation, see Gloege, *Guaranteed Pure,* 27–29.

126. For an overview of the changes to which premillennial theology responded, see Sutton, *American Apocalypse,* 10–16.

127. Moody himself lent public support to dispensationalism around 1897. Gloege, *Guaranteed Pure,* 107.

128. Arthur T. Pierson, *Many Infallible Proofs: A Series of Chapters on the Evidences of Christianity* (New York: Fleming H. Revell Co., 1886), 20. For more on Pierson's dispensationalism, see Pietsch, *Dispensational Modernism,* 113–117.

129. Robert Cameron, *The Doctrine of the Ages* (New York: Fleming H. Revell Co., 1896); Len Gaston Broughton, *The Second Coming of Christ* (New York: Fleming H. Revell Co., 1907).

130. "Publisher's Note to the Second Edition," in *Heaven: Where It Is, Its Inhabitants, and How to Get There,* by Dwight L. Moody, 2nd ed. (Chicago: Fleming H. Revell, 1884).

131. David Harrington Watt, *A Transforming Faith: Explorations of Twentieth-Century American Evangelicalism* (New Brunswick, NJ: Rutgers University Press, 1991), 138–139. Kathryn Lofton makes a related point in "Gospel," in Aubry and Travis, *Rethinking Therapeutic Culture,* 34–45, esp. 42.

132. Henry P. Robinson, "Hours with Publishers," *New York Evangelist,* May 19, 1898; see also "The New Publishing District," *New York Evangelist,* November 29, 1894, 48.

133. Kristen Doyle Highland, "In the Bookstore: The Houses of Appleton and Book Cultures in Antebellum New York City," *Book History* 19, no. 1 (2017): 214–255, esp. 240.

134. Sutton, *American Apocalypse,* 35.

135. "Mr. Moody on the Unemployed," *Christian Statesman,* September 23, 1893, 4.

136. On "the problem of the masses," see Gloege, *Guaranteed Pure,* chap. 2. On Moody's ultimate failure to reach the working classes, see chap. 4, esp. 99–113.

137. Anne Blue Wills, "Imagination beyond Belief: The Cultural Sources of Hannah Whitall Smith's Devotional Writing" (PhD diss., Duke University, 2001), esp. chap. 1.

138. Hannah Whitall Smith, *The Christian's Secret of a Happy Life* (New York: Fleming H. Revell, 1888), 31. See also Randall Balmer, "Keswick Movement," in *The Encyclopedia of Evangelicalism,* rev. ed. (Waco, TX: Baylor University Press, 2004), 380–381.

139. Smith, *Secret of a Happy Life,* vi, 55, 167.

140. Ibid., 33. On the composition of Smith's intended public, see Wills, "Imagination beyond Belief," 151.

141. See Debra Campbell, "Hannah Whitall Smith (1832–1911): Theology of the Mother-Hearted God," *Signs* 15, no. 1 (1989): 79–101.

142. Smith, *Secret of a Happy Life,* 197.

143. On authors' citations, see Campbell, "Hannah Whitall Smith," 79–80. See also Allan Fisher's remark that Smith became "a prototype of successful women authors of inspirational books." "Revell: Seventy-Five Years of Religious Book

Publishing," 2234; Fisher, *Fleming H. Revell Company*. For sales records, see Alice Hackett's *Fifty Years of Best Sellers* (New York: R. R. Bowker, 1945).

144. Arthur P. Fitt, "Preaching the Gospel in Print: The Work of the Bible Institute Colportage Association, Chicago," ca. 1905, folder: BICA Promotional Material, MBI-ED; also see "Colportage Beginnings," ca. 1948, folder: Moody Press History, MBI-ED.

145. February 9, 1903, 36, book 1, BICA.

146. Arthur P. Fitt to Dwight L. Moody, January 24, 1898, vol. 6, DLM-MBI; "The Spread of Gospel Literature," *New York Observer and Chronicle,* March 21, 1912, 378; Pollock, *Moody,* 287.

147. "Some Interesting Cases of Reform Known to Our Acting Committee," *Journal of Prison Discipline and Philanthropy,* nos. 35–36 (January 1897): 17.

148. Gloege, *Guaranteed Pure,* 96–99.

149. With $2,306.24 on deposit at the end of 1901, the Prison Book Fund nearly doubled the other funds, combined. February 3, 1902, 30, book 1, BICA.

150. Arline Harris, "Moody's Silent Missionaries," unpublished manuscript, written during 1950s while Kenneth Taylor served as director of Moody Press, folder: Moody Press Promo Material, MBI-ED.

151. Dale Carnegie to Mr. Hitt, May 25, 1943, folder: Moody Press Promo Material, MBI-ED.

152. In 1903, Fitt secured quotes from other printers, who offered him prices as low as 2.6 cents per book. Revell charged 3.5 cents, in addition to an addition 0.5 cents per book as a rental charge on its printing plates. November 9, 1903, 44, book 1, BICA.

153. E. T. M., "What People Are Reading," 429. A few years earlier, the *New York Times* had published an article with a similar theme. Citing an interview with a "New York man" who was "prominent" in publishing, the article reported the publisher as having said, "Let a panic come on, however. At first our business feels it as keenly as any other line. People suddenly cease buying everything except what they are obliged to have. As times fail to improve, people take more to going to church. Attendance increases very perceptibly. In a few weeks we can tell it in our business. There is a greatly increased demand for devotional books of all kinds. The business increases, and at the very height of the financial troubles we do the largest business. As times get better, you can see our trade in this line of publications gradually drop off, until, when prosperity again comes round we settle down to a normal business quite different from the boom we had been enjoying." "Panics and Religious Books," *New York Times,* March 17, 1901, 16.

154. Arthur P. Fitt to A. F. Gaylord, January 3, 1900, folder: Letters by A. P. Fitt, APF.

155. United States Post Office Department, *Annual Report of the Postmaster General* (Washington, DC: U.S. Government Printing Office, 1892), 69.

156. February 3, 1902, 26–32, book 1, BICA.

157. January 26, 1904, 51, book 1, BICA.

158. March 30, 1904, 65–69, book 1, BICA.

159. Doran, *Chronicles of Barabbas,* 26–32.

160. Paul Boyer describes the book as "the most popular of a spate of reform-minded religious novels which appeared in the 1880–1910." Boyer notes that the book "is cited repeatedly (and exclusively) in histories of the Social Gospel movement." Paul S. Boyer, "In His Steps: A Reappraisal," *American Quarterly* 23, no. 1 (Spring 1971): 61.

161. "Ralph Connor Advertisement," *Washington Post,* November 17, 1906; "A Handful of Fiction," *The Independent,* January 29, 1891, 94.

162. John Kelman, *The Faith of Robert Louis Stevenson* (New York: Fleming H. Revell Co., 1903), xv–xvi.

163. "Robert Louis Stevenson's Faith," *New York Times,* April 11, 1903. See also "Stevenson's Faith," *New York Times,* July 18, 1903.

164. Doran, *Chronicles of Barabbas,* 25–32; "Books and Bookmakers," *The American Bookseller: A Semi-Monthly Journal Devoted to the Interests of the Book, Stationery, News, and Music Trades* 29, no. 9 (April 25, 1891): 243; "The New Publishing District," *New York Evangelist,* November 29, 1894, 48; "Revell's Book Store in a New Home," *New York Observer and Chronicle,* February 3, 1898, 150. For a discussion of New York's status as the center of American publishing, see "Hours with the Publishers," *New York Evangelist,* May 19, 1898, 13.

165. "Revell: Seventy-Five Years."

166. Newell D. Hillis, *A Man's Value to Society* (New York: Fleming H. Revell Co., 1899), 255.

167. Harry Emerson Fosdick, *Christianity and Progress* (New York: Fleming H. Revell Co., 1922). On Fosdick and "liberal evangelicalism, see Matthew Burton Bowman, *The Urban Pulpit: New York City and the Fate of Liberal Evangelicalism* (New York: Oxford University Press, 2014), e.g., 2–5, 253–254.

168. Matthew S. Hedstrom, *The Rise of Liberal Religion: Book Culture and American Spirituality in the Twentieth Century* (New York: Oxford University Press, 2013), 22–27.

169. Ibid., 28, 34.

170. "Zondervan to Sell Revell, Chosen Books," *Publishers Weekly,* August 1, 1986, 15; William Griffin, "A New Lineup for Dallas," *Publishers Weekly,* June 8, 1992, 29.

171. "How to Increase the Income of the B.I.C.A.," June 9, 1939, folder: MP/BICA Business Records, 13, MBI-ED.

172. Ibid., 20.

173. Ibid., 6.

2. Brands of Distinction

1. As Kathryn Lofton notes, the fundamentalist posture finds its center in "a claim of reinstated order after a named destabilization." Kathryn Lofton, *Consuming Religion* (Chicago: University of Chicago Press, 2017), 24.

2. For background on Billy Sunday and his stature among fundamentalist Protestants during the early decades of the twentieth century, see Robert Francis Martin, *Hero of the Heartland: Billy Sunday and the Transformation*

of American Society, 1862–1935 (Bloomington: Indiana University Press, 2002). Martin highlights how Sunday's style of revivalism displayed humor, sentimentality, and an athleticism that reflected his background as a baseball player. These characteristics allowed Sunday to playfully "instruct, entertain, and manipulate an audience's emotions with consummate skill" (53). See also Matthew Bowman, *The Urban Pulpit: New York City and the Fate of Liberal Evangelicalism* (New York: Oxford University Press, 2014), 178–189.

3. Mara Einstein, *Brands of Faith: Marketing Religion in a Commercial Age* (London: Routledge, 2008), 70.

4. Jörg Stolz and Jean-Claude Usunier, "Religions as Brands: New Perspectives on the Marketization of Religion and Spirituality," in *Religions as Brands: New Perspectives on the Marketization of Religion and Spirituality,* ed. Jean-Claude Usunier and Jörg Stolz (Burlington, VT: Ashgate, 2014), 4, 8.

5. See Andrew Pettegree, *Brand Luther: 1517, Printing, and the Making of the Reformation* (New York: Penguin Press, 2015), xi, 161–163.

6. Harry S. Stout, *The Divine Dramatist: George Whitefield and the Rise of Modern Evangelicalism* (Grand Rapids, MI: William B. Eerdmans, 1991), xvi–xviii; Douglas L. Winiarski, *Darkness Falls on the Land of Light: Experiencing Religious Awakenings in Eighteenth-Century New England* (Chapel Hill: University of North Carolina Press, 2017), esp. 15–17, 138–141.

7. See Eugene Exman, *The House of Harper: One Hundred and Fifty Years of Publishing* (New York: Harper and Row, 1967); John William Tebbel, *Between Covers: The Rise and Transformation of Book Publishing in America* (New York: Oxford University Press, 1987), 43.

8. William Eerdmans's nephew, Johannes Eerdmans—known as "Jaguar" Jo on account of his work as the president of Jaguar Cars North America—would claim that his uncle entered the religious book business due to little more than the profit potential those books possessed. Larry ten Harmsel with Reinder Van Til, *An Eerdmans Century: 1911–2011* (Grand Rapids, MI: Eerdmans, 2011), 39. Although Ten Harmsel quotes extensively from Jo Eerdmans, he does not share Jo's reflections on his uncle's commercial motivations. Ten Harmsel shared this aspect of the story with me in a conversation in November 2010. For biographical details on Johannes, see "Johannes Eerdmans, Ex-Auto Importer, 85," *New York Times,* November 9, 1990, B9.

9. Candy Brown notes that "the Harpers saw themselves as sanctifying the print market by publishing religious texts and by using their influence to reinforce religious and moral standards." Candy Gunther Brown, *The Word in the World: Evangelical Writing, Publishing, and Reading in America, 1789–1880* (Chapel Hill: University of North Carolina Press, 2004), 75.

10. See Laura J. Miller, *Reluctant Capitalists: Bookselling and the Culture of Consumption* (Chicago: University of Chicago Press, 2006), e.g., 84.

11. Randall H. Balmer, "Warfield, B(enjamin) B(reckinridge) (1851–1921)," in *The Encyclopedia of Evangelicalism,* rev. ed. (Waco, TX: Baylor University Press, 2004), 718–719; Molly Worthen, *Apostles of Reason: The Crisis of Authority in American Evangelicalism* (New York: Oxford University Press, 2013), 21–24.

12. When Eerdmans studied there, the seminary was known officially as the Theological School at Grand Rapids. Before enrolling in the seminary, Eerdmans had studied at John Calvin Junior College, which later became the four-year institution known today as Calvin College. I have heard this story from Williams Eerdmans Jr. as well as several other current company employees. Illustrating the story's longevity, Eerdmans Sr. told it to an interviewer around 1965. But Eerdmans Sr. divided the story in two; he mostly repeated the Warfield story as I heard it decades later, but he attributed the Kok suggestion to a professor whom Eerdmans claimed to have met while visiting Amsterdam. William B. Eerdmans Jr., interview by author, Grand Rapids, MI, June 16, 2008; William B. Eerdmans, interview by Herbert J. Brinks, 3, ca. 1965, box 1, folder 1, WBE-HH. Ten Harmsel and Van Til also relate the Warfield Story in *An Eerdmans Century*, 19–20. For more on Warfield, see Balmer, "Warfield, B(enjamin) B(reckinridge)," 718–719.

13. William B. Eerdmans to Harry J. Albus, October 24, 1944, box 1, folder A, WBE. On family members' perceptions of Eerdmans's motivations, I rely on Larry Ten Harmsel, interview by author, Grand Rapids, MI, April 6, 2011. Ten Harmsel shared information and stories that he discovered in the course of writing his history of the Eerdmans Company.

14. Eerdmans Jr. interview; Ten Harmsel and Van Til, *An Eerdmans Century*, 14, 29–30.

15. David Cornel De Jong, *With a Dutch Accent: How a Hollander Became an American* (New York: Harper and Brothers, 1944), 261.

16. James D. Bratt, *Dutch Calvinism in Modern America: A History of a Conservative Subculture* (Grand Rapids, MI: Eerdmans, 1984), 8.

17. Ibid., 15–22.

18. "Importer Notes Changes in Demands," *Grand Rapids Press*, August 1, 1923, 1.

19. W. B. Eerdmans, *De Ramp Van de Titanic* (Grand Rapids, MI: Eerdmans-Sevensma Co., 1912), box 1, folder 2, WBE-HH; Eerdmans to Albus.

20. "An American Publisher of Books for the Hollanders," *Publishers Weekly*, May 29, 1920, 1173; For a commentary on the insularity of the Dutch community in Grand Rapids, see De Jong, *With a Dutch Accent*.

21. James D. Bratt, *Abraham Kuyper: Modern Calvinist, Christian Democrat* (Grand Rapids, MI: Eedmans, 2013), 13–14.

22. Ibid., xvi, 15–22, 48–51, 198–203.

23. James A. DeJong, *Henry J. Kuiper: Shaping the Christian Reformed Church, 1907–1962* (Grand Rapids, MI: Eerdmans, 2007), 232–235. Historians have debated Kuyper's direct influence on segregationist policies, with some scholars seeking to criticize any conflation between Afrikaner nationalism and Kuyperian Neo-Calvinism. Yet even if Kuyper did not advocate regularly for segregation on the basis of race, his separationist theology would come to complement segregationist policy. Gerrit J. Schutte, "The Netherlands, Cradle of Apartheid?," *Ethnic and Racial Studies* 10, no. 4 (October 1987): 392; George Harinck, "Abraham Kuyper, South Africa, and Apartheid," *Princeton Seminary Bulletin* 23, no. 2 (2002): 184–187. For an overview of this debate, see

Ernst M. Conradie, ed., *Creation and Salvation: Dialogue on Abraham Kuyper's Legacy for Contemporary Ecotheology* (Leiden: Brill, 2011), chap. 2. For a discussion of "the historical myth of a primitive Afrikaner Calvinism," see Andre du Toit, "No Chosen People: The Myth of the Calvinist Origins of Afrikaner Nationalism and Racial Ideology," *American Historical Review* 88, no. 4 (October 1983): 920.

24. Hendrik Edelman, *The Dutch Language Press in America: Two Centuries of Printing, Publishing and Bookselling* (Nieuwkoop: De Graaf, 1986), 32–33.

25. Suzanne M. Sinke, *Dutch Immigrant Women in the United States, 1880–1920* (Urbana: University of Illinois Press, 2002), 175–197.

26. "A Transaction in the Book World," *The Banner,* April 17, 1931, 356–357; Eerdmans interview by Brinks, 21.

27. Eerdmans to Albus.

28. Joseph Hill Hall, "The Controversy over Fundamentalism in the Christian Reformed Church, 1915–1966" (ThD diss., Concordia Seminary, 1974), 8.

29. "An American Publisher of Books"; "Importer Notes Changes."

30. De Jong, *With a Dutch Accent,* 259; DeJong, *Henry J. Kuiper,* 61–62.

31. Bratt, *Abraham Kuyper,* 265–267.

32. "Two More Aspire to Legislature," *Grand Rapids Press,* August 9, 1922, 7; Ten Harmsel and Van Til, *An Eerdmans Century,* 31.

33. "The Kind of Books We Need," *The Banner,* February 27, 1931, 189; "What the Undenominational Movement Should Teach Us," *The Banner,* March 14, 1930, 244.

34. Advertisement, *The Banner,* September 19, 1930, 834.

35. Quote in Bratt, *Dutch Calvinism,* 59–61; Mark T. Mulder, *Shades of White Flight: Evangelical Congregations and Urban Departure* (New Brunswick, NJ: Rutgers University Press, 2015), 25.

36. Henry Beets, "Billy Sunday—a Near-by View," *The Banner,* September 28, 1916, 608–610.

37. Bratt, *Dutch Calvinism,* 59–60; Barend K. Kuiper, "Orthodoxy and Christianity," *Calvin College Chimes,* June 6, 1910, suppl., 11, box 1, BKK.

38. Kathryn Lofton, "Queering Fundamentalism: John Balcom Shaw and the Sexuality of a Protestant Orthodoxy," *Journal of the History of Sexuality* 17, no. 3 (2008): 439–468, esp. 447–448. George Marsden famously defines a fundamentalist as "an evangelical who is angry about something." George M. Marsden, *Fundamentalism and American Culture,* 2nd ed. (New York: Oxford University Press, 2006), 235.

39. "Modernism in the Southern Presbyterian Church," *The Banner,* January 31, 1930, 100; see Bratt, *Dutch Calvinism,* 130–131.

40. DeJong notes that Henry and R.B. were not brothers, but R.B. and B. K. Kuiper were brothers. See DeJong, *Henry J. Kuiper,* 63.

41. R. B. Kuiper, "Fundamentalism and We," *The Banner,* December 2, 1932, 1048.

42. Hall, "The Controversy over Fundamentalism," 13–16, 25–30, 59–65.

43. Kuiper, "Fundamentalism and We."

44. See James R. Adair, *M. R. DeHaan: The Life behind the Voice* (Grand Rapids, MI: Discovery House, 2008); James D. Bratt, *Gathered at the River: Grand*

Rapids, Michigan, and Its People of Faith (Grand Rapids, MI: Eerdmans, 1993), 136–137.

45. "What the Undenominational Movement"; Bratt, *Dutch Calvinism,* 131.

46. "A Bible Reading Marathon," *The Banner,* February 16, 1939, 148. Daniel Poling would become editor of the *Christian Herald,* an influential evangelical periodical.

47. "Advertisement: From the Office of Wm. B. Eerdmans Publishing Co.," *The Banner,* January 8, 1932, 43.

48. "Should We Read Only the Bible?," *The Banner,* May 5, 1938, 412.

49. "The Kind of Books."

50. "Advertisement: From the Office."

51. "What Shall I Read?," *The Banner,* January 8, 1932, 35.

52. "The Kind of Books"; "A Transaction."

53. Bratt, *Dutch Calvinism,* 128; Hall, "The Controversy over Fundamentalism," 19; Mark A. Noll, *Between Faith and Criticism: Evangelicals, Scholarship, and the Bible in America* (San Francisco: Harper and Row, 1986). On the secession from Princeton and the founding of Westminster, see Bradley J. Longfield, *The Presbyterian Controversy: Fundamentalists, Modernists, and Moderates* (New York: Oxford University Press, 1991), esp. chap. 7.

54. Worthen, *Apostles of Reason,* 31.

55. "Praise for Dr. Machen," *The Banner,* December 9, 1932, 1068–1069.

56. S. Volbeda, "Review of *The Power of God unto Salvation,*" *The Banner,* January 30, 1931, 104.

57. Bratt, *Abraham Kuyper,* 263–264.

58. Ten Harmsel and Van Til, *An Eerdmans Century,* 39–40; Matthew S. Hedstrom, *The Rise of Liberal Religion: Book Culture and American Spirituality in the Twentieth Century* (New York: Oxford University Press, 2013), 82–83.

59. Keith A. Ives, *Voice of Nonconformity: William Robertson Nicoll and the British Weekly* (Cambridge: Lutterworth Press, 2011), 42, 60.

60. William Robertson Nicoll, *The Expositor's Bible* (New York: Funk and Wagnalls, 1900), xiv; on attitudes toward the Bible, see Bowman, *The Urban Pulpit,* 176.

61. "Maclaren's Expositions of the Holy Scripture," *The Banner,* December 9, 1932, 1069.

62. Tebbel, *Between Covers,* 282–284.

63. Henry Beets, *Elementary Christian Doctrine for Bible Classes* (Grand Rapid, MI: William B. Eerdmans Publishing Co., 1926), box 64, folder 3, HB.

64. Joel A. Carpenter, *Revive Us Again: The Reawakening of American Fundamentalism* (New York: Oxford University Press, 1997), 15.

65. On the CBMC, the Gideons, and the "entrepreneurial evangelicals" who led them, see Sarah Hammond, *God's Businessmen: Evangelicals in Depression and War,* ed. Darren Dochuk (Chicago: University of Chicago Press, 2017), esp. chap. 3.

66. Carpenter, *Revive Us Again,* 22. On popular Bible conferences, see also Brendan M. Pietsch, *Dispensational Modernism* (New York: Oxford University Press, 2015), esp. 68.

67. *Winona Lake Program for 1941,* box 2: C-G, folder: Conferences, HJO.

68. "Doctrinal Platform of Winona Lake Christian Assembly," box 15: Zondervan correspondence misc. files of 1965–1970, folder: General Annual Appeal Letters, WLCA; Kathryn Lofton, "The Methodology of the Modernists: Process in American Protestantism," *Church History: Studies in Christianity and Culture* 75, no. 2 (2006): 374–402, quote on 401.

69. Ten Harmsel and Van Til, *An Eerdmans Century,* 88.

70. Mark Sidwell, "'Come Apart and Rest a While': The Origin of the Bible Conference Movement in America," *Detroit Baptist Seminary Journal,* no. 15 (2010): esp. 81.

71. WLCA Program for 1944, box: Winona Lake info 1943–1952, folder: 1944, WLCA.

72. Robert P. Swierenga, *Dutch Chicago: A History of the Hollanders in the Windy City* (Grand Rapids, MI: Eerdmans, 2002), 472; R. B. Kuiper, "What Is Truth?," in *Winona Echoes: Notable Addresses Delivered at the Thirty-Sixth Annual Bible Conference* (Winona Lake, IN: Winona Lake Institutions, 1930).

73. William G. McLoughlin, *Billy Sunday Was His Real Name* (Chicago: University of Chicago Press, 1955), 9–13, 157; Sidwell, "'Come Apart and Rest,'" esp. 94.

74. Billy Sunday, *Billy Sunday Speaks! Sentence Sermons* (Grand Rapids, MI: Zondervan, 1937), 9, 16. On Sunday's view of cities and their corruptive effects, see Bowman, *The Urban Pulpit,* 178–180.

75. See Kelly J. Baker, *Gospel according to the Klan: The KKK's Appeal to Protestant America, 1915–1930* (Lawrence: University Press of Kansas, 2011); see also Dwight W. Hoover, "Daisy Douglas Barr: From Quaker to Klan 'Kluckeress,'" *Indiana Magazine of History,* June 1991, 171–195.

76. "Program for Winona Lake Bible Conference, August 11–25, 1940," box 2: C-G, folder: Conferences, HJO.

77. Frederick Flavell to Harold John Ockenga, June 11, 1943, box 2: C-G, folder: Conferences, HJO.

78. Ray S. Harris to Harry Ironside, November 7, 1946; Ironside to Harris, November 12, 1946. Both sources consulted in box 25, folder 1: H, 1946, RMC.

79. Paul Hutchens to William B. Eerdmans, September 27, 1934; Hutchens to Eerdmans, October 4, 1935. Both sources consulted in box 2, folder H, WBE.

80. Mignon Brandon Rimmer, *Fire Inside: The Harry Rimmer Story* (Berne, IN: Publishers Printing House, 1968), 160, 218.

81. On evangelical experts, see Randall J. Stephens and Karl Giberson, *The Anointed: Evangelical Truth in a Secular Age* (Cambridge, MA: Belknap Press of Harvard University Press, 2011).

82. "Kanawha Valley Bible Conference Program, July 4th–18th 1943," box 2: C-G, folder: Conferences, HJO. For more on Rimmer's self-aggrandizing titles, his debating prowess, and his educational endeavors, see Edward B. Davis, "Fundamentalism and Folk Science between the Wars," *Religion and American Culture: A Journal of Interpretation* 5, no. 2 (Summer 1995): 220.

83. Rimmer, *Fire Inside,* 98, 227. Mignon Brandon Rimmer relates this story in his biography of Harry Rimmer: "A Christian woman living in Baltimore

wrote me about two years ago, telling of her continuing distribution of this book. She lives on a small income, but buys it periodically, sending it to prominent people as a gift. She prays over her choice of recipients and follows each book with prayer. She considers it 'the finest presentation of Christ' that she has ever read, and 'the most valuable Christian book in print.' One famous person who received a copy was Princess Margaret of England" (*Fire Inside*, 227).

84. Paul Hutchens, *From the Pulpit to the Typewriter: An Autobiographical Sketch* (Waterloo, IA: Sugar Creek Book Room, 1946), 14–15, copy consulted in folder: Hutchens, Paul, WBEC.

85. Paul Hutchens to William B. Eerdmans, July 10, 1934; Hutchens to Eerdmans, July 17, 1934; Hutchens to Eerdmans, July 21, 1934; Hutchens to Eerdmans, September 10, 1934. All sources consulted in box 2, folder H, WBE.

86. "Our Authors," *Eerdmans Quarterly Observer* 1, no. 1 (Grand Rapids, MI: Eerdmans, 1945), 10, WBEC; Eerdmans to Hutchens, December 30, 1935, WBE.

87. "A Complete Publishing Service for Authors," William B. Eerdmans Company Catalog for 1940, WBEC.

88. Eerdmans to Hutchens, July 10, 1934; Hutchens to Eerdmans, July 21, 1934.

89. Victorious Life Conference Program for 1941, folder: Conferences, box 2: C-G, HJO; "We Visit the Firs Book Store," *Firs Fellowship* 7, no. 1 (December 1943), box 2: C-G, folder: Conferences, HJO; *Winona Lake Bible Conference Program for 1940,* box 2: C-G, folder: Conferences, HJO.

90. William B. Eerdmans to Norman Kellow, June 16, 1943, box 2, folder P, WBE.

91. Rene Cappon, "Forgotten Books Boost Business," *Grand Rapids Press,* September 16, 1957.

92. James E. Ruark, *The House of Zondervan,* 2nd ed. (Grand Rapids, MI: Zondervan, 2006), 17–29; Richard Baker, interview by author, Grand Rapids, MI, June 16, 2008.

93. Homer Rodeheaver to Mrs. Billy Sunday, March 30, 1937, box 2, folder 54, WBS; Hyman Appelman to Pat Zondervan, July 15, 1942, box 1, folder 7: Correspondence with Pat Zondervan & Miscellaneous Materials, 1942–1949, HJA; Pat Zondervan to Harry Ironside, September 6, 1941, box 7, folder 9: XYZ, 1941, RMC.

94. *Autumn Book List for 1941,* ZPH; Ruark, *The House of Zondervan,* 37; *WLBC Program for 1940,* box 2: C-G, folder: Conferences, HJO.

95. "Executive Committee Winona Lake Christian Assembly, Inc.," February 15, 1958, box 43: 1953–1969, folder: 1958, WLCA.

96. Waldo Yeager to Pat Zondervan, October 30, 1963, box 43: 1953–1969, folder: 1963, WLCA.

97. Moore to Yeager, July 6, 1967, box 43: 1953–1969, folder: 1967, WLCA.

98. Pat Zondervan to Russell Dunlap, December 16, 1969, box 43: 1953–1969, folder: 1969, WLCA; Dunlap to Pat Zondervan, December 23, 1969, box 43: 1953–1969, folder: 1969, WLCA.

99. Paul E. Chappell to Peter Kladder, February 20, 1973, box 1985–1988, folder: Zondervan Bookstore, WLCA.

100. Winona Lake Christian Assembly, *Report to the Director of Business Affairs by the Controller,* June 20, 1979: 13, box 1965–1970, folder: WLCA Planning File, WCLA.

101. "Zondervan Sales," ca. 1985, Winona Lake Christian Assembly, box 1985–1988, folder: Zondervan Bookstore, WLCA.

102. Percy Crawford to William B. Eerdmans, April 4, 1945, box 1, folder C, WBE.

103. William B. Eerdmans to Norman Kellow, April 24, 1945, box 2, folder P, WBE; Eerdmans to James Starr, May 9, 1944, box 2, folder S, WBE.

104. William B. Eerdmans to Wilbur Smith, July 4, 1949, box 10, folder W. Smith / Eerdmans, WS.

105. Eerdmans to Kellow, July 12, 1943, box 2, folder P, WBE.

106. Eerdmans to Kellow, April 24, 1945.

107. Kellow to Eerdmans, April 20, 1945, box 2, folder P, WBE.

108. Kellow to Eerdmans, April 16, 1945, box 2, folder P, WBE.

109. Robert J. Wells to William B. Eerdmans, June 12, 1945, box 2, folder S, WBE.

110. F. J. Wiens to William B. Eerdmans, April 10, 1937, box 2, folder W, WBE.

111. Wiens to William B. Eerdmans, September 7, 1937, box 2, folder W, WBE.

112. Zondervan Publishing House to Peter De Visser, October 4, 1938, box 2, folder Z, WBE.

113. Bertha Moore to William B. Eerdmans, February 2, 1952, box 2, folder M, WBE.

114. Eerdmans Catalog for 1945–1946, WBEC.

115. In the preface to his history of Fuller Seminary, Marsden notes that Eerdmans was the "obvious choice" to publish the book because "not only are they a publisher of distinguished books; they have also had a long and mutually beneficial relationship with Fuller Theological Seminary that deserves to be honored." George M. Marsden, *Reforming Fundamentalism: Fuller Seminary and the New Evangelicalism* (Grand Rapids, MI: Eerdmans, 1987), viii.

116. Henry, *The Uneasy Conscience of Modern Fundamentalism* (Grand Rapids, MI: Eerdmans, 1947), 68–70. On criticism from fundamentalists, see Henry to Ockenga, January 22, 1948, box: 40, folder: Henry, Carl, 1947–1948, HJO.

117. William B. Eerdmans to Graham, December 26, 1964, box 1, folder G, WBE; Billy Graham, *The Jesus Generation* (Grand Rapids, MI: Zondervan, 1971), 47–48, 178–181.

118. Quoted in Erin A. Smith, *What Would Jesus Read? Popular Religious Books and Everyday Life in Twentieth-Century America* (Chapel Hill: University of North Carolina Press, 2015), 209.

119. Quoted in Ruark, *The House of Zondervan,* 35–36. Although the Gideons initially welcomed only traveling Christian businessmen as members, they broadened their guidelines in 1937 to admit all businessmen. "Professionals" such as doctors and lawyers were not welcomed until the 1960s. Initially focused on man-to-man proselytizing, the Gideons began placing Bibles in hotel rooms in 1908. As early as 1910, local camps worked together with revivalists and ministers to hold citywide revivals. The CBMC, by comparison, focused more concertedly on city evangelism. It functioned less as a hierarchical

institution than as a rubric for local cooperation, with groups of businessmen in each city drawing up their own chapter constitutions. See Hammond, *God's Businessmen*, 77–84.

120. Pat Zondervan to Appelman, July 20, 1944, box 1, folder 7, HJA.

121. Presenting the notions of Christianity, Islam, Judaism, and Christian Science as "brand names," Stolz and Usunier insist: "There can be no doubt that *branding as a concept* is applicable to religious phenomena." Stolz and Usunier, "Religions as Brands," 16. Such a statement invariably invites a reader to posit exceptions to this supposed rule, but the point of this claim is that brands not only conjure social constituencies but also solicit modes of affiliation, belief, and identity, which we often recognize as "religion" and associate with particular religions. "Religions are everywhere," Kathryn Lofton explains in her analysis of Oprah Winfrey's media empire and personal brand, "available to everyone, in every color of the conceivable theological, ritual, and experiential rainbow." Kathryn Lofton, *Oprah: The Gospel of an Icon* (Berkeley: University of California Press, 2011), quote on 6.

122. Fred Inglis, *A Short History of Celebrity* (Princeton: Princeton University Press, 2010), 3–4.

123. Will H. Houghton, J. Palmer Muntz, and E. Schuyler English to William B. Eerdmans, July 22, 1946, box 2, folder Z, WBE. Ten Harmsel and Van Til also reproduced the correspondence in *An Eerdmans Century*, 82–85.

3. Trade Associating

1. Dwight D. Eisenhower to John F. Fish, June 1, 1956. Copy of letter available in Jerry B. Jenkins, *Twenty-Five Years of Sterling Rewards in God's Service: The Story of Christian Booksellers Association* (Nashville: Thomas Nelson/ Christian Booksellers, 1974), 32.

2. On the relationship between religion, national identity, and the Cold War, see T. Jeremy Gunn, *Spiritual Weapons: The Cold War and the Forging of an American National Religion* (Westport, CT: Praeger, 2009), esp. chap. 4.

3. David L. Holmes, *The Faiths of the Postwar Presidents: From Truman to Obama* (Athens: University of Georgia Press, 2012), 37–38.

4. "Books for the President," *Christianity Today*, September 25, 1964, 50.

5. Ibid.

6. See Matthew Avery Sutton, "Was FDR the Antichrist? The Birth of Fundamentalist Antiliberalism in a Global Age," *Journal of American History* 98, no. 4 (March 2012): 1052–1074; Daniel K. Williams, *God's Own Party: The Making of the Christian Right* (New York: Oxford University Press, 2010), esp. chap. 1.

7. National Industrial Conference Board, *Trade Associations: Their Economic Significance and Legal Status* (New York: National Industrial Conference Board, 1925), 7.

8. See, for example, Randall H. Balmer, *Mine Eyes Have Seen the Glory: A Journey into the Evangelical Subculture in America*, 5th ed. (New York: Oxford University Press, 2014), 6.

9. Ronald Edward Frank, William Francis Massy, and Yoram Wind, *Market Segmentation* (Englewood Cliff, NJ: Prentice-Hall, 1972), 4–5.

10. R. William Kotrba, "The Strategy Selection Chart," *Journal of Marketing* 30, no. 3 (July 1, 1966): 22–25, esp. 22–23; Wendell R. Smith, "Product Differentiation and Market Segmentation as Alternative Marketing Strategies," *Journal of Marketing* 21 (1956): 5. On the "mass market," see Steven C. Brandt, "Dissecting the Segmentation Syndrome," *Journal of Marketing* 30, no. 4 (October 1966): 22–27, esp. 22. See also Lizabeth Cohen, *A Consumer's Republic: The Politics of Mass Consumption in Postwar America*, 1st Vintage Books ed. (New York: Vintage Books, 2004), 294–295.

11. Timothy Gloege, *Guaranteed Pure: The Moody Bible Institute, Business, and the Making of Modern Evangelicalism* (Chapel Hill: University of North Carolina Press, 2015), 164–168, 173.

12. William B. Eerdmans to Norman B. Kellow, November 28, 1944, box 2, folder P, WBE.

13. William B. Eerdmans to Harry J. Albus, October 24, 1944, box 1, folder A, WBE; Matthew S. Hedstrom, *The Rise of Liberal Religion: Book Culture and American Spirituality in the Twentieth Century* (New York: Oxford University Press, 2013), 35.

14. Eerdmans to Kellow, November 28, 1944.

15. On the notion of normative whiteness, see David R. Roediger, *Colored White: Transcending the Racial Past* (Berkeley: University of California Press, 2002), e.g., 17.

16. Coined during the 1920s, the term "middlebrow" originally served primarily as an elite term of derision for art and literature that aspired to be more than "lowbrow" popular entertainment yet failed to meet "highbrow" intellectual or aesthetic standards. Historians also have used the term, however, to describe initiatives devoted to circulating shared knowledge and cultural sensibilities among an expansive American middle class through the mass market. Joan Shelley Rubin, *The Making of Middlebrow Culture* (Chapel Hill: University of North Carolina Press, 1992), xii–xv. As the historians Matthew Hedstrom and Erin Smith both have documented, "religious middlebrow culture" became an essential component of a broader middlebrow culture, and liberal religious leaders, media companies, and public figures served as its advocates. Hedstrom, *Rise of Liberal Religion*, 53–55. See also Erin A. Smith, *What Would Jesus Read? Popular Religious Books and Everyday Life in Twentieth-Century America* (Chapel Hill: University of North Carolina Press, 2015), 10–11.

17. Joanne P. Sharp, *Condensing the Cold War: Reader's Digest and American Identity* (Minneapolis: University of Minnesota Press, 2000), xii, 10, 12, 45.

18. "Editorial Policy," *Religious Digest*, October 1935, 2; "Editorial," *Religious Digest,* January 1936, 2.

19. See Darren E. Grem, "Christianity Today, J. Howard Pew, and the Business of Conservative Evangelicalism," *Enterprise and Society* 15, no. 2 (June 2014): 337–379; Molly Worthen, *Apostles of Reason: The Crisis of Authority in American Evangelicalism* (New York: Oxford University Press, 2013), 56–60.

20. *Complete Catalog of Zondervan Publishing House*, ca. 1945 (n.d.), 2, ZPH.

21. Eric Tranby and Douglas Hartmann, "Critical Whiteness Theories and the Evangelical 'Race Problem': Extending Emerson and Smith's *Divided by Faith*," *Journal for the Scientific Study of Religion* 47, no. 3 (September 2008): 341–359, esp. 347.

22. "Wm. B. Eerdmans Publishing Company," *Christian Life and Times*, February 1948, WBEC. I encountered this article and the former press releases in a large scrapbook that Eerdmans Company maintained in the 1940s.

23. Eerdmans Company Scrapbook, 51, WBEC.

24. R. L. Decker, "Who Are the Evangelicals?," *United Evangelical Action*, December 5, 1945, 5.

25. Henry J. Kuiper, "Fiction Contest," *The Banner*, January 18, 1946, 68.

26. As one survey of the history of trade associations notes, the modern trade association emerged after the Civil War, when trade associations helped take stock of regional and national production capacity during Reconstruction. Trade associations also helped revive industry after the panics of 1873 and 1893. National Industrial Conference Board, *Trade Associations*, 9–26.

27. *Rules and Regulations of the Association of the Boston Booksellers*, Early American Imprints, ser. 2, no. 217 (Boston: n.p., 1801).

28. Leonard H. Lynn and Timothy McKeown, *Organizing Business: Trade Associations in America and Japan* (Washington, DC: American Enterprise Institute for Public Policy Research, 1988), 6.

29. "American Booksellers' Association," *The Bookseller*, June 1904, 188.

30. John Tebbel, "A Brief History of American Bookselling," in *Bookselling in America and the World: Some Observations and Recollections in Celebration of the 75th Anniversary of the American Booksellers Association*, ed. Charles B. Anderson (New York: Quadrangle / New York Times Book Co., 1975), 17–21; Michael Winship, "The Rise of a National Book Trade System in the United States," in *Print in Motion: The Expansion of Publishing and Reading in the United States, 1880–1940*, ed. Carl F. Kaestle and Janice A. Radway, vol. 4 of *A History of the Book in America* (Chapel Hill: American Antiquarian Society / University of North Carolina Press, 2009), 65.

31. Laura Phillips Sawyer, "Trade Associations, State Building, and the Sherman Act: The U.S. Chamber of Commerce, 1912–1925," in *Capital Gains: Business and Politics in Twentieth-Century America*, ed. Richard R. John and Kim Phillips-Fein (Philadelphia: University of Pennsylvania Press, 2017), 25–42, esp. 28–33.

32. Charles B. Grannis, "More than Merchants: Seventy-Five Years of the ABA," in Anderson, *Bookselling in America*, 84–85.

33. "'Evangelicals' Launch Association to Push Costly Program—Say Liberals Have Sapped Evangelistic Power," *Christian Century*, May 19, 1942. I accessed the article as a manuscript copy of the printed article's text. This copy was located in box 13, folder: National Association of Evangelicals Minutes and Reports, 1942, HJO.

34. Elias Benjamin Sanford, *Origin and History of the Federal Council of the Churches of Christ in America* (Hartford, CT: S.S. Scranton Co., 1916), 466.

35. Robert A. Schneider, "The Federal Council of Churches and American Presbyterians, 1900–1950," *Journal of Presbyterian History* 84, no. 2 (2006): 103–122, esp. 113–114; *National Association of Evangelicals: What Is It and How Does It Function?* (Boston: National Association of Evangelicals, n.d.), 3, box 13, folder: National Association of Evangelicals Minutes and Reports, 1942, HJO.

36. R. L. Decker, "Cooperation among Conservative Christians: Setting Forth Some Reasons Why Evangelical Churches Should Cooperate with the National Association of Evangelicals for United Action," 16, box 13, folder: National Association of Evangelicals, Minutes and Reports, 1942, HJO.

37. Worthen, *Apostles of Reason,* 38.

38. Bettye Collier-Thomas, *Jesus, Jobs, and Justice: African American Women and Religion* (New York: Knopf, 2010), 315–316. See also John F. Piper, "The Formation of the Social Policy of the Federal Council of Churches," *Journal of Church and State* 11, no. 1 (1969): 63–82.

39. *National Association of Evangelicals for United Action: Constitution and Policy* (Boston: NAE, n.d.), box 13, folder: National Association of Evangelicals, Minutes and Reports, 1942, HJO.

40. Tisa Wenger, *Religious Freedom: The Contested History of an American Ideal* (Chapel Hill: University of North Carolina Press, 2017), 194.

41. "Board of Administration Meeting of the National Association of Evangelicals, September 21–22, 1943," 5, box 13, folder: National Association of Evangelicals, Minutes and Reports, 1943, HJO. On explicit and implicit racism among fundamentalists in the era immediately preceding the NAE's founding, see Mary Beth Swetnam Mathews, *Doctrine and Race: African American Evangelicals and Fundamentalism between the Wars* (Tuscaloosa: University of Alabama Press, 2017). To be sure, the NAE's founders did not counter the FCC's interracial initiatives by articulating explicitly racist policies. During the 1960s, however, its leaders generally sought to distinguish between desegregation, which they supported timidly, and integration, which they insisted should not be "forced." Williams, *God's Own Party,* 30–31; Randall J. Stephens, "'It Has to Come from the Hearts of the People': Evangelicals, Fundamentalists, Race, and the 1964 Civil Rights Act," *Journal of American Studies* 50, no. 3 (August 2016): 559–585, esp. 575–576; Curtis J. Evans, "White Evangelical Protestant Responses to the Civil Rights Movement," *Harvard Theological Review* 102, no. 2 (2009): 245–273.

42. See Garth Rosell, *The Surprising Work of God: Harold John Ockenga, Billy Graham, and the Rebirth of Evangelicalism* (Grand Rapids, MI: Baker Academic, 2008), 13. See also D. G. Hart, *Deconstructing Evangelicalism: Conservative Protestantism in the Age of Billy Graham* (Grand Rapids, MI: Baker Academic, 2004).

43. Decker, "Cooperation among Conservative Christians."

44. Ted Benson to Harold John Ockenga, May 11, 1943, box 13, folder: National Association of Evangelicals, Correspondence 1942, HJO.

45. See Mathews, *Doctrine and Race,* 5–6; Gloege, *Guaranteed Pure,* 130–137; Gastón Espinosa, *William J. Seymour and the Origins of Global Pentecos-*

talism: A Biography and Documentary History (Durham, NC: Duke University Press, 2014), esp. chap. 6; Worthen, *Apostles of Reason,* 138.

46. Tona J. Hangen, *Redeeming the Dial: Radio, Religion and Popular Culture in America* (Chapel Hill: University of North Carolina Press, 2002), 22. See also Heather Hendershot, *What's Fair on the Air? Cold War Right-Wing Broadcasting and the Public Interest* (Chicago: University of Chicago Press, 2011); Matthew Avery Sutton, *Aimee Semple McPherson and the Resurrection of Christian America* (Cambridge, MA: Harvard University Press, 2007).

47. Between free "sustaining time" and airtime that religious broadcasters purchased, religious programming represented about 8 percent of all radio programming in 1932. Quentin J. Schultze, "Evangelical Radio and the Rise of the Electronic Church, 1921–1948," *Journal of Broadcasting & Electronic Media* 32 (1988): 292–296.

48. Harold John Ockenga to Lenox R. Lohr, January 6, 1940, box 2, folder 6: Federal Council of Churches, HJO.

49. William Ward Ayer, "Evangelical Christianity Endangered by Its Fragmentized Condition," in *Evangelical Action! A Report of the Organization of the National Association of Evangelicals for United Action* (Boston: United Action Press, 1942), 42–43.

50. For a more extended study of evangelical responses to liberal book cultures, see Daniel Vaca, "Meeting the Modernistic Tide: The Book as Evangelical Battleground in the 1940s," in *Protest on the Page: Essays on Print and the Culture of Dissent,* ed. James L. Baughman, Jennifer Ratner-Rosenhagen, and James P. Danky (Madison: University of Wisconsin Press, 2015), 137–160.

51. Pat Beaird, "Religious Books and the War," *New York Times,* March 28, 1943; see also Hedstrom, *Rise of Liberal Religion,* 126; Trysh Travis, "Books as Weapons and 'The Smart Man's Peace': The Work of the Council on Books in Wartime," *Princeton University Library Chronicle* 60, no. 3 (Spring 1999): 361–362.

52. Hedstrom, *Rise of Liberal Religion,* 143–150.

53. "Religious Book Week Opens," *New York Times,* March 28, 1943. See also Rubin, *Making of Middlebrow Culture;* Janice Radway, *A Feeling for Books: The Book-of-the-Month Club, Literary Taste, and Middle-Class Desire* (Chapel Hill: University of North Carolina Press, 1997), esp. 177–178.

54. Wilbur M. Smith, "The Urgent Need for a New Evangelical Literature," *United Evangelical Action,* June 15, 1946, 4, 20–21. For background on Moody Bible Institute and Wilbur Smith's career as a fundamentalist and evangelical leader, see George M. Marsden, *Reforming Fundamentalism: Fuller Seminary and the New Evangelicalism* (Grand Rapids, MI: Eerdmans, 1987). See also George M. Marsden, *Fundamentalism and American Culture,* 2nd ed. (New York: Oxford University Press, 2006).

55. Will H. Houghton, *Let's Go Back to the Bible* (New York: Revell, 1939), 21, 45.

56. For more on fundamentalist attitudes toward the Bible, see Peter Johannes Thuesen, *In Discordance with the Scriptures: American Protestant Battles over Translating the Bible* (New York: Oxford University Press, 1999).

57. The new organization was modeled in part on the New England Fellowship (NEF), a Boston-based organization founded in 1929 by J. Elwin Wright, a prominent lay member of Ockenga's Park Street Church. A kind of Rotary Club for conservative New Englanders who dissented from what they saw as the deep-seated liberalism of the region's denominations, the Fellowship pursued initiatives designed to nurture New England's conservative subculture. Randall Balmer, "New England Fellowship," in *The Encyclopedia of Evangelicalism*, rev. ed. (Waco, TX: Baylor, 2004), 488. In addition to Bible conferences, Christian education programs, and a daily radio broadcast, those initiatives included two "Fellowship Bookstores"—in Boston and Portland, Maine. Describing the bookstores as a premier "outlet for Christian literature," the NEF often placed advertisements in popular conservative periodicals, touting the bookstores' "books by outstanding Bible teachers." *What the NAE Is Doing* (Chicago: NAE, n.d.). Located in folder: "National Association of Evangelicals Minutes and Financial Reports, 1945," box 13, HJO. See also "Advertisement: Fellowship Book Store," *United Evangelical Action*, April 1943, 3.

58. Smith, "The Urgent Need," 20–22.

59. Carl F. H. Henry, *Successful Church Publicity: A Guidebook for Christian Publicists* (Grand Rapids, MI: Zondervan, 1943), 56.

60. Carl F. H. Henry, *The Uneasy Conscience of Modern Fundamentalism* (Grand Rapids, MI: Eerdmans, 1947), 68–70.

61. Carl F. H. Henry, "The Year in Books," *United Evangelical Action*, March 15, 1950, 9.

62. Alfred R. McIntyre, "The Crisis in Book Publishing," *Atlantic Monthly*, October 1947, 107; William Barbour to Harold John Ockenga, January 20, 1947, box 5, folder: Publishing: Revell, HJO; Barbour to HJO, March 19, 1946, box 5, folder: Publishing: Revell, HJO.

63. Barbour to Ockenga, December 6, 1946, box 5, folder: Publishing: Revell, HJO.

64. In 1943, for instance, Harper & Brothers began a conversation with the Eerdmans Company about having Eerdmans use 140,000 pounds of its paper quota to print Harper & Brothers books. Although Eerdmans expressed interest in the idea, Harper & Brothers eventually backed out of the agreement when Eerdmans expressed reservations about allowing Harper to select which books to print, for fear of undermining its brand. In a letter canceling the contract, Harper's representative admitted that Eerdmans "acted quite properly in restricting the use of your imprint to editorial material meeting your particular standards." But the representative insisted that "it would be quite awkward, if not impossible, to make the fullest use of the additional paper quota . . . within the limits which you might wish to have us operate." Barbour to Ockenga, January 20, 1947; Raymond C. Harwood to William B. Eerdmans, October 16, 1943, box 1, folder H, WBE.

65. McIntyre, "Crisis in Book Publishing," 107.

66. The five committee members included Louis Finkelstein, president of Jewish Theological Seminary; Arthur Cushman McGiffert, president of Pacific School of Religion; and Edna Hull, head of the philosophy and religion division of

the Cleveland Public Library. "Religious Books Picked for Worth," *New York Times,* June 20, 1943, 34.

67. Sutton, "Was FDR the Antichrist?," esp. 1070.

68. "Minutes of the Meeting of the Board of Administration, N.A.E., North Shore Hotel, Evanston, Ill., Sept. 19–20," box 13, folder: National Association of Evangelicals, Minutes and Financial Reports, 1944, HJO.

69. "Minutes of the Meeting of the Executive Committee, National Association of Evangelicals, LaSalle Hotel, Chicago, Ill., March 2, 1945," box 13, folder: National Association of Evangelicals Minutes and Financial Reports 1945, HJO; "Evangelical Book Project Launched," *United Evangelical Action,* April 4, 1945, 3.

70. Carl F. H. Henry, "N.A.E. Book List," *United Evangelical Action,* June 15, 1945, 12; Henry, "Literature for Our Time," *United Evangelical Action,* June 15, 1946, 14; Henry, "Another Year in Books"; Henry, "Year in Books," 9.

71. Carl F. H. Henry, "A Look at the Year in Books," *United Evangelical Action,* April 1, 1951, 10.

72. "Re: Standard Publishing Company," February 24, 1954, box 12, folder: Standard Publishing (Sale of), JDM.

73. James DeForest Murch to John Bolten, August 29, 1952, box 13, folder: N.A.E. Standard Publishing Co., HJO.

74. "Re: Standard Publishing Company," JDM.

75. O. A. Ohmann, "'Skyhooks': With Special Implications for Monday through Friday," *Harvard Business Review* 33, no. 3 (June 1955): 34. Bolten sent the article to Murch in 1955. Bolten to Murch, June 7, 1955, box 12, folder: Standard Publishing Sale (Bolten Correspondence), JDM.

76. "Erretts Transfer Control; No Change in Policy," *Christian Standard,* January 23, 1955, 2; "Religious Foundation Buys Standard Publishing Co.," *Cincinnati Times-Star,* January 8, 1955, 2; Murch to Aldis L. Webb, January 19, 1955. Each of these preceding items was consulted in box 12, folder: Standard Publishing (Sale of), JDM. Clyde Taylor to John Bolton, February 5, 1954, box 13, folder: N.A.E. Standard Publishing Co., HJO.

77. See Darren E. Grem, *The Blessings of Business: How Corporations Shaped Conservative Christianity* (New York: Oxford University Press, 2016); Sarah Hammond, *God's Businessmen: Evangelicals in Depression and War* (Chicago: University of Chicago Press, 2017).

78. Murch to Billy Graham, February 16, 1953, box 12, folder: Standard Publishing (Sale of), JDM. Murch proclaimed this hope in a note titled "New Evangelical Movement," undated, box 12, folder: Standard Publishing (future plans), JDM. On the cultural authority of the *Christian Century,* see Elesha J. Coffman, *The Christian Century and the Rise of the Protestant Mainline* (New York: Oxford University Press, 2013).

79. Note titled "Present Status," undated, box 12, folder: Standard Publishing (future plans), JDM.

80. "Give a Book to the White House Library," *Publishers Weekly,* March 29, 1930, 1779. Experts included the librarians of Stanford and Chicago's Newberry Library, Congresswoman Ruth B. Pratt, a professor of Southern

literature from the University of North Carolina, and the head of the National Geographic Society.

81. Hedstrom, *Rise of Liberal Religion,* 7–11, 27, 49.

82. On Religious Book Week, see ibid., 32. See also Smith, *What Would Jesus Read?,* chap. 3.

83. James L. W. West III, "Price Control and the Publisher," *Sewanee Review,* May 27, 2015, quote on 272.

84. Jenkins, *Twenty-Five Years,* 19.

85. O. H. Cheney, *Economic Survey of the Book Industry, 1930–1931* (New York: R. R. Bowker, 1949). Cheney's assessment would prove so influential that R. R. Bowker republished it in 1949, in response to "continued interest in the material collected and its present value as a base from which to evaluate current conditions."

86. Ibid., 278.

87. Ibid., 34, 50–51, 300–302.

88. Kenneth Nathaniel Taylor and Virginia J. Muir, *My Life: A Guided Tour: The Autobiography of Kenneth N. Taylor* (Wheaton, IL: Tyndale House, 1991), 161–162, 172–173.

89. John Bass and Robert DeVries, *The Christian Book Store* (Homewood, IL: Christian Booksellers Association, 1968). During the year when he helped co-author this book, DeVries left his position as editor in chief of Moody Press and became Zondervan's director of publications. "Zondervan Appoints New Director of Publications," *Bookstore Journal,* September 1968, 22.

90. Sid Zullinger, "My Eighteen Years as a Salesmen to the Christian Booksellers," *Bookstore Journal,* September 1968, 10–11; Peter Hewitt, "An Interview with John T. Bass of the Christian Booksellers Association," *Publishers Weekly,* September 26, 1977, 69–70.

91. Jenkins, *Twenty-Five Years,* 12–13.

92. Ibid., 18–19, 27; James E. Ruark, *The House of Zondervan,* 2nd ed. (Grand Rapids, MI: Zondervan, 2006), 96.

93. Shirley Kauffman to Revell Publishing Company, August 19, 1975, folder: Complaints, FHRC.

94. Shirley Koppenal to "Mr. Revell," August 13, 1980, folder: Complaints, FHRC.

95. Dwight Baker, interview by author, Grand Rapids, MI, October 13, 2016. On the rise of large bookstores such as Barnes & Noble during the early 2000s and their growing dominance over Christian bookstores, see Rachel Elinsky, "Religious Publishing for the Red State Consumers and Beyond," *Publishing Research Quarterly* 21, no. 4 (Winter 2005): 11–29, esp. 26.

96. William B. Eerdmans to Kenneth Taylor, November 19, 1953, box 2, folder M, WBE; Eerdmans to Taylor, November 23, 1953, box 2, folder M, WBE; "Evangelical Christian Publishers Association: Statement of Purpose," October 11, 1974, folder: Evangelical Christian Pub. Assn., FHRC.

97. Christian Booksellers Association, Inc., "Christian Booksellers Convention Report for 1950," box 2, folder M, WBE.

98. Quoted in Jenkins, *Twenty-Five Years,* 34; John F. Fish, "CBA International," *Bookstore Journal,* July–August 1968, 16.

99. Kenneth L. Woodward, "Born Again!," *Newsweek,* October 25, 1976, 68.

100. Before surveys and sales figures linked survey statistics to "the Evangelicals" and helped transform evangelicalism into what seemed like a discrete social group, a more nebulous evangelicalism had drawn social significance from other statistical sources. Attendance figures at large, public revivals provided one source. For centuries, revivals often had received coverage in the popular press. In the twentieth century, for example, revivals like the Youth for Christ gatherings of the 1940s and revivalists like Billy Graham had received credit for bringing together tens of thousands of Protestants—especially younger Protestants. See, for example, popular media coverage of Billy Graham's revivals and gatherings such as the "Explo" convention of 1972. John G. Turner, *Bill Bright and Campus Crusade for Christ: The Renewal of Evangelicalism in Postwar America* (Chapel Hill: University of North Carolina Press, 2008); Darren Dochuk, *From Bible Belt to Sunbelt: Plain-Folk Religion, Grassroots Politics, and the Rise of Evangelical Conservatism* (New York: W. W. Norton, 2011); Grant Wacker, *America's Pastor: Billy Graham and the Shaping of a Nation* (Cambridge, MA: Belknap Press of Harvard University Press, 2014). For more comprehensive figures, journalists often counted the members of denominations that neither affiliated with the NAE nor claimed the evangelical appellation. Although the head of the Southern Baptist Convention's Christian Life Commission insisted in 1976 that "evangelical" is "a Yankee word," Billy Graham's Southern Baptist affiliation led the *New York Times* to report in 1967 that "the evangelicals—there are believed to be 20 million to 25 million in this country—find most of their strength in the Southern Baptist Convention, the Lutheran Church–Missouri Synod and the National Association of Evangelicals, a loose federation of many smaller bodies." George Dugan, "Evangelical Leaders Map National Campaign: Conservatives Stress Bible Authority rather than the 'Social Gospel,'" *New York Times,* October 7, 1967, 32; Woodward, "Born Again!"

101. Notably, Gallup considered himself an evangelical. He described surveys as "a very important tool in God's work," and his own views oriented both his survey questions and his interpretations of the responses those questions generated. Quoted in Robert Wuthnow, *Inventing American Religion: Polls, Surveys, and the Tenuous Quest for a Nation's Faith* (New York: Oxford University Press, 2015), 109, and esp. chap. 5.

102. Acknowledging *Newsweek*'s status as a magazine of political and cultural record in its heyday, historians often have cited 1976 and Woodward's article in particular as reference points to mark evangelicalism's cultural ascent. Historians regularly have implied that *Newsweek* itself gave 1976 this title, but the magazine merely was quoting Gallup. Robert Wuthnow notes, "Had it not been for *Newsweek*'s article, the Gallup results about evangelicals could easily have been missed or quickly forgotten." Ibid., 105.

103. Alice Payne Hackett, "Bestsellers in the Bookstores, 1900–1975," in Anderson, *Bookselling in America,* 136–137; on Marabel Morgan and *The Total Woman,* see Steven P. Miller, *The Age of Evangelicalism: America's Born-Again Years* (New York: Oxford University Press, 2014), 24–25.

104. On survey figures, see Russell Chandler, "50 Million 'Born Again' in U.S.: Third of Adults Have Had Experience, Gallup Poll Finds," *Los Angeles Times,* September 23, 1976: A3.

105. McCandlish Phillips, "Protestant Book Publishers' Sales Rise," *New York Times,* August 2, 1970.

106. To support his claim, Chandler quoted an article from *Publishers Weekly,* which served as a primary source of statistics about evangelicals before surveys became commonplace. Russell Chandler, "Religious Book Sales Soaring to New Heights: Sales of Religious Books Skyrocket," *Los Angeles Times,* July 28, 1975, C3. See also Glenn Armon, "Twice-Told Tale: Book Publishers Are Setting One Record after Another," *Barron's National Business and Financial Weekly,* August 23, 1976, 3; "Religious Books Doing a Heavenly Business," *Chicago Tribune,* August 23, 1976, E8.

107. Chandler, "Religious Book Sales Soaring."

108. Johnny Cash, *Man in Black* (Grand Rapids, MI: Zondervan, 1975), quotes on 38 and 208.

109. George W. Cornell, a writer for the Associate Press, wrote a piece about "silent censorship" that was syndicated in dozens of small-town newspapers. Zondervan's clipping file includes "Religion in the News," September 17, 1983, from the "Worchester-Fitchburg Metro Area," and "Dealers Protest 'Censorship' of Books Oriented to Religion," *Detroit News,* November 11, 1982. ZPH.

110. For more on representation on best-seller lists, see Smith, *What Would Jesus Read?,* 217–221.

111. Cornell, "Religion in the News," ZPH.

112. Cal Thomas, *Book Burning* (Westchester, IL: Crossway Books, 1983), 99–100.

113. On the New Christian Right's efforts to mobilize political constituencies on behalf of moral and religious reform, see J. Brooks Flippen, *Jimmy Carter, the Politics of Family, and the Rise of the Religious Right* (Athens: University of Georgia Press, 2011); Neil J. Young, *We Gather Together: The Religious Right and the Problem of Interfaith Politics* (New York: Oxford University Press, 2015); Axel R. Schäfer, *Countercultural Conservatives: American Evangelicalism from the Postwar Revival to the New Christian Right* (Madison: University of Wisconsin Press, 2011); Miller, *The Age of Evangelicalism.*

114. Ed Kotlar, "Zondervan Modernizes in Search of Christian-Oriented Readers," *Grand Rapids Press,* July 30, 1980.

4. Righteous Retail

1. To be clear, the correspondence between Moody and Hero Bratt, Eerdmans's credit manager, does not explicitly identify Moody as the owner of the store. But that status is implied through her correspondence with Bratt. In addition to confirming receipt of a payment, Bratt raised an ongoing discussion with Moody about her potential decision to sell her store, and Moody spoke authoritatively about that decision in her response. Daisy Moody to Hero Bratt, November 11, 1947, box 2, folder M, WBE.

2. See, for example, R. Laurence Moore, *Selling God: American Religion in the Marketplace of Culture* (New York: Oxford University Press, 1994); Mark R. Valeri, *Heavenly Merchandize: How Religion Shaped Commerce in Puritan America* (Princeton: Princeton University Press, 2010); Devin Singh, *Divine Currency: The Theological Power of Money in the West* (Stanford, CA: Stanford University Press, 2018), esp. chap. 5.

3. Frances E. Gardner, "The Witnessing Store," *Bookstore Journal,* November/December 1969, 10–11.

4. "What Is a Christian Bookseller?," *Bookstore Journal,* July/August 1968, 4.

5. See, for example, Douglas Abrams's study of business and fundamentalism, in which he insists that fundamentalists' "adjustments to mass culture did not alter the essentials of the Christian message." Douglas Carl Abrams, *Selling the Old-Time Religion: American Fundamentalists and Mass Culture, 1920–1940* (Athens: University of Georgia Press, 2001), 123–129. See also Jeremy R. Carrette and Richard King, *Selling Spirituality: The Silent Takeover of Religion* (London: Routledge, 2005), esp. chap. 3.

6. Despite a rising tide of scholarship about religion and media, sales practices rarely are treated as an aspect of mediation, or as modes of mediation in their own right. To be sure, scholars of religion increasingly have examined the relationship between how audiences understand media and the means by which media circulate, acknowledging the principle behind Marshall McLuhan's pithy claim that "the medium is the message." Studies of Islamic, Christian, and Jewish devotional cultures have illustrated that listeners and viewers respond differently to sermons read in print, heard in a religious gathering, listened to via radio, or viewed on television. Such comparisons have demonstrated that mediation and perception depend not just upon forms of media technology but also upon the social systems within which those technologies function. Fewer scholars have explored, however, how media technologies themselves carry and cultivate social values. As the anthropologist David Graeber explains, "human action, or even human thought, can only take place through some kind of material medium and therefore can't be understood without taking the qualities of that medium into account." David Graeber, "It Is Value That Brings Universes into Being," *HAU: Journal of Ethnographic Theory* 3, no. 2 (2013), quote on 222. On religion and varied modes of mediation, see Charles Hirschkind, *The Ethical Soundscape Cassette Sermons and Islamic Counterpublics* (New York: Columbia University Press, 2006); Leigh Eric Schmidt, *Hearing Things: Religion, Illusion, and the American Enlightenment* (Cambridge, MA: Harvard University Press, 2000); Harry S. Stout, *The Divine Dramatist: George Whitefield and the Rise of Modern Evangelicalism* (Grand Rapids, MI: Eerdmans, 1991); Jonathan L. Walton, *Watch This! The Ethics and Aesthetics of Black Televangelism* (New York: NYU Press, 2009); Isaac Weiner, *Religion Out Loud: Religious Sound, Public Space, and American Pluralism* (New York: NYU Press, 2013); Jeremy Stolow, *Orthodox by Design: Judaism, Print Politics, and the ArtScroll Revolution* (Berkeley: University of California Press, 2010); Marla Frederick, *Colored Television: American Religion Gone Global* (Stanford, CA: Stanford University Press, 2015).

7. My use of the term "infrastructure" is indebted to the media theorist John Durham Peters, who proposes "the doctrine of *infrastructuralism*," which he defines as an effort to "make environments visible." John Durham Peters, *The Marvelous Clouds: Toward a Philosophy of Elemental Media* (Chicago: University of Chicago Press, 2016), 36–38.

8. Anne L. Borden, "Making Money, Saving Souls: The Christian Bookstore Field in the United States" (PhD diss., Emory University, 2006), 36.

9. Emily Johnson shows how the evangelical culture industries that blossomed during the second half of the twentieth century "served to socialize women into traditionalist gender roles while also providing space for women to negotiate the boundaries of traditionalist gender systems." Emily S. Johnson, *This Is Our Message: Women's Leadership in the New Christian Right* (New York: Oxford University Press, 2019), 7–8.

10. William Norton, "Teachers, You May Do It!," *Moody Monthly*, July 1922, 1127.

11. "The Bookstore Manager as a Missionary," *Bookstore Journal*, September 1968, 29.

12. Attributing the origins of the missionary ideal to sixteenth- and seventeenth-century Jesuits, Luke Clossey notes that "the characteristic of 'mission' referred less to the target (Protestant or Catholic or pagan) than to the target's location (here or there)." Luke Clossey, *Salvation and Globalization in the Early Jesuit Missions* (New York: Cambridge University Press, 2008), 12–15.

13. By highlighting the process of sending, I do not discount the violence that missionizing institutions and missionaries have meted out among the peoples to whom they have been sent. As the historian William Hutchinson once remarked, Christians often have acted as though they "had a 'right' not only to conquer the world, but to define reality for the peoples of the world." In the Americas, Christian missionaries in both rural and urban settings recurrently treated their outreach as an opportunity and obligation to subject indigenous and immigrant peoples to campaigns of moral discipline, cultural erasure, and physical violence. William R. Hutchison, "A Moral Equivalent for Imperialism: Americans and the Promotion of 'Christian Civilization,' 1880–1910," in *Missionary Ideologies in the Imperialist Era: 1880–1920*, ed. William R. Hutchison and Torben Christensen (Aarhus: Christensens Bogtrykkeri, 1982), 167–178, quote on 174. See also Dana Lee Robert, *Christian Mission: How Christianity Became a World Religion* (Chichester, UK: Wiley-Blackwell, 2009), esp. chap. 4; Laurie F. Maffly-Kipp, "Assembling Bodies and Souls: Missionary Practices on the Pacific Frontier," in *Practicing Protestants: Histories of Christian Life in America, 1630–1965*, ed. Laurie F. Maffly-Kipp, Leigh Eric Schmidt, and Mark R. Valeri (Baltimore: Johns Hopkins University Press, 2006), 51–76.

14. Clossey, *Salvation and Globalization*, 229; Amy DeRogatis, *Moral Geography: Maps, Missionaries, and the American Frontier* (New York: Columbia University Press, 2003), 63–65; Hui-Tzu Grace Chou, "Mormon Missionary Experiences and Subsequent Religiosity among Returned Missionaries in Utah," *Social Sciences and Missions* 26, nos. 2–3 (January 2013): 199–225.

15. Lee Gessner, "Bookselling in the Religious Marketplace," in *Inside Religious Publishing: A Look behind the Scenes,* ed. Leonard George Goss and Don M. Aycock (Grand Rapids, MI: Zondervan, 1991), quote on 260.

16. Robert, *Christian Mission,* 118–119.

17. See Laurel Thatcher Ulrich, *Good Wives: Image and Reality in the Lives of Women in Northern New England, 1650–1750* (New York: Vintage Books, 1991).

18. Sally K. Gallagher, *Evangelical Identity and Gendered Family Life* (New Brunswick, NJ: Rutgers University Press, 2003), 32.

19. Colleen McDannell, *The Christian Home in Victorian America, 1840–1900* (Bloomington: Indiana University Press, 1986), 7, 36; for a criticism of the notion of separate spheres, see Linda K. Kerber, "Separate Spheres, Female Worlds, Woman's Place: The Rhetoric of Women's History," *Journal of American History* 75, no. 1 (June 1988): 9–39; Nancy F. Cott, *The Bonds of Womanhood: "Woman's Sphere" in New England, 1780–1835,* 2nd ed. (New Haven: Yale University Press, 1997); Karin E. Gedge, *Without Benefit of Clergy: Women and the Pastoral Relationship in Nineteenth-Century American Culture* (New York: Oxford University Press, 2003).

20. Tracy Fessenden, *Culture and Redemption: Religion, the Secular, and American Literature* (Princeton: Princeton University Press, 2007), 89, 91. Amy DeRogatis notes that "the most vicious attacks against Catholics . . . arose from what Protestants deemed to be the 'perverse' gender practices of Catholic priests and nuns." See DeRogatis, "Gender," in *Themes in Religion and American Culture,* ed. Philip Goff and Paul Harvey (Chapel Hill: University of North Carolina Press, 2004), 197–226, esp. 212–213.

21. McDannell, *The Christian Home,* 100.

22. Robert, *Christian Mission,* 125.

23. Ibid., 128–129, 138.

24. Margaret Lamberts Bendroth, *Fundamentalism and Gender: 1875 to the Present* (New Haven: Yale University Press, 1993), 15, 26.

25. McDannell, *The Christian Home,* 100.

26. Michelle Levy, "Do Women Have a Book History?," *Studies in Romanticism* 53, no. 3 (Fall 2014): 297–317.

27. "Reaching the Masses with Good Literature" and "A Pastor Utilizes Opportunities," *Moody Monthly,* December 1921, 741.

28. *Confidential Instructions and Suggestions to the Authorized Agents of the Bible Institute Colportage Association,* undated, folder: BICA Promo Material, 3, 16–17, MBI-ED; William Norton, "The Gospel in Print," *Moody Monthly,* October 1925, 95.

29. Norton, "Teachers, You May Do It!"

30. *A Primer on "Book Missionary" Work,* undated, folder: BICA Promo Material, 11, MBI-ED.

31. Monica Lynn Mercado, "Women and the Word: Gender, Print, and Catholic Identity in Nineteenth-Century America" (PhD diss., University of Chicago, 2014), 24; see also Monica L. Mercado, "'Have You Ever Read?': Imagining

Women, Bibles, and Religious Print in Nineteenth-Century America," *U.S. Catholic Historian* 31, no. 3 (Summer 2013): 1–21.

32. "A Vast Soul-Winning Opportunity in Rural Public Schools," undated, folder: BICA Promo Material, MBI-ED.

33. *Primer on "Book Missionary" Work,* 4, 17.

34. "Present Aims of the American Tract Society," *Weekly Messenger,* July 19, 1843, 1.

35. Quote in David Paul Nord, *Faith in Reading: Religious Publishing and the Birth of Mass Media in America* (New York: Oxford University Press, 2004), 99.

36. February 13, 1905, book 1, BICA; "Out of Work?," *Moody Monthly,* October 1921, 624.

37. *Primer on "Book Missionary" Work,* 10.

38. *Confidential Instructions,* 4–5.

39. Reflecting in 1969 upon his fifty-year career as a Canadian bookseller, Hugh Hull boasted that his store in a downtown Winnipeg shopping center had consistently grown in sales volume and even physical size. Accompanying that profile, a portrait of his staff of seven included five women and just two men. Hugh Hull, "My 50 Years in Christian Bookselling, *Bookstore Journal,* June 1969, 10; other examples: "The House That Jack Built," *Bookstore Journal,* October 1974, 10–13.

40. Cliff Dudley, "Let's Sell Books," *Bookstore Journal,* October 1969, quote on 19; Ruth Y. Hackman, "Read!," *Bookstore Journal,* April 1970, 22; John Bass and Robert DeVries, *The Christian Book Store* (Homewood, IL: Christian Booksellers Association, 1968), 28.

41. On Anita Bryant and how the New Christian Right "politicized the domestic spaces that were the centers of conservative evangelical women's expertise," see Johnson, *This Is Our Message,* 39. As a number of anthropologists insist, social values produced in domestic spheres ultimately are "absorbed into personal identities in the public, communal sphere, accessible to everyone." David Graeber, *Toward an Anthropological Theory of Value: The False Coin of Our Own Dreams* (New York: Palgrave, 2001), 78. Michael Lambek also asks how and where values are stored. See Michael Lambek, "The Value of (Performative) Acts," *HAU: Journal of Ethnographic Theory* 3, no. 2 (2013): esp. 147–148.

42. Fleming H. Revell to Helen T. Sunday, October 25, 1913, reel 1, WBS.

43. Hendrik Edelman, "A History of Religious Publishing and Bookselling in the United States and Canada, 1640–1985," in *Christian Book Publishing and Distribution in the United States and Canada,* ed. John P. Dessauer, Paul D. Doebler, and Hendrik Edelman (Tempe, AZ: CBA/ECPA/PCPA Joint Research Project, 1987), 7–70, esp. 58; "The Phenomenon of the Religious Bestseller," *Publishers Weekly,* July 14, 1975, 45–47, esp. 47; John P. Dessauer, "Statistical Analysis and Forecast," in Dessauer, Doebler, and Hendrik Edelman, *Christian Book Publishing,* 125.

44. "Phenomenon of the Religious Bestseller," 45.

45. Jean McLaren, "Window Displays Sell the Store," *Publishers Weekly*, May 25, 1940, 1980–1982; "The Scribners Bookstore Increases Business by Good Retail Methods," *Publishers Weekly*, January 31, 1942, 416–422.

46. Rachel Bowlby, "Supermarket Futures," in *The Shopping Experience*, ed. Pasi Falk and Colin Campbell (London: Sage, 1997), esp. 96–97.

47. Ibid., 98.

48. Carl William Dipman, *The Modern Grocery Store* (New York: Progressive Grocer, 1932), 11; Bowlby, "Supermarket Futures," 98–104; Shane Hamilton, "Supermarkets, Free Markets, and the Problem of Buyer Power in the Postwar United States," in *What's Good for Business: Business and American Politics since World War II*, ed. Kim Phillips-Fein and Julian E. Zelizer (New York: Oxford University Press, 2012): 177–194, esp. 180.

49. Richard Powell, "It's a Kind of Supermarket," *Publishers Weekly*, March 11, 1957, 25–27.

50. "Shop Talk," *Publishers Weekly*, November 29, 1952, 2178.

51. Theodore G. Striphas, *The Late Age of Print: Everyday Book Culture from Consumerism to Control* (New York: Columbia University Press, 2009), 57–58.

52. "Show-Case for Low-Priced Series: K&B's Big New Super Book Mart," *Publishers Weekly*, February 19, 1955, 1196–1202.

53. "Zondervan's New Store Geared for Self-Service," *Publishers Weekly*, January 5, 1959, 69–70.

54. See Bruce Bickel and Stan Jantz, *His Time, His Way: The CBA Story, 1950–1999* (Colorado Springs: Christian Booksellers Association, 1999), 98.

55. "Market Transformation," *Bookstore Journal*, November 1968, 8; "CBA Annual Meeting," *Bookstore Journal*, March 1969, back cover.

56. Edith Jones, "Building an Image of Excellence," *Bookstore Journal*, July–August 1968, 22.

57. Robert O. Self, *All in the Family: The Realignment of American Democracy since the 1960s* (repr., New York: Hill and Wang, 2013), 4, chap. 1.

58. Susan Porter Benson, *Counter Cultures: Saleswomen, Managers, and Customers in American Department Stores, 1890–1940* (Urbana: University of Illinois Press, 1988), 130, 134.

59. Elizabeth Beardsley Butler, *Saleswomen in Mercantile Stores: Baltimore, 1909* (New York: Russell Sage Foundation, 1912), vii; Helen Rich Norton, *A Textbook on Retail Selling* (New York: Ginn and Co., 1919), 4–5.

60. Bethany Moreton, *To Serve God and Wal-Mart: The Making of Christian Free Enterprise* (Cambridge, MA: Harvard University Press, 2009), 74–76.

61. Ruth Y. Hackman, "For the Manager's Wife Only!," *Bookstore Journal*, November 1968, 14.

62. Gardner, "Witnessing Store"; "What Is a Christian Bookseller?"

63. Abraham Kuyper, *Women of the Old Testament* (Grand Rapids, MI: Zondervan, [1933] 1964), 9–12.

64. Harold John Ockenga, *Have You Met These Women?* (Grand Rapids, MI: Zondervan, 1940), foreword.

65. John Meredith and Charlotte Meredith, "The Zondervan Brothers," *Christian Life and Times,* January 1947, esp. 32, copy consulted in ZPH.

66. Mrs. Ray E. Busch to Paul Hutchens, February 5, 1935, folder H, box 2, WBE. I describe the author of this letter as "Mrs. Ray E. Busch" because she identified herself that way.

67. D. Keith Stonehocker, "The Living Bible: A Market Research Survey, Sept. 1972," box 6, folder 18, KT.

68. Charles Marvin Brown, "The Culture of Culture Industries: Art, Commerce, and Faith in the Christian Retailing and Entertainment Industry" (PhD diss., Southern Illinois University at Carbondale, 2002), 91.

69. Natasha Zaretsky, *No Direction Home: The American Family and the Fear of National Decline, 1968–1980* (Chapel Hill: University of North Carolina Press, 2007), 6–11. As Zaretsky reports, less than a quarter of American women worked outside the home in 1950, but more than 40 percent of all married women did so by 1972.

70. On the evangelical preoccupation with "family values," see Seth Dowland, *Family Values and the Rise of the Christian Right* (Philadelphia: University of Pennsylvania Press, 2015).

71. On books and efforts to save the evangelical family, see Self, *All in the Family,* 348–349.

72. "Fleming Hewitt Revell: Nearly 100 Years of Religious Publishing," *Bookstore Journal,* July/August 1969, 22, 58.

73. "New Corporation Formed to Operate Zondervan Stores," *Publishers Weekly,* November 9, 1964, 68.

74. Self, *All in the Family,* 348.

75. On women entering the workplace, see ibid., chap. 4.

76. Gallagher, *Evangelical Identity,* esp. 46–47, 53–54.

77. George Parson, "The Future of the Industry—Healthy and Growing," *Bookstore Journal,* February 1974, 8.

78. Bass and DeVries, *The Christian Book Store,* 28.

79. F. J. Wiens to William B. Eerdmans, September 25, 1937, box 1, folder B, WBE.

80. Thompson quoted in Paul Hutchens to William B. Eerdmans, July, 21, 1934, box 2, folder H, WBE.

81. Sue Smith, interview by author, Grand Rapids, MI, October 11, 2016; Eric Tiansay, "Sue Smith Elected as Next CBA Chairman," *Christian Retailing,* September 30, 2012. The name change reflected the fact that books were not the only preoccupation of Christian retail. In 1997, the CBA's *Bookstore Journal* also became *CBA Marketplace.* See Michael D. Goldhaber, "Gospel Gifts," *Dayton Daily News,* October 11, 1997.

82. Interview with Sue Smith. On women in evangelical ministry, see Catherine A. Brekus, ed., *The Religious History of American Women: Reimagining the Past* (Chapel Hill: University of North Carolina Press, 2007); Brekus, *Strangers and Pilgrims: Female Preaching in America, 1740–1845* (Chapel Hill: University of North Carolina Press, 1998); Elizabeth Hill Flowers, *Into the Pulpit: Southern Baptist Women and Power since World War II* (Chapell Hill: Uni-

versity of North Carolina Press, 2012); Priscilla Pope-Levison, *Building the Old Time Religion: Women Evangelists in the Progressive Era* (New York: NYU Press, 2013); Bendroth, *Fundamentalism and Gender.*

83. Maisha T. Fisher, "Earning 'Dual Degrees': Black Bookstores as Alternative Knowledge Spaces," *Anthropology & Education Quarterly* 37, no. 1 (March 2006): esp. 97. See also Fisher, *Black Literate Lives: Historical and Contemporary Perspectives* (New York: Routledge, 2009).

84. Michelle M. Nickerson, *Mothers of Conservatism: Women and the Postwar Right* (Princeton: Princeton University Press, 2012), quote on 56; see also ibid., 37, 142–149; Verna M. Hall, ed., *Christian History of the Constitution of the United States of America* (San Francisco: American Christian Constitution Press, 1960), v.

85. Johnson, *This Is Our Message,* 27.

86. Matthew D. Lassiter, *The Silent Majority: Suburban Politics in the Sunbelt South* (Princeton: Princeton University Press, 2006). See also Dowland, *Family Values,* 7.

87. Nickerson, *Mothers of Conservatism,* 148; see also Susan B. Ridgely, *Practicing What the Doctor Preached: At Home with Focus on the Family* (New York: Oxford University Press, 2016).

88. Fessenden, *Culture and Redemption,* chap. 3; Anne M. Boylan, *Sunday School: The Formation of an American Institution, 1790–1880* (New Haven: Yale University Press, 1988); Adam R. Shapiro, "Civic Biology and the Origin of the School Antievolution Movement," *Journal of the History of Biology* 41, no. 3 (October 2008): 409–433; Nickerson, *Mothers of Conservatism,* 71–72.

89. "Editorial: Good Books . . .", *Eerdmans Quarterly Observer,* Fall 1945, 3, WBEC.

90. William B. Eerdmans Company, *Complete Catalog and List of Publications, Fall and Winter 1945–1946,* 17, 21, WBEC.

91. Edwin Wilbur Rice, *A Short History of the International Lesson System* (Philadelphia: American Sunday-School Union, 1902), 3–4. See also Brendan M. Pietsch, *Dispensational Modernism* (New York: Oxford University Press, 2015), 37–39.

92. In the 1930s, for example, Wilbur Smith had become editor of Francis Peloubet's popular *Peloubet's Select Notes on the International Sunday School Lessons.* Writing to Harold Ockenga in 1943, Smith complained that the Moody Bible Institute professor Clarence Benson had begun selling a different system. "Everywhere he goes," Smith fumed, "he attempts to thrust this particular lesson system, and all of his printed literature, upon those who are listening to him, or those who are writing to him." Wilbur M. Smith to Harold Ockenga, December 23, 1943, box 13, folder: National Association of Evangelicals Correspondence, 1944, HJO.

93. As evidence of their suspicion, some dispensationalists noted that the system included relatively few lessons from the book of Revelation. Wilbur M. Smith to Harold Ockenga, December 29, 1943, box 13, folder: National Association of Evangelicals Correspondence, 1944, HJO.

94. "Minutes of the Meeting of the Executive Committee, National Association of Evangelicals, December 13, 1944," 5, box 13, folder: National Association of Evangelicals, Minutes and Financial Reports, 1944, HJO.

95. Almost immediately after the conference, Zondervan began sending Ockenga somewhat sycophantic letters, congratulating him on the NAE's work, asking him to visit Grand Rapids, and soliciting manuscripts. B. D. Zondervan to Harold Ockenga, April 19, 1944, box 13, folder: National Association of Evangelicals Correspondence, 1944, HJO.

96. Fernando Arzola, *Evangelical Christian Education: Mid-Twentieth-Century Foundational Texts* (Eugene, OR: Wipf and Stock, 2014), viii.

97. Eileen Luhr, *Witnessing Suburbia: Conservatives and Christian Youth Culture* (Berkeley: University of California Press, 2009), 69–71.

98. For more on YFC and the evangelical businessmen who supported it, see Sarah Hammond, *God's Businessmen: Evangelicals in Depression and War*, ed. Darren Dochuk (Chicago: University of Chicago Press, 2017), esp. chap. 4.

99. Mervin E. Rosell, *Challenging Youth for Christ* (Grand Rapids, MI: Zondervan, 1945), 2, 7, 37–39, 83. Zondervan also published the early official histories of the movement. See Mel Larson, *Youth for Christ, Twentieth Century Wonder* (Grand Rapids, MI: Zondervan, 1947); Larson, *Twentieth Century Crusade: The Story of Youth for Christ* (Grand Rapids, MI: Zondervan, 1953).

100. O. H. Cheney, *Economic Survey of the Book Industry, 1930–1931* (New York: R. R. Bowker, 1949), v–vi, 1–3, 70, 76. See Chapter 3 for more on Cheney's findings regarding distribution.

101. Kenneth Nathaniel Taylor and Virginia J. Muir, *My Life: A Guided Tour: The Autobiography of Kenneth N. Taylor* (Wheaton, IL: Tyndale House, 1991), 161–162, 172–173.

102. Moore had become familiar with the American Booksellers Association by working for eleven years at Brentano's Book Store in Chicago, one of Chicago's largest and most prominent bookstores. When it ultimately closed in 1995, the victim of low-margin bookstore chains like Barnes & Noble and Borders, the *Chicago Tribune* described it as Chicago's "oldest and best-known book dealer." Genevieve Buck, "Kroch's & Brentano's Closes the Book on 2 More Stores," *Chicago Tribune*, April 29, 1995.

103. W. F. Moore to William B. Eerdmans, February 27, 1947, box 2, folder M, WBE.

104. Jerry B. Jenkins, *Twenty-Five Years of Sterling Rewards in God's Service: The Story of Christian Booksellers Association* (Nashville, TN: Thomas Nelson/Christian Booksellers Association, 1974), 12–13.

105. For more detailed information about Kenneth Taylor's biography, early publications, and interest in creating versions of the Bible for children, see Daniel Vaca, "Selling Trust: The Living Bible and the Business of Biblicism," in *The Bible in American Life*, ed. Philip Goff, Arthur E. Farnsley II, and Peter J. Thuesen (New York: Oxford University Press, 2017), 169–182.

106. Taylor and Muir, *My Life*, 208–216.

107. Tyndale House Publishers, "Their Future Lies in Your Hands," advertisement, n.d., folder 23, box 6, KT.

108. Laura J. Miller, *Reluctant Capitalists: Bookselling and the Culture of Consumption* (Chicago: University of Chicago Press, 2006), 91.

109. *The Zondervan Corporation 1980 Annual Report*, ZPH.

110. Jonathan Petersen, "Family Bookstores/Zondervan Publishing House Christmas Party Speech—1994," ZPH.

111. Lizabeth Cohen, "From Town Center to Shopping Center: The Reconfiguration of Community Marketplaces in Postwar America," *American Historical Review* 101, no. 4 (October 1996): 1055–1056.

112. Lizabeth Cohen, *A Consumer's Republic: The Politics of Mass Consumption in Postwar America* (New York: Vintage Books, 2004), 196, 202. On the ideological transformations that suburban relocation required, see Darren Dochuk, "'Praying for a Wicked City': Congregation, Community, and the Suburbanization of Fundamentalism," *Religion and American Culture* 13, no. 2 (Summer 2003): 167–203, esp. 178.

113. Cohen, *A Consumer's Republic*, 202–206, 214, 221, 241.

114. Kevin Michael Kruse, *White Flight: Atlanta and the Making of Modern Conservatism*, Politics and Society in Twentieth-Century America (Princeton: Princeton University Press, 2005), esp. chap. 3; Lassiter, *The Silent Majority*; Cohen, *A Consumer's Republic*, 197.

115. Luhr, *Witnessing Suburbia*, 8. Because the term "suburb" describes a residential area's *sub*ordinate relationship with an *urb*an center, some sociologists note that postwar suburbs should be reckoned more accurately as "postsuburban space," insofar as they are not connected to any single city but instead connected contingently to multiple urban centers and suburbs. Justin Wilford explains that "places like Lake Forest, California, South Barrington, Illinois, Alpharetta, Georgia, Fort Lauderdale, Florida, and Edmond, Oklahoma, are not necessarily connected to any dominant urban core. They are part of what the urban sociologist Mark Gottdiener calls a 'multinucleated metropolitan region'—deconcentrated, functionally differentiated, and fragmented." Wilford, *Sacred Subdivisions: The Postsuburban Transformation of American Evangelicalism* (New York: NYU Press, 2012), 60.

116. Thomas W. Hanchett, "U.S. Tax Policy and the Shopping-Center Boom of the 1950s and 1960s," *American Historical Review* 101, no. 4 (October 1996): 1082–1110, esp. 1095–1098. See also Kenneth T. Jackson, "All the World's a Mall: Reflections on the Social and Economic Consequences of the American Shopping Center," *American Historical Review* 101, no. 4 (October 1996): 1113.

117. Vicki Howard, *From Main Street to Mall: The Rise and Fall of the American Department Store* (Philadelphia: University of Pennsylvania Press, 2015), 141–143.

118. Linda M. Scott, "Markets and Audiences," in *The Enduring Book: Print Culture in Postwar America*, ed. David Paul Nord, Joan Shelley Rubin, and Michael Schudson, vol. 5 of *A History of the Book in America* (Chapel Hill:

American Antiquarian Society/University of North Carolina Press, 2009), 83; Miller, *Reluctant Capitalists,* 35–38, 90.

119. Bass and DeVries, *The Christian Book Store,* 18–23.

120. He later would found Spring Arbor. Carlson initially told his store's story at an InterVarsity Press workshop at the 1970 CBA convention, and popular acclaim led Carlson to publish it as a series of articles in three successive issues of *Bookstore Journal* in 1971. In his story, Carlson recounts how he had served as a counselor for InterVarsity Christian Fellowship. When Gordon Van Wylen, dean of the University of Michigan's Engineering School, gathered $12,000 in capital and set out to establish a Christian bookstore, Van Wylen asked InterVarsity to manage it, and the organization tapped Carlson to lead the initiative. The experience ultimately gave Carlson expertise not just in Christian retailing but also in distribution. After his time at Logos, Carlson founded Spring Arbor Distributors, which became one of the two most powerful Christian book distributors of the 1980s. John P. Ferré, "Searching for the Great Commission: Evangelical Book Publishing since the 1970s," in *American Evangelicals and the Mass Media: Perspectives on the Relationship between American Evangelicals and the Mass Media,* ed. Quentin J. Schultze (Grand Rapids, MI: Academie Books/Zondervan, 1990), 99–117, esp. 107.

121. *1980 Annual Report,* ZPH.

122. Miller, *Reluctant Capitalists,* 49, 57.

123. Jim Harger, "Family Bookstores Back in Local Ownership," *Grand Rapids Press,* November 18, 1994, C7.

124. Charles B. Grannis, "More than Merchants: Seventy-Five Years of the ABA," in *Bookselling in America and the World: Some Observations and Recollections in Celebration of the 75th Anniversary of the American Booksellers Association,* ed. Charles B. Anderson (New York: Quadrangle/New York Times Book Co., 1975), 74.

125. Blessings Book Store, *Summer Book News,* 1941, box 1, folder: Books, HJO; Baker Book Store, *Catalog of Used Books on Biblical and Theological Subjects,* no. 8., 1941–1942, box 1, folder: Books, HJO.

126. Neil J. Young, *We Gather Together: The Religious Right and the Problem of Interfaith Politics* (New York: Oxford University Press, 2015), 151–154. See also Barry Hankins, *Francis Schaeffer and the Shaping of Evangelical America* (Grand Rapids, MI: Eerdmans, 2008).

127. Heather Hendershot, *Shaking the World for Jesus: Media and Conservative Evangelical Culture* (Chicago: University of Chicago Press, 2004), 13.

128. Francis A. Schaeffer, *The God Who Is There* (Downers Grove, IL: InterVarsity Press, 1978 [1968]), 14, 19.

129. Matthew Engelke, "Angels in Swindon: Public Religion and Ambient Faith in England," *American Ethnologist* 39, no. 1 (2012): 155–170, esp. 164–167. "The direction of our glance," the media theorist Michael Warner argues with a similar model of sociality in mind, "can constitute our social world." Warner argues that social publics "commence with the moment of attention, must con-

tinually predicate renewed attention, and cease to exist when attention is no longer predicated." Michael Warner, *Publics and Counterpublics* (New York: Zone Books, 2002), 88.

130. James E. Ruark, "Meeting the Evangelical Needs," *Publishers Weekly,* September 26, 1977, 66.

131. James E. Ruark, *The House of Zondervan,* 2nd ed. (Grand Rapids, MI: Zondervan Publishing House, 2006), 50, 68, 100–105.

132. Dessauer, Doebler, and Edelman, *Christian Book Publishing,* 130; Brown, "Culture of Culture Industries," 115; Quentin J. Schultze, "The Invisible Medium: Evangelical Radio," in Schultze, *American Evangelicals,* 171–195. Stowe explains that "the impact of the Jesus Movement popular music was felt less through album sales and radio playlists than through new styles of boomer-friendly worship music." Such Christian music pioneers as Larry Norman and Amy Grant began their careers playing music in the Jesus Movement's coffeehouses. But the practices of listening to and engaging in worship music began coming together as far back as the 1940s. In addition, although Singspiration recordings may seem old-fashioned today, their sensibilities share much in common with the staid popular music of their own day. David W. Stowe, *No Sympathy for the Devil: Christian Pop Music and the Transformation of American Evangelicalism* (Chapel Hill: University of North Carolina Press, 2011), 8. See also Brown, "Culture of Culture Industries," 67.

133. See Jay R. Howard and John M. Streck, *Apostles of Rock: The Splintered World of Contemporary Christian Music* (Lexington: University Press of Kentucky, 1999), esp. chap. 4 on "transformational" Christian music. On Jars of Clay and their reach "beyond the boundaries of the evangelical subculture," see Randall H. Balmer, *Mine Eyes Have Seen the Glory: A Journey into the Evangelical Subculture in America,* 5th ed. (New York: Oxford University Press, 2014), chap. 16, esp. 308.

134. "William R. Barbour, Jr., Revell President, Talks about 'Getting Our Books Out There Where the Unbeliever Action Is,'" *Publishers Weekly,* March 14, 1977, quote on 57. On "color-blind racism," see Eduardo Bonilla-Silva, *Racism without Racists: Color-Blind Racism and the Persistence of Racial Inequality in America* (Lanham, MD: Rowman and Littlefield, 2013).

135. Andy Butcher, "New Strategic Alliance Builds Retail Opportunity," *Christian Market,* July 18, 2016, https://cbaonline.org/new-strategic-alliance-builds -retail-opportunity.

136. Ann Byle, "Christian Books Selling Well at Hobby Lobby," *Publishers Weekly,* March 22, 2017, https://publishersweekly.com/pw/by-topic/industry-news /religion/article/73142-christian-books-selling-well-at-hobby-lobby.html.

137. Ibid.

138. "Family Christian Closing All Stores," *Christian Market Weekly,* February 23, 2017, https://cbaonline.org/family-christian-closes-stores/. On Hobby Lobby, see Candida R. Moss and Joel S. Baden, *Bible Nation: The United States of Hobby Lobby* (Princeton: Princeton University Press, 2017).

139. See Darren E. Grem, *The Blessings of Business: How Corporations Shaped Conservative Christianity* (New York: Oxford University Press, 2016), esp. chap. 4.
140. Sam Binkley, "The Seers of Menlo Park: The Discourse of Heroic Consumption in the 'Whole Earth Catalog,'" *Journal of Consumer Culture* 3, no. 3 (November 1, 2003): 283–313, esp. 290; see Axel R. Schäfer, *Countercultural Conservatives: American Evangelicalism from the Postwar Revival to the New Christian Right* (Madison: University of Wisconsin Press, 2011).
141. Note that Wal-Mart renamed itself Walmart in 2017. Sarah Nassauer, "Wal-Mart's New Name: It's Not Just a Store Anymore," *Wall Street Journal,* December 6, 2017, sec. Business.
142. Jones, "Building an Image of Excellence," 22.

5. Financial Faith

1. *The Zondervan Corporation 1985 Annual Report,* ZPH.
2. Mark Potts, "Zondervan Corp. Signs Consent Agreement with SEC," *Washington Post,* March 7, 1985.
3. Jim Harger, "3rd Investor Buys Large Holding in Zondervan," *Grand Rapids Press,* February 28, 1986.
4. See J. A. Fichtner, "Tradition (in Theology)," in *New Catholic Encyclopedia,* 2nd ed. (Detroit: Gale, 2003), 14:133–138, esp. 133–134; John R. Franke, "Scripture, Tradition and Authority: Reconstructing the Evangelical Conception of Sola Scriptura," in *Evangelicals and Scripture: Tradition, Authority and Hermeneutics,* ed. Vincent E. Bacote, Laura Miguelez Quay, and Dennis L. Okholm (Downers Grove, IL: IVP Academic, 2004), 192–210, e.g., 200. See also Gary Dorrien, *The Remaking of Evangelical Theology* (Louisville, KY: Westminster John Knox, 1998), 21–22.
5. On evangelicals denying tradition's authority, see Daniel H. Williams, *Retrieving the Tradition and Renewing Evangelicalism: A Primer for Suspicious Protestants* (Grand Rapids, MI: Eerdmans, 1999), esp. chap. 2; Stanley J. Grenz, "Nurturing the Soul, Informing the Mind: The Genesis of Evangelical Scriptural Principle," in Bacote, Quay, and Okholm, *Evangelicals and Scripture,* 21–41, esp. 32–37. During the 1970s, the Bible professor and editor of *Christianity Today* Harold Lindsell argued that the essence of evangelical identity lay in devotion to the incomparable authority of an inerrant Bible. See Harold Lindsell, *The Battle for the Bible* (Grand Rapids, MI: Zondervan, 1976). Molly Worthen discusses Lindsell's attempt to sound a theological alarm in *Apostles of Reason: The Crisis of Authority in American Evangelicalism* (New York: Oxford University Press, 2013), 200–202.
6. R. Ward Holder, "The Reformers and Tradition: Seeing the Roots of the Problem," *Religions* 8, no. 6 (May 2017): 1–11; Grenz, "Nurturing the Soul," 36.
7. Second Vatican Council, *Dei Verbum: Dogmatic Constitution on Divine Revelation,* 1965, http://www.vatican.va/archive/hist_councils/ii_vatican_council /documents/vat-ii_const_19651118_dei-verbum_en.html.

8. See Gerald F. Davis, *Managed by the Markets: How Finance Re-shaped America* (New York: Oxford University Press, 2009), esp. chap. 1. Although Davis focuses primarily on the era after 1980, he notes that "the passing of industrial society" was apparent by the early 1970s.

9. Quoted in Wendy Wall, *Inventing the American Way: The Politics of Consensus from the New Deal to the Civil Rights Movement* (New York: Oxford University Press, 2008), 59. Melinda Cooper argues that neoliberal inheritors of free enterprise created their policies especially in response to a "novel politics of redistribution" that undermined "the sexual normativity of the family wage as the linchpin of welfare capitalism." Melinda Cooper, *Family Values: Between Neoliberalism and the New Social Conservatism* (New York: Zone Books, 2017), 21. On "Christian free enterprise," see Bethany Moreton, *To Serve God and Wal-Mart: The Making of Christian Free Enterprise* (Cambridge, MA: Harvard University Press, 2009); Elizabeth A. Fones-Wolf, *Selling Free Enterprise: The Business Assault on Labor and Liberalism, 1945–60* (Urbana: University of Illinois Press, 1994), esp. chap. 8.

10. Sarah Ruth Hammond, *God's Businessmen: Evangelicals in Depression and War*, ed. Darren Dochuk (Chicago: University of Chicago Press, 2017), 17–18; Ted W. Engstrom, ed., *"This I Know . . .": Testimonies from Men Successful in Business* (Grand Rapids, MI: Zondervan, 1947).

11. Laura J. Miller, *Reluctant Capitalists: Bookselling and the Culture of Consumption* (Chicago: University of Chicago Press, 2006), 24, 31–32.

12. Ibid., 5, 18.

13. John P. Dessauer, *Book Publishing: What It Is, What It Does*, 2nd ed. (New York: R. R. Bowker, 1981), 6–7; Linda M. Scott, "Markets and Audiences," in *The Enduring Book: Print Culture in Postwar America*, ed. David Paul Nord, Joan Shelley Rubin, and Michael Schudson, vol. 5 of *A History of the Book in America* (Chapel Hill: American Antiquarian Society/University of North Carolina Press, 2009), 72–90.

14. See Matthew S. Hedstrom, *The Rise of Liberal Religion: Book Culture and American Spirituality in the Twentieth Century* (New York: Oxford University Press, 2013). On conservative corporate interest in religion, see Fones-Wolf, *Selling Free Enterprise*, esp. chap. 8, e.g., 223.

15. Philip Benjamin, "Publishers of Books Are Turning to Mergers," *New York Times*, July 31, 1960, sec. Business; Davis, *Managed by the Markets*, 75–76; Lewis A. Coser, Charles Kadushin, and Walter W. Powell, *Books: The Culture and Commerce of Publishing* (New York: Basic Books, 1982), 26. See also Elin B. Christianson, "Mergers in the Publishing Industry, 1958–1970," *Journal of Library History* 7, no. 1 (January 1972): 5–32, figures on 10. On books as "big business," see Henry Raymont, "Book Publishers Feel Economy Pinch," *New York Times*, February 3, 1971, 30.

16. Coser, Kadushin, and Powell, *Books*, 22–25.

17. "The Big Story in Books Is Financial," *Business Week*, May 16, 1970, 68–74; Benjamin, "Publishers of Books."

18. "Baker Book House Purchases Publishing Division of W. A. Wilde Co.," *Bookstore Journal*, July–August 1968, 20.

19. "News from Convention: Word, Inc. Acquires the Assets of Rodeheaver Company," *Bookstore Journal,* October 1969, 24.
20. Advertisement in *Bookstore Journal,* January 1972, 71.
21. Pat Zondervan's *Harper Bible Booklet,* 65–66, ZPH.
22. "Zondervan Starts New Program," *Bookstore Journal,* October 1968, 14.
23. Sherwood Wirt, "Direction Signs for Christian Literature," *Bookstore Journal,* October 1969, 12–15. Originally delivered as an address at the Christian Booksellers 20th Annual Convention, Cincinnati, July 30, 1969.
24. James E. Ruark, *The House of Zondervan,* 2nd ed. (Grand Rapids, MI: Zondervan, 2006), 119–120.
25. *Complete Trade Catalog, 1965–1966,* ZPH.
26. "John Knox and Westminster Join Sales Forces," *Bookstore Journal,* October 1969, 25; "More on Bethany Fellowship Distributors," *Bookstore Journal,* July–August 1968, 20.
27. On the charismatic renewal movement, see Worthen, *Apostles of Reason,* 139–141. For an example of partnerships with and acquisitions of charismatic publishers, see "Re-drawing the Religious Publishing Map," *Publishers Weekly,* August 10, 1992, 45. The article details Word's partnership with Creation House, the publishing division of the charismatic corporation Strang Communications. Word's CEO explained that Creation House had "a particular appeal . . . to that part of the church body that is not immediately accessible to evangelicals or mainliners."
28. Coser, Kadushin, and Powell, *Books,* 26. On stunted "organic growth" during the recession of the 1970s, see Davis, *Managed by the Markets,* 80.
29. Raymont, "Book Publishers Feel Economy Pinch," 30.
30. Robert DeVries, "Evangelical Publishing—A Gamble?," *Bookstore Journal,* September 1970, 26–27.
31. "Countdown Capsule News: Volume of Christian Book Sales Amazes Those in Trade," *Bookstore Journal,* January 1972, 2.
32. Fabrice Collard and Harris Dellas, "Monetary Policy and Inflation in the 70s," *Journal of Money, Credit and Banking* 40, no. 8 (2008): 1765–1781.
33. Coser, Kadushin, and Powell, *Books,* 26.
34. On "degrees of conglomerateness" and conglomerate "node commonality," see John C. Narver, *Conglomerate Mergers and Market Competition* (Berkeley: University of California Press, 1967), 4–5. See also Richard C. Clark, "Conglomerate Mergers and Section 7 of the Clayton Act," *Notre Dame Law Review* 36, no. 3 (1961): 255–275.
35. Louis Galambos, "The U.S. Corporate Economy in the Twentieth Century," in *The Cambridge Economic History of the United States,* ed. Stanley L. Engerman and Robert E. Gallman (Cambridge: Cambridge University Press, 2000), esp. 958; John P. Dessauer, "Coming Full Circle at Macmillan: A Publishing Merger in Economic Perspective," in *The Structure of International Publishing in the 1990s,* ed. Fred Kobrak and Beth Luey (New Brunswick, NJ: Transaction, 1992), 29; Raymont, "Book Publishers Feel Economy Pinch"; Winson B. Lee and Elizabeth S. Cooperman, "Conglomerates in the 1980s: A Performance Appraisal," *Financial Management* 18, no. 1 (Spring 1989): 45–54.

36. Ruark, *The House of Zondervan,* 139.

37. "President Kladder Extends Seasons Greetings to All," *Zondervan Corporation News,* December 1973, 2, ZPH.

38. *Thomas Nelson Annual Report for 1995,* 32, U.S. Securities and Exchange Commission, https://www.sec.gov/Archives/edgar/data/71023/0000950144-95-001801.txt.

39. Lynn Andriani, "Hello My Name Is . . . ," *Publishers Weekly,* October 2, 2006, 31–32; Lynn Garrett and Jana Riess with reporting by Daisy Maryles, "Trade Houses Find More Religion," *Publishers Weekly,* July 17, 2006, 12; Lynn Garrett and Cindy Crosby, "Evangelical Publishers Flourish in 'The Springs,'" *Publishers Weekly,* November 20, 2006, 10–13, esp. 13.

40. Examples of popular books on prayer include Stormie Omartian's *The Power of a Praying Wife* (Eugene, OR: Harvest House, 1997). For more on what the historian Kate Bowler describes as the "bright-sided faith" of Wilkinson's book, see *Blessed: A History of the American Prosperity Gospel* (New York: Oxford University Press, 2013), 228. On the success of Wilkinson's book, see Heidi Schlumpf, "Answered Prayers for Booksellers," *Publishers Weekly,* April 15, 2002, 30–31; Daisy Maryles, "Setting a New Record," *Publishers Weekly,* November 5, 2001, 18.

41. Angie Kiesling, "'Jabez' Enlarges Multnomah's 'Territory,'" *Publishers Weekly,* April 1, 2002, 17; Dale Buss, "Multnomah Publishers Cuts 15 Positions," *Publishers Weekly,* February 9, 2004, 8.

42. "Murdoch Buys Bible Printer," *Newsday,* July 14, 1988, sec. Business; Cynthia Crossen, "Harper & Row Says It Will Acquire Zondervan, Expand Religious Line," *Wall Street Journal,* July 14, 1988. Harper & Row became HarperCollins in 1990, when Harper & Row merged with the British publisher William Collins. See Roger Cohen, "Birth of a Global Book Giant," *New York Times,* June 11, 1990, sec. D. For the Thomas Nelson acquisition, see Julie Bosman, "HarperCollins to Acquire Religious Publisher," *New York Times,* November 1, 2011, sec. B; David Gelles, "News Corp to Create Holy Alliance with Thomas Nelson Deal," *Financial Times,* November 1, 2011, sec. Companies-UK; Lynn Garrett, "Stunned Reaction to HarperCollins's Acquisition of Thomas Nelson," *Publishers Weekly,* November 4, 2011. On HarperCollins Christian's profile, see "Company Information: HarperCollins Christian Publishing," HarperCollins Christian Publishing, accessed July 25, 2019, http://www.harpercollinschristian.com/info/.

43. Allan Fisher, "The Man Who 'Owns' the News—and the Bible: Rupert Murdoch, HarperCollins, and the Recent History of Bible Publishing" (unpublished paper delivered at the 2014 annual meeting of the Society for the History of Authorship, Reading and Publishing, Antwerp, Belgium), 12.

44. Dwight Baker, interview by author, Grand Rapids, MI, October 13, 2016.

45. Dwight Baker, "How I Learned to Love Media Conglomerates," *Christian Retailing,* September 3, 2014, http://www.christianretailing.com/index.php/features/27409-how-i-learned-to-love-media-conglomerates.

46. Dwight Baker interview.

47. Louis Hyman, "Rethinking the Postwar Corporation: Management, Monopolies, and Markets," in *What's Good for Business: Business and American Politics since World War II*, ed. Kim Phillips-Fein and Julian E. Zelizer (New York: Oxford University Press, 2012), 195–211, esp. 196.

48. See Daniel Silliman, "Publishers and Profit Motives: The Economic History of *Left Behind*," in *Religion and the Marketplace in the United States*, ed. Jan Stievermann, Philip Goff, and Detlef Junker (New York: Oxford University Press, 2015), esp. 172.

49. Jim Harger, "Zondervan's President Leads Effort to Buy the Company," *Grand Rapids Press*, April 29, 1992.

50. Linda E. Connors, Sara Lynn Henry, and Jonathan W. Reader, "From Art to Corporation: Harry N. Abrams, Inc., and the Cultural Effects of Merger," in Kobrak and Luey, *Structure of International Publishing*, 39–70, quotes on 66–67.

51. Coser, Kadushin, and Powell, *Books*, 24–25; Frederick M. Scherer, *Industrial Market Structure and Economic Performance* (Chicago: Rand McNally, 1970), 354.

52. James Buick, interview by author, Grand Rapids, MI, October 11, 2016.

53. Scott Bolinder, interview by author, Grand Rapids, MI, October 11, 2016.

54. "Zondervan Appoints Brunswick Executive as New Operating Chief," *Grand Rapids Press*, July 5, 1984, C3.

55. James Buick interview.

56. Collin Hansen, "The CEO Who Takes Greek Exegesis," *Christianity Today*, April 22, 2008, 42–43; "Girkins Named Zondervan CEO," *Publishers Weekly*, December 10, 2007, 6. Girkins had a relatively brief tenure. Her contract was not renewed in 2011, with the company's other leaders citing insufficient return on digital investments and poor handling of criticism over controversial publications, including the Today's New International Version of the Bible (see Chapter 6). Supporters have insisted that she became a scapegoat for the inevitable struggles that came with the digital transition and Zondervan's reach for broader religious audiences. Sarah Pulliam Bailey, "Moe Girkins to Leave Zondervan CEO Post," *Christianity Today*, February 17, 2011, https://www.christianitytoday.com/news/2011/february/moe-girkins-to-leave-zondervan-ceo-post.html.

57. Marx makes this observation throughout the *Grundrisse*. See Cooper, *Family Values*, e.g., 16, 21, 63.

58. Ruth Moon and Ted Olson, "NRB Forces Out WaterBrook Multnomah over Sister Imprint's 'Gay Christian' Book," *Christianity Today*, May 16, 2014, https://www.christianitytoday.com/ct/2014/may-web-only/nrb-waterbrook-multnomah-god-and-gay-christian.html.

59. John Z. DeLorean, *DeLorean*, with Ted Schwarz (Grand Rapids, MI: Zondervan, 1985), 226–235. On the advance, see Betty Cuniberti, "DeLorean—'Every Person Has His Price,'" *Los Angeles Times*, October 7, 1985, E1.

60. By request of my sources, I have withheld the name of the celebrity in question. Buick interview; Bolinder interview.

61. Andrea Karin Muehlebach, *The Moral Neoliberal: Welfare and Citizenship in Italy* (Chicago: University of Chicago Press, 2012), 26.

62. Ron Harris, "Spread of Legal Innovations Defining Private and Public Domains," in *The Cambridge History of Capitalism,* ed. Larry Neal and Jeffrey G. Williamson, 2 vols. (Cambridge: Cambridge University Press, 2013), 2:127–168, esp. 143.

63. Harger, "3rd Investor."

64. Harris, "Spread of Legal Innovations," 143.

65. Adam Smith, *An Inquiry into the Nature and Causes of the Wealth of Nations* (1776), 4.2.9.

66. Karen Zouwen Ho, *Liquidated: An Ethnography of Wall Street* (Durham, NC: Duke University Press, 2009), 175. See also Milo Bianchi and Magnus Henrekson, "Is Neoclassical Economics Still Entrepreneurless?," *Kyklos* 58, no. 3 (2005): 353–377.

67. Emphasis in original. Maxwell J. Mangold, *How Public Financing Can Help Your Company Grow: A Guide to the Advantages and Ways of Securing Equity Capital through Sales of Stock to the Public, Including 25 Case Histories of Actual Public Offerings* (New York: Pilot, 1959), 13.

68. Ibid., 9, 14.

69. Quoted in Ruark, *The House of Zondervan,* 140–141.

70. "The Zondervan Corporation: Preliminary Prospectus for 363,883 Shares," ZPH.

71. *Zondervan Corporation Annual Report for 1982,* 7, ZPH.

72. See Davis, *Managed by the Markets,* 84–89.

73. "A Religious Publisher Gets More Worldly about Management," *Business Week,* June 18, 1984, 92.

74. "Publishers Spread the Word to the World," February 1983, ZPH. I encountered this article as a newspaper clipping in a scrapbook that Zondervan kept in its archives; although the clipping included an indication of the month and year of publication, it did not include an indication of the periodical from which it came.

75. Ed Kotlar, "Zondervan Modernizes in Search of Christian-Oriented Readers," *Grand Rapids Press,* July 30, 1980; "A Religious Publisher."

76. Chris Meehan, "Words and Music (& Zeal) by Zondervan," *Grand Rapids Press,* February 4, 1984, sec. D1.

77. Nanine Alexander, "Religious Empire: Zondervan Expands from Publishing to Bookstores and Music," *Barron's National Business and Financial Weekly,* January 24, 1983; John Mutter, "Zondervan to Buy Revell from SFN," *Publishers Weekly,* August 5, 1983.

78. "The 'House of Best Sellers,'" *Zondervan Corporation News,* June 1984, 1, ZPH; Alexander, "Religious Empire"; "A Religious Publisher."

79. Sam Moore, *American By Choice: The Remarkable Fulfillment of an Immigrant's Dream* (Nashville, TN: Thomas Nelson, 1998), 106.

80. Ibid., xvii–xviii, 28, 35, 76, 83–84, 100, 106.

81. "Who Are Our Customers?," *Zondervan Corporation News,* November 1984, 2, ZPH.

82. David W. Bebbington, *Evangelicalism in Modern Britain: A History from the 1730s to the 1980s* (London: Unwin Hyman, 1989), 2–17.

83. Kotlar, "Zondervan Modernizes."

84. Erin Smith recognizes Zondervan's self-conscious embrace of "nominal Christians" in *What Would Jesus Read? Popular Religious Books and Everyday Life in Twentieth-Century America* (Chapel Hill: University of North Carolina Press, 2015), 203, 206.

85. Alexander, "Religious Empire"; Meehan, "Words and Music"; "A Religious Publisher."

86. Dale D. Buss, "Zondervan's Loss Came as Old News to Some Analysts," *Wall Street Journal,* October 26, 1984.

87. "SEC Is Said to Study Big One-Day Decline in Zondervan's Stock," *Wall Street Journal,* October 31, 1984.

88. Matthew Schifrin, "Bible Bungle," *Forbes,* March 11, 1985, 123.

89. Although Catherine Bell wrote on belief, I apply her insights to the concept of faith. For my purposes here, the processes of "believing" and "being faithful" or "having faith" are synonymous. For Bell, belief involves "the ways that contradictions are maintained, rather than truths affirmed." Quoted in Kevin Lewis O'Neill, "Pastor Harold Caballeros Believes in Demons: Belief and Believing in the Study of Religion," *History of Religions* 51, no. 4 (May 2012): 299–316, quote on 308. Rebecca Bartel builds on both Bell's work and O'Neill's, identifying the difference between belief and knowing as belief's need for "the suspension of return on an act of belief." Rebecca C. Bartel, "Giving Is Believing: Credit and Christmas in Colombia," *Journal of the American Academy of Religion* 84, no. 4 (December 2016): 1006–1028, esp. 1013. Bell's understanding of belief can be seen as an extension of Michel de Certeau's notion that "belief . . . concerns 'what makes it run.' " Michel de Certeau, "What We Do When We Believe," in *On Signs,* ed. Marshall Blonsky (Baltimore: University of Maryland Press), 192–203.

90. Gerald Davis shows how advocates of shareholder capitalism defined corporations as "nothing but a nexus of contracts." *Managed by the Markets,* 91.

91. Ho, *Liquidated,* 186.

92. Naomi R. Lamoreaux, "Entrepreneurship, Business Organization, and Economic Concentration," in Engerman and Gallman, *Cambridge Economic History of the United States,* 403–434, esp. 427–428.

93. Ranald Michie, "Financial Capitalism," in Neal and Williamson, *Cambridge History of Capitalism,* 2:230–263, quotes on 236–238.

94. Harger, "3rd Investor."

95. Lynn Turner, "Moran Renews Offer to Buy Zondervan Corp.," *Grand Rapids Business Journal,* August 4, 1986.

96. "British Broker Intent on Pursuing Zondervan," *New York Times,* May 9, 1986, sec. D; Lauren A. Rublin, "Do Zondervan Shareholders Have a Prayer? The Unorthodox Behavior of a Bible Publisher's Stock," *Barron's National Business and Financial Weekly,* October 19, 1987, 18.

97. Dale D. Buss, "Fight to Take Over Religious Publisher Becomes a Holy War," *Wall Street Journal,* August 14, 1986.

98. James Buick, "A Christmas Message from Jim Buick," *Zondervan Publishing House News*, December 1987, ZPH.

99. "Employee Information Meetings," *Zondervan Corporation News*, August/September 1988, 1–2, ZPH. On later layoffs, see W. Griffin, "Dozens Laid Off in 'Restructuring' at Zondervan," *Publishers Weekly*, March 16, 1992, 20. A team of former Zondervan executives purchased the bookstore division from HarperCollins. Dan Calabrese, "Family Bookstores Gets New Ownership in Zondervan Break," *Grand Rapids Business Journal* 12, no. 50 (December 12, 1994): 3.

100. Crossen, "Harper & Row Says." To generate its list, four male executives reviewed all of the books that HarperCollins sold through the religious distributor Spring Arbor. "There were disagreements about certain titles," explained the Book and Bible Division's vice president for sales, but "we came to some conclusions and tended to be rather conservative in our selection process." On the process and Craig's remarks about cross-selling, see "The Way Ahead," *Grapevine: An Employee Publication of the Zondervan Corporation and Its Subsidiaries*, October/November 1988, 1–3, ZPH.

101. *Zondervan: A Division of HarperCollins Publishers*, 1–4, ZPH.

102. Scott Bolinder interview.

103. Davis, *Managed by the Markets*, 83.

104. Allan Fisher, interview by author, Wheaton, IL, August 17, 2016. Other members of the industry also expressed surprise. See Garrett, "Stunned Reaction."

105. Journalists sometimes mentioned Thomas Nelson during the 1990s to describe Zondervan's relative size. See Jim Harger, "Zondervan Splitting into Two Companies," *Grand Rapids Press*, September 1993, ZPH. I encountered this article as a newspaper clipping that included the month and year but not the day of publication.

106. Bowler, *Blessed*, 3. For examples of Thomas Nelson titles by Hinn and Jakes, see Benny Hinn, *The Anointing* (Nashville, TN: Thomas Nelson, 1992); Benny Hinn, *He Touched Me: An Autobiography* (Nashville, TN: Thomas Nelson, 1999); T. D. Jakes, ed., *Holy Bible: Woman Thou Art Loosed! Edition* (Nashville, TN: Thomas Nelson, 1998).

6. The Spirit of Market Segmentation

1. Stan Gundry to Jim Ruark, "Sequence of Events Leading up to the Release of *Under Fire*, Oliver North with Bill Novak," December 20, 1991, folder: Oliver North—Under Fire, 3, ZPH-ED; see also James E. Ruark, *The House of Zondervan*, 2nd ed. (Grand Rapids, MI: Zondervan, 2006), 174.

2. After acquiring Harper & Row in 1987, Murdoch acquired the British publisher William Collins in 1990. That acquisition produced the merged company HarperCollins. Edwin Mcdowell, "Murdoch to Buy Harper & Row in Surprise Deal," *New York Times*, March 31, 1987, sec. Business; Roger Cohen, "Birth of a Global Book Giant," *New York Times*, June 11, 1990, sec. Business.

3. "Sequence of Events Leading up to the Release of *Under Fire,* Oliver North with Bill Novak," ZPH-ED.

4. Oliver North and William Novak, *Under Fire: An American Story* (New York: HarperCollins; Grand Rapids, MI: Zondervan, 1992), 147.

5. Ruark, *The House of Zondervan,* 174.

6. North, *Under Fire,* 411.

7. Axel R. Schäfer, *Countercultural Conservatives: American Evangelicalism from the Postwar Revival to the New Christian Right* (Madison: University of Wisconsin Press, 2011), 111, 145–147.

8. Wendell R. Smith, "Product Differentiation and Market Segmentation as Alternative Marketing Strategies," *Journal of Marketing* 21 (1956): 3–8, esp. 5. On the "mass market," see Steven C. Brandt, "Dissecting the Segmentation Syndrome," *Journal of Marketing* 30, no. 4 (October 1966): 22–27, esp. 22. See also Cohen, *A Consumer's Republic,* 294–295.

9. Jack B. Weiner, "Myth of the National Market," *Dun's Review and Modern Industry,* May 1964; James F. Engel, Henry F. Fiorillo, and Murray A. Cayley, "Segmentation: Its Place in Marketing Management," *Business Quarterly* 36, no. 1 (Spring 1971): 64; Kotrba, "The Strategy Selection Chart," 23.

10. Ronald A. Fullerton, "How Modern Is Modern Marketing? Marketing's Evolution and the Myth of the 'Production Era,'" *Journal of Marketing* 52, no. 1 (January 1988): 113. See also Susan Strasser, *Satisfaction Guaranteed: The Making of the American Mass Market,* 2nd ed. (Washington, DC: Smithsonian Institution, 2004).

11. "Eighteenth Annual Report (1834)," in *Annual Reports of the American Bible Society,* vol. 1 (New York: American Bible Society, 1838), 715.

12. *Complete Catalog of Zondervan Publishing House: Books, Plaques, and Novelties,* Fall 1943–Spring 1944, 52–54, ZPH; "Eighteenth Annual Report," 715.

13. Brandt, "Dissecting the Segmentation Syndrome," esp. 22.

14. Arthur E. Swanson, "The Harvard Bureau of Business Research," *Journal of Political Economy* 22, no. 9 (1914): 896–900; Sarah Elizabeth Igo, *The Averaged American: Surveys, Citizens, and the Making of a Mass Public* (Cambridge, MA: Harvard University Press, 2007), 8.

15. Ibid., 119, 140.

16. Gina A. Zurlo, "The Social Gospel, Ecumenical Movement, and Christian Sociology: The Institute of Social and Religious Research," *American Sociologist* 46, no. 2 (June 2015): 177–193, esp. 184–188.

17. Robert Wuthnow, *Inventing American Religion: Polls, Surveys, and the Tenuous Quest for a Nation's Faith* (New York: Oxford University Press, 2015), esp. chap. 2.

18. Robert Staughton Lynd, *Middletown: A Study in Contemporary American Culture* (New York: Harcourt, Brace, 1929), 7. On the reception of *Middletown* and its influence on the marketing business, see Igo, *The Averaged American,* chap. 2, esp. 85–88.

19. J. Waskom Pickett, *Christian Mass Movements in India* (Cincinnati: Abingdon Press, 1933), 11, 330.

20. Donald A. McGavran, *Understanding Church Growth*, ed. C. Peter Wagner, 3rd ed. (Grand Rapids, MI: Eerdmans, 1990), 163. In 1965 McGavran's Institute of Church Growth became part of Fuller Theological Seminary's School of World Mission. See Arthur F. Glasser, "Church Growth at Fuller," *Missiology* 14, no. 4 (October 1986): 401–420, esp. 402–403. On the development of McGavran's Church Growth principles, see Molly Worthen, *Apostles of Reason: The Crisis of Authority in American Evangelicalism* (New York: Oxford University Press, 2013), 128–134.

21. Eugene A. Nida, *Customs and Cultures: Anthropology for Christian Missions* (New York: Harper and Row, 1968).

22. C. René Padilla, "The Unity of the Church and the Homogeneous Unit Principle," *International Bulletin of Missionary Research* 6, no. 1 (January 1982): 23–30, quotes on 23, 29.

23. C. Peter Wagner, *Church Growth and the Whole Gospel: A Biblical Mandate* (Eugene, OR: Wipf and Stock, 1998), 169, 180–181.

24. C. Peter Wagner, *Our Kind of People: The Ethical Dimensions of Church Growth in America* (Atlanta: John Knox Press, 1979). See also Michael O. Emerson and Christian Smith, *Divided by Faith: Evangelical Religion and the Problem of Race in America* (New York: Oxford University Press, 2000), 150.

25. C. Peter Wagner, "Vision for Evangelizing the Real America," *International Bulletin of Missionary Research* 10, no. 2 (April 1986): 59–64, quote on 61.

26. Worthen, *Apostles of Reason*, 131.

27. Rick Warren, *The Purpose Driven Church: Growth without Compromising Your Message and Mission* (Grand Rapids, MI: Zondervan, 1995), 170.

28. Wuthnow, *Inventing American Religion*, 113–114.

29. See Eugene A. Nida and Charles R. Taber, *The Theory and Practice of Translation* (Leiden: Brill, for the United Bible Societies, 1969), e.g., 27.

30. Paul C. Gutjahr, "Crowning the King: The Use of Production and Reception Studies to Determine the Most Popular English-Language Bible Translation in Contemporary America," and Daniel Vaca, "Selling Trust: The Living Bible and the Business of Biblicism," both in *The Bible in American Life*, ed. Philip Goff, Arthur E. Farnsley II, and Peter J. Thuesen (New York: Oxford University Press, 2017), 283–291, esp. 286, and 169–182; Peter J. Thuesen, *In Discordance with the Scriptures: American Protestant Battles over Translating the Bible* (New York: Oxford University Press, 1999), 137.

31. "Newest Bible Said to Appeal to Evangelicals," *Washington Post*, November 10, 1978, E18.

32. "The New International Version: Its Background and Its Character," undated manuscript, series 1, box 18, folder: History, CBT.

33. "Position Paper of the Committee on Bible Translation," July 11, 1967, series 1, box 18, folder: History, CBT.

34. A. Larry Ross & Associates, Inc., "When the 'Good News' Becomes Bad News," May 7, 1997, 20, series 4: Unprocessed, box 2012-0204, CBT.

35. "Position Paper of the Committee on Bible Translation," July 11, 1967, series 1, box 18, folder: History, CBT.

36. The RSV began in 1937 as an initiative of the International Council of Religious Education (ICRE), which fundamentalists long had portrayed as a modernist ally of the Federal Council of Churches and its successor, the National Council of Churches. Although the RSV New Testament appeared under the ICRE's auspices in 1946, the copyright for the full RSV ultimately belonged to the NCC, which absorbed the ICRE in 1950. A variety of publishing firms purchased licenses to print the RSV, including Harper & Row. Avoiding association with institutions like the NCC, many fundamentalists simply continued using the KJV, which had entered the public domain in the United States. Zondervan became licensed to print the RSV in 1965, when it purchased Harper & Row's Bible division. See Thuesen, *In Discordance with the Scriptures*, 79–87; "Harper-Row Bible Unit, Half of British Firm to Be Sold," *Wall Street Journal*, December 3, 1965; "Zondervan Acquires Harper Bible Department," November 12, 1965, box 5, folder: Publishing: Zondervan, HJO; Thatcher to HJO, November 17, 1965; "Zondervan Registers Offering," *Wall Street Journal*, September 28, 1973.

37. "Minutes of the Meeting of the Executive Committee, N.A.E., December 16, 1952," box 13, folder: National Association of Evangelicals, Minutes and Reports, 1952–1958–1959, HJO.

38. Thuesen, *In Discordance with the Scriptures*, 126.

39. James DeForest Murch, "Evangelicals and the 'New Version,'" *United Evangelical Action*, January 15, 1953, 5–6, JDM.

40. "NAE List of Significant Books," *United Evangelical Action*, June 15, 1946, 6; Thuesen, *In Discordance with the Scriptures*, 129–130. Wilbur Smith compared Lindsell's Bible to Scofield's in a review in *Eternity* magazine. "Wilbur Smith Reviews RSV Study Bible," *Eternity*, November 1964, 64–68. Accessed in box 6, folder 7: Harper Study Bible 1964–1977, HL.

41. Harold Lindsell, "The Making of a New Study Bible," *Christian Life*, November 1964. Accessed in box 6, folder 7: Harper Study Bible 1964–1977, HL.

42. Quoted in Thuesen, *In Discordance with the Scriptures*, 133.

43. A group of fifteen white, male, evangelical scholars from a variety of denominations, the CBT required its members to join by invitation. "The New International Version" (undated) and "Committee on Bible Translation Constitution" (January 5, 1968), both series 1, box 18, folder: History, CBT.

44. The former NYBS has been renamed a number of times. After becoming the International Bible Society in 1988, it became Biblica in 2009. Ruark, *House of Zondervan*, 152; Thuesen, *In Discordance with the Scriptures*, 148. On the contract extension, see Phyllis Tickle, "Zondervan Signs Long Extension of 'NIV Bible' License," *Publishers Weekly*, June 19, 1995, 13.

45. "The translators here have usurped the reader's right to an accurate, even if ambiguous and obscure, rendering of the text," a critic explained with reference to a passage in the Gospel of John. Ed L. Miller, "The 'New International Version' on the Prologue of John," *Harvard Theological Review* 72, nos. 3/4 (1979): quote on 309.

46. Francis A. Schaeffer, *How Should We Then Live: The Decline of Western Thought and Culture* (Old Tappan, NJ: Revell, 1976); Worthen, *Apostles of Reason,* 84–85.

47. James S. Bielo, *Words Upon the Word: An Ethnography of Evangelical Group Bible Study* (New York: NYU Press, 2009), 64.

48. Advertisement, *Christianity Today,* February 16, 1979, back cover; "New International Bible, N.T. Edition Ready for C.B.A. Introduction," *Zondervan Book News,* June 1973, ZPI I; "Committee on Bible Translation Constitution," CBT.

49. Tanya M. Luhrmann, *When God Talks Back: Understanding the American Evangelical Relationship with God* (New York: Knopf, 2012), 14, 92. James Bielo affirms this point, noting that evangelicals often insist that "a close, personal relationship with God is accomplished best by establishing the relevance of biblical texts" to readers' lives. Bielo, *Words upon the Word,* 86–87.

50. Dwight Chappell, "A Readability Report on the New International Version" (Grace Theological Seminary, 1976), series 1, box 18, folder: History, CBT.

51. "Do-It-Yourself Bible Campaign Successful," *Trade News and Views: Zondervan Bible Publishers,* Winter 1977, ZPH.

52. Reuben Archer Torrey, *How to Study the Bible for Greatest Profit* (New York: Fleming H. Revell Co., 1896), 16–18, 23, 34, 54, 86.

53. "A Bible for Everybody: The Niche Phenomenon," *Publishers Weekly,* October 9, 1995, 58.

54. "NIV Strategy," 1998, series 4: Unprocessed, box 2012-0204: tNIV, folder: IBS Policy, CBT.

55. Chris Meehan, "Many Messages: New Niche Bibles Boost Business, Fill Many Needs," *Grand Rapids Press,* December 12, 1997.

56. On the financial value of bible-related products, see "Special Situation Report: Zondervan Corporation," First Michigan Corporation, ZPH.

57. "The *NIV*—Now What?," June 1998, 4, series 4: Unprocessed, box 2012-0204: tNIV, folder: IBS Policy, CBT.

58. International Bible Society, "NIV/NIrV Marketing Update," March 24, 2000, series 4: Unprocessed, box 2012-0204, CBT.

59. R. L. Harris, "Comments on an Article in *World* 3/29 on Proposed NIV Revision," April 15, 1997, series 4: Unprocessed, box 2012-0204: tNIV, CBT.

60. On gender and the relevance of the Bible to readers' lives, see Bielo, *Words upon the Word,* 60.

61. Emily S. Johnson, *This Is Our Message: Women's Leadership in the New Christian Right* (New York: Oxford University Press, 2019), 73.

62. Fleishman Hillard International Communications, "Conference Report," June 19, 2000, series 4: Unprocessed, box 2012-0204: tNIV, folder: IBS Policy, CBT.

63. "NIV Inclusive Language," February 25, 1993, series 4: Unprocessed, box 2012-0204: tNIV, folder: Inclusive Language Misc., CBT.

64. "Baptists Irate over Zondervan Plan for New Bible," *Grand Rapids Press,* May 14, 1997, A1; L. Roy Taylor to Jonathan Peterson, March 20, 2002, series 4: Unprocessed, box 2012-0204: tNIV, folder: IBS Policy, CBT.

65. "International Bible Society Halts Revision Process of NIV Bible," *World,* May 27, 1997.

66. "When the 'Good News' Becomes Bad News."

67. "Project Onward: Task List," undated (ca. 1997), series 4: Unprocessed, box 2012-0204: tNIV, CBT.

68. "The *NIV*—Now What?"

69. "The Politically Incorrect Bible," in "When the 'Good News' Becomes Bad News."

70. "The *NIV*—Now What?"

71. "When the 'Good News' Becomes Bad News."

72. Discovery Market Research, "Zondervan Publishing House: Inclusive Language Research," June 15, 2000, 35–37, series 4: Unprocessed, box 2012-0204, CBT.

73. "NIV/NIrV Marketing Update."

74. They entertained a number of solutions. One solution called for publishing a new brand under the title "New Millennium Bible," which the proposal suggested launching on January 1, 2001. "The *NIV*—Now What?"

75. Discovery Market Research, "Zondervan Publishing House," 36; Timothy C. Morgan, "Revised NIV Makes Its Debut," *Christianity Today,* February 4, 2002, 19.

76. "NIV/NIrV Marketing Update."

77. Scott Bolinder to L. Roy Taylor, May 9, 2002, series 4: Unprocessed, box 2012-0204: tNIV, folder: IBS Policy, CBT.

78. Crossway Bibles, "The Holy Bible: English Standard Version," series 4: Unprocessed, box 2012-0204, CBT.

79. For a sympathetic overview of the ESV translators' strategy, see Michael D. Eldridge, "A New Addition to the King James Family," *Expository Times* 114, no. 7 (April 2003): 241–244. For a more critical discussion, see Scot McKnight, "The New Stealth Translation: ESV," *Jesus Creed* (blog), September 12, 2016, https://www.patheos.com/blogs/jesuscreed/2016/09/12/the-new-stealth-translation-esv/. McKnight focuses especially on the ESV translators' complementarian decision to translate Genesis 3:16 in a way that underlines the need for men to rule over women.

80. Packet prepared for "Zondervan Editorial Advisory Council," August 19, 1966, box 5, folder: Books, HJO.

81. Connie Goddard, "Zondervan: Looking Ahead at 60," *Publishers Weekly,* March 15, 1991, quote on 34.

82. Brantley W. Gasaway, *Progressive Evangelicals and the Pursuit of Social Justice* (Chapel Hill: University of North Carolina Press, 2014), 77, 97–98; for more on Wallis and the "young evangelicals," see Worthen, *Apostles of Reason,* 181–183.

83. On the declaration, see Worthen, *Apostles of Reason,* 189.

84. Peter Goodwin Heltzel, *Jesus and Justice: Evangelicals, Race, and American Politics* (New Haven: Yale University Press, 2009), 136. See also Milton G. Sernett, "Black Religion and the Question of Evangelical Identity," in *The*

Variety of American Evangelicalism, ed. Donald W. Dayton and Robert K. Johnston (Pasadena, CA: Wipf and Stock, 1998), 135–147, esp. 143–144.

85. See Judith Weisenfeld, *New World A-Coming: Black Religion and Racial Identity during the Great Migration* (New York: NYU Press, 2016). On black religion and the historical and historiographical problem with overemphasizing African Americans' affiliation with a monolithic "black church," see Barbara Dianne Savage, *Your Spirits Walk Beside Us: The Politics of Black Religion* (Cambridge, MA: Belknap Press of Harvard University Press, 2008), esp. 9.

86. See Mary Beth Swetnam Mathews, *Doctrine and Race: African American Evangelicals and Fundamentalism between the Wars* (Tuscaloosa: University Alabama Press, 2017).

87. As sociologists long have noted, "individualistic priorities" are correlated with opposition to "redistributive policies." See Lawrence Bobo, "Social Responsibility, Individualism, and Redistributive Policies," *Sociological Forum* 6, no. 1 (1991): 71–92, quote on 88.

88. Heltzel, *Jesus and Justice,* 138; Gasaway, *Progressive Evangelicals,* 96–97.

89. Lerone A. Martin, *Preaching on Wax: The Phonograph and the Shaping of Modern African American Religion* (New York: NYU Press, 2014), 4–8.

90. See Jonathan L. Walton, *Watch This! The Ethics and Aesthetics of Black Televangelism* (New York: NYU Press, 2009), esp. 171; Marla Frederick, *Colored Television: American Religion Gone Global* (Stanford: Stanford University Press, 2015); Carolyn Moxley Rouse, John L. Jackson Jr., and Marla F. Frederick, eds., *Televised Redemption: Black Religious Media and Racial Empowerment* (New York: NYU Press, 2016).

91. Joan Neufeld to Joni Eareckson Tada, October 12, 1976, folder: Tada, Joni—Old Contracts, etc., ZPH-ED.

92. "Best of Spring '78," *Publishers Weekly,* February 13, 1978, 34; "Religious Best Sellers," *Publishers Weekly,* February 13, 1978, 90.

93. Sernett, "Black Religion," esp. 144.

94. According to one 1996 report, two-thirds of all Christian retail sales occurred through CBA-affiliated stores. Packaged Facts, *The Market for Religious Publishing and Products* (New York: Packaged Facts, June 1996), 5.

95. Soong-Chan Rah, "In Whose Image: The Emergence, Development, and Challenge of African-American Evangelicalism" (PhD diss., Duke University, 2016), 204.

96. Howard O. Jones, *Shall We Overcome: A Challenge to Negro and White Christians* (Old Tappan, NJ: Revell, 1966), 7–9, 144.

97. Grant Wacker, *America's Pastor: Billy Graham and the Shaping of a Nation* (Cambridge, MA: Belknap Press of Harvard University Press, 2014), 252–254; Jones, *Shall We Overcome,* 120.

98. William E. Pannell, *My Friend, the Enemy* (Waco, TX: Word Books, 1968), 121, 123.

99. Tom Skinner, *Black and Free* (Grand Rapids, MI: Zondervan, 1968).

100. James R. Adair, *The Story of Scripture Press: "The Whole Word for the Whole World"* (Glen Ellyn, IL: SP Ministries, 1998), 225.

101. Theon Hill, "Melvin Banks Had a Dream," *Christianity Today*, June 22, 2017, http://www.christianitytoday.com/ct/2017/june-web-only/melvin-banks-had -dream.html.

102. Adair, *Story of Scripture Press*, 227.

103. "A Bible for Everybody," 58.

104. Mark Rice, interview by author, Grand Rapids, MI, October 13, 2016.

105. On LifeWay's creation, see Frances Meeker, "Baptist Publisher Renamed to Show Change," *Nashville Banner*, September 17, 1997, A15. Announced in 1997, the name change was finalized in 1998.

106. Gayle White, "Tailoring the Message," *Publishers Weekly*, November 8, 1993, 32.

107. Jonathan Walton argues that ministries are neo-pentecostal if they combine traditional pentecostal beliefs with an emphasis on "participation in the cap- italist economy, culture industries, and wealth attainment." See Walton, *Watch This!*, chap. 3, quote on 81.

108. Shayne Lee, *T. D. Jakes: America's New Preacher* (New York: NYU Press, 2005), 39–40.

109. On the forms of the prosperity gospel, see Kate Bowler, *Blessed: A History of the American Prosperity Gospel* (New York: Oxford University Press, 2013), e.g., 5; Lee, *T. D. Jakes*, 38, 104; Sridhar Pappu, "The Preacher," *Atlantic*, March 2006. See also Bowler, *Blessed*, 91.

110. Walton, *Watch This!*, 23. See also Tona J. Hangen, *Redeeming the Dial: Radio, Religion and Popular Culture in America* (Chapel Hill: University of North Carolina Press, 2002), esp. chap. 6; Jeffrey K. Hadden, "The Rise and Fall of American Televangelism," *Annals of the American Academy of Political and Social Science* 527 (May 1993): 113–130.

111. Lee, *America's New Preacher*, 68–69; John H. Wigger, *PTL: The Rise and Fall of Jim and Tammy Faye Bakker's Evangelical Empire* (New York: Oxford Uni- versity Press, 2017). On the ministries of Dollar and Jakes, see Mary Hinton, *The Commercial Church: Black Churches and the New Religious Marketplace in America* (Lanham, MD: Lexington Books, 2011).

112. Jakes originally published his book with Destiny Image, a small publisher of charismatic books that operated as an outlet for self-publishing. Lee, *Ameri- ca's New Preacher*, 67–68. On Jakes's early ministry, see Walton, *Watch This!*, 104–106.

113. Lee, *America's New Preacher*, 145; "Evangelical Christian Bestsellers," *Pub- lishers Weekly*, April 10, 1995.

114. Daniel Ramírez, *Migrating Faith: Pentecostalism in the United States and Mexico, 1906–1966* (Chapel Hill: University of North Carolina Press, 2015), 28–29. The Society for Promoting Christian Knowledge revised and reissued the Reina-Valera in 1856–1857, and the American Bible Society subsequently undertook their own revision, which they released in 1893. J. M. Lopez Guillen, "Versions of the Bible in Spanish," *Bible Society Record* 39, no. 11 (November 15, 1894): 161–164.

115. Dwight Lyman Moody, *El Cielo* (Mexico City: Impr. de la Iglesia Metodista Episcopal, 1882); John Wesley Butler, *History of the Methodist Episcopal*

Church in Mexico: Personal Reminiscences, Present Conditions (New York: Methodist Book Concern, 1918), 79.

116. "A Million Neglected Souls Given a Message of Life," folder: Moody Press History, MBI-ED.

117. Lynn Garrett, "Christian and Spanish: Rooted in Missions," *Publishers Weekly,* September 3, 2012, 31–33.

118. W. Dayton Roberts, "The Legacy of Harry and Susan Strachan," *International Bulletin of Missionary Research,* July 1998, 127–131; also see the finding aid for "Records of Latin American Mission—Collection 236," BGC.

119. Garrett, "Christian and Spanish," 31.

120. David Coyotyl, interview by author, Grand Rapids, MI, October 11, 2016.

121. Ramírez, *Migrating Faith,* 28.

122. Ibid., 27, 28, 67; Arlene M. Sánchez-Walsh, *Latino Pentecostal Identity: Evangelical Faith, Self, and Society* (New York: Columbia University Press, 2003), 38.

123. David Smilde, *Reason to Believe: Cultural Agency in Latin American Evangelicalism* (Berkeley: University of California Press, 2007), 7, 13.

124. Philip Wingeier-Rayo, "The Transculturalization and the Transnationalization of the Government of 12: From Seoul to Bogotá to Charlotte, North Carolina," in *Engaging the World: Christian Communities in Contemporary Global Societies,* ed. Afe Adogame, Janice McLean, and Anderson Jeremiah (Eugene, OR: Wipf and Stock, 2014), 153–168.

125. Ilan Stavans, "Bilingual Nation: Spanish-Language Books in the United States since the 1960s," in *The Enduring Book: Print Culture in Postwar America,* ed. David Paul Nord, Joan Shelley Rubin, and Michael Schudson, vol. 5 of *A History of the Book in America* (Chapel Hill: American Antiquarian Society/University of North Carolina Press, 2009), esp. 393–394.

126. Arlene Dávila, *Latinos, Inc.: The Marketing and Making of a People,* updated ed. (Berkeley: University of California Press, 2012), 50.

127. Rahel Musleah, "Reaching a Vast Market," *Publishers Weekly,* October 12, 1992, esp. 45.

128. Margaret Langstaff, "Making Cross-Cultural Connections," *Publishers Weekly,* September 23, 1996, 537–543.

129. Advertisement, *Publishers Weekly,* October 12, 1992, 47.

130. See Luciano Jaramillo, *De Sacerdote a Hombre de Dios* (Grand Rapids, MI: Zondervan, 2014).

131. Musleah, "Reaching a Vast Market," 46.

132. Leylha Ahuile, "Dealing with Change: Spanish Publishers in the U.S.," *Publishers Weekly,* September 3, 2012, 28.

133. Despite this claim, Telemundo's content often has featured a high proportion of light-skinned, Mexican actors and comparably few black Latinos. Arlene Dávila, "Talking Back: Spanish Media and U.S. Latinidad," in *Latino/a Popular Culture,* ed. Michelle Habell-Pallán and Mary Romero (New York: NYU Press, 2002), 47–65, esp. 51–52.

134. Antonio Guernica and Irene Kasperuk, *Reaching the Hispanic Market Effectively: The Media, the Market, the Methods* (New York: McGraw-Hill, 1982).

135. Dávila, *Latinos, Inc.,* 2, 61; Langstaff, "Making Cross-Cultural Connections."

136. "Mission / Vision Statement," *NHCLC,* May 9, 2017, https://nhclc.org/about -us/missionvision-statement/.

137. National Hispanic Christian Leadership Conference, "Hispanic Minister, Wilfredo De Jesus, Emerges as Pastor of Assemblies of God Largest Congregation," Cision: PR Newswire, June 2, 2017, https://www.prnewswire.com/news -releases/hispanic-minister-wilfredo-de-jesus-emerges-as-pastor-of-assemblies -of-god-largest-congregation-102800499.html.

138. Emma Koonse, "Religion Book Deals: July 2016," *Publishers Weekly,* July 27, 2016, https://publishersweekly.com/pw/by-topic/industry-news/religion/article /71029-religion-book-deals-july-2016.html.

139. Choco De Jesus, *Move into More: The Limitless Surprises of a Faithful God* (Grand Rapids, MI: Zondervan, 2018).

140. See Lucia Hulsether, "The Grammar of Racism: Religious Pluralism and the Birth of the Interdisciplines," *Journal of the American Academy of Religion* 86, no. 1 (March 2018): 1–41; Courtney Bender and Pamela E. Klassen, eds., *After Pluralism: Reimagining Religious Engagement* (New York: Columbia University Press, 2010).

141. Ruark, *The House of Zondervan,* 174.

142. John P. Dessauer, Paul D. Doebler, and Hendrik Edelman, eds., *Christian Book Publishing and Distribution in the United States and Canada* (Tempe, AZ: CBA/ECPA/PCPA Joint Research Project, 1987), 102–104.

143. See Matthew Avery Sutton, *American Apocalypse: A History of Modern Evangelicalism* (Cambridge, MA: Belknap Press of Harvard University Press, 2014); Darren Dochuk, *From Bible Belt to Sunbelt: Plain-Folk Religion, Grassroots Politics, and the Rise of Evangelical Conservatism* (New York: W. W. Norton, 2011); Daniel K. Williams, *God's Own Party: The Making of the Christian Right* (Oxford: Oxford University Press, 2010).

144. Worthen, *Apostles of Reason,* 4.

145. Schäfer, *Countercultural Conservatives,* 111. Molly Worthen explains that, by the mid-1970s, "the happy vines of compromise had begun to grow over their internal divisions." Worthen, *Apostles of Reason,* 198.

146. Robert Wuthnow, *The Restructuring of American Religion: Society and Faith since World War II* (Princeton: Princeton University Press, 1988), 185.

147. Ibid., 192.

148. Schaefer to Lindsell, May 9, 1976, series I, box 1, folder: Battle for the Bible; Correspondence and Notes; 1975–1978, HL.

149. Williams, *God's Own Party,* 137–143.

150. Francis A. Schaeffer, *Whatever Happened to the Human Race?* (Old Tappan, NJ: Revell, 1979).

151. Schäfer, *Countercultural Conservatives,* 152–154.

152. DeVries to Lindsell, October 8, 1975, series I, box 1, folder: Battle for the Bible; Correspondence and Notes; 1975–1978, HL.

153. DeVries to Lindsell, October 24, 1975, series I, box 1, folder: Battle for the Bible; Correspondence and Notes; 1975–1978, HL.

154. "The Moral Majority in the CBA Market," *Publishers Weekly,* August 21, 1981, 30–31; Randall H. Balmer, *Mine Eyes Have Seen the Glory: A Journey into the Evangelical Subculture in America,* 5th ed. (New York: Oxford University Press, 2014), 205.

155. "CBA in Denver: A Big Show—with an Attitude," *Publishers Weekly,* July 18, 1994, 14–15.

156. Michael Reagan and Jim Denney, *The City on a Hill: Fulfilling Ronald Reagan's Vision for America* (Nashville, TN: Thomas Nelson, 1997); D. James Kennedy and Jerry Newcombe, *What If America Were a Christian Nation Again?* (Nashville, TN: Thomas Nelson, 2003); Richard D. Land, *The Divided States of America? What Liberals and Conservatives Are Missing in the God-and-Country Shouting Match!* (Nashville, TN: Thomas Nelson, 2007).

157. Angela McGlowan, *Bamboozled: How Americans Are Being Exploited by the Lies of the Liberal Agenda* (Nashville, TN: Thomas Nelson, 2007); R. Emmett Tyrrell, *The Clinton Crack-Up: The Boy President's Life after the White House* (Nashville, TN: Thomas Nelson, 2007); David N. Bossie, *Hillary: The Politics of Personal Destruction: The Multimedia Expose, Includes Full-Length DVD Documentary* (Nashville, TN: Thomas Nelson, 2008); Stephen Mansfield, *The Faith of Barack Obama* (Nashville, TN: Thomas Nelson, 2008); Kevin McCullough, *No He Can't: How Barack Obama Is Dismantling Hope and Change* (Nashville, TN: Thomas Nelson, 2011).

158. Dochuk, *From Bible Belt to Sunbelt,* xxii, 52.

159. Narramore to Zondervan et al., May 13, 1960, folder: Narramore, Clyde, The Psychology of Counseling, ZPH-ED.

160. Nicole Hemmer, *Messengers of the Right: Conservative Media and the Transformation of American Politics* (Philadelphia: University of Pennsylvania Press, 2016), xiv.

161. Ibid., 235–251.

162. On the putatively apolitical quality of evangelical social claims, see Emily Suzanne Johnson, "God, Country, and Anita Bryant: Women's Leadership and the Politics of the New Christian Right," *Religion and American Culture: A Journal of Interpretation* 28, no. 2 (Summer 2018): 238–268, esp. 244.

163. Hemmer, *Messengers of the Right,* 265–266.

164. Audrey Roloff, "Marriage Is Hard Work—Here's How We Protect Ours," *Fox News,* March 28, 2019, https://www.foxnews.com/opinion/jeremy-and-audrey-roloff-marriage-is-hard-work-heres-how-we-protect-ours; Candace Cameron Bure, "Candace Cameron Bure: How to Set Your Life's GPS and Find Your Purpose," *Fox News,* April 27, 2018, https://www.foxnews.com/opinion/candace-cameron-bure-how-to-set-your-lifes-gps-and-find-your-purpose; Steve Green, "The Incredible, Unexpected Journey That Led to the Museum of the Bible," *Fox News,* November 4, 2017, https://www.foxnews.com/opinion/steve-and-jackie-green-the-incredible-unexpected-journey-that-led-to-the-museum-of-the-bible; "Publisher to Issue Revised Edition of Ben Carson Book," *Fox News,* May 26, 2015, https://www.foxnews.com/politics/publisher-to-issue-revised-edition-of-ben-carson-book.

165. For an overview of Murdoch's sustained commercial devotion to conservative publics, see Jonathan Mahler and Jim Rutenberg, "Planet Fox," *New York Times Magazine*, April 7, 2019.

166. For studies of Fox News and the ideas and ideologies that it has emphasized, see Jeffrey P. Jones, "Fox News and the Performance of Ideology," *Cinema Journal* 51, no. 4 (Summer 2012): 178–185; Colleen E. Mills, "Framing Ferguson: Fox News and the Construction of US Racism," *Race & Class* 58, no. 4 (April 2017): 39–56; Reece Peck, "Usurping the Usable Past: How Fox News Remembered the Great Depression during the Great Recession," *Journalism: Theory, Practice & Criticism* 18, no. 6 (July 2017): 680–699; William E. Connolly, "The Evangelical-Capitalist Resonance Machine," *Political Theory* 33, no. 6 (December 2005): 869–886.

167. Attributing support for Donald Trump among white evangelicals to Trump's "unexpected orthodoxy," the sociologist Gerardo Martí explains that "profession of belief is not most important among white Evangelicals but rather support for policy initiatives that would enforce white Evangelical priorities in all sectors of government." Gerardo Martí, "The Unexpected Orthodoxy of Donald J. Trump: White Evangelical Support for the 45th President of the United States," *Sociology of Religion* 80, no. 1 (January 9, 2019): 1–8. See also John Fea, *Believe Me: The Evangelical Road to Donald Trump* (Grand Rapids, MI: Eerdmans, 2018). On responses to particular survey categories as metonyms for other sensibilities and attachments, see Wuthnow, *Inventing American Religion*, 200–203.

168. Mark Labberton, ed., *Still Evangelical? Insiders Reconsider Political, Social, and Theological Meaning* (Downers Grove, IL: InterVarsity Press, 2018), 3–5.

Epilogue

1. Randall H. Balmer, *Mine Eyes Have Seen the Glory: A Journey into the Evangelical Subculture in America*, 5th ed. (New York: Oxford University Press, 2014), xiv–xvi.

2. Christian Smith and Michael Emerson, *American Evangelicalism: Embattled and Thriving* (Chicago: University of Chicago Press, 1998), 118–119.

3. "Integrated Marketing Communication Strategy," November 4, 1996, 2, folder: Graham, Billy, ZPH-ED.

4. Tish Harrison Warren, "Who's in Charge of the Christian Blogosphere?," *CT Women*, April 2017, http://www.christianitytoday.com/women/2017/april/whos-in-charge-of-christian-blogosphere.html.

5. Eric Stanford, "Book Trends 2003," *CBA Marketplace*, March 2003, 24–27.

6. Packaged Facts, *U.S. Market for Religious Publishing and Products* (New York: Packaged Facts, 2000), 16; on Logos, see Cindy Crosby, "How to Save the Christian Bookstore," *Christianity Today*, April 2008, 22–27.

7. Sarah Eekhoff Zylstra, "All 240 Family Christian Stores Are Closing," *Christianity Today*, February 23, 2017, https://www.christianitytoday.com/news/2017/february/all-family-christian-stores-closing-fcs-liquidation.html; "LifeWay to Focus on Digital Retail, Close Brick-and-Mortar Stores," *LifeWay*

NewsRoom, March 20, 2019, https://blog.lifeway.com/newsroom/2019/03/20/lifeway-to-focus-on-digital-retail-close-brick-and-mortar-stores/; Emma Wenner, "One Year after UNITE, CBA Is Dead," *Publishers Weekly.com,* June 26, 2019, https://www.publishersweekly.com/pw/by-topic/industry-news/religion/article/80507-one-year-after-unite-cba-is-dead.html.

8. Ann Byle, "To Market, with Strategies Old and New," *Publishers Weekly,* February 28, 2011, 8–9.

9. David Coyotyl, interview by author, Grand Rapids, MI, October 11, 2016.

10. Kate Shellnutt, "Celebs from Michael Phelps to Kim Kardashian Want a Purpose-Driven Life," *Christianity Today,* August 12, 2016, https://www.christianitytoday.com/news/2016/august/celebs-from-michael-phelps-to-kim-kardashian-want-purpose-d.html; Michael E. Ruane, "The Rise (and Fall, and Rise) of Michael Phelps," *Washington Post,* June 9, 2016; Joyce Chen, "First 25 Things You Don't Know about Me Ever: Kim Kardashian," *Us Weekly* (blog), April 29, 2016, https://www.usmagazine.com/celebrity-news/pictures/first-25-things-you-dont-know-about-me-ever-with-kim-kardashian-w204117/gifted-knowledge-w204139/.

11. Suzanne Sataline, "In Prayer, Warren Calls for Tolerance," *Wall Street Journal,* January 21, 2009; Katharine Q. Seelye, "Inaugural Role for 'Purpose Driven' Pastor," *International Herald Tribune,* December 19, 2008; Jon Cohen, "61% in Poll Back Rick Warren as Invocation Pick," *Washington Post,* January 20, 2009.

12. "Rick Warren, Obama and the Left," *Wall Street Journal,* December 29, 2008. In his 2006 profile of Warren's Saddleback Church, in Orange County's Lake Forest, Randall Balmer reported that "twenty-four thousand people attend Saddleback's services on a typical weekend." Balmer, *Mine Eyes Have Seen the Glory,* 331. The *International Herald Tribune* described Warren as "the evangelical pastor and author of 'The Purpose Driven Life'"; the *Wall Street Journal* reported that "the popularity of his 2002 bestseller, 'The Purpose Driven Life,' with roughly 30 million copies in print, made Mr. Warren influential in Protestant and Catholic churches and homes world-wide"; the *Washington Post* explained that Warren "gained prominence for his book 'The Purpose Driven Life'"; the *Boston Globe* profiled Warren as "the evangelical minister and bestselling author of 'The Purpose Driven Life.'" Seelye, "Inaugural Role"; Sataline, "Warren Calls for Tolerance"; Cohen, "61% in Poll Back Rick Warren."

13. Kathryn Lofton, "Considering the Neoliberal in American Religion," in *Religion and the Marketplace in the United States,* ed. Jan Stievermann, Philip Goff, and Detlef Junker (New York: Oxford University Press, 2015), 269–288, esp. 275, 285; on neoliberalism's characteristics and its conceptual vagueness, see Catherine Kingfisher and Jeff Maskovsky, "The Limits of Neoliberalism," *Critique of Anthropology* 28, no. 2 (June 2008): 115–126, esp. 116–117.

14. Marcia Z. Nelson, "Losing Their Religion," *Publishers Weekly,* January 21, 2013, 16–17.

Acknowledgments

Every book requires countless individuals and institutions to believe and invest in its creation. This fact is a fundamental premise of this book. Knowing this, I acknowledge and thank some of the people and organizations who have taught me this lesson by believing and investing in my work.

Several mentors shaped my approach to this project in profound ways. Randall Balmer and Courtney Bender have offered guidance since my earliest attempts to identify and explore this book's landscape. David L. Holmes first taught me how to ask questions that the academic study of religion and history could answer, and Kathryn Lofton continually has prodded me to ask yet another question. I am glad to have their voices perpetually in my head.

A number of esteemed colleagues and friends generously offered feedback on portions of the manuscript. They include Timothy Gloege, Elayne Oliphant, James Bratt, Kate Bowler, Sonia Hazard, Charrise Barron, David Watt, Linford Fisher, Darren Dochuk, David Bratt, Eden Consenstein, Alda Balthrop-Lewis, David Newheiser, Seth Perry, Geoffrey Pollick, and Leigh Schmidt. The members of my cohort of Young Scholars of American Religion also responded to my work with insight and encouragement. They are Brandon Bayne, Cara Burnidge, Emily Clark, Brett Grainger, Rachel Gross, Cooper Harriss, Justine Howe, Elizabeth Jemison, and Nicole Turner. I also thank the anonymous reviewers for Harvard University Press for their helpful suggestions on improving the manuscript, and I am grateful to my editor, Andrew Kinney, and to Olivia Woods at Harvard University Press, as well as to Wendy Nelson for all their help in transforming my manuscript into this book.

This project benefited tremendously from the illuminating questions and comments I received at a variety of scholarly conferences and workshops. I am especially grateful for feedback I received at large and small gatherings on topics related to this book, including those convened at Yale University (2013), the Center for the Study of Religion and American Culture (2014), the University of Toronto (2016), Princeton University (2016), Michigan State (2017), the Center for Contemporary Buddhist Studies (University of Copenhagen, 2018), the Obama Institute for Transnational American Studies (Johannes Gutenberg University, 2018), and the Jonathan M. Nelson Center for Entrepreneurship (Brown University, 2018). For hosting me at these events or responding to my work, I particularly thank Heather Curtis, Lucia Hulsether, Michael Hamilton, Seth Dowland, Matthew Sutton, Mary Beth Mathews, Brendan Pietsch, Pamela Klassen, Rebecca Bartel, Judith Weisenfeld, Jessica Delgado, Jon Keune, Amy DeRogatis, Sara Moslener, Jane Caple, Elizabeth Williams-Oerberg, Axel Schäfer, Heather Hendershot, and Jennifer Nazareno.

I owe significant debts to a number of institutions that have funded my work. I am especially indebted to the Louisville Institute for its generous First Book Grant, which enabled me to complete much of this project. I sincerely thank Princeton University's Center for the Study of Religion for a postdoctoral fellowship, and I am grateful to the Center for the Study of Religion and American Culture for accepting me into its Young Scholars program (2016–2017). Thank you to the leaders and administrative staffs of these institutions, including Edwin Aponte, Pam Collins, Philip Goff, Anita Kline, Jenny Wiley Legath, Keri Liechty, Don Richter, Lauren Schmidt, and Robert Wuthnow.

Since I began teaching at Brown, I have been fortunate to be surrounded in the Department of Religious Studies by thoughtful and generous colleagues and students, all of whom have nourished my thinking and writing. I am especially indebted to Susan Harvey, Nancy Khalek, Paul Nahme, and Andre Willis, who read parts of the manuscript and celebrated its progress along the way. Thank you also to my other colleagues, including Shahzad Bashir, Stephen Bush, Mark Cladis, Jae Han, Thomas Lewis, Saul Olyan, Jason Protass, Hal Roth, Michael Satlow, and Janine Sawada. Undergraduate and graduate students who read portions of this manuscript or informed its creation include Elizabeth Carlson, Christine Collins, Hannah Santos, Abraham Westbrook, and Nicholas Andersen. Nicole Vadnais, Tina Creamer, William Monroe, and James Dorian offered invaluable administrative support.

Throughout my research for this book, I was welcomed with generosity and hospitality in a wide range of academic and corporate settings. Current and former employees of Zondervan, Eerdmans, and Baker graciously agreed to share their insights and archives with me. Thank you to William B. Eerdmans Jr., Reinder Van Til, Jon Pott, Larry ten Harmsel, James Ruark, Robert Hudson, Stanley Gundry, Sandy Vander Zicht, David Coyotl, Mark Rice, Scott Bolinder, James Buick, Allan Fisher, Dwight Baker, Richard Baker, Jim Kinney, Sue Smith, Marilyn Gordon, Sara Harlow, Robert Hosack, and Judith Markham. I am also indebted to numerous archivists, librarians, journalists, and scholars for sharing insights and pointing me toward resources that I would not otherwise have discovered. Thanks especially to Garth Rosell, Adam Gossman, Meredith Sommers, Corie Zylstra, Rhoda Palmer, Jared Burkholder, and Marcia Z. Nelson for opening up resources at Gordon-Conwell Theological Seminary, Fuller Theological Seminary, Milligan College, Moody Bible Institute, and Grace College and Seminary.

It always has seemed odd to me that authors typically wait until the end of their acknowledgments to thank the people who have proved most instrumental to the book's creation, but I am perpetuating this peculiarity now by turning to my friends and family. For as long as this project has gestated, I have received intellectual enrichment as well as unwavering affection from members of my graduate school cohort. For this and more, I thank Susan Andrews, Patton Burchett, Joseph Blankholm, Todd French, Matthew Pereira, and Gregory Scott. Alongside these and all of the other friends whom I have not named here, my family has continually been a source of inspiration. Although I could name virtually every one of my family members, I thank Daniel Vaca Jr., Lourdes Vaca, Stephen Vaca, Jessica Vaca Reeve, Jonny Reeve, Richard Powers, and Lucy Powers. I also thank my grandparents—Natalia Molina, Alberto Solis, and Concepcion Solis—for being models of imagination and perseverance.

Most of all, I thank Julia Vaca and our children, Samuel and Sylvia. This project has stretched across the entirety of Sam and Sylvia's lives, and they have filled that time with laughter and joy. But Julia has been my partner through every second of this book's development. For making everything possible, I dedicate it to her with love.

Several sections of this book have been informed by arguments first developed in other publications. Portions of Chapters 1 and 5 are informed by arguments that appear in my "Believing within Business: Evangelicalism, Media, and Financial Faith," in *The Business Turn in American Religious History,* ed. Amanda Porterfield, Darren Grem, and John Corrigan (New York: Oxford University Press, 2017), 20–45. Part of Chapter 3 is informed by an argument I developed in "Meeting the Modernistic Tide: The Book as Evangelical Battleground in the 1940s," in *Protest on the Page: Essays on Print and the Culture of Dissent,* ed. James L. Baughman, Jennifer Ratner-Rosenhagen, and James P. Danky (Madison: University of Wisconsin Press, 2015), 137–160. A brief section of Chapter 4 is informed by research I discussed in "Selling Trust: The Living Bible and the Business of Biblicism," in *The Bible in American Life,* ed. Philip Goff, Arthur E. Farnsley II, and Peter J. Thuesen (New York: Oxford University Press, 2017), 169–182.

Index